Choosing Our Destiny

By the Same Author

The Sorcerer's Apprentice: An Anthropology of Public Policy

Towers Besieged: The Dilemma of the Creative University

The Conditions of Social Performance: An Exploratory Theory

Under the Ivi Tree: Society and Economic Growth in Rural Fiji

The Great Village: The Economic and Social Welfare of Hanuabada, an Urban Community in Papoua.

Choosing Our Destiny

*Creating the Utopian World
in the 21st Century*

Cyril Belshaw

Copyright © 2006 by Cyril Belshaw.

ISBN 10:   Hardcover   1-4257-2244-X
             Softcover   1-4257-2243-1

ISBN 13:   Hardcover   978-1-4257-2244-9
             Softcover   978-1-4257-2243-2

All rights reserved. No part of this book may be reproduced or transmitted in any form or by any means, electronic or mechanical, including photocopying, recording, or by any information storage and retrieval system, without permission in writing from the copyright owner.

This book was printed in the United States of America.

To order additional copies of this book, contact:
Xlibris Corporation
1-888-795-4274
www.Xlibris.com
Orders@Xlibris.com

34845

CONTENTS

I	Prologue	11
II	The Process of Innovation	15
III	The Search for the Soul, the Spirit, and a Model of Who we Are	43
IV	The Responsibilities of Education	59
V	The Family and the Generations	114
VI	Of Crime, the Law and Ill-Health	153
VII	Community and Diversity	192
VIII	Language, Media and Communication	211
IX	Humans in Nature	235
X	The Pursuit of Knowledge	243
XI	Terrorism and Freedom	279
XII	Of Work and Poverty	292
XIII	Fiscal Balance	305
XIV	A Note on Organisation, especially of capitalism	314
XV	The Poorer World	330
XVI	Bureaucracies and the Archaic State	349
XVII	Global Government	381
XVIII	Epilogue: How to Get There	407
	Acknowledgements	419
	Endnotes	421

C'est une promesse faite à Maître feu Felix Paschoud

And a gift for Eleanor Belshaw-Hauff, and Juniper Belshaw

If people would dare to speak to one another unreservedly, there would be a good deal less sorrow in the world a hundred years hence.
— *Samuel Butler*

The future enters into us, in order to transform itself in us, long before it happens.
— *Rainer Maria Rilke*

Visionary people are visionary because of the very great many things they don't see.
— *Berkeley Rice quoted in the Globe and Mail*

Although there are many who attempt to predict the future, and others who discuss ethical and policy issues based upon such predictions, there is considerably less discussion of where we want to arrive. We have the means. It is time to have the will.
— *This book*

I

Prologue

Studies of Utopia have in the past primarily focussed on imaginative literary expression, without worrying about the practicality of achieving what the mind conceives. There is a sense in which such work, valued in creating Alice in Wonderland mirrors and critical appraisals of inadequate human society, were precursors of later science and fantasy fiction.

In the nineteenth and twentieth centuries the focus partially shifted. On the one hand entrepreneurs endeavoured to create living, real, Utopian societies, localized in space, through colonies and communes. At the same time, led by Marxism or religious fervour, ideologies—the governance of behaviour through fundamental principle—took on an even stronger role in guiding political and socio-cultural action.

It is my contention that the twenty-first century can celebrate the evolution of Utopian propositions into forms which provide practical guidance for those of us who wish to create the best of possible worlds. This book is intended to be another step in that direction.

An underlying premise is that we have at our fingertips all the technical apparatus that we need to achieve whatever goals we decide upon. (This does not mean that we know everything—we certainly do not, but we know enough for change to be desirable). Another is that most of humankind wants a peaceful globe without violence of any kind, yet respecting and valuing cultural difference and variety. Since we have the means, it is not unreasonable to have the ambition to reach the kind of global Utopia I envisage by the year 2100, that is within the next century. Such is the current momentum of societal change. We have the choice of letting that momentum run its chaotic way unchecked, or of consciously deciding to guide it into paths we want to follow. It is, as never before, up to us.

There are multiple ways of arriving there, and billions of value-laden decisions to take along the way. Here the premise is that we, as peoples, must take steps to examine, evaluate, discuss the intermediary objectives—the ones to be defined as we move forward. However definitive I may seem in my ideas, they are just that. Ideas. I believe in them at this moment. But they need to be discussed, amended, replaced. All I ask is that in the discussion, the implication of any amendments be thought out, and traced through the rest of the argument for inconsistencies and further amendment. We must never forget the holistic pattern, that one decision affects all others. What you and I do now, individually and intimately, affects the 2100 outcome. In making decisions, however personal, we must never forget that.

Another premise is that cultures, whether local, professional or global are dynamic. The changes which took place in the twentieth century—little more than one lifetime—were fundamental to all societies in the world[1]. Some would argue, persuasively, that the rate of change increased exponentially, leading to inequities and anxieties about our ability to absorb the innovations. What is more, the changes have not been limited to technology or commercial practice or instruments designed to kill. In a very uneven way, they have included the most basic elements of human culture, from religious belief to marriage and sexual practice.

One major comment on the human conditions is that it is a result of tension between Krishna's idealisation of duty and Arjuna's belief that our actions will be judged rather on their consequences. Krisha wins the argument in practice, which violence and disaster for his victims. As Amartya Sen points out, the Bhagavad Gita, where this drama classically unfolds, may be interpreted as a warning about the blind devotion to duty, for its consequences may be successful in the short term, but dire in the long term. This essay comes down firmly on the side of consequences, but also argues that duty in fact implies precisely that—duty to humankind means being awar of and respectful of consequences.[2]

Up to the present, despite the existence of pressure groups, powerful politicians and CEOs, the changes have been blind. There is one relevant rule of human life. However much we plan, scheme, and rationalize policies, the results of any action, public or private, contain unforeseen elements. Sometimes these are trivial, sometimes they completely frustrate the given objective.

Thus we cannot be 100% certain about what we do. This is not a plea for more research—we must accept uncertainty and, its concomitant, the learning experience of failures along the way. We cannot wait for the completion of a major study; we must act in good faith, with the best knowledge and sensitivity we can muster.

The cliché has it that the movement of a butterfly's wings in the Amazon will influence the state of mind of a hermit in the Himalayas. We cannot detect that tiny influence. What the cliché says is that what we do has ramifying effects on the thoughts, actions, emotions, planning, of others both near and far. We do not normally extrapolate the consequences of our individual acts to the analysis of the nature of the world order. Yet the pond ripples, and it would be good to judge the effects of our own actions, however humble, in terms of their rippling consequences.

At an intimate level, there is much that can be done. We can judge our own actions in terms of what we know about their effects. This of course is already being done. Husbands and wives ponder the effect of their words and behaviour on their partners. Sincere environmentalists amend their private actions, consciously working if not to improve, at least not to further damage, the environment as they know it. Parents work with theories and ideas about what works best for their children, and in doing so have at least some wider respect for social responsibility. The exercises will be the more effective the more they become spontaneous, as natural results of attitudes towards life. To handle this is of course a prime goal of activities which create maturity in youth.

The vast differences between the rich countries and the poor, not only in commercial wealth but in the opportunities presented to the human spirit, create obvious targets for action. Too often, this takes the form of "Let them be like us". Put baldly, the gross flaws in such an argument are obvious to all except the proselytizers of U.S. style capitalism. I have claimed elsewhere[3] that the more centralized and detached a political entity, the more humans value small scale associations of great variety (from Churches to carnavals and cultural associations) within which they may find an identity.

Thus what we may call global values (e.g. embodied in international law and policy) both emerge from and impinge upon systems of significant localized values. Adaptation, resistance, judgement, positive excitement and anger are part of the dialectic. No great work can emerge which can take into account all the variations. But principles, such as those of understanding the nature and ramifications of change, the implications of reform, may be applied and respected.

I base my hope and optimism on several features.

The first is that we are already arguing, not following the structure of this book, but in our daily lives and politics. The second is that intimate and global societal changes have taken place in the past fifty years with a speed that perhaps is not as great as with technology, but is nevertheless mind boggling, chaotic, and needing popular control. The third is the rise of people power in the first years of this century. often indicating that the popular will is in advance of the political. The fourth is the effect of growing education and enquiry for all.

II

The Process of Innovation

There are some general principles which underlie my optimism and belief that Utopia is possible in the twenty-first century. These are the principles which govern and account for innovation and change. The recognition of them demonstrates that Utopia has moved from science fiction and fairy tales to reality.

How does societal change occur? As a boy with left wing ideals my critics often said to me "But human nature will never change". Biologically there are limits. But in fact, culturally, there are none, with one exception. Where we go is dependent on where we are and have been. In the past, that has put limits on our imagination of where we *can* go. But today so many options are open to us that such a limit is now of minimal importance.

If we wish to play our part, as individuals, in the movement of society we may preach (as perhaps I am doing) or, to the extent that it is in our ability, to live our beliefs. Not many of us can be political leaders of countries, let alone of world "government". But in family, business, or creative life we can do so insofar as the world around us permits. As more and more are doing, we can, if it suits our temperaments, exercise influence in associations and in whatever political process is open to us.

Since, by definition, we are working toward change (or such behaviour would not be an issue) it is not going to be easy, as I shall show. It is hard to think of changes in ourselves—managing the control of depression, working fewer hours, dealing with conflict—that will not be noticed by others, thus giving rise to comments and judgement. We put ourselves on the line, we are stating who we are, exposing our identities.

Those who run the gauntlet of possible criticism, however, can be comforted by the phenomenon that *any* action or belief, at least in industrialised society, will be criticised, open to the charge that it is mistaken, immoral or evil. (The obverse is not true: murder, child abuse, rape, are not likely to be approved by anyone, though killing is often condoned, ethnocide is often advocated, and some may excuse sexual assault.) A good football player, idolised by crowds, is condemned as a macho bonehead by others. Mother Theresa has her critics, as did Albert Schweitzer. A computer whiz or brilliant mathematician is scorned for being outside the real world. Giving to charity is blessed to some and tabbed as posturing by others. Discipline a child in the family circle, and neighbours will comment—when does it become abuse? A manager who promotes an able woman attracts gossip and jealousy. How many are they who have been hurt and disappointed when they find that their well-meaning, generous, or innocent actions have attracted derision, hostility or suspicion?

In many small societies in which I have worked, success is both highly sought after and dangerous. A successful person is one of power, manipulating the ties of kinship, friends, or compadres to create obligations. The reciprocal bonds of indebtedness ensure that the successful person is one who is owed much by others, ensuring that he gets material, moral or political support when he needs it. It is his generosity that makes this possible, for to give creates an obligation. But too much success attracts competition, envy, hostility, so that it must continually be managed sensitively. The successful person must speak in the idiom of family, tribe, community, ancestors, not of himself alone. If generosity falters, then it can be seen to be blatant, self-serving, and selfish. Dislike of aspects of behaviour—failure to perform a ritual properly, slighting a relative, the failure of a crop—leads to resentment that masks envy. Of a sudden, success is dangerous. There is illness or a string of bad luck attributed to sorcery or the success of competitors. The mana, the power, is gone. The high are toppled.

Complex societies have not evolved very far from reciprocal dependencies and the levelling influence of envy. We sometimes mistakenly think this to be so because of the ideology of individualism, and the perception that "simpler" societies were somehow non-competitive because they had ideologies of kinship, family, clan, tribe. We must address this issue, the way in which *ideologies mask the empirical realities*, the way in which they can disguise the realities of the system they represent. Until I raise that question more systematically it must be reserved as part of the background to some of my arguments, held as a continuous modifier to interpretations.

Anthropologists do not have much difficulty in demonstrating this. The public pretends reciprocity is not there. Yet ceremonial events—birthdays, weddings, Christmas—tie in dramatically with each other. The intensity, or lack of it, in personal and family relations, by which is meant personal interactions, create networks of giving that are dynamic, and in which what happened before influences what happens now. That the giving is generous does not remove the fact that it recognises past obligations, and creates new moral ones too. And the proportion of consumer spending that can be attributed to ceremony and friendship is enormous.

The impersonal market system of commerce and industry is not impersonal. Yes, contracts may be up for bidding. Yes, they are usually awarded on price and quality. The strict rules that apply to governmental contracts demonstrate, by the very "need" for them that something other than "objectivity" is significant. Of course it is. Reliability, the return of a favour, security based on personal knowledge, are of key significance. Entrepreneurs want to *know* their clients and suppliers, both to favour them and to exploit their weaknesses. Why else should there be business clubs, entertainment accounts, golf and horse racing?

I see pros and cons as I make judgements about such features. As a "scientist" my orientation is to understand without judging, to try to elucidate *how* it is that societies and cultures work the way they do, *how* did present conditions arise, *what* makes phenomena functional or dysfunctional within the system that is presented to me. By attempting to understand what goes on in one society and culture I may be able to arrive at principles or intuitions which can be applied to the interpretation of others. Some principles may be extended to apply to numerous, even all, societies.

Indeed it has happened already. The study of the classical prestatory (gift-obligation) societies—North West Coast Indians engaged in potlatch, Trobriand Islanders, then many others throughout the world—enabled anthropologists to hypothesise, in fact predict, the occurrence of such dynamics in as yet undescribed cultures, and, as mentioned above, in a re-interpretation of what goes on in the"individualistic" West. Clearly, because so many things are otherwise different, prestatory dynamics will not, empirically, be identical or even similar. But they will be there, in some form or another, in all societies, because giving (not only in material forms, but in emotions and communication) and receiving, and the psychological demands and moralities of the exchanges, are the essential bricks out of which the regularities of social organisation and of social predictability are built.

I am writing not as a "scientist" but as a citizen attempting to give shape to my ideas, values and prejudices, and to justify them by at least the minimum of logic and comparative empirical experience. And I am attempting to determine which features of the present have to be considered in order to tip socio-cultural evolution in the direction I feel to be satisfying. Hence I am making judgements about the viability and utility of the phenomena I write about. This is normative. What do we, I, value in life; what does it mean for designing the Utopia to which we will, I argue, strive?

Let us continue, bearing in mind that we are leading up to thoughts about the nature of innovation, for we have determined that the necessity for change is pretty well axiomatic, and change rests upon it.

The dynamics of prestation suggest that individuals pursue their goals through the creation of networks of social exchange with others. In some societies the networks may be hierarchical or kin-oriented. In the industrialised world the networks are far more open, although hierarchy and kinship are still very much there.

It seems difficult for many, including some of those in the intellectual community, to apply the concept of social exchange that underlies prestation. Most economists, with the exception of those who follow Gary Becker, have escaped from their ancestors into narrower concepts of exchange, confined to goods and (commercialised) services, or to market, that is monetised, transactions. Even many of my fellow anthropologists still speak of "the economy" or "the economic" as being related to material things, relegating services such as the provision of ritual to some other domain. The concept can be not only confining, but mistaken and ethnocentric.

It is mistaken, from the point of view of the subject matter of this argument, because such separations are artificial rather than real, because the material and the non-material are inextricably blended together by webs of value and meaning, and because ideas, values, concepts, emotions, spiritual thoughts, philanthropy, the search for power are all there, in competition, both as instruments for a satisfying life (resources) and as competing goals.

It is ethnocentric, for the ideas of money and the market are used to separate "market economies" from the rest, a separation that denies continuities between the two categories, postulates the near impossibility of the one evolving naturally into the other, and obscures analytical similarities. I have argued elsewhere that "money" is a matter of degree, not of kind[4]. It is not coinage and bank balances, but the *degree* to which whatever it is (materially) serves such functions as medium of exchange, store of value, and so on, in which other elements such as liquidity and confidence are embedded. There is nothing new in this; indeed it is old-fashioned.

So, as it were, we must turn things on their head. In the context of innovation, we talk of *exchange* not market, and we recognise that the things that are exchanged are not simply commercialised goods and services but all those other things that link one person to another, the immaterial, the intangibles, power and love, altruism as a goal, those other things that are never "equal".

Almost by definition, human beings cannot be totally in isolation from one another. Some groups can separate themselves more or less, and some individuals may opt to be hermits. These are decisions which result from previous histories of social interaction. Furthermore, in this day and age, supplies are almost always, if minimally, required from elsewhere.

The desire of individuals to link with groups is among their decision-making goals, and as such will be a subject of later discussion. Here it is sufficient to note the tension between the individual and the group, whether that group be a family, an association, a church, an ethnos or whatever. At one end of the spectrum, the group in question may succeed in subduing the individual and creating authoritarian conformity.[5] (Even here individuals are not carbon copies of each other, so that some degree of tension is present.) At the other end the individual attempts to reject a group, to find his own path, to seek isolation, to be a total rebel—or to find another association.

For by far the majority of persons on this earth, linkage with one or more groups is an essential element in the construction of personal identity. We cannot live alone; the choice of whom we associate with, in varying contexts, is part of our self-expression. This is true of even abstract communication, such as my writing this book.

At present it is almost an accepted truism in therapeutic ideology that it is not an appropriate goal for an individual to be so surrounded by inescapable group influences that he or she has lost his or her identity. Such individuals must seek their identities from a renewed consciousness of what lies within—especially if pressuring group has been a dominating family. Early family influences, once regarded as almost the inescapable creators of the persona, are now seen as the enemy, to be rejected in order to find one's self. The specifics of such an argument are for later chapters. Here, let us simply note that this is an example of the tension to which I refer. Moreover, the individual is in fact often replacing one group with another—the family (which he or she has probably already lost) with the cultural group constituted by therapists and their clients and like-minded others.

Tensions taken to this degree can be horrendously destructive. But some degree of tension is the source of creativity, since tension implies that there is a problem to solve. Awareness of a problem, its solution, is part of the process of innovation, of change. An alertness comes with reasonable tension, an alertness in which the mind identifies ranges of problems.

Problem solving, that is creativity, however modest, can draw its ideas from within the identified group, for this is where the idioms of communication will be fairly clear. In such groups there are shared languages. Mostly, a modicum of security is needed for the innovator to take the risky step of not only thinking, but of doing, something new. That security comes from group membership. And the innovation comes from mixing the ideas that lie within the group in new ways, and is extended when ideas enter the group from the neighbouring cultures. We can see the tensions, opportunities and restrictions at work very clearly in immigrant groups—not only now, but over the centuries. Overseas Chinese constitute the most well-known and marked example, reinforced by immense international networks of friends and persons who can be called kin. But almost every migration has had its stimulating effects—Huguenots, the nineteenth century movement of Swiss, English, Scots, and German; Lebanese, Punjabi, Ismaili, the list goes on.

Of course, the group can be self-limiting and inward-turning. If it is not open to outside influences, absorbing and using them, the capacity to innovate will be limited to the mix of ideas already present, and that limitation will be reinforced if there is an isolationist ideology. This is particularly true of some religious groups, who place an emphasis on their uniqueness, and the superiority of their ideology and ethics.

Another significant aspect of group identification is the use of innovation to reinforce that very identity. We must be very careful not to confuse innovation with only so-called "utilitarian" considerations. Spectacular ceremonies and extravagant festivals are the most cogent of examples of other kinds of pervasive innovation.

In a world where so much of our living is related to the anonymity of functionaries, where we interact with people of whom we know very little, when we must make meanings for ourselves as tiny particles in an infinite universe of others, where we are lumped together as being of a certain age, or sex, or tax bracket, we must, the therapists tell us, know ourselves. What better way than to see ourselves not as part of the whole world, but as a member of an association, an individual who can make a creative contribution in a cultural group—when "out there" we pass almost unnoticed?

When western developers first pondered the potential of Third World communities to "grow", they almost unanimously decried the existence of "wasteful" ceremonial. It took time before they could understand the anthropological truism that such ceremonial was often a way of re-distributing wealth and socio-political power; that it created dynamics of social exchange without which the economy would be dead; that it embodied positive goals, part of the economists' "competing ends" to which "scarce resources" would be allocated.

Surprise, surprise. As income increased, so did the amount of resources devoted to ceremonial—even to the extent of re-inventing activities that had been apparently gone, as with the famous medieval football game of Florence, proscribed under Mussolini.

And most such activities are still further segmented. In Florence and Siena the activities are organised—over months—in parishes of the city, to which loyalties are addressed. In Rio and Basle the competing carnival enterprises are handled by long term associations. Throughout the world there are events of a similar kind, let alone weddings, funerals, and Christmas giving. Embedded in them are values of power, fame, pride in the group, self-identity (look at me, I belong here), companionship—and often spectacular innovation. Are the competitions of sports, both professional and amateur, not similar—for athletes, "owners", coaches, advertisers, and the home fans?

But wait. Competition is dangerous. Associations have their own charters, their own rules, the procedures that set themselves apart from others. Like professions, which are restrictive by definition, they set boundaries to acceptable activities. An innovator may get away with enormous power; or by contrast the very fact of being too ambitious may lead to him being dragged down by envious rivals. To be successful, he must work within cultural rules and norms. Go too far beyond them and the power slips away. Nowhere is this more clear than in Industrialised political parties—both internally, and externally as the electorate expresses envy at perks and the symbols of power, and stretches out claws to tear them down. But it is everywhere.

An innovator, then, must often express a different kind of personality from his fellows to give expression to his ideas. He must often break with his group; his creativity is perhaps first expressed by doing just that. He may even be expelled or excluded by suspicion as to his motives, his intellectual nature, even his strange powers. He may find that the group with which he is associating simply does not have the imagination, the resources, the drive, or the interest, to support him when he needs it.

His risk taking assumes a new dimension. It is not only the risk of failure in the eyes of those who have trusted him, but the risk of self-failure. It is not only the risk of bankruptcy, or that his ideas are not functional or ahead of their time, that they won't work, that others won't recognise them. His own self is on the line. Can he fight through the reverses and disappointments? Can he find the niche in society that will allow his talents to flourish?

So many innovators discover themselves to be different, must live with those differences, become outcasts at least for the moment. In this age when we study almost everything, writers have drawn attention to two kinds of individuals who, except for a few perceptive observers, are somewhat like this. One set consists of those many differing individuals who have brain damage or sensory handicaps. The fact that "normally" equipped people have difficulty communicating sensitively with them hides their interior lives from all but the closest companion-observers. Those who do communicate find enormous resources of intellectual activity, artistic sensitivity, and creativity that comes from the narrower but more intense focus of their perceptions, which, when expressed, may be highly compulsive, yet innovative and valuable when made known to the rest of society.

And there are the "eccentrics", people who in effect say to the world "I'm me. I shall concentrate on behaving the way I like. If you wish to learn to live with my foibles, good. If not, I'm sorry, but I laugh." Britain was once renowned as a country that valued its eccentrics, turned them into the subject of warm satire and playful cartoons. Britain defended their right to be eccentric to the hilt. The most recent small example I ran into was at a pedestrian crosswalk in London. A tweedy gentleman with a cane stepped forth. The oncoming car kept moving at the crosswalk. The gentleman stepped into its path, waved his cane angrily, went to the driver's window and gave him a dressing down.

Take that little incident for a moment. Trivial? Not at all. To an observer like myself it was a warmingly welcome incident, with which I identified, but perceived as unusual, hence eccentric, probably part of a personality that would express many other similar actions. In some parts of the world, doing that would have been a high risk matter. Here, in this part of London, it seemed to carry little risk, denoting the thought that such behaviour was still tolerated. But it carried another thought, namely that if there were a growing number of incidents of that kind, if it were on the rise, so to speak, then drivers would begin to realise that infractions of this kind, the inherent threat of danger within them, was no longer a matter to be taken for granted. In other words, the eccentric act of one individual at one time, if repeated and taken up by others, could become the norm. Is this why, now, I do whatever I can to make my anger known to drivers of rowdy motor-cycles, unsuppressed car mufflers, and heavy metal emerging from 4 x 4s.

Individual actions *are* significant. It is through them that norms become established.

Are there any general principles which account for innovation, out of which we may derive some enlightenment about how our norms, behaviour, and material world, change?

"Eureka" he shouts in the bath tub, "I have it!" The dramatic flash of insight that in a moment changes the world . . . Coming from nowhere, into a brilliant mind.

Not so fast. There are many components to innovation. An innovation is, by definition, a new cultural artefact. Innovations flower in a thousand ways. But they all have one characteristic.

They make use of *already* known cultural components. The components must be *recognised* by the innovator, they must have meaning for him. Even in dreams, in the wildest imagination, the elements that combine to make the fantasy are each, if taken apart one by one, known. The angels do not send down a flash of lightning with the message here is something, dear innovator, for you to use, something that is beyond the comprehension of your culture. Even if that were so, the innovator could not be expected to understand its significance unless he were mentally ready, unless the novelty were composed of elements he recognised, unless he had some understanding of how it fitted into already established life or thought. An innovation may be revolutionary, may have uncomprehended consequences, but in itself it combines in a new way characteristics that are already there. The novelty may come from accidental observation, the insight of a dream awakening, but the components of what is observed must have meaning; or it may come from painfully elaborated abstract logic.

Whoever first used fire to cook something, maybe meat, already knew that fire burned, already knew that meat was good to eat. Perhaps he dropped the meat in, but his senses were ready for the result. Obversely, it is no use preaching the value of platinum to a culture which does not yet recognise the uses of the substance, directly or in trade. And the outcome of mathematical logic depends on the elaboration and manipulation of concepts that have already been developed, doing so in new combinations. Each concept, once established, adds to what is there, expands it, becomes a stepping stone for the next stride.

That axiom is at the root of what follows.

For it follows that if you have very few components in your culture the likelihood of recombination will be slim, the changes slow. But if you have limitless components, then the possibility of recombination is also limitless, and the pace of innovation is fast.

It used to be argued that "traditional" societies were "innately" conservative, lacking an "achievement orientation". Not so. In the first place, *all* societies value achievement—where they differ is in the objectives of achievement. It may be good hunting, producing children, warfare, riches, spiritual attainment, leisure, or of course in combination. It is true also that some societies, or social groups, value the security of stability or unchanging continuity; but so strong is the appeal of innovation that they can only do so by attempting to place strict boundaries around themselves, trying to prevent the enlargement of their cultures. And there, of course, in this modern world at least, they fail, with the result of change, of schism, or of loss of population.

In a previous work I wrote, confusingly, of an "orientation" toward innovation. It is probable that it would be more useful to place innovation within the list of societally valued goals as a variable. This is most easily illustrated with art. In some societies new pieces of work are valued for their continuity with past forms; in others they are valued for their "originality", their change from the past. Such goals have to be balanced with, and to compete with, other goals—perhaps some aesthetic principle—to become effective.

Certainly, *individuals* differ the one from the other in their ability to create the recombinations, to innovate, that is they differ in their creativity. In the simplest of societies there are those who think, who tell stories imaginatively, who philosophise, who tinker, who adventure, who explore, and thus stand out as different.

A new idea or artefact is not in itself an innovation. It must somehow spread beyond the individual's own world, be communicated to others, and embraced into the cultural world of others. If it stays privately with the individual, it is lost to culture. It is the individual's private toy.

The individuals to whom a new idea or artefact is presented judge it from the point of view of their own thoughts, interests and goals. That is, does it somehow fit into their conceptual frameworks? A proposal that is "ahead of its time" may simply not fit well; it must wait until the rest of culture has changed to make the fit more apt, more useful, more acceptable.

The impact does not have to be acceptable to everyone. On the contrary, its value may be in stimulating further debate, further change. The point is that it has entered the pool of ideas, become part of the capital stock of culture, available for yet further recombination, known to other minds.

There must be hundreds if not thousands of material inventions which are in themselves inherently sound, but which have not been recognized, or have been rejected because their creation does not fit into the mind set of those to whom it may be targeted. One current example is that of the Skegway. This is a battery operated device which moves the human body making use of the body's own inherent attributes of balance and adjustment which come into play when we walk. Its foundation is a platform on two specially tired wheels which the user's body manipulated by linking the body to the device through a rigid handle. It replaces the single occupancy car, is environmentally safe and energy efficient and, with adaptations, can be used all terrain. The inventor could not get financiers, policy makers, and certainly not vehicle manufacturers to take up its production and distribution. Despite this, through his own efforts, the device has been successfully demonstrated in many contexts, is now in manufacture, and is being adopted in numerous industrial contexts (such as the Vancouver International Airport) as well as for individual use (despite its current expense).

In other words it is more likely that not that initial inventions will meet nay-sayers who have vested interests in reducing competition, or who, unlike the inventor, are still thinking blindly within a dark box.

If this is true of material inventions, how much more true it can be of non-material and policy innovations. Don't rock the boat, there are too many risks and uncertainties, are common objections to the most innocent of proposals, let alone those which have world changing attributes. Indeed, innovative ideas in this book are bound to attract opposition as a matter of blind principle as well as a matter of genuine thinking. It will be a task of what follows to shoe that such objections are open to challenge and that they can have consequences which are often dire as well as obstructive. Nevertheless it behoves the innovator to consider the socio-cultural context in which heshe is working, and to bring the ideas and proposals into touch with those elements of culture and knowledge which are already in place to be tapped and recognised.

To sum up, the rate of innovation in a culture is a function of the size of the cultural stock, that is the pool of ideas, knowledge and material resources, interpreted widely, plus another factor I will introduce shortly.

Material resources are included for two reasons. The obvious one is that material resources provide some of the raw materials for innovators to play with, to help them communicate their ideas, and to put them into effect.

For this to happen the resource must be recognised in some form. When a resource crosses from one culture to another, it is frequently the case that its meaning, and therefore its function, will also change. Guitars will be used for different purposes in Nova Scotia and Pernambuco—the outflows in music and in the social context are not identical. The aluminium and wires of an abandoned aircraft in Kenya will not go to a recycling depot, but will be turned into articles of bodily adornment. To sell the benefits of oil production to a culture that does not know the concept "oil" as it applies to underground liquids and industrial use or consumption requires conversation and persuasion to introduce the relevant notions, that is to add to the stock of cultural capital.

In other words the material is never just the material. It does not consist of objects isolated from cultural linkages. Whether it be coins or a chair or women's adornments, or a rock by the side of a road, or a road itself, it is irrelevant except insofar as it has meaning, can be interpreted, and unless it communicates that meaning, which may have utilitarian, aesthetic, personal, or even spiritual overtones. It is with the manipulation of such meanings that material innovation takes place. Hence, from an innovative point of view, the elements of the material that are significant are those that are immaterial. Remove the legs of a table and replace them with rollers; change the shape of the table; replace the wood with glass; etch the glass; place flowers on it; put a Japanese screen behind it; place food on it; put your feet on it; all these changes take place through the use of concepts. Put the table in a Melanesian thatch hut and it may be out of place, not wanted—unless another idea comes into play, that of prestige, one-upping the neighbours. The material consists of concepts, then, and those concepts are available to the innovator in the same way as are the ideas translated into a book or a painting.

I have already pointed out that the size of the cultural stock affects the chances of innovation taking place, that is the quantity of innovation. Let us do a bit of innovation along the lines of the principles I have been enunciating. From economics we know the concept that the size of the money supply consists of the quantity of money modified by its *velocity of circulation*. It seems sensible to borrow the concept here.

For surely if two men sit side by side, each with differing ideas, but don't talk to each other, i.e. with a velocity of circulation of ideas of zero, the size of the sum of ideas of each of them will be minimal if not zero. Minimal rather than zero because mew thought combinations may be occurring in their brains. Zero velocity, minimal innovation. Even if one of the men has enough ideas in his head to think up something new, he is not communicating by talk, hence minimising the potential innovatory impact.

Once they start talking, the chances increase. Expand the conversation to others, they increase further. Circulation is happening within the pool of ideas. And so it goes on. It is no accident that the exponential innovation growth of the twentieth century was founded on profound changes in communication. And it is no accident, either, that mediaeval scholars, often quite isolated in their own communities, placed enormous emphasis on travel to scholarly centres to expand the limits of their communication. Was not the need for communication, for disputation, for the interacting of minds, in times when travel was inefficient, a most powerful impetus for the founding of universities? And did not a lingua franca, Latin, contribute to that possibility?

So, the rate of innovation is a result of the size of the pool of ideas modified by the velocity of communication.

In later argument I will be writing of cultures as entities, that is as being in some sense bounded, a concept that raises many issues. For the moment, however, let us assume that this is so.

If so, we can conceive of culture as something like a liquid containing millions of moving cells—not people, but ideas, concepts, values, moving through talk, gestures, facial expressions and embodied in recognised natural entities and items of man-made material culture. To conduct empirical research on culture, in connection, say, with my theses, it would be ideal to be able to quantify the number of those cells. To do that one would have to break down everything—ideas, elements of material items—into both their smallest parts that can conceptually stand alone and into those combinations (a table, a table leg, a table top, a mathematical equation, each of the concepts which make up the equation) that also have meaning. An enormous and literally impractical task.

Failing that, and failing the ability to conduct hypothesis testing on the basic of such a necessity, a major conclusion stands out nevertheless, which will have an impact on later chapters. We have come across one of many limitations to the certainty of knowledge. Our knowledge about the kinds of matters we are discussing cannot be perfect. It can be indicative, approximate, subjective. As individuals facing the future we must reconcile ourselves to **the certainty of imperfect knowledge**.

To return, however, to the concept. If a cultural boundary is tight, with no movement over it (almost an impossibility as is the economist's "perfect competition") the number of cultural cells contained within the boundary is finite at any given time. But there are more of some than of others. There may be ten mathematicians and a hundred boat builders and five thousand lovers. The number of cells related to these conceptual domains will be affected by the complexity of the thoughts in each domain (let us say 1,000 cells mathematics, 500 boat building, and 50,000 lovemaking—not very realistic, but illustrative), by the number of individuals sharing those thoughts, and by the velocity of circulation, that is communication.

To draw up an account of what is going on, one would in fact be drawing up an inventory of the cultural stock, and analysing modes, patterns and intensities of communication (which would have to allow for the possibility that the receiver did not absorb the communication in precisely the way it was sent—that it, filtered it). This inventory I call a *profile of culture*.

Profiles of culture do, approximately, exist. They are called thick ethnographies. Most of them, for the non-specialist, are terribly dull to read, because they describe in minute detail elements of the daily life of a people, as completely as possible, preferably based on participant observation, a technique in which the observer merges as closely as he can within the daily life, using the language as the medium of talk. They are indeed inventory-like, and they make interpretations and generalisations based upon the way in which elements in the inventories relate to each other, that is, communicate.

Because such profiles describe the here and now of the observation, they are also the *only* data that approximate what the economist calls effective demand, that is what people actually do with their resources at any given time, whether that be of a material or non-material nature. In practice, economists deal with only little bits of effective demand, treating some of the most important wants (or goals in life) as outside their models, or as "other things being equal". Not many of them read ethnographies, even of modern communities.

In fact the ethnographies also fall far short of the objective. The writers do not have, at least in these decades, the scientific objectives that would be implied in the questions of this Chapter. Paradoxically, once upon a time the objectives would not have seemed so strange, for anthropologists in the early part of the century were obsessed by what they called "cultural traits" that correspond very roughly to the cells, and they were guided in doing so by a search for the influence of cultural traits upon each other within and across cultural boundaries. Many of them did so out of sociological context, that is without observing meaning working *in practice*, and with inadequate attention to context.

Studies of profiles of culture are also hampered by manpower, its training and its distribution. Doctoral candidates are seldom given the finances to employ research assistants to gather data in ways that permit quantification. Their theoretical orientation suggests, anyway, that this is less worthwhile than the creation of a range of studies, each focusing on a theoretical problem which does not require such minute quantification. In most cases, discussion is by way of *example*, minutely dissected. If there were enough of these examples, the data would be there, but there cannot be through these methods.

I myself, in looking at the interlinkages between ceremonies in parts of Fiji, in which scores of individuals were involved, with the massive exchange of goods, and large feasting, and working alone, could not cover all the significant detail of any one marriage, for example. I had to attend several, and combine the observations. And then do the same with funerals and other events for they were all interlinked. But I did not count the *number* of such ceremonies in the observation period. It could have been done, quite simply. But other things . . . the number of first fruits ceremonies performed? I would have had to redirect my four Fijian part-time assistants, who were very busy doing household budgets and tracking cargoes on the trucks going to market . . .

We can improve, if the questions are deemed important enough. We are not likely to improve enough to give certainty, even in the quantification mad twentieth century. I have argued before, and state again, that in the absence of appropriate techniques we can never truly know the operable values in a culture or predict its movement. We can only approximate.

I think the questions *are* important, because I believe there are significant generalisations about the way in which innovation translates into societal change, which are capable of being investigated more closely. (I first expressed the ideas in the late 'forties as a result of thinking about agriculture in the Solomon Islands, and tinkered with them from time to time later. No one has told me I'm wrong, nor yet debated them.)

Begin with the notion that the profile of culture is not a random hodge podge of cells accidentally linked to each other. The cells are linked by communication, which is the electricity that attracts or repels them, and by the power of thought that binds those that are attracted into conceptual nuclei. Add to this the notion that societal change takes place not when a single nucleus is altered, but only when it spreads within the system to some degree. The system is just that, a system, its parts influencing each other.

A changed nucleus can bring about ramifying consequences. For example, the introduction of reading skills can bring about a demand for reading materials, newspapers, books, libraries; can lead to changes in other ideas as a result of the fusing of concepts contained in the written word with ideas already in place, and so on and on. It can also have multiplying effects, that is for more reading instruction given to other persons, children or adult. However, such effects may be no more than potentials, if the means of satisfying them are not there, or are too onerous to be used. When I was in the Solomon Islands in the 'forties the ramifying effects were primarily limited to religious literature and the writing of letters which sometimes had almost mystical connotations of power, for there was almost no other reading material. (Paperbacks from the U.S. forces were snapped up, and a typewritten "newspaper" I created engendered a flow of story and article contributions which totally surprised me.) But after the war the resource base changed, and the potential demand was translated into a vigorous and effective search for highschool and university learning.

To disentangle a viable *potential* profile of culture, in precise terms, is almost impossible, but in approximate terms it must be attempted. If asked, individuals will certainly express their hopes, fears, goals, values. But when it comes to the point, when actually confronted with the possibility of achievement, many of the thoughts fall by the wayside. The precise costs, the alternatives that have to be downplayed or given up, the price in terms of time, emotion, or material things, turn out to have a reality that differs from the fantasy. Such conundrums are the bane of social workers, community developers, political activists, reformers of all kinds. Many of the suggestions that come later in this book will be wrecked, at least in the short term, on this sharp rock. If this were not so, we might already have reached Utopia . . .

There are conceptual ways of getting around this problem. The economists' notion of *elasticity* of demand, adequately re-arranged for sociological purposes, provides a framework. It would postulate that the true measure of valuation of a thing or an activity consists in the degree to which individuals are willing to suffer costs to get more of it, or to pay increased costs (including the psychological and emotional ones) to hold on to it. The empirical test of values through elasticity runs up against the problem of differing kinds of costs, of measurement of changes, and of the fact that it is *ex post facto*, which limits the power of predictability. Nevertheless, more serious attention to the concept could result in approximate advances in what we know, and some data observed from segments of the population might provide bases for predicting what could happen in others.

Certainly, if we wish to know more about future innovation, attention to the concept is essential. At the very least, it indicates that assertions about the future, and about what is *likely* in fact to happen, whether by politicians, by pundits or by preachers, must be taken with mountains of salt. *The harsh truth is that they do not know what the consequences of their actions will be, and nor do I.*

We must live with approximation. We cannot stand back from the world or fail to act because our informed guesses about the future are just that. Further, the limitations of predictability increase, the desirability of normative analysis. We *can* articulate where we *think* we want to go. We *can* change our minds if we find the costs too high, or the satisfactions of achieving the goal are less than we had anticipated. We can and do live with uncertainty, and that does not and should not prevent us from doing things that we imagine, anticipate, will bring about a better world. Dealing with uncertainty is an adventure, an emotional challenge, a value in itself. Uncertainty is no excuse for sitting on one's butt.

Note that a profile of culture contains conceptions of values, moral positions, goals. Treated as a system, the profile is not just a weighted list. Nuclei reinforce one another, because they represent the logical and emotional connections between goals and values of different people. Those who stand on one side or another of the abortion debates are, as individuals, different one from another, in the source of their opinions, in their other goals, in the way their emotions work. Perhaps there are regularities of background—religious assumptions, for example—which tie some together. But there are likely to be many more variants, coming together on this issue. Insofar as the nuclei come together in a reinforcing, ramifying or multiplying manner, they may be said to be *complementary*.

Given the complexity—that is the size and variety of nuclei in the pools of culture—of the modern world, the differences are as significant as the complementarities. Even within a group of persons who are united to pursue one goal, or who seem in sympathetic agreement on issues, differences, subtle or major emerge. The differences have a variety of consequences, which strongly influence or inhibit the innovatory path.

Competition between concepts is obvious. The competition reveals itself in the fight for a place in human minds, in the search for the prepotency which will control action, within one individual as within those of a group. This leads to varying mixtures of ideas from time to time as different nuclei find a place in a single group of thoughts, and one's "thinking" about an issue changes.

As this happens, within one or between several, individuals there are perceptions of the result. Some are stimulating, satisfying—the problem has, for the time being, been resolved. But whatever the resultant concepts are, others are also present, on the verge of consciousness, or on the verge of communication. As they come to the fore, the perception, intellectually or emotionally driven or both, can arise that something is not right, there is discomfort, there is a *perceived inconsistency* with other sets of nuclei.

We all learn to live with our inconsistencies. We handle them, tell ourselves they don't matter, or we follow one idea at one time and another at the next. There may be objective inconsistencies that observers could agree are manifest in our expressions or behaviour. We can ignore them, and are usually unaware of them.

Sometimes, though, they become uncomfortable, to the point of interfering with our actions, rising to obsessive dominance in our thoughts, and arguments with our fellows. The inconsistencies demand resolution. We seek to amend our thoughts and our world until our internal peace is reconstituted; we are in equilibrium again. *Incompatabilities* are once again reduced to compatibility, by some adjustment in the cultural nuclei. This is a constructive path to societal change, one that, ideally, we would all like to follow, since it posits an outcome, a psychological resolution. Peace and well-being return. There is a sense of having achieved something. There are some of us who innovate in this way continuously, thriving on the succession of problems, resolution, problem, resolution—and sometimes other related rewards, such as the respect and prestige it can bring. (Don't forget the costs: failure, envy.)

Here we are on the very edge of *dysfunction*. There is no law that states that a cultural system has to be perfectly adjusted. If it were, there would be no demand for change whatsoever. Functional (and its offshoot structural) anthropology reacted to the popular conception that many cultural traits were irrational, strange, inexplicable, savage. It was and is a major tool of understanding to actively seek the explanations, the rationalities that underlay the apparently irrational, the common sense of what was being done in the light of the total context, the damage that systems would suffer if one such significant trait were to be destroyed by outside thoughtlessness. The sources of change to functional or structurally sound systems did not come from stresses within. They came from without, and caused pain and problem-solving as the outside influences ramified through the culture, creating inconsistencies and incompatibilities that cried to be resolved.

In the modern world, there is still much to be said for the humanistic values of such an approach. But it needs to be amended. As analysts were quick to show, what came from outside did not descend on an inert body waiting for injections of new nuclei. The body of culture had its own immune systems, and chose from the invading viruses those they could handle and those they rejected. (Not literally: individuals did not have the power to resist biological viruses . . .) Of course, power played a part, the power of the outsider to use force and blandishments; and the power the insider sought to gain by adopting new strengths. And while this was happening, the functional systems had their own problems to handle, and were involved in the ongoing adaptations of their cultures. Invading ideas had to fit the dynamic, force the dynamic into another path, or be adapted to fit the dynamic.

When competitive nuclei refuse to accommodate in such ways, when individuals hold to them as precious, as so highly valued that they will pay high costs to keep them, and the accommodations can be resolved only by a clash, often of titans, sometimes of dwarfs, we are led straight into *dysfunction*. In individuals it manifests itself in depression, alienation and the like, which, if treated, can return to the functionality of solutions. But as a manifestation of a cultural system, or two in a clash, we have measures of adjustment which aim at control, an inability to compromise, and often force in one form or another. Divorce, violence, anti-social behaviour, war, totalitarianism, racism, family violence, the attempt by groups to *impose* their will on others, the list goes on.

The processes I have mentioned in this summary form all imply that one can abstract a culture, talk about it as an entity, and think of it as being composed of a multitude of interacting parts, which not merely gear together in some mechanical way, but rather influence and change each other. The conceived culture is *articulated* insofar as rules can be discovered which guide the effects of nuclei upon each other. One such theme is that the powers of nuclei to adapt and to change others are based on their psychological component, manifested most significantly in perceptions. It is the *perception* of compatibility or incompatibility that counts, not some outside idea of functionality. Would-be reformers must constantly be reminded of this. An idea is much more likely to move into the system, or through it, if the persons involved *perceive that it fits*, and, based on that perception, judge that it will be good for them. Good for them usually means that it brings a benefit to their thought or behaviour that is worth the costs and sacrifice involved.

Here we are close to the ends-means relationship that is essential to the thinking of economists and some other social scientists. I adhere to the use of this relationship in the form I understood it to mean among the *pionee*r economists. That is, what is an end and what a means is not an objective external definition, but depends upon the personal evaluations and concepts of the actor. Influenced by their need to measure and to manipulate quantities, economists have largely dropped this notion, and they themselves attempt to define what is a means and what an end, what is productive capital and what is a consumption good.

There are signs of trends back to what I regard as basics. This is coming about because economists have been forced to become interested in factors of production and social objectives that link with finance but have non-material components—health, social policy, education to take the most obvious. Once seen as social objectives and thus calculated as "ends", they are now recognised to have effects on "production", must be picked apart as "factors of production" *as well as* ends in themselves.

The circumstance that education has both characteristics, that is as a valuable end in itself, and as a means to greater productivity, should give us pause for thought. It impinges on arguments in various sections of these essays. But more profoundly, it raises the hypothesis that ***all** behaviour and objects contain **mixtures** of means and ends.*

A grand cathedral is a means to spirituality, but it is also a direct provider of awe and aesthetic satisfaction in itself. Tourists are shown Gaudi's buildings in Barcelona, not because they are functional but because they challenge the eye. A craftsman carves or builds a boat to make money for his family; but the activities are chosen because he loves them, he is prepared even to take a loss or a pittance of profit because he values the work in itself.

Once again, reform has often stalled because the element of satisfaction in something the reformers define as having only pain can so easily be overlooked, or put down to "innate conservatism". Why should shifting cultivators give up their forest digging sticks for "more effective" spades and shovels, and their clearings for fields, when they *like* the way their bodies move in traditional agriculture, enjoy the leaves around them, are happy with the schedules of work and rest in their present system? There can be good reasons, but reformers need to be absolutely sure that the benefits they dream up are real ones, do not have hidden unexpressed costs, and above all fit well into the perceptions of the cultivators about what they want from the world.

If there is confusion about ends and means, there is equivalent confusion about the material and non-material. The distinction seems so straight-forward: the material is something I can touch. If I can't touch it, it is non-material.

Material objects are, though, a collection of symbols put together in material form. In that, they are at one with non-material symbols like language and thought. They are in fact composed of thoughts, of the recognition of meanings. Buildings are libraries of concepts, so are coal mines, so are piles of grain waiting to be shipped, so is a pavement. Without their embodied concepts they are meaningless, they do not exist, they rot away.

And the meanings and concepts are subject to change according to the same rules we have been discussing. All the things we think about them, all the recognitions, ambiguities and puzzles, are nuclei in the profiles of culture. At one time a building is ripe for demolition; at another a historical treasure. At one time it is a school, another a warehouse. Coal is something dirty for domestic fires; or an alternative source of energy. The mine is dangerous and dirty, or a work place with perhaps high wages, or a source of tourist dollars, or something to be closed down. The pavement is hard on the feet and needs replacing, it is the route to the nearest good restaurant, it is composed of ugly stones, it is the embodiment of the history of the feet which have passed over it. The house on the corner is environmentally destructive, to some its staircase is beautiful and functional, to others it is something to be taken away to an antique market, what happened to the trees?, it accommodates too many people, it interferes with my view, I don't like the idea it is a half-way house . . .

Once my father and I had to invent a new word for a building, where my grandfather preached. It was built as an ordinary house, to which someone had added a belfry. We couldn't decide whether it was a "chouse" or a "hurch". (His innovation was for the family only)

Is it not a common complaint about certain "functional" buildings that we don't know from the outside whether they are supermarkets, schools, hospitals, or prisons?

Material innovation and cultural innovation are one and the same. Cultural and social changes arise from the dynamics contained in the profiles of culture. The move to, or from, Utopia, is a cultural event. Within that context, politics and economics are not even sub-divisions. They do not exist except as part of the changing cultural whole.

You may of course be wondering why I have used the word "innovation" instead of "creation" or "creativity". One reason is pragmatic. The word "innovation" focuses on a process which results in something new. Much of creation does too. But in my view quite significant creation does not. A woodworker may turn out chair after chair of quite skilled handcraft. His original concept may have been innovative, but thereafter it is repetitive. Yet he is a creator of good things.

The other reason is that much confusion surrounds the analysis of creation, so that there is good reason to break away from it. One of the most recent compilations of perspectives and analysis, with the words :Theory and practice" in the title is almost encyclopaedic in its range of examples[6]. It even suggests that the religious stories of "Creation" are part of the subject, not because they are creative fables, but because the subject they deal with is one form of creation—that is not due to human hand. This is going to far, but the author correctly notices that the approaches of creative individuals differ widely according to subject matter—in literature, music, engineering, for example. Then the matter is left up in the air—there are many creativities and no over-arching theory[7] A set of propositions which accounts for the process? Considering innovation in all domains of human endeavour enables us to approach understanding in a theoretical way. And having undertaken such an approach, we can use it to inform ourselves or our own innovative behaviour, and that of the institutions of which we are a part.

There is also a psychology of innovation. Studies of innovative individuals ha ve revealed that for the greatest of them psychological props help. My favourite example is that of writers or composers who must settle to their work at a particular time of day, must have their pen or keyboard just so, with a cup of favourite coffee of just the right blend and strength, and the page open at the end of an unfinished sentence which gets them back in the mental swing. If any of these items is missing, it takes time to get settled. Thinkers are noted for their walks in the words. A sculptor or a painter must have the work space arranged (however chaotic it may seem to an outsider) to hiser satisfaction, and maybe spend some moments reflecting on how his creation meets his ambitions in the new morning. And should we speak of chefs with their *batterie de cuisine*. So it goes on. Each one of us can fins ways to refine our innovative actions and thoughts.

An understanding of and an application of a theory of innovation gives us the opportunity to be more effective in changing our world towards that of a Utopia in the 21st century.

III

The Search for the Soul, the Spirit, and a Model of Who we Are

The spiritual searching that is characteristic of all cultures is now a part of the search for one's self. It does not apply to all individuals by any means; secular values appear to predominate.

Writing on this subject is heavily fraught. The range of religious and spiritual beliefs globally and within modern cultures is enormous. So is the range of spiritual experience, from ecstasy to psychological exploration. As with almost everything else, I see embedded contradictions, oppositions, values and social and personal dysfunctions. The task for Utopia is to support and emphasise the positive human values in the spiritual search, and to weed out the dysfunctions[8].

Phrases such as "freedom of religion" as with "freedom of the press" and "the right to organise", once of enormous significance, power, and necessity, which I thought I would defend to the death, have, unfortunately, become the banal refuge of a misplaced absolutism, slogans which hide uncomfortable thought. In fundamental ways they are still there, to be used wisely, and are among the foundations on which Utopian society must rest.

But they are not absolute. We made them nearly absolute because we could not trust authorities to distinguish between the valuable and the damaging. This was not a right we wished to pass over to someone else; and because we also distrust our neighbours, not to them either; we wished as a public to rise to their defence. Yet when the chips are down, we place limits. No to cults which engage in strange habits, brainwashing, sexual autocracy, and forced membership. No to child pornography. No to organisations, even unions, which put the public safety in danger. What those limits should be is a cause for continuous argument and disagreement, with wide cultural variation.

The spiritual search is creative, innovative, and often an essential ingredient in psychological balance. Formal studies of innovation have concentrated mostly on material culture, scientific and technical ideas, and management practices. Yet the great variety of religious beliefs, the continuity of schism and debates about theology and religious practice, indicates that many of the same processes are at work—the diffusion of ideas; their acceptance, modification or rejection; the link of acceptance to a search for psychological, aesthetic, and intellectual equilibrium; multiplying effects throughout the systems of belief.

The search for one's soul and its spiritual expressions is, like all other searches, a combination of religious belief and scientific enquiry.

By religious, I mean holding onto a belief through faith; by scientific I mean examining and testing belief sceptically through logical tools and empirical evidence. If a patient seeks advice from a doctor, and accepts that advice without question, the patient is acting on faith. The doctor is in the role of priest, his theories a theology; the patient confesses and gets absolution through the rituals of medication; religion is at work. If, on the other hand, the patient questions the doctor, wants to know the basis for hiser advice, and then makes up hiser mind independently as to whether he orshe will take the advice or not, and to what degree, h or shee is using sceptical enquiry, as in science. It is a mistake to think of science as a package of experimental paraphernalia, or as a technology. It is an attitude, just as religion embodies particular kinds of attitudes.

In real life, most specific actions emerge from *both* religious and scientific attitudes, in these senses. It is not so much a question of categorising actions as *either* religious or scientific, as if they were separated. In theology there is a great deal of sceptical searching, and of applying theory to ends (both worldly and other-worldly) and practices. Some churches engage in bodily healing as well as the curing of the soul, and promise rewards on this earth as well as in the hereafter. There is a continuum of such beliefs. If the sceptical searching were not there, there would be but one, the originally invented, religion. Paradoxically, the search for new faiths, for amending old ones, may be intensified by the spread of scientific questioning, and by the principle, if something doesn't seem to work, try something at least a little different: experiment.

At the same time, faith is an essential component of most action. It may come about through entrenched belief, through the successful repetition of actions, through accepting ideas. It embraces, and frequently unites, what seem to be disparate fields of action. Belief in an almighty, judgmental, merciful God can coalesce quite well with faith in the stock market or in the wisdom of doctors or witch doctors. True, outsiders can comment upon seeming contradictions in behaviour; the humble church-goer co-existing with the predatory competitor and merciless manager. Psychological equilibrium, however, is attained internally, from the believer's own faith, logic, and sense of compatibility. It may be well-merged; it may be a source of stress; either. It is not for the lay outsider to judge by projecting his or her own logic onto the believer's mind, though the outsider may very well use the data before him to think and speculate about the phenomenon.

The less faith in one's actions, the greater the probability of internal tension. How often we do something, doubting its wisdom, not knowing whether the outcome will be what we can expect. If scepticism about our own actions goes too far, we become unable to act, confused, depressed. We need a modicum of faith. It does not have to be of the organised sort, though that helps many.

It has been said that the power of guilt is particular to the Judeo-Christian tradition. That cannot be so. Guilt is linked to worry over a moral dilemma and the exercise of personal responsibility. There are those who manifest very little by way of guilt, strong spokesmen for or members of a Church. Their faith absolves them, for they do what they do in its name. In non-Christian societies, a father who causes the death of his son grieves not only for the son, but for the failed responsibility of his actions. Guilt is a universal variable. From this point of view, I see little difference between a Thai Buddhist business man donning the saffron robes for a lengthy spiritual revival, and westerners who retreat for meditation. Guilt may be linked to a code of sinning, or it may stem from the perception of an inadequate exercise of responsibility. It may come from a feeling that one should know one's soul better, and ought to do something about it. Psychologically and theologically speaking, it requires redemption; the path to redemption is eased by faith.

I find too that the need for redemption or absolution is linked to two of the most dominant themes in our personal lives: the desire to be in tune with one's fellows (that is to live in social harmony), and to be in concord with one's inner being, away from the strains of guilt and self-doubt. We will see that dealing with such principles are significant preoccupations for sexual and inter-personal relationships and the Utopian education. They are an important part of the struggle to redeem those whom we define as criminals, or even those who are ill. Guilt about over-weight or smoking?

Whether the personal spiritual journey is part of those systematic organised beliefs we call religion, or whether it is part of a secular rationalisation of ethics and psychology, it is thus an inescapable and fundamental part of Utopian dynamics.

It is here that religion, ethics, philosophy, and psychology meet. Many formal religions have moved to recognise this, making use of therapeutic techniques such as role playing, Jungian analysis, gospel singing, the use of incense, the hypnotic moving of the heads during recitations, group meditation and discussion of religious themes and personal inner conflict. Whatever one may feel about the validity of specific techniques and the way they may modify the religious messages, they represent, at this stage, positive innovations in our search for social and individual peace.

The last word about such methods has not yet been written, and will not be for a long time. Pushed to extremes, and reinforced by other elements of faith, the methods can be manipulated to install dogma, to place boundaries around movements and cults, and to ossify the freedom of the spirit. To reach Utopia implies attaining balance, and greater skills in *helping* the open mind.

The way forward is sign posted by extreme danger. It is extraordinary that society almost everywhere places strict regulations and training requirements on those who profess to heal the body, but far less on those whose task it is to heal the mind. Counselling, searching for one's troubled self, dealing with everyday emotions, depressions, involve troubles of the mind, the interplay between feeling and thought. In this sense the mind is the most precious thing we have, much more precious than the body. Our knowledge and feeling about the body is located in the mind. The body and its sensations affect, indeed largely control, what goes on in the mind, yet it is through the mind that the senses manifest themselves.

To influence the mind, especially in our present state of knowledge, is one of the most dangerous activities there is, however well meaning the purpose. At this point psychotherapeutic techniques are little more than experiments, and mostly uncontrolled ones at that. We do know that talking out one's problems can be beneficial; we know too that it is often useless, even harmful. The techniques that therapists use to elucidate self-expression, to recapture images, or to reveal the sub-conscious, have not been shown, by controlled examination, to bring about the results claimed for them. Their dynamic is based on faith; to that extent we know that faith can help heal. The operative word is "can". We do not know how, when, in what circumstances. The work of the great masters, Freud, Jung, Adler, are uncontrolled experiments, and the thousands of therapists who make use of their techniques and the hundreds of variants and opposing techniques, are in the same boat—frequently with far less training or control and also loaded with the baggage of self-sustaining movements, in fact cults, in which the leader-priests hand down their rituals and organising myths to acolytes.

There is one common theme. For therapy to "succeed" it is necessary to have faith—faith in the therapist and his or her methods. The beginnings of consultation are devoted to this end. Somehow, scepticism must be put aside, or it won't work. Faith. Religion. Only the strictest supervision and ethical standards can prevent such dynamics from turning into dominant-subordinate power, manipulation, and worse. Since there are few effective regulations, since it is relatively easy to set up some sort of "shingle", and since many of the abuses are behind closed doors and unreported, the dangers are severe. All therapists have their own agendas, professional and personal.

The power of faith should never be under-estimated. The critics of a particular faith should never treat faith as "strangely irrational". Once the premises of a faith are discerned, its consequences follow logically. There is considerable rationality. Millennial and messianic movements throughout the ages have been well studied.

Consider Melanesian cargo cults. Faced with the overwhelming evidence of industrial power, in the form of wartime navies, warehouses full of supplies, food appearing in cans, powerful flying machines, radio communication, Melanesians, hitherto isolated from the industrial world, sought explanations, which came from a mix of indigenous mythology and ritual with elements learned through interaction with "agents" of the west—missionaries, administrators, the military. Those explanations were, by definition, innovations.

In accordance with the principles described in Chapter II, such innovations had to be pulled out of the spectrum of knowledge which they possessed. It was naive to expect, as administrators did, that the explanatory ideas would include factories, Victory Bonds, sophisticated commerce, the loading and unloading of ships. The explanations had not merely to explain the arrival of such materials but *why*. Why did the materials come to the fighting troops, and not to them, the Melanesians?

Prophets emerged to provided explanations, totally consistent with the world view then present. The techniques of prophecy were drawn from tradition; the power of dreams. The content of the prophetic dreams embraced two themes: symbolic ideas from Christianity, and the evident wrongness of what was happening before their eyes. Christianity provided the messianic and millennial story, validated through messages from Jesus, angels, or biblical figures. The wrongness provided substance; the goods were in fact intended for the Melanesians, but had been purloined by Whites, who diverted them to their own uses. Why was this happening? Because the Melanesians were behaving badly; not listening to the messages. What to do about it? Two things: change life and adopt appropriate ritual.

The intellectual and psychological problem was so great, so dramatic, that only a huge change in ways of living could be effective. Thus, *in mostly unconnected* cults, the prophets called for a complete reversal of social norms. Sexual taboos abandoned, gardens uprooted, valuables destroyed; faith would take the place of work. The prophets preached the overthrow of government: the millennium would place the Melanesians at the top, Whites at the bottom. In the search for appropriate rituals, where else to turn but to the successful purloiners of wealth? Obviously they had the right rituals. Search then for inexplicable magical behaviour. That was not difficult. Bits of cloth called flags that the military put into the sky at dawn and pulled down again at dusk, with ceremonial salute. Marching up and down with rifles, pack drill, the instantaneous construction of airfields to receive cargo planes. These apparently mindless rituals (to the Melanesians) must have religious significance. The prophets, aided by their administrators, saw to it such rituals were followed.

Given the images that were in their minds and those which were assaulting them from every direction; given the lack of other images and knowledge; given the sudden idea that newer, richer, ways of life were possible on this earth; I find nothing irrational about the interconnectedness of beliefs.

It is true that the *methods* used to attain the adherence of believers and move them to appropriate action involved not only what we would call administration, but the involvement of emotion—of which hope and joy were significant—excitement, ecstasy, mass hysteria, sometimes deliberately engendered, sometimes the dynamic result of belief that the Messiah was at last coming, the millennium would result from their rituals and efforts, the evils of the world were at last coming to an end. If you systematically go about reversing every social convention, with powerful sexual implications, the emotions are certainly going to become predominant.

Quickly, those who are concerned with law and order inject and expand the political implications. The leaders were considered to be manipulative exploiters preaching the overthrow of government and the subversion of power. In the Solomon Islands, then a colonial Protectorate, where I first became directly involved with this phenomenon, the government became alarmed, imported an expeditionary force from Fiji, and arrested the "ring-leaders". Then they did a highly intelligent thing.

They sent the leaders abroad, to Australia and Fiji, for on-hands education, showing them how in fact the outside world worked. At the same time, local government responsibilities were being created for the first time. The returned cult leaders became, in many instances, leaders in the new local governments. The images had changed. There were new ideas for the leaders to develop. The approach became secularised.

With major differences of content, millennial movements similar to this have occurred in all parts of the world and at all historical periods where Judeo-Christian-Muslim ideas have rooted—Africa, Europe, the Americas, parts of Asia. They typically arise where there is the strong idea of a better life, and frustration because conventional methods don't bring it about. The way to get there uses the one alternative, a belief in the power of faith and ritual and a major change in social conventions (conceived as rituals), since clearly secular methods have failed.

When external power attacks such movements, and those like them, power has almost always ignored history and anthropology and has gone for the repressive jugular. Power itself mixes its rationalities (derived from power's own premise's) with emotion and even hysteria, nowadays fuelled by the media. Because it ignores knowledge, power underestimates the strength of the beliefs, and the determination of the believers to go to the final step, to die through fighting or through ritual suicide. The tragedy of Waco, Texas, is the outcome of a failure, a refusal, on either side to accept the beliefs of the other.

I have written of cults, a word which has now in North American English come to equate movements in which a prophet is believed to dominate his believers with anti-social consequences. Cult, however, simply means a form of worship. By extension, it also refers to variants of a received religion. In a further, secular and ironic, extension, it refers to a ritualistic worshipful attachment of people to a figurehead—the cult of Madonna, of Elvis Presley.

Where mainstream religions operate with similar elements in their ideology and in similar social conditions similar results occur. The most dramatic example is in parts of contemporary Islam. It is an unfortunate fact that much of the Islamic world is living in material conditions far below its potential and is surrounded by religions and cultures which many Islamic religious leaders define as evil. A major difference in ideas is that Paradise is replete with what we might call earthly delights, and that Paradise is attainable by dying in the cause of Islam. Those who have the courage and faith can offer themselves up to God in an act of what the rest of the world would call terrorism. The majority do not normally have that individual commitment and drive, but it is there to be called upon in time of crisis, whipped up in time of a need to coalesce. Short of that level of self-sacrifice, the masses are ripe for co-ordinate action based on religious faith and spurred on by a world that has, it seems, hitherto passed them by. It is a wake-up call that inspires hope. In the process, the awakening of fundamentalist Islam finds in the faith anger, intolerance and aggression, in danger of transforming what has been at times one of the world's most tolerant religions.

*It is nowadays a truism that major ideological movements use and have used the power of religious dynamics to create the their loyalties and faiths. Nazism, fascism and communism did so. Ecological movements do so. Far right militias and organised neo-nazis do so. Charismatic politico-religious leaders do so. Belief, faith, override scepticism throughout life. This is natural and inescapable. But when belief and faith *destroy* questioning and scepticism, the kind of civilisation we want is in danger[9].

Thought control in the name of religion is as anti-Utopian as thought control in the name of politics. Utopian faiths must be based on the free commitment of individuals and the continuing quest for *further* enlightenment, understanding, and truth; on the theme that what we believe will, in the light of further knowledge and experience, prove to have been ephemeral. Faith without questioning is extreme and becomes fanaticism. My Utopia does not include fanaticism; it *does* include religious, or spiritual, commitment.

Religions contain within them models of the individual human, ideas about how persons are constructed. A major element in many models is the concept of the soul. Recent expositions have argued forcefully that the soul cannot exist in nature. The debate, if that is what it is, is significant not only intellectually but practically.

If we indeed have souls in the theological sense, the knowledge of what constitutes that soul would have profound consequences for how we go about handling attitudes and behaviour in education, crime, and ethics.

In the face of the trillions of words and thousands of concepts that argumentative religious and scholars and ordinary people have devoted to the soul, it would be naive of me to think of adding anything new. My task, rather, is to set forth notions that are consistent with the thrust of my argument. It is also to suggest, by implication, that the inconsistencies between my notions and those of theology on the one hand and of science on the other ultimately require resolution. The popular concepts of "soul" and "spirit" are at best fuzzy, and my own presentation is arbitrary, though designed to sort out aspects of being so that they might be enquired into further.

By "soul" we can mean an entity that is essential to our humanity, profoundly based within us and governing who we are, yet separate from the body in, frequently, an everlasting way. The everlasting nature of the soul may allow it to arise to heaven or descend to hell, or to continue in the world through rebirth. The last sentence contains propositions that, at present, are incapable of being disproven; hence, in Popperian logic, are non-scientific.

I see no support, other than belief, for the existence of a soul in this sense. At the same time, I do not categorically deny its existence. I have little emotional sympathy for the heaven/hell dichotomy, but there is aesthetic merit in the rebirth approach. There is much knowledge yet to be obtained, an issue with which I shall link up again in a later Chapter X, and scientists can be premature in writing off the possibilities simply because they are inconsistent with what scientists presume to know at this moment.

If we remove the "everlasting" criterion as a *necessary* condition for that which is called the soul, we are left with something that is an internal nucleus around which we are organised as humans. That nucleus contains the spark of life itself, a spark which still resists the certainties of definition and explanation. The remaining elements contain the *unchanging* principles *if there are any* that drive our behaviour, including our thoughts, feelings and values, from birth to death. I think they are there, partly inherited and partly already individuated through biological processes. They are within us, waiting for maturation, for external conditions to stimulate their expression, for interpretation in the real world.

It is difficult to resist a biological checklist, including, for example, involuntary reactions, and sensory perceptions. These are, if you will, the soul's use of its tools. But a soul is not that; it is much more. It embraces the strength or otherwise of various kinds of feelings, the ways in which sensory experience, from tactility to sound, affect our emotions or stimulate thought and action. It contains the ways in which we think, the type of logic or intuition that come naturally to us. It includes the manner in which we dream awake or "asleep". It takes in those subconscious regularities that emerge in psycho-analysis. It is fundamental to our being. It is our source of humanity, of living.

The concept I am describing, or at least parts of it, can also be referred to as "spirit", a term which has many other meanings as well. In my personal schema I like to select a more commonsensical and distinguishable meaning, keeping "spirit" for a different concept that is necessary for the interpretation of behaviour and its dynamics. "Spirit" is the energy and style with which the soul's principles express themselves in conduct. Depression, writer's block are negative styles of spirit. Joy, aggression, affection, addiction to work, cold-hearted manipulation, determination to survive pain and crisis, describe variations of the spirit. Spirit is malleable, subject to influence as externals interact with the steady soul. Spirit is open to cultural influence, therapy, drugs. It describes regularities which may be long or short lasting.

It is a matter of great debate as to whether aspects of the soul—for example, manifestations of the sub-conscious—are carried genetically. In September 2005 the international press was full of reports that scientists discovered that genes which seem to control intelligence are evolving almost globally and fast, with expected major improvements in IQ. Much depends on the meaning of intelligence, a fraught subject into which I will not delve too deeply. Let us say that it means the power to deal with facts and concepts effectively and creatively. It is different from moral intelligence which means addressing that power to a sensitivity toward ethics.

Thus if the observation is true, it does not mean automatically a better world, for intelligent creativity can be used for good or evil. But it might make an advance toward an agreed Utopia more feasible. Some have taken the observation as a proof that Creationism is false. That depends on the kind of Creationism. One might cynically argue that if God had created evolution, it would have been nice for him to have inserted the evolution of the intelligence gene a little earlier in human history.

And it can still be argued persuasively if not definitively that any improvement in intelligence is caused not by the gene but by the huge cultural expansion that is going on, which forces the brain to deal with ever expanding sets of data with exercising challenges to the creative process.

The extrapolation of Jung into contemporary scientific models would suggest that he would lean towards a genetic interpretation, although his religious background might prompt him to reject it as too biological, and lead him toward mysticism. The collective unconscious, as a concept, requires a verifiable statement of the process by which it moves from one generation to another and is embedded in individuals.

Jung and Freud's intellectual milieu contained an anthropology which was in process of being invented. The comparison of symbols, concepts and ideas in differing cultures was based on information mostly gleaned with little or no knowledge of the indigenous language, isolated from the processes of everyday life, and specifically from those which were responsible for social change and continuity. "Socialisation", "acculturation" and similar ideas did not emerge seriously in anthropology until the 'thirties. Nor did the integrated study of societies through the enquirer's use of language and long-term residence, nor the method of participant observation.

This does not necessarily invalidate Freudian or Jungian ideas. It suggests, however, that they need modification and re-interpretation, a procedure that is taking place, mostly outside the restricted circles of their followers.

In the model I am developing here, the collective unconscious has no substantive merit as an influence on brain processes outside of culture, unless and until its elements are shown to be passed biologically from one generation to another, probably through genes, or unless there are non-material soul-like influences at work. It has even less merit because it over-complicates simpler, readier, ideas.

Of course ideas, concepts, symbols move from one generation to another. They do so through socialisation. They vary in their strength over time, an issue that collective unconscious and similar constructs (remember "national character"?) avoid. They are frequently modified. They are re-invented. In our present world, we literally have almost the whole variety and history of ideas to draw upon. It is natural that themes will reappear in our innermost thoughts. We are excruciatingly open to suggestion, as to what we think and imagine—and dream.

It is not a mystery that themes in Egyptian, Greek, Celtic, Maori, thought have similarities. On the one hand there is strong reason to believe that similar imponderable questions will give rise to similar imaginative answers. Where did the world come from? Heroes and Gods. The old world explanations had limited, repetitive themes, embodying specific images and relationships, because the fundamental questions were limited, not in significance, but in number. The stock of cultural ideas was, by comparison with today, limited, and hence placed a restriction on innovation. Origins, gender, relationships, anxieties. The number of images that could be brought into play with meaning were also limited—and still are. Father, mother, son, daughter, authority and sex happen to be in *all* cultures. It is not surprising that similar thoughts and images should be present

And on the other hand, not all, but many of the cultures were linked by continuity. The east and middle-east impinged on both Egypt and Greece, the Celts were not isolated but Europe-wide, and interacted with Christianity. Far back in pre-history, Maori ancestors split from Asia.

There is no need for the construction of a collective unconscious as an independent *deus ex machina*. Under such circumstances, the processes set out in Chapter II, and others like them, provide an adequate, observable, framework. On the other hand a *deus ex machina* is an old imaginative and literary device which has been handed down through the generations, frequently popping up in the natural and social sciences as well. Our search for a single causative factor gives us intellectual and *emotional* satisfaction. If there is an accident or a natural disaster, let a sorcerer be found to explain its specific occurrence in time, place, and personnel. Or the anger of a God. Or, nowadays, personal inadequacy. Could this, I wonder, be the root genetic inheritance? The collective unconscious is not something to be reified and given a life of its own. It consists of those signs and concepts and themes that have been handed down in patchwork fashion from one generation to another, and passed from one culture to another through association. Dreams and myths are artifacts of thought without special mystical relevance, created in, admittedly, not yet fully understood ways that seem similar to any other thinking.

To soul and spirit let us add that component to the human being which represents his learned, adaptive, cultural resources; his specific ideas, thoughts, dreams, imaginings, the way in which his emotions pour out, his ethics, philosophy, knowledge, his concept of himself, his thoughts about others, just about everything that has meaning for his life. His *personal culture* embedded in the culture of his people.

From his personal culture, modified by his spirit, we can discern, over relatively steady periods, regularities in the way he expresses himself and responds to situations and, through investigation, his regular modes of thought. Character or personality.

One of humankind's major characteristics is the sensitivity to the presence of and interactions with others beyond the family who share his concepts—a cultural group. Bronislaw Malinowski, the pioneering anthropologist, in one of his rare forays into theory as distinct from interpretive ethnography, suggested that culture was an expression, in particular circumstances, of a range of basic needs—such as shelter, food intake, sexual reproduction, group defence. I think he missed the main one—to be associated with and supported by, a cultural group beyond the family. In any event, while humanity does need these kinds of things, there are many humans who reject them—hermits, cloistered monks, ascetics, extreme dieters. While humankind is concerned about such matters, individual humans may not be, and hence "basic needs" cannot constitute a definition of humanity.

The reason I give attention to these matters is that a conceptual framework of the elements of human behaviour is indispensable for tackling almost every issue that I am addressing. If Utopia is to be achieved, it requires the modification of attitudes, thought and behaviour. The problem is not that there is no framework available. It is that there are too many, competing without resolution. I am arguing, not necessarily for the framework here presented, but for arriving at the simplest one consistent with what we know, not the most complicated. My own discipline of anthropology is as bad a sinner as any other when it comes to making simple things falsely complicated.

Each element in such a conceptualisation will have its own methods of investigation, and particularly a different weight between the biological, the theological, and the cultural. Curiously, the deeper we enquire into the nature of the soul, the more theology and science will interact. Our conceptions of what will go on within Utopia will be modified fundamentally by investigations that are now racing ahead. Amongst these are studies of the mind and the brain, of the physiological nature of consciousness, the emotions and the senses. Hardly begun as yet are disciplined enquiries into other unexplained phenomena in nature connected, yes, to our old concepts of the soul, studies which could indeed open up new paradigms for science itself.

Watch for explosive debates. Milestones on the road to Utopia? The unknown future?

IV

The Responsibilities of Education

It will become apparent as my argument progresses that education of youth is the foundation upon which the future depends. Weak education, no Utopia. So we begin here.

[10]It is my intention to examine critically the ways in which official policies relate to the maturation of youth, primarily through the educational system, primarily but not only in richer countries. More and more frequently schools are being confronted by manifestations of societal ills—violence, depression et al. This is not new. But they have not been equipped to remedy the problems they face, and there are bureaucratic and communication difficulties bringing other community resources to bear on the issues.

Once we identify the tasks and challenges necessary to optimize the ways in which youths mature into responsible citizens, we may then design appropriate institutions to do the job. That design will be the Utopian goal to achieve prior to 2100—in my view it should be achievable fifty years before that—indeed very soon—in much of the world. Special adjustments will be required to modify the institutions and ensure that they are effective in the poorer countries. In all instances the interaction of these ideas with indigenous values and systems will need careful culture-specific appraisal.

I start with suicide in its several forms.

In many parts of the industrial world, high school age youths are committing suicide in increasing numbers. As their age group rises as a cohort in the demographic scale, so the general figures of attempted suicide rise. In other words, the tendency toward suicide carries on into higher age groups.

Recently—I do not know for how long—the elderly had the highest suicide rates in such countries. Now the rates among the youth cohorts match those for the elderly. Unless there are fundamental transformations, the changing attitudes towards euthanasia coupled with the entry of present youth cohorts into the ranks of the elderly could produce a suicide explosion in forty years[11], if not before, that could shake the capabilities of society to respond.

I accept and advocate the right of the elderly to take their own lives, though I would prefer it to be in the context of psychological peace rather than age-induced depression. I do not accept it as a necessity in other age groups, for which the future is still an open possibility. That would not be my idea of the Utopia toward which we strive.

In Japan and other countries suicides take place as the young take their lives for fear of failing examinations or similar tests. Family and peer pressure play a role: so do induced or real feelings of self-worthlessness in a demanding society.

A further form of suicide is ideological. This is particularly the case in Arab society, where young, well-educated people, notably including women, undertake acts of terrorism in which their own deaths are virtually certain—acts of martyrdom.

Close to suicide, perhaps virtually the same, are thousands of young boys and girls who are recruited into guerrilla and sometimes national armies, indoctrinated with the fever of killing, and thrust into the front lines where they are most in danger. It is well documented that many, indeed the majority, have been kidnapped to serve as cannon fodder. They are often in hysterical or drug-induced excitement, at the dangerous age of susceptibility. They take risks, voluntarily or under pressure, in which the likelihood of death, before or after episodes of looting and socially destructive seemingly inhuman acts, is high. They are removed from the world of normal society, pariahs to civilisation.

And then there are those whose alienation is not that of the body, but of the mind and its spirit. These are the habitual criminals, so often so long behind bars that they are totally unable to function outside of prison, and who, when freed, commit acts so that they return. They do not kill their bodies, but their way of life has become virtually suicidal—often, at a young age, because of experiences "inside" prison, that breeding ground of anti-social behaviour.

The correction of the tendency among those who have already moved beyond school and university can only be modified by a changes throughout culture, especially in the institutions which are held to be responsible for social control—including police and prisons—an issue that is fundamental to Utopia, as we shall see in Chapter VI.

However, the first step in tackling the issue *throughout all age groups* lies with education.

Suicide is part of the nexus of concerns that include violence and harassment in schools, truancy, youth prostitution, youth homelessness, the recourse of youth to violence and gangs on the streets, abuse in the family, and drugs. These are not just urban problems. Until the idealisation of rural life in the second half of the last century, it was well known that sexual abuse, family instability, incest, and violence were typical phenomena of **rural** living. They are more dramatic, more concentrated, less hidden, more newsworthy, and more frequently observed because the populations are higher, in cities. Although this is so, it is doubtful whether the statistical incidence is higher than in earlier years of the century, and it is certain that there have been periods in modern history, for example the nineteenth century, when the situation was much worse.

That is, though, beside the point. It doesn't matter what the trends are, except insofar as wrong publicity over-creates immoderate anxieties and backlashes. What is to the point is that there should be zero tolerance of any of these phenomena in a civilised society. I am not referring to the superficial remedies of authoritarian crackdown. I mean getting to the remedial basics.

The basics consist in the *positive* upbringing of youth, presently a joint responsibility of family, schools, youth organisations, religions and the State.

The family is having great difficulty. It has *always* had great difficulty, among rich *and* poor. Let us be freed from "traditional family values" which have done such a horrible job, and been the cover up for abuse. That does not mean throwing everything out. It means re-thinking responsibilities and dynamics.

Guilt. Anxiety. Hopelessness. From time to time these strike at all parents who take their responsibilities seriously. What, oh what, am I doing wrong?

What parents tend to do is to bring forward the learning that they acquired in their family of origin, and as they acquired a philosophy of parenting in their twenties and thirties. Parents themselves survived troubled times, in the late 'sixties and 'seventies battling authority with the assertion of permissiveness. When adults become responsible for loved children themselves, the two themes fight for dominance and balance. Parents blame themselves for not getting the balance right, for not foreseeing.

They cannot get the balance right. Nobody knows what that balance is, for each individual child. The outside influences are also so powerful. Parents must count themselves fortunate and extraordinarily sensitive if their offspring make the transition to adulthood reasonably well. Quite frequently, the path is first of natural rebellion which can take extremely dangerous turns beside the abyss of drugs and alienation. Quite frequently, parents find that the children, now "friendren", have survived, matured, found new solid roads.

This is not to argue that, if parents do not *know* they should not try. Of course they will. Their efforts, whether misguided or highly sensitive, *will* have an effect, a positive one, when guided by love and support, come what may. It is almost the only principle that counts for sure. Parents, after all, are not the only variables.

There is the child itself. Life never will be a cakewalk. Despite the incidence of trouble, by far the majority of children become reliable adults. Even when they have inner pains, they function well, even creatively.

And they live in a challenging environment in which they are led by a myriad of influences toward a myriad of choices.

In what follows I am somewhat neglecting the influence of religion. This is a pity, but I can't do everything at this moment. Despite refusing the concept of a God or gods in human form, I am not one of those who believes that religion, or at least the search for spirituality, is insignificant. On the contrary, the search for spirituality, within or without the churches, is a major preoccupation, a resource, an intellectual and emotional drive, that has a major part to play in the lives of an increasing number of men and women. On the other hand, the influence of formal religion and the spiritual beliefs of parents on children is a part of family life, determined by parents. Further, the range and variety of belief and of the types of searching are now so great as to defy summary. For the growing young, seeking their own paths as they enter the enquiring teens, the range and variety are part of the almost infinity of choice with which they are confronted. It is that infinity of choice which evokes creativity, thoughtfulness, anxiety and despair, an infinity that continues well beyond school into adulthood. As each decade passes, the conscious part of that infinity expands, life juxtaposing simplicity and resounding chaos, in which the ears as well as our other senses defend themselves against both aggression and sensuality, often not being able to distinguish this from that.

The school is the place in which family influence confronts the perspectives of other families through the filter of other children's presence. It is the place where the influences of the media, of adult role models, of professional teachers, the contributions of churches and voluntary youth organisations, and the policies of the State, come together, working out their pressures and contradictions in the minds and behaviour of children.

It is inevitable that education should thus be the focus of power rivalry, conflict and co-operation, demands and compromise. Ideally, the State should be in a position to take a detached view, to consider the meaning, objectives, philosophies and methods of education. This is not the case. The State is governed by men and women whose basic philosophies are *a priori*, joined with those of political allies in a mostly confrontational competition with oppositions. The State is strongly advised by bureaucracies who control data and implementation, who are a force for conservative continuity which fortunately somewhat counterbalances the potential swings of elected political opinion. Powers are variously filtered through intermediary bodies down to the school, or in some instances tightly controlled by the central government or a recognized religious hierarchy. Powers relate to the official objectives and philosophy of education, the curriculum, and budgetary influences on school practice.

Teachers, like any other professional corpus, have the responsibility for the direct contact with their client-pupils, and to a lesser extent with the semi-client-parents. It is this responsibility, together with their common experience of professional training, that binds them together, and constitutes the reality of their power base. Furthermore, the most significant reality in the exercise of educational policy is what teachers do with it. A fiat from above is useless if it does not fit well with the perceptions that the teachers themselves have of their realities, their philosophy, their responsibilities, and, increasingly, their material conditions. Even unintentionally teachers internalise their beliefs and practices in ways that are difficult to change, and of course sometimes they don't want to change, because what they do is a sacred pursuit.

It might be said that the way to change teaching is to change teacher training. Indeed, without this, change would be even more difficult. But if serious changes are to be contemplated—and I have not yet made my case for them—we must recognise that young newly trained teachers have limited influence and, perhaps, none at all within a religious hierarchy. It is not only that time must pass before they rise in seniority and their proportions increase—with the consequence that even newer ideas must enter the system with the young cohorts now the conservatives. It is that they are posted to schools as individuals, surrounded by those whose training belongs to an earlier period. They meet in committees, socialise, discuss issues, are rewarded, with and by those who belong to an earlier generation. Inevitably, most of them will unintentionally modify their positions to conform to those of their peer group. Their impact is reduced. (They could have greater impact if posted en bloc to specific schools, more or less taking them over, at the expense of experience.)[12]

Some of this can be modified by major refresher training. This is not readily achieved by North American style "professional days", or by uncontrolled sabbaticals. It would require periodic freedom from classroom activities for substantial blocks of ***required*** refresher education.

There are other difficulties in teacher formation. What is to be taught to them? Subject matter? Pedagogical philosophy? The State's requirements? In these matters, wherein lies the "academic freedom" of the teacher? Does the teacher in fact have "academic freedom" that a university professor is supposed to have? I think not. The teacher has a responsibility for the vulnerable children of parents, and is thus morally responsible to those parents, whereas university faculty are supposedly guiding young adults. The teacher interprets responsibility by using skills the best way possible to influence young minds. In my view, those skills have technical components that can be taught, and personal, human components that training can influence but not control. Because of the latter limitation, the effectiveness of the classroom has, ultimately, to depend on the individual teacher who makes the institutional framework operate through personal qualities which technical skills support but do not suffocate. The freedom of the teacher lies in his or her application of those skills, *not in deciding what the ultimate classroom goals should be.*

Ultimately, then, I argue that innovation in the school system is the same as in any other context. It comes through the interplay of ideas and concepts that can come in all forms, formally and informally, which the individual teacher rejects or accepts. The rate of acceptance will be proportional to the degree to which the concept or practice "fits" the profile of culture of individual teachers, and can be incorporated into that profile.

You will find only a few small countries—some Pacific Islands, perhaps—where the main corpus of teachers individually share more or less identical cultural profiles. In all others, there is considerable variety. Within that variation, individuals who approximate each other in ideas and point of view may be grouped, more or less categorised. If one wished to do so, one could identify such groups. Educational innovation would have differing impacts on each such group. This is one potential influence towards diversity in the school system. Teachers with differing philosophies and methods can, theoretically, operate schools with differing philosophies and methods.

If there is truth in this, how much more so is it true of the third power group, the parents. Whereas teachers, despite their differences, have some common ground derived from occupational considerations, parents do not. Their variability is much greater, except in rural tribal communities. And in developed and developing countries they increasingly demand more variation in education. States, and teachers, confront increasingly multi-faceted parental cultures.

Some argue that the more varied and complex a society, the more important it is to use schooling as a cohesive force. (In some times and places, compulsory army service was justified in this way.) I confess to doubts about this, if the objective is Utopian, for we have seen that diversity adds to the size of the profile of culture, and hence to innovation, and because, as I shall argue in a later context the State is not, fundamentally and as we know it, holy. Yet in the shorter term, this is a practical consideration. Do we want the cohesiveness of the State to be weakened? Let us keep this in mind.

What should be the functional objectives of the school? Do they imply major innovation? In approaching these questions I am not implying that, for any function, the school is the only influence that is relevant or that is needed. The school, however, works with children for long hours, day after day. Its potential influence, through both teaching and the influence of peers, is as great as that of parents and it may be identified as the primary institution which exposes children to non-family society in a societally coordinated way[13].

Such influences embody major ethical problems. If State schools were fully effective in carrying out their mandate, they would be imposing a single universal philosophy on children. The authoritarian and centralising dangers are modified by the essential individuality of both teachers and children, the existence of programme choices, and the counterbalancing effects of family and other outside influences. Yet a single, universal, little modified, State system could move in the universalising direction and is contrary to my sense of the Utopian goal of a diverse culture.

There is also an incipient conflict between the goals of particular schools and the goals of parents, individually or collectively. One of the most dramatic illustrations came from special Indian schools in British Columbia in the nineteenth and early twentieth centuries. A now discontinued type of school, known as "residential schools", deliberately removed young children from their parents and communities (considered to be retrograde influences), transferring them to boarding schools. Later, in more subtle ways, Indian community day schools were sometimes staffed by dedicated, earnest and responsible non-Indian teachers who, as individuals, considered it their duty and mandate to be agents of change. In itself, this indeed might have been a legitimate mandate—it would in effect have been impossible for a school to have operated *without* engendering change of some sort. The issue here, though, is that, at least to begin with, many of the teachers did not have the skills or incentives to match their ideas about the goals of change to those of the parents. The child, unintentionally, became the location of a battleground between two sets of adults, overt or unseen. Even teachers in village schools were drawn into such conflicts. In extreme cases the tensions and misplaced mandates brought despair, neurosis in both teacher and pupil, and revolting abuse.

This is an extreme form of a tension which is frequent, teachers considering some parents to be irresponsible, uncaring, harmful to their offspring, ignorant about the educational needs and strengths of their children, causing anti-social behaviour; parents considering teachers to be using wrong methods, presenting irreligious values, encouraging laziness or pushing children too far.

To advocate no tension at all would be unrealistic and false. A major part of learning, as I shall reinforce, is to deal with tension and to work out the implications of inconsistency and conflict. It is from such bases that innovation takes place. However, whatever I may suggest by way of resolving issues, I am in no doubt that differences will continue in Utopia, and that, in reasonable ways, they should. When I set forth ideas about objectives for ultimate achievement I know I shall be establishing a battleground or, I would rather hope, a platform for debate.

By way of opening the subject, I once had ideas about an ideal base curriculum for a modern world. It was oriented toward mobility and the growth of the individual. The underlying theme was to maximise the child's potential for communication as an adult. Thus the three-r's were essential—few disagree about that today. To literacy, numeracy and communication skills (including logic and rhetoric) were added those languages which worked as *linguae francae* across major segments of the world—English, German and Russian (for much of eastern Europe), Arabic, Spanish, French (for parts of Africa and Asia), written Mandarin, Malay, and Swahili (for East Africa). To this would be added comparative anthropology, world social and political history and geography, medical diagnosis, data searching and processing, and, for real mobility, basic motor mechanics, horse riding, sailing (with navigation) and outdoor skills. Such a curriculum was predicated on one specific goal—making it possible for young adults to move through the world anywhere with confidence and to move forward (with specialised advanced education) into their professions anywhere.

While such a model programme may be teasing to some, **all it does** is to demonstrate that current curricula are not writ in stone; that what is taught depends entirely on objectives. The major limitation of the above imagined programme was that the objective was narrow, too much based on instruction and too little on the nature of the child, and not suited to the needs of Utopia. But the limitations of the above extreme case are also present, if to a lesser degree, in **all** curriculum models. The very idea that one curriculum serves the needs of all students in all parts of society is and should be a non-starter. The major thread running through all good curricula is that they establish standards of rigour, discipline, clear thinking, and the processes of continuously acquiring and using knowledge.

Of the above is not satisfactory, then what should most, if not all, schools do, in principle? There is a great deal.

Particularly in the second half of the twentieth century, schools have been experimenting with our children, often in the light of general theories which can be misinterpreted when put into practice, theories which, in the nature of things, have not been properly tested in terms of results. What I write now is of the same order. It is opinion, linked to some observation, some experience, and, I hope, some logic. In particular, *it is linked to ideas about what the end results should be.* Recall one of my foundation statements. There is no complete knowledge; anything put into practice will lead to unexpected results. What we do in schools will have profound effects on the future. The cautions of this paragraph will have major implications for the organisation and dynamics of schools.

In 'fifties Canada I saw schools in which uniforms had been abandoned as a matter of theory. Uniforms were felt to be authoritarian, representing an expense for those not so well off. At the same time schools emphasised the skills of social interaction, the ability to get on with one's fellows. The solitary pupil was an anachronism. The children themselves stepped into the gap. Peer pressure dictated clothing, both boys and girls decided that what they wore had to be what youthful fashion dictated. Those who wore different clothing were open to derision. Within the peer dictates, some of the better off were seen to be better off by the expense of the clothes, the cars driven, the hair-dos and makeup of the girls. The concern for the visible aspects of group personality seemed to take priority over the content of school work, where conformity emerged naturally.

By the 'nineties more individuality was expressed. But the use of externals and clothing is still an identifier. This time it identifies group *difference* as well as juvenile peer-conformity. Gangs have their markers. Certain conformist schools mistakenly attempt to enforce clothing standards which reduce ethnic identification.

The most marked change in school ethos in many industrialised countries since the late 'sixties has been the formal redefinition of the appropriate tension between conformity and individuality, a redefinition which affects major changes in adult perceptions. In one sense, the group is re-asserted. Group projects frequently take the place of individual ones. Seating arrangements create eye-to-eye contact in the classroom, emphasising interactions, and hence peer control, in place of the more individualistic lines of desks.

On the other hand, the self is re-asserted. Therapies dealing with relationships in adult society often emphasise self-awareness, self-knowledge, the discovery of the past and of the child within; and self-assertion. Mishandled, as therapy often is, the "other" becomes secondary. The right kind of concern for the "other" will emerge only after the "self" has been discovered.

So in the school. In both schools and universities, there have been times, teachers, and classes for which self-expression is valued simply because it is the expression of self, with little or no regard to the quality of the expression. The fact that I thought it is quite sufficient to give me top marks. Indeed, since everyone in the class thought something, let's give them all top marks. Such caricatures have been realities.

However, even where such naive extremes have been in place, it is interesting to see both teachers and the public striving to establish something else, "standards". And it is more interesting to see children discovering that there is more to creativity than simple effort; discovering, as they step into the world, that they have been betrayed because they were not prepared for "standards"; that much of peer pressure "out there" is indeed about standards and performance rather than superficialities; and that there is excitement to be obtained from meeting intellectual challenges. The cliché has it: if there are rigorous and demanding standards in sports, why not in thinking?

Both themes need expression, and never will either disappear. To equip children for a world in which there is extensive adult non-work that I envisage for Utopia[14], it is essential that they know themselves. It is a fundamental part of creative education that children learn how to explore, out of their own interests. They will not fully discover themselves in high school. Currently, most children do not discover their creative capacities until well into young adulthood. No school can place before a young person the whole total richness of the world and what the human capacity is capable of; no school can provide the total basis for choice[15]. But all schools can aim at encouraging intellectual—in which I include artistic and psychological—exploration, the discovery that one is capable of entering undreamed-of realms of creativity, the knowledge that the search for self-fulfilment is never-ending and wondrous. The emphasis on the mind and spirit implied in my last sentence does not reduce the significance of the bio-physical.

The truism that healthy minds emerge from healthy bodies is only partly true. Many great minds belong to those who are or have been physically and emotionally warped. Touch a great philosopher and you will find a troubled soul. What *is* true, on the other hand, is that *all* thought and self-expression arrives through the senses, is filtered internally as a result of sensory experience. Especially in the puritanical parts of the world, where the creative uses of some senses are denied, the ability of teachers to encourage sensory experience is strictly limited—and rightly so, since maturing children are especially vulnerable to sensory abuse and dysfunctional influence. Yet a balance can surely be attained in which sensory experience is valued, and individually encouraged, and the links between experience, creativity, and damage are made known.

Furthermore, the world of physical activity intersects directly with the mind, its expression, and its choices. The physical and the mental are not opposites; they are part of one state. The choice of physical activity over desk activity is not a choice of body over mind. It is a choice in which body and mind unite to go in a specific direction. The application of thought and knowledge to sport and recreation makes this clear. Some children will make physical activity a greater part of their lives than others; almost all children should understand that this is not a separate, classified as different, part of life, but an integrated aspect. It will, like every other aspect, be used creatively by some and less by others, just as is music or scientific experimentation. But the bio-physical and the mental are fundamental, part of every single one of us, in a way that music or scientific experimentation is not.

To start the process of knowing one's self, then, is a primary goal of school education. The search for that knowledge will never end.

And at the same time, it is of utmost significance to limit that search for self. This will be done by placing it in context. But without balance and context an over-emphasis on the ego is likely to be hurtful, to the child, and to others. It will engender the continuous life-long question, the dominance of Who-am-I? Anxiety because I do not know myself, perpetual introspection, inhibition from action because it might not be right for me. In this field, even more than in all others, it is of major necessity to indicate also that I will *never* know fully who I am; that *why* I am who I think I am doesn't matter so much—it can't be changed retrospectively—as *who* I am. I must learn when to think about it and when to stop thinking about it. The importance of the search is to find out what my values are, what I would like to do in living my life, how I can get on with others, how I can communicate myself to others, and how to make some reasonable choices for myself.

Education is replete with paradoxes, contradictions, and oppositions. Successful education does not allow one theme to dominate, but to balance the contradictions in ways that alert the child without creating improper anxiety, that make use of the paradoxes for creativity, and that meet the needs of different children in different ways.

Thus self-expression is counter-balanced by awareness of and concern for others. I personally feel that **the primary underlying issue is courtesy, understanding and respect for others.** And I feel that somehow, all over the world, schools have limited success in conveying this message, and that very frequently the concern is treated as peripheral rather than fundamental. If there is no courtesy and respect for others a school simply cannot function adequately. An adult society cannot exist.[16] The issue links to so many other aspects of society—violence, crime, autocracy, self-interest pressure groups, attitudes to work are rather obvious. I shall identify others.

Hence self-expression should not be confused with selfishness and egotism.

In my elderly superficial observations I see small examples of the confusion. Young people at all times and places have difficulty in defining their personal space. Anyone who encounters young people on public transport, in shopping areas, in souks, anywhere where there is a strong possibility of physical contact, is bound to get an elbow in the ribs, toes stepped on, the sensation of being pushed aside as the energetic young, in groups, steam ahead. One remarks on the natural courtesy of a youth who gives his, or more usually her, seat to an elderly person of no matter what ethnic community. One often feels that in such a case it is parental, not school, influence that has been responsible;

and that peer pressure is against it through derision, especially amongst boys.

Trivial. Not at all. Fundamental. Which is why I repeat the point.

If courtesy is not taught in little ways, the large ones, when there, are hypocritical.

Some schools, of course, do in fact stress courteous behaviour. All should. How?

I do not like the word "tolerance" in multi-ethic or cross-religion contexts.[17] It implies that there is something about another's behaviour that I don't particularly like, but will tolerate. Yes, indeed, we often do run across behaviour which we dislike and tolerate. Often when we run across behaviour that we dislike and should *not* tolerate; we should do something about it.

What I object to is the easy way in which we can think of tolerance of rather than respect for **or understanding** of others. It is not tolerance that should be emphasised in schools, but respect and understanding. Tolerance implies "Real weird he digs classical music. Who cares?" or "They have such weird customs. I don't mind, though, that's for them". Patronising. On the contrary, respect for others implies "I wonder what he gets out of classical music? Makes him interesting." or "What they do makes considerable sense for them. Even though it's not for me, I'd like to know about it." And understanding means just that, figuring out the reasons behind the behaviour in question and placing them in cultural and "philosophical" context.

One of the results of the late 'sixties was the re-emphasis of the idea that discipline, however valued in sports, was unnatural in mental activity, and that "failure" was an assault on the persona. On the contrary, both discipline and failure are essential experiences for a truly civilised person who wishes to be capable of the fullest self-expression and the fullest contribution to total well-being. Blaming others, or circumstances, or upbringing, can too easily slide over into excuses for failures which should be faced up to and learned from, The "culture of complaint" as one writer perceptively put it, Is very far from Utopia, fort both adults and children.

However much a creative person enjoys the outcome of his chosen activity, there will be costs involved. To commit to the chosen outcome requires the payment of those costs. They include not only the material, but the psychological. If you are not prepared to pay the costs, you do not value the activity as highly as you thought. To summon the resources, internal and objective, to pursue a goal, it is necessary to have the discipline to pay, in effort, in materiel, in mental concentration, and, quite often, in going through boring and seemingly pointless stages and bits of training. You may have to suffer through boring instructors. To get to the fullest enjoyment of achievement it is necessary to be prepared to go through times when you ask yourself, is this all worthwhile?

You do not simply get an answer out of the air. There has been groundwork laid for those flashes of insight, of intuition, of bodily achievement, of controlled logic.

As I have said, and will repeat, there is no greater betrayal of a child's capabilities that to pretend to him or her that whatever they think is objectively as good as what someone else thinks, just because it is thought. That any thought is as good as another. That what matters is to do the thinking, and that the skills of communicating that thinking are insignificant. This sort of betrayal is not to be confused with the genuine attempt to encourage the emergence of the child's thoughts—and then to show, skilfully and gently, that those thoughts can be extended by the application of discipline—even by going through disliked procedures.

The betrayal I have mentioned is matched by another equal treachery,—the denial of "failure", the belief that the term "failure" has to mean the denigration of the individual, that it is somehow shocking and should never occur. It is true that in the past, and still in the present, failure has been used as a punishing stick in that way; it has discouraged and destroyed individual talents.

The word "failure" should be brought back into current dialogue. It should be used with understanding as a positive element in life. To "fail" means that you have *tried*, that you have attempted something that is for some reason at this point beyond you. To fail gives you guidance. It tells you what to work on—it may even be lassitude or lack of discipline, but it can also be lack of a technical mastery, of understanding. It may even tell you that the subject matter will not, eventually, be for you.

Placed in a positive context, failure should be a challenge. It should alert both teacher and child that something requires attention. As a child I failed in both mathematics and French. My teachers dealt with the other pupils who understood and were not so mentally lazy. My father bought me a French tutor and in a couple of months I was top in the city's schools. I wish he had thought to do that in mathematics, for in later life I found, without knowing any math, that symbolic logic has an extraordinary appeal and value that my laziness undermines.

In my case the teachers did not have the will or the interest to advise someone who, to them, was a bit of an idiot and lazy to boot. Literature recounts many tales of dedicated teachers whose avocation is to find and nurture the wandering child, to bring him through the tests of discipline and failure. It is also full of accounts of harsh disciplinarians who have little interest but to give vent to their own internal problems, and in doing so stifle the growth of others. For many talented men and women the suffering of school is something to eventually be put behind them, for adult life is their real school, the place where they find an outlet for their skills and even achieve fame. True. But many others fall by the wayside. And what a waste of school resources and energy to let the opportunity slip by.

Embrace failure. Let teachers resurrect it as a positive force. It will be there throughout life; it is a step on the path to achievement; it must be understood, not fled from. He who does not fail does not try; indeed is not alive.

The question of sex education is fraught and highly controversial. It needs serious addressing because, as I shall be arguing in connection with the family, and with health and the law, sexual ills are at the source of many or most of personal dysfunctions and inter-personal troubles. Far from being a subject addressed on tip toe it should be font and centre in the concerns of Youth Maturity Institutes which I advocate later to replace schools. We choose to downplay or hide such facts as that the relationship between mother and child at the breast is highly sexual; that babies are tactile; that young children are curious and interested in the body, experimenting with it and investigating. Add to that the perception, perhaps the fact, that sexual experiment is going on amongst teens and in pre-teen friendships.

Our attitudes to sex are cultural, and we need cultural adjustments to handle them. Except for some of the potential medical consequences and the psychological effects of repression, there is little biological about our thoughts about sex. What indeed is a sex act? Voyeurism? Playing with one's own genitals? Intimate caressing? On a small island in the southern Solomons I witnessed young girls below the age of ten dancing a hissing dance, in which the rhythms and hisses coincided—as did the rubbing of genitals on genitals and genitals on thighs. Sex act or fun? The licentious ribaldry of cross cousins of opposite genders in some parts o Fiji would get close to sexual harassment if performed in a Canadian bureaucracy—yet they are designed to say "no copulation allowed" and to emphasize the delightful but forbidden danger, A Western phenomenon emerging as I write is that of the daisy chain, in which young pre-teens of both sexes join their naked bodies in a circle and play with the one next in the chain.

Repression makes behaviour with sexual content seriously damaging. It often removes the highly desirable supportive and warm touching that should exist between appropriate adults and troubled children. And it turns sensuous or insecure children into dysfunctional adults in many psychological areas.

So Youth Maturity Institutes must do something about it. They will focus on parents (see Chapter V on the family). But they will also investigate and innovate in sexual education.

Sex education today is primarily biological—how the reproductive system functions—medical—for example, the dangers of sexually transmitted diseases and unprotected sex—the moral, psychological and social implications, and how to get help. It is inescapable that the emphasis is on danger and discomfort rather than pleasure and joy. Is it any wonder that searching teens ignore the warning and take risks.

The problem is that the truths about sex as joy are ignored, and young people are too often experiencing the fumblings, discomforts and ignorances of sexual pleasure as they try their hands at it. Guilt, fear and ignorance turn the experiences into distaste and repeated searching for something better. Pity the young girl faced with a would be lover who doesn't know how to stimulate her before he satisfies himself. And pity the self-confidence of the young boy who discovers his inadequacy, or the arrogant young man who thinks that this is what it is about. And for that read, at least for a while, almost 100% of young intercourse.

What to do. Don't raise your eyebrows. I'm serious because the implications are serious. People engage in sex for enjoyment. That characteristic is given to us so that as we engage in sex we can also procreate.

It is not even certain that the evolutionary function of sex is limited to procreation. For example, various theories of female orgasm are rooted in the assumption that that is what sex is about. But studies have shown that the biological theorems underlying such a postulate are quite mistaken and that the female orgasm has no bearing on the power to conceive. And while male orgasm and ejaculation go, shall we say, hand in hand, once again there is little of any relationship between its physical manifestation and rate of conception.[18]

While sexual activity has a bearing on procreation it is also there, deeply embedded, for its own sake. It is an activity which can be, should be, joyous and wholesomely rewarding, engendering compassion, love, delight, and the renewal of the body and the senses. It can go seriously wrong, become nasty, evidence of sickness, fumbling and crude. To keep it in balance and to gain the most from it, young people *need to be coached* in sex as an art form, just as they are taught the essence of aesthetics in art or the beauties in mathematics. Vestal Virgins and other priestesses undertook this task for young men as a religious duty. In numerous cultures young men were and are initiated by engaging prostitutes. Neither of these institutions engenders more than some technical knowledge for the satisfaction of the male. Rarely does it educate the male in the desires of the woman.

Girls are marginally better off. Self experimentation and playfulness with other girls can create considerable sensual satisfaction, so that lesbianism may be a pleasing outcome. But many grow into women who are overcome by guilt, dry dissatisfaction and "frigidity" so that even sex for procreation becomes an unpleasant chore.

So how can Youth Maturity Institute undertake appropriate coaching and education? Get with it, pedagogues. The blackboard alone will not do. And it needs to completely avoid exploitation by and the perversion of instructors. It must be entirely sensitive to the individual child, yet skin to skin, body to body teaching of ways to satisfy the other partner and retain one's own integrity.

One must inset an obvious warning. If adults are to teach younger adults the arts of sex, is there not a risk of perversion and abuse? Most certainly there is. But remember we are dealing with such matters within the context of Youth Maturity Institutes. With the expectation that there will, in time, be fundamental changes in the behavioural ethics of youths becoming in their turn adults.

Even then there are certain principles to be observed, rigorously and sensitively. Biologically, young people become pubescent at different ages. There are some who, for whatever reason, resist and dislike sensual touching. It would be disastrous if sexual education, in the sense in which I am using it, became a classroom exercise to be administered mechanically to a specific age group. At the very least, this has to be something in which the individual child's readiness is assessed accurately For some it may be almost from birth, for others not until the late teens or not at all.

Below I shall be opening the challenges for pedagogy. This is clearly one of them. Should instruction be given in clinical surroundings, as if it were an extension of hygiene? Should there be and to what degree, an enhancement of sensuous atmosphere—lighting, music, scent. How far should group instruction be desirable, effective? Is it possible that for some sexual activity will be repulsive, and for what reasons, and with what consequences? Should homosexuality be included and under what conditions if any? Should instructors/instructresses be given a special *cachet* and perhaps privileged and circumscribed status?

Whatever your, the reader's views, this is not a matter to be ignored. Give it deep, constructive thought.

For it is fundamental to many many aspects of a Utopian world, well beyond the confines of the sex act itself—family life, equanimity, peace with one's self and the world, self-confidence, anger control, even crime. We must face up to it, and follow through with determination.

At present we are going through what I hope is a blip on the hidden screen of Utopia. We are, quite properly, tying education to social goals; but the blip on the screen tells us that the primary goal is to train young people for employment. Vocational and/or practical education is, will be, and should be of as much concern as the so-called academic, for this is the path that many will choose in life, and it is significant for the full life and recreation of many whose primary occupation will be less definable.

So here I address a problem of pedagogy. Let me illustrate. Many years ago I administered an educational programme for the United Nations which consisted of extending the horizons and knowledge of senior civil servants from developing countries, in almost all substantive fields, from social work to hydraulic engineering. The previous director of the centre, with great perspicacity, set in place a system in which he talked with each of the fellows to determine what, in their *theoretical* understanding they were lacking. At first the fellows resisted. What they wanted were the latest practical techniques and gimmicks. Each individually tailored programme, however, was designed to reinforce the *principles* from which the practical techniques were created, to create professional on-going contacts with the world of advanced knowledge, and to help the candidate to control, throughout hiser life, the flow of new information, techniques and ideas. He faced the issue that the "latest" today is the "out-dated" tomorrow; that education in the "latest" will be démodé by the time the student returned home. In other words, he aimed instead at broadening capabilities for life-long development, individually, instead of making the experience a one-shot, classroom kind of quickly out-dated and ephemeral instruction. In that context the experiment, for that was what it was, was "too expensive" to last, yet it was in truth a most efficient and long-lasting expenditure of resources.

Similar principles apply to "practical" instruction in high schools.

The reasoning is simple. If you train children with employment in mind, what precisely is that employment? You begin educating in that manner in the teens, but it will be four years (more if tertiary education follows) before the child is offering his or her services. In the present and future world, changes in the work place, in both technique and distribution of tasks, move so fast and unpredictably that you may be training for dead ends. Furthermore, unless there is a very close liaison with the *whole range* of employers, it will be inevitable that the skills represent only a portion of what is needed. How many schools train butchers in sushi techniques? (Some do.) How far behind were schools in adapting auto mechanics courses to the electronic age?

Furthermore, it is obvious that the work place itself will change many times during the career of the employee, and that an employee is likely to change jobs more frequently than at present. How can schools keep up with the fast changes and movements in occupation? They can't, unless they specialise as technical high schools, which is not always to be recommended, and may not be what employment needs require.

What the school can best do is to educate, not train. Even for those whose major aptitude is practical, it is still the mind that counts. Skilled tradesmen and secretaries can adapt. They understand what lies behind the practice, they play with alternatives in their minds, they are not shocked but challenged if there is a technological revolution, and they have psychological command of what is needed to go through the adaptation. Schools that build programmes on the concept of a survey of employer-specific needs are doomed to fall short.

This is not to say that school and the work-place should be separated. Children should *know* what the workplace entails— not as a fixed static entity, but one that is always in fluctuation. Since time is limited, not all careers can be demonstrated by class activities. The notion of dynamics needs to be extended by indications that there are other worlds out there, other kinds of industry and commerce. And, especially for the more academically inclined, that boring subjects are sometimes of great advantage, from languages to abstract mathematics.

If the school is to combine practice and theory in generalisable ways, employers will still fret about the lack of trained applicants to do immediate tasks. As most Europeans have known—but maybe are losing sight of—that is the task for the employer himself. For that kind of training, there is no substitute for it being on the job, linked precisely to the issue of earning a living. A modernised concept of apprenticeships—which will have to be followed time and again by refresher training—still makes sense. Some large industries may be able to support class activities, either in-house or in association with training or technical post-high schools.

But don't dump this on secondary schools. They have too much to do to create the dynamic fundamentals and to nurture creative aptitudes.

One of the concomitants of undisciplined self-expression is the inability to communicate effectively and to discriminate between incoming messages. Disturbingly, many adults take manipulatory advantage of this.

Before World War II ideology was linked to political propaganda. Both the left but especially the right honed the skills of communicating falsity and manipulating half-truth. Crowd behaviour, mass rallies, manipulation of mass theatrical devices, endless repetition, slogans instead of thought—all these were common. Mostly, educators could see them for what they were. As a youth and young man I found that classes in logic and books which showed the nature of the techniques and the logical *leger-de-main* quite fascinating—of course using what I had learned to support my own prejudices!

It is extremely difficult to find such classes and books today, especially for high schools. States still manipulate with propaganda, but, save for those which are ideologically founded, their positions are more subtle. They make use of PR firms and techniques, with communication models derived from advertising, but now being cynically distrusted as "spin". In the industrialised world the techniques of propaganda have been taken over by a kaleidoscope of pressure groups. Pressure groups organised around particular points of view and philosophies are a natural outcome of democratic life. But it behoves the citizen to see clearly the relationship between argument and data, to know the empirical base of points of view, the logic and assumptions with which it is upheld. Youth is particularly vulnerable to the power of repeated assertions, the mis-use of emotion, and loud slogans—yes, even when teachers use them.

And this applies, even more, to nurturing the ability to appraise critically the numerous ideologies and unsupported scientific and folk claims with which all of us are confronted today. Without sacrificing independence of thought and respect for mavericks, youth needs to be able to make judgements about balderdash, mumbo-jumbo, "obscurantist bunkum, swirling hogwash, mendacious codswallop" and to be guided to simple expressions in their own language, avoiding the obscure language which is nowadays typical of corporations, politicians and academics[19].

Utopianly, a citizen society equipped to judge and think and appraise would, by its own standards and criticisms, reveal the strengths and weaknesses of arguments, and hence punish by scepticism those who try to win by playing tricks on the mind.

There is evidence that the public senses much of this. There is widespread cynicism about political statements, derision about the way the media fasten on a limited aspect of a "story" and repeat it *ad infinitum* until it goes away, neglecting the balancing data. While many fasten upon visual scenes of horror and distress, others know that this is manipulative, replacing thought and balance with blood and tears.

A few recognise that, while it is proper for children to know what demonstrations are about, what lies behind them, it is exploitative to include very young children in those demonstrations; it is abusive and brain-washing, especially at primary school age. By the secondary level, lessons in logic and rhetoric become essential for the formation of critical citizens, and teachers must be prepared to have their values and perspectives openly challenged and debated.

I am disturbed about other phenomena. The movements of the late 'sixties in the "West" properly shook up received ideas in almost all public fields, from sex to the environment. In part they did so by affirming the significance of the emotions, of feelings, of the subjective, and did indeed provide a much-needed corrective to the idea that logic is detached from the senses and is the only path to understanding[20]. Paradoxically, however, one result was to create group tyrannies, ideologies that built dogma and used emotion, particularly anxiety, alienation and anger, to bind adherents together.

Out of that came positions that held certain beliefs to be absolutely right, positions shared by some, not all, parents and teachers. Schools become the loci for the transmission of such beliefs, whether they were about the dangers of nuclear catastrophe, global warming, over-population, depletion of non-renewable resources, crime, sexual harassment, and much more.

Here enters a matter of difficult judgement. Such issues are indeed a matter for study and education. They will not be understood in their complexity and balance at very young ages. They must be approached at later ages. By the end of high school, pupils should be in a position to approach such topics *independently* from the teacher and with an ability to work out their position after having looked at argument and data—they should be becoming adept at finding and thinking about both.

My problems are two-fold.

Many of the issues are presented in a highly charged emotional context in which adults transmit their own fears, *creating* anxieties, fears and even emotional upset in personae who are not ready for it. If this matter is not dealt with, goes the message, the apocalypse will arrive. And it is going to be *your* task to deal with it. It will be on *your* consciences. Can anyone forget the strained faces of *primary school* children in the 'fifties and 'sixties as they expressed fears of nuclear catastrophe? Now the fear that strikes home most immediately is fear of sex=AIDS, of poverty; of violence on the street, of terrorism, of unemployment, even, in some parts of the world, of the possibility that the United States will destroy our religion and culture. Fear permeates the schools. Somehow we must replace it, not with over-confidence, but with balance, thought, belief that we *can* and *will* make a difference, not by taking the whole world on our shoulders, but by playing thoughtful roles where our capabilities count.

The second problem is that even well-meaning and just positions are frequently tainted by dogma; slogans replace thought. Time and again I see high school students praised in public when they trot out the latest fashionable position on a complicated issue, repeating *ad nauseam* already-tired clichés. We do not expect world-shattering innovation from high school students. But by the end of high school clear individual, even original, statements of position, which are not simply the regurgitation of a teacher's or parent's ideology, should be the norm. This is even more serious an issue in those parts of the world where the basis of learning is by rote, and based on fundamentalist beliefs.

My own statements here are condensed and hence somewhat simplistic. I must go further, although even then the legitimate debate will only be opened up, by no means concluded. I would like to see schools consciously and clearly organise their approach to teaching and engendering thought around the following kinds of ideas.

Children can be helped to comprehend that understanding can be achieved through two alternative but interlinked processes. The one is subjective, intuitional and aesthetic, making use of words *and other signs* (harmonies, shapes) characteristic of "the arts". The other is rational, logical and communicable through words or similar (mathematical) signs. In making judgements about the efficacy of what is revealed, ideally the nature of the mix of the modes should be assessed. In dealing with the more subjective, it is of course interesting to pursue the influence of the creator's history and personality. This, though, is a part of knowledge itself, as revealing how it came to be, *not* part of the judgement of the significance or otherwise of the ideas themselves. Youth must understand that *ad hominem* arguments are not arguments. Whatever the nature of the communicator, it is his or her statements that count, in themselves. (It is nevertheless legitimate to interpret the *meaning* of the statements, where they are ambiguous, in terms of other signals the communicator may have given by his or her other statements and behaviour. Behaviour is then identified as a part of the statement.)

Both methods deal with ideas which consist of relationships, though differing in how they go about presenting them. Music consists of types of sound, notes, tones, movement, rhythm, harmonies, volume, all knit together into relationships which are the obverse of chaotic. Natural science includes the teasing out of explanations, that is relationships between this and that variable. So do the social sciences. Painting and architecture involve form. So it goes on. The horror of Hiroshima or 7-11 can be approached through art, communicating through visual form, the connotations of music, poems which link the act to feeling and experience, statements that show the relationship between nuclear action and catastrophe. It can also be placed in the context of, that is it can be related to, total war, generalisations about the dynamics of war and international politics, the state of the world society at the time, the linkage between that and the present, the proximal and fundamental causes of the events. All these and many more relationships are there to be explored, and full understanding needs them all. Although it is a statement of a relationship, it is superficial indeed for children simply to say "I think it was horrible". They must know there are other relationships involved, other generalisations to think about, approached through well constructed modes of thought and expression which we call disciplines. Disciplines are tools, tools that the young need to learn to use.

Within that mastery they may learn to criticise, be dissatisfied, with what the disciplines can do. There may here be the seeds of creative endeavour. But most of us cannot create, cannot innovate, unless we have the kinds of building blocks that schools can provide. (Yes, it is true that some creators and innovators find their building blocks away from school, even rejecting the institution. But disciplinary building blocks they do find, nevertheless.)

Even subjective assessments involve statements about more or less, that is about quantity, whether or not the quantities can be enumerated. There is more or less beauty, subjectively speaking. Ugliness is negative beauty.

When explanations are involved there is an inherent significance in the quantities. The arts deal with single representations, unique cases—the original painting is not more or less interesting because it is replicated in prints; it is unique in its statements. The same applies to a theatrical or musical performance, a sculpture, a book. That is, the single case has a certain validity, which is *dependent upon its success in communicating*. The communication may be contemporaneously ineffective, but received at some future time, which makes immediate judgement problematic. Popular approval may be ephemeral, yet the relationships involved, for example in "hard metal", are in communication, and are thus there to be teased out, examined, as part of "knowledge", both subjectively and objectively. Youth needs to know these things as part of the fundamental basis of what they are "learning".

In the critical examination of what is being communicated, teachers dealing with human affairs seem to place considerable emphasis on trying to reveal the hidden agendas, the unstated values, of what is there. Quite often I feel that such revelations sometimes come from teachers' own hidden agendas and political perspectives (in some parts of the world, not so hidden). Yet the validity of the principle is indisputable. My reservation can be dealt with by teachers inviting and respecting the same critical attention to their own presentations.

Matters of equal importance, however, are not so frequently addressed. We have already noticed the value of the single case, the unique and non-replicated statement. It is important to relate this to and distinguish it from, *explanation* in the more formal sense, not because of the nature of the revealed assertions, but because of the demands of the methodology.

This morning I was reading a front page story in a well respected and carefully presented newspaper. It dealt with ozone thinning for the coming summer, a matter of great concern and certainly a matter for school discussion. The main space in the story was contained in a full column on the front page. That consisted of repeated statements of concern, linked to such phrases as "It has been shown that". The identification of who had done the showing and how was not mentioned until a very short column concluding the story on an inside page. There was not the slightest attempt to communicate any reason for accepting or rejecting the findings by representing the pros and cons of the methodology and its locus in general scientific knowledge. The implication was that the results should be accepted because they came from a reputable scientific organisation—and because the newspaper presented them. One assumes the results to be valid until someone comes along later with another story. This is unacceptable. It is as *ad hominem* as the dismissal of a politician's ideas because of his sexual peccadillos.

Even where data *are* presented quite fully, citizen-children need to learn how to evaluate them. This applies especially to anecdotal and statistical material. Is the anecdotal to be considered as a unique work of art? Quite possibly. No more and no less. Since it is unique one can draw legitimate conclusions *subjectively*. Within the media anecdotal evidence does not have the same seriousness or sincerity of purpose as a major work of art. Most frequently the portrayal of incident communicates to the emotions on subjects—for example crime—that are open to consideration from the other, more logical, more enumerative methods. A citizen-youth must be aware of the values and emotional impact of the unique instance; but also to be able to place that in the context of knowledge obtained by other methods.

Frequently the media give the appearance of quantifying through repetition of unique cases. Day after day of attention to similar violent acts, for example. In doing so they usually, except for responsible articles and documentaries, ignore the disciplines that the implication of quantification demand. Statistical controls. Control of variables. Margins of error. Comparison in time and place.

There is another problem, which I find particularly in the presentation and methodology of medical research. Time and again we learn of a causative relationship discovered on the basis of a statistical enquiry, sometimes minimal, sometimes massive. Later, we find another study which, with similar methodology but a different set of variables, provides alternative or contradictory causation. Tucked away in a footnote you often find that the researchers are puzzled as to *how* the relationship comes about.

Statistics deal with *probability* not final proof. A statistical statement is almost useless *in itself*. It has meaning *only* as providing a serious hypothesis, unless and until it is embedded in the context of a wider theory of explanation, linked to *other* relationships by abstract general statements, which could, in principle, be disproven. If the researchers admit they don't know *why* the relationship exists statistically, their data must be treated with the utmost caution, as the subject for further research, *not* the presentation of a conclusion which has enormous implications for human life. The recent history of medicine surely shows this. At one time margarine not butter, now butter not margarine. What is the cholesterol implication of consuming eggs? Milk, dairy products, the effects of digesting fish. Generalisations about these and so many more technical nutritional and medical matters have, literally, been upset or modified within the past few *weeks* of my writing this.

To my relief—for I am never certain about what I say—an entry in *The Economist* for September 3rd, 2005 refers to a significant study by Dr.John Ioannidis of the University of Ioannina published in *PLOS Medecine*[21]. He looked at studies in the *Journal of the American Medical Association* and found that a third of them were later refuted. The problems were rooted into a misunderstanding of the meaning of "statistical significance" and to un professional use of the statistical methods.

And again, especially in medicine, while the statistical norm certainly matters, it is the individual organism which is at issue. The variations from the norm are as significant as the norm itself. Probability is just that, probability. It is *not* certainty about each and every instance. In many areas of study, the fact is that even one single instance which does not conform to the norm implies that the theoretical basis for the norm has been disproven as a generalised statement. There is something else at work. The human organism—and so many other fields of investigation—contains so many variables that the essential tool of statistics has to be treated with great caution, the only certainty being that it cannot remove doubt. Indeed, the single seemingly aberrant instance, if closely examined, may yield more theoretical innovation and understanding than the instances that are statistically normal.

Doubt. Uncertainty. Yet acting on the basis of what we know. These are major conundrums that youth have to be prepared for, have to understand if they are to live with the huge changes in knowledge that are being thrust at them.

Youth need that understanding, *and the acceptance of it* more than ever for psychological reasons. The unknown has always been a threat. Deep within ourselves, in primitive, perhaps irrational, fear, we do not know how to deal with it. It impinges on our personal lives every day, it is thrust upon us as a characteristic of the world, indeed of the universe. We correctly discuss the possibility of annihilation by projectiles from outer space.

What is troublesome is the serious anxiety and stress that comes from fear of the unknown. I am not concerned here with the modes of dealing with it, from religion to witchcraft, alternative therapies or fatalism, many of which at least have the possibility of relieving stress. What are more serious are the inhibiting features, the negative pessimism, inhibition of activity, chronic anxiety and depression, which flow. Suicide among youth. Alienation.

It is fundamental to serious education that children learn to deal with the unknown, especially before a personal crisis hits them. They must examine the validity and limitations of unique experience, learning from it but not turning it into dogma. A teacher who is sick may be ill because of the effects of a new detergent in the washroom. That is a matter for investigation. But if it turns into a dogma it can dangerously deflect investigation from some other causative possibility—even one that is at present not identified.

"Hey hey, ho ho! Get rid of Mr. Joe!" Slogans, demonstrations. The one thing they are *not* is argument. Unless on a massive scale, they are not even an indication of popular support. Sometimes, as perhaps in France, they are so predictable and frequent that they have little effect on the electorate (as distinct from a nervous prime minister) beyond satisfying the emotions of the demonstrators. In most cases they are so lacking in imagination that they do not qualify as theatre, and, like much of advertising, are counter-productive. In another sense, of course, they are an exercise in power; possibly creative. Here I am more concerned with what they communicate. They do not replace either the objective study or the artistic representation of "truth" and "belief". It is certainly possible for youth to understand this and to analyse slogans objectively, whether or not they agree with the point of view.

It is a primary responsibility of school education to engender clear individual judgements about the presentation of information, and to show how youths can get to the sources themselves and at least be sceptical about inadequate materials, however persuasive the cause. What I have argued for is complex. In its sources, like everything else taught in school, it is embedded in subject matter which belongs in universities and beyond, which high school students cannot normally be expected to fully master. That in itself is not a reason for dismissing it. The principles *can* be (and often have been) taught directly in high school. And, with good pedagogical attention, they can be communicated indirectly as an aspect of normal studies.

To move toward the informed citizenship that is necessary in our Utopia, we must re-emphasise, especially in high school, the arts of logic, discourse, debate and rhetoric; the relationship between data, theory and judgement; the ability to search for, assess, and use data; the positive force of constructive criticism, both logical and aesthetic; the role of sensory experience in arriving at observations and judgements; and the ability both to speak and to write well-marshalled ideas. School children should be able to test the statements of teachers with confidence and skill, but on the basis of reasoned argument and data, and mutual respect.

We want our children (grandchildren) to be educated in such a way that they utterly reject slogans, false jargon, and improperly communicated data.

The social purpose of the school links, as I have said, with other objectives than the vocational. I have pointed out the distress of the elderly who find themselves unstimulated, bored, and alienated. We know of the unemployment of youth. We know that most countries have high steady rates of unemployment and that one of the major difficulties in developing countries is linked to chronic under-employment. In other words, perhaps fifty per cent of the world's population has *unwanted* time on its hands[22]. To the extent that this is true—I ask you to suspend judgement on that issue for the meantime—the primary institution for properly handling the situation is, once again, the school. To be stated bluntly, schools must be able to help children to find ways to stimulate their leisure time and to obviate *boredom*, one of the most depressing characteristics of old age, unemployment, and youthful crime.

For this reason the educational system has a major responsibility, at least equal to the others I have outlined, to assist children in the task of discovering their self-directed creative and recreational capacities. Modern schools do some of this, by including courses in the arts, from music to theatre, and practical skills such as carpentry and metal-working, or transmitting cultural materials. However, when such activities are simply slotted into the timetable problems arise. They inevitably compete with one another for rare time slots, which include what most consider to be the basics, and the artistic courses become the target of parents who see them as "frills". The "practical" courses are almost always justified by vocational rather than avocational considerations.

To remedy this schools must be able to plan and justify the activities in terms of the principles I have outlined before. Most adults will have a hard time agreeing, since the underlying argument runs counter to the philosophy, which I shall continue to dispute throughout my theses, that Work is King. Hence those responsible for educational policy will have an uphill struggle to make those policies clear, consciously advocated, and fully planned. Creative Leisure is Queen.

Lying behind the discovery of the creative self is the challenge to learn to occupy oneself when not being supervised. A number of cultures deliberately used isolation in stressful conditions as a rite of passage. Self-reliance, even in highly interdependent communities, was necessary to survival. Isolation forced the young candidate for adulthood to know his inner being, and to know that being in its relationship to a potentially threatening nature, a nature with which the candidate learned also to be at peace. It was an exercise in being, and in spirituality. Such procedures could well be studied and adapted. So too could modes of meditation, relaxation, and emotional control.

Similar exercises can expose the values and dangers of living with small groups, the mutual dependencies under stress, the uselessness of making a habit of ascribing blame to others or giving dysfunctional expressions of aggression, and learning the ways of small group diplomacy. For some young people will find their creativity not in the private actions of solitude but in the co-operation of acting with others toward a common outcome.

It will be for the pedagogues to work out such possibilities. The objective of drawing out self-reliance and unimposed creativity carries the additional benefit of improving self-knowledge and becoming sensitised to small group interactions which have implications for family life and the workplace as well as for unpaid positive activity.

The issues lead to the conclusion that the school course-ridden day is inadequate. Good schools already intrude into family life through the demands of home study. Perhaps more of that should be done in current school class time, moving some of the avocational activities—as is done with sports—outside the conventional school day, allowing creative home activity to take place in its natural setting, involving parental judgements about the possibilities, and permitting, for example, more inclusion of evening and weekend cultural activities in the youth's overall preoccupations.

Carrying this theme to its ultimate conclusion will require major changes in the organisation and operation of what we now call schools in our 21st century Utopian society.

Since the school has children in its care for such an enormous proportion of their time, and since those children are subjected to so many confusing, worrying and contradictory influences in their lives, the school cannot avoid being in a position of *nurturing*. It may not want to do so, it may not be mandated to do so, and it is almost certainly not equipped to do so. Yet in this responsibility it is almost equal to that of the family.

What I have written so far has dealt mostly with the mind. But the mind is inseparable from the body, the senses, the emotions, the influences, the interactions, and the memories. *Pace* some forms of psychoanalysis, the child is far from completely formed in infancy. What happens in school will be a major influence in creating the ever-dynamic or statically-confined persona.

A great deal of this cannot be *controlled* by the individual teacher, for it is a result of the complexities of the institutional *ambience*, peers and other teachers. Individual teachers do, frequently, detect problems of concern which range from attention disorders to malnutrition and the possibility of crime. They give of themselves through advice, discipline, listening and referral. By role definition they must give priority to the effects of what they detect to the operation of the classroom and the formal work of teaching itself. Very commonly the child's personal problems can show through surly indiscipline, avoidance of work, theft, obscenity, anger, nonchalant insolence, gang behaviour, bullying and violence—all the problems, in fact, that are found in the adult world, but in more vulnerable forms.

Consultation with parents may, but mostly are unlikely to, help, since teachers are not in a position in to enter into family therapy. Teachers by themselves cannot create the remedies. Yet schools have to deal with concerns, just as they are now learning to deal with the "physically and mentally challenged"—oh, what wonderful and inadequate jargon to obscure the reality that the child, deprived or contorted with respect to hiser capabilities may or may not feel "challenged" but certainly needs attention and help. It is an inescapable responsibility that has serious consequences for school (what we shall call Youth Maturity Institute) mandates and organisation.

All of which intersects with the issue of behavioural discipline. There has been a school of socialisation that asserts that the only legitimate form of control is that of argument. The problem is that it doesn't always work . . . And when it does it can sometimes breed conformity rather than courtesy.

Hit 'em and learn 'em in righteous anger and its sadistic extremes has gone by the board in many parts of the world. There, teachers must control their reactions, however provoked. On the other hand some parents encourage their children to express their angers, which can mean placing the self before others with insolence, refusal to heed, and rejection of what the school is trying to do—just as disruptive reactions as the surly introversion of unexpressed problems. More frequently than not, minor irritants of these kinds move through the classroom, as peers delightedly cheer the culprit on. Then follows open defiance, the use of appeal procedures to undermine the teacher, and the intervention of angry parents convinced they are not themselves responsible, or frustrated ones who do not know how to deal with situations that are out of control.

Indeed, in some areas I know of the school in effect has no effective powers of discipline and control, and would be totally lost if it were not for the decency of the majority of the children. There are, it is true, possibilities of assigning extra work or detentions, which the hard core can simply refuse to honour. When that happens, when violence breaks out, when there is habitual absence from the classroom, when there are drugs or weapons, the ultimate threat is there. Exile, banishment from the school. What a game! A game that tempts others who are toying with the lure of dropping out. To be officially pronounced unwelcome in the school, no longer hassled by authority, officially able to roam the streets—exactly what such delinquents want . . .

We do not want this in Utopia. Not only does it represent the loss of an individual to the common good, but it is an example to the half-alienated and is disruptive of those who have other ideals. It is an instance, potentially, of the spread of an anti-school innovation. Since parental responsibility is either not there or is insufficient, the school itself must develop other tools, even though, without outside help, it cannot get at root problems such as dysfunctional family life.

There are two methods at least which might help. As I write this I read of an experiment in Toronto. Youths expelled for violence are identified as such and transferred to another specialist programme for them only. Instead of roaming the streets each student works (expensively) with a psychiatrist and a programme co-ordinator. In the pilot programme, fifty per cent of the students have been judged ready to return to regular schooling. At least for the others some education is achieved. My information does not reveal what happens if the youths refuse to cooperate, nor what kind of family involvement is in place. Nevertheless the thought behind such approaches deserves attention.

Another method, also being experimented with in various contexts, is to involve the children themselves in peer responsibility, and to give them some of the tools to do so. As in so many other cases, older methods which have gone out of psychological fashion (such as the use of prefects) have been ridiculed on the basis of extreme caricature. All methods, old or new, have their defects. Perhaps one should look again, and tease out the positive from the negative.

Many schools nowadays have some form of student council, a useful way of enabling, usually the better, pupils to voice difficulties and to organise events. There are also emergent student-teacher initiatives, such as plays and discussions, which aim at demonstrating such topics as the handling of violence when it occurs, the difficulties of sex, or the release of anger. Even in primary schools selected children are trained in mediation, intervening in quarrels to persuade quarrellers to look at each others' points of view, to find ways out of the situation before it explodes.

Experiments of these kinds are novel, welcome, and full of hope. But they cannot deal effectively with every situation, and cannot always be on top of day to day incidents.

It seems that the old idea of a "school spirit" based on identification with the school, pride in what it attempts to do, rivalry with others, and internal pupil-based discipline, is worth another look. As with any other type of cultural or sub-cultural identity, it can go too far, with autocracy emerging, too much interference in private acts, too much peer pressure, and, in extreme instances, schools becoming rivalrous gangs. What is different nowadays, and even more we hope in the future, is that in the developed world the teachers who have the ultimate responsibility are better informed about such dangers and are likely to be more sensitive to their emergence.

Let us then consider re-inventing (where it has to be re-invented) the system of prefects for day schools. Let there be chosen leaders at various levels in the school, with responsibilities according to the degree of maturity that their age can handle. Senior prefects might very well act as disciplinary agents and intervenors under policies formulated by, or with the assistance of, the student council. Let them have the authority to discipline for designated infractions—giving detentions for example; to maintain order and respect on school premises and at school functions; to report serious infractions; to present constructive ideas to council and staff; in short to supervise, *on behalf of the student body*, standards of good order and courtesy.

One of the primary tools that street gangs use to reinforce solidarity and identity, is dress and body decoration. They do so naturally, out of spontaneous recognition of principles that are as old as human groups. Schools in many parts of the world, and especially North America, deliberately gave away this reinforcing tool. In some form, whether through simple uniforms or badges, it needs to return. It is one way of enhancing pride. I am on my mettle because I can be seen to be a *member* of the school that has a great team, organises volunteers for a social cause, puts on an exciting art show, or perhaps, even, is the place where academic achievement gets us going. At least when I'm wearing that uniform outside of school I behave; I'm noticeable and proud of it. [I'm well aware that the wearing of uniforms at schools where state schools do *not* wear them is an identifier of difference that is often not acceptable and is even embarrassing to the wearers. Acceptance changes when the custom is *general*.]

The easiest part of this discussion is to write the words; the most difficult to interpret the principles in specific contexts, to give them pedagogical content and reality, to make them work. None of my statements can be considered as an absolute.

First and foremost it is the teachers who have the responsibility for method and content, for the specifics of classroom and school. They claim to be, and are, and should be, the professionals. It is what they have learned, their experience, their skills, that makes the difference. But those skills, as with any profession, must work in context, the context of societal aims, immediate culture, and changing knowledge.

One of the realities is that henceforth they will be working in a society that changes ever more rapidly, and that they must second-guess what the needs of the future may be. Is that to be toward some vision of Utopia, a world in which we wish ourselves to live, even though we may never see it in our lifetimes? Some vision of a better world? I hope so. But if so that kind of ultimate purpose needs discussion, needs teacher attention, needs definition, even though that definition is bound to change over the decades.

This is a area that lies beyond the horizons of teachers alone. Teachers are in a position to be arbiters of society, communicating (deliberately or without noticing it) their own values. But they do not have the mandate to *decide* where society should go. In that they are simply one set of citizens. Who then does? The interplay of parents, non-parent voters, political and community leaders, teachers, other professionals who, as we shall see, are involved with the same objectives.

Teachers then, as it were, interpret the objectives. The trouble is that the objectives, at this stage in our evolution, are not spelled out for society as a whole (except, for example, in fundamentalist religious schools or autocratic state systems), and can only be defined in simplistic and programmatic terms, tinged with political ideology. Just the same, some observations can be made.

One is that in a future world, in a Utopian view, society and culture not only *will* consist of varying groups, cultures or subcultures, with non-uniform ideas, but *should* do so. The reality of the statement for contemporary societies is beyond dispute. Look within your country. It is there.

To the extent that this is so, it follows that schools **must** themselves vary. The concept that each State school must have an identical, centrally determined, philosophy, curriculum, and pedagogy is now revealed for what it is, an ideology based upon a false socio-cultural premise, upon a false Utopian view that we should all be the same, and upon an impractical establishment.

Ideally, varying schools should match variations in child response to varying methods, varying parental philosophies, and variations in cultural realities, at least. Such clear matching is seldom practicable, but close approximations are possible. Perhaps the following principle is worthy of thought: schools and teachers within schools should have the utmost flexibility to exercise their ideas in directions which link with a recognised Utopian dream and educational philosophy; but no child should be forced into a particular school. Choice that is now available to some (the better off) should be available to all.

Such a principle implies that variation should not merely be between state schools and private schools, religious schools, schools for the rich and the not so rich. State systems themselves need to abandon the assignment of children to schools on the sole criterion of geographical proximity, a policy which derives from the false notion that equity and equality of opportunity imply pushing every child into the same cauldron. Equity and equality of opportunity imply the opposite, that every child should be in the school that suits him or her best. The identification of what is "best" will not be accurate. It involves parents' ideals and parents' knowledge both of the child and of the nature of each possible school, a knowledge that will undoubtedly change with time.

Hence movement of pupils between schools must be possible. And schools must provide parents with information—documentation, for example, about its educational philosophy and goals, its methods, its achievements, what it is trying to do better. *Every school in the system should be required to formulate and enunciate its point of view.* Every piece of data that bears on the parents' potential evaluation of the school should be public.

One specious argument against the idea is that once it is known that one or two schools meet needs better than others they will become elite, based on restricted entry. Of course that is possible, but it reveals inflexibility in the school system. (It may also involve prejudice and lack of knowledge of the alternatives.) It may encourage other schools to emulate. But in addition it will be the case that there will be no single definition of "better". Parents will not be like lemmings, moving in one single direction. Schools that meet children's varied educational needs best require replication; others require down-sizing.

The two most difficult sources of inflexibility are teachers and buildings. If choice reveals that certain wanted types of teaching are not reflected in the distribution of teacher skills, then, at least in an adjustment period, some individual teachers will be in difficulty. The implications are that in the long run teacher education itself should teach less dogma and more adaptability; that there should be maximum support for teacher re-education; and that unadaptable teachers will have to go or be assigned elsewhere.

At present the conditions under which teachers do their work are highly variable, country to country, sometimes responding to bargaining conditions, sometimes to social status, sometimes to poverty, sometimes to religious ideology. However I do not know of any countries in which the conditions of work and education, except in some of the most expensive private schools, and then not in a Utopian sense, correspond to the need. Sometimes good principles have been subverted by union action and bargaining into privileged "rights".

Days off for professional education, in which the school closes; long summer vacations, originally to permit children to undertake agricultural tasks—such arrangements, fiercely union protected, are inflexible, inefficient, rule-bound, misused, and archaic. The first, for example, are often boring, not observed by individual teachers, and, while sometimes useful, are not administered to face up to improving and updating the skills of *individual* teachers. That requires more than the occasional discussion or lecture, but weeks of analysis and education. Teaching, especially in high school, is an ever-moving profession, in the roles required, and in the subject matter.

It is a normal fact of employment that teachers in most systems take their classes home with them, figuratively and also literally. Much of their work consists of out-of-class paper work, including marking and preparation. When classes take place throughout the day, either they stay very late at school, or work at home, with effects on their domestic arrangements. The short breaks between classes, or class time off, are seldom adequate to do serious work. Despite what the public regards as soft and privileged work time, teachers in most advanced systems are typically stressed out, under constant emotional and psychological pressure, especially when dealing with under-motivated, tumultuous children; to say nothing of those with severe personal problems. Moves in several systems to mix "special needs" children into conventional classes, while highly desirable in theory, add to teacher stress (especially when the teacher has no education in the specialty of the needs) and divert him or her from attention given to the ordinary, who, in their own ways, are just as needy. Unless very special measures are taken, such moves are typical of the ways in which principles can come to grief because the material and organisational resources are not adjusted sufficiently.

If to these present difficulties we add the requirements of Utopia, without other adjustments, mayhem and breakdown could destroy what little is left of the high school system. Any reforms must be built around the capacities, physical and mental, of the staff—teachers *and others*—whose task it is to deliver.

In many systems the school year is built around terms divided by short breaks—one, two, or three weeks—instead of a concentration of holidays on a long two month summer break typical of others, during which the dynamic of school progress can be threatened. A number of breaks of around two weeks enables the progression of teaching with little interruption of the dynamic, especially if some of the breaks are designated for projects, independent study, alternative creative activities. Such breaks provide an opportunity for teacher refresher courses as well.

Teachers are not only over-worked but also inefficiently directed. Some systems provide, not just the occasional class off during the week, but up to an equivalent of classroom time for study and preparation. Initially, in systems where teachers are not accustomed to that, the provision of such time could be significantly abused. Many teachers are simply not used to the idea that handling the subject matter requires continual research and reading. Such teachers would not know what to do with their time, except paper work, until guided into its effective use. (Are there still teachers who have the time, the drive, the energy, the knowledge, to *contribute* to the growth of knowledge, to undertake research, however modest; even perhaps to involve their classes in that activity? Yes there are. They should be among the role models, though it is too much to make that a formal requirement until Utopia is here.)

An efficient educational system requires a surplus of resources beyond those immediately used in the classroom. Contrary to the drives of budget-minded administrators, if you show me an educational institution of serious intent in which all classrooms are being used at every minute of the day, and in which there are no teachers outside the classroom, I will show you a static, unresponsive, bureaucratised, anti-educational operation, unable to meet society's needs.

Why? When considering the distribution of teachers, it should be obvious that they should be pedagogically sound and know their subject matter. In secondary schools particularly, it is not good enough to say, as some have, "Give me a class and I'll teach it anything." That is the sure way to superficiality. But teachers take ill, the Utopian system would require them to take time off for formal re-education, and they must have an opportunity to take real holidays that would involve being absent for terms. Redistribution among existing teachers, re-posting, now often means assigning teachers to subject areas of which they know little or nothing. Short term replacements are often temporary substitute teachers, which may often be effective in individual cases. But as a *system* it cannot be efficient. Such substitutes usually have to have other sources of income and cannot afford to place themselves in a one-line teaching career position; their standards and updating cannot therefore be rigorously controlled. Both these situations *require a pool* of subject-oriented teachers in the career stream available for replacement allocation. Members of the pool would not be in the classroom until called upon, but would be salaried.

I have been referring to refresher education. The movement of school responsibilities into non-vocational and therapeutic fields will increase the range of required specialties, of differing combinations of skills. School professionals, just like health professionals, will in some instances be stimulated to re-combine their skills: a combination of language teaching and family therapy might be a case in point. And just like health professionals, or university professors in North America who are seeking promotion, they will require formal certification, from time to time, of their continued pedagogic and coexistent subject area skills.

As I write I am living in an urban area in which the distribution of the population is changing fast. Immigrants are arriving in substantial numbers, finding living space in new areas, and needing educational courses (such as language) which differ from those of the past. Some locations are no longer affordable for new growing families in the same numbers. Changing technology requires new subject matter which is unevenly developed and which requires altered forms of teaching and working space. New interactive multi-media teaching tools again require new forms of space to be effective—even bringing the home into the classroom (especially with web based distance learning). Old school buildings are sometimes emptying, and some cannot be adapted easily to new teaching needs.

Demographic forecasts are notoriously affected by value and political judgements and are seldom reliable in detail. Educational authorities are thus reluctant to spend large capital sums on new buildings when the trend that demands them may be applicable only, say, for six or seven years. They meet the need by throwing up temporary port-a-classrooms, which parents immediately identify as sub-standard and discriminatory.

Yet the flexibility afforded by mobile classrooms is clearly more desirable than the inflexibility of monuments hewed in stone. The unresolved problem suggests that the expenditure of money, efficiency of operation, and educational flexibility and quality will be best where buildings can respond to need from decade to decade instead of dominating and freezing the delivery of service. If this is so, then there is a major architectural challenge to design school buildings which can easily be moved from one location to another, which consist of modules of differing functions which can be combined and recombined to fit changing educational needs, and which, probably, are less expensive than conventional structures. Paradoxically, this may be more easily achievable in developing tropical countries, making use of traditional structures which can be removed and rebuilt with less cost. Here is a field for UNESCO innovation.

Someone has to take decisions and to provide resources in an environment in which, at least in the short term, resources are getting scarcer. The Utopian specifics will vary so much from one system to another that I can only write in generalities. But it should be clear by now that we need to re-think the structure and operation of what we now call schools, if they are to properly educate, nurture and create cohorts of well-adjusted future citizens. This is the Utopian, but achievable, goal.

The initiative to establish and design variable schools will come mostly from parents, from some teachers, and from some citizens. Since it is the community providing the funds, it is likely that what I will call the Youth Maturity Institute management authority will be vested in an overall area board which allocates funds and authorises establishments. The board will need to represent the taxpayers and those who elect the political authority; it should also have representatives of parents and teachers (not in their self-seeking but in their professional capacities); and it might be beneficial to have representatives of senior high school classes. The danger in such a board is that each of these constituencies will provide members, elected or chosen, whose debates will result in some sort of majority opinion. The danger then is that the majority will be seen as having a political mandate to exercise that opinion throughout the system, giving no voice to alternative philosophies and styles. This is the opposite of what we are endeavouring to achieve. Hence it seems essential that the terms of reference for such a board require as a matter of law that the board recognises the principles of school, now Youth Maturity Institute, variation.[23]

As I have said, each individual Institute should be required to establish and publicise its philosophy and methods, paying special attention to its unique character. The initiative for doing this should come from both parents and teachers *and other professional contributors* acting in concert. Until Utopia becomes less confrontational there will undoubtedly be conflict between opposing philosophies; someone will lose out. The area supervisory board needs to ensure that the Institute management council losers will be accommodated, that there is a school for them to join, or that one can be organised. Considerable initial adjustment is likely to take place, a necessary price for the achievement of the ultimate goals.

I deliberately placed the phrase "other professional contributors" in this context. There are now in fact examples not only of private schools in the conventional sense but of schools established by large industrial firms. Such schools are in response to two drives. One is the improvement in working conditions when working parents have on-premise schools (especially for younger children) with recreational as well as classroom space. Parents can visit in their breaks, and their children will be occupied instead of returning home to an empty house.

Another motivation, for upper year youth, is vocational training. It is very doubtful if adequate applied training for the workplace can be conducted effectively in conventional schools. It is often best done on site. Large firms can do this with either narrowly focused classes, in association with and supplementing Institutes, leading to apprenticeships or by actually locating and financing upper year broad education on their premises.

The feasibility of such schemes does not have to be limited to commerce and industry. The civil service, hospitals, universities, large public service and charitable organisations also have roles. Education affects us all; it percolates throughout; the barriers should be of malleable rubber.

A similar principle works in reverse. The objectives of the Utopian Institutes run far beyond the capacity of conventional schools to honour. This implies not that the objectives are wrong but that school capabilities must be altered to meet them. The most ineffective way of doing this is to throw money at schools and teachers. For most teachers are not educated to carry out many of the tasks (such as therapy for a suicidal youth), and do not have the time or energy even if they were equipped to do so. And school management would have to undergo a revolution to assess and address the broadened role; managers notoriously find this difficult although there are many innovative school heads and principals trying new approaches which have to be dubbed "experimental".

We are dealing with the "whole" child. We are seeking a holistic education. The state of knowledge and professionalisation of society create more and more specialists who are dealing with various parts of that whole. Their perspectives need to be brought together, and *the use of their manpower optimised*. There is dreadful duplication, waste, uncoordination, and confusion, not in the best interests of the child.

In order to achieve our Utopian vision, the concept of "school" as an institution with a narrow mandate needs to be jettisoned. They should be replaced by organisations which are mandated and equipped to nurture children and youths in a holistic manner toward the objectives of individual maturation.

As I have hinted, let us call these, until a better term is devised, "**Youth Maturity Institutes**."

First, each Youth Maturity Institute should have a management committee in which teachers, parents and representatives of youths from the final class should be represented. The task of the management committee should be to ensure that the teachers and staff in their day to day operation, act in accordance with the approved school philosophy, and to organise the operation of the Institute.

Second, each Youth Maturity Institute should have an advisory committee consisting of members appointed by the various bodies in the community concerned with the welfare of youth. To the extent that they bear upon the philosophy of the school and the needs of its operation, there could be included, for example, representatives of churches, youth organisations, social services, the media (not for "stories" but as being perceived as partly "responsible" for what goes on), police, medical services, employers, unions, and high school pupils. It would consider identified problems (such as drugs, violence, for example), the bearing of all of the services on each of those problems, possible co-ordination and changes of policy, not only in the Youth Maturity Institute but in the institutions which surround it.

As an example, in this committee it might be that representatives of the media are confronted with the ways in which their "stories" bear upon the objectives of the Institute.

Third, there would need to be a fundamental reappraisal of financing, the conception of "school hours", and personnel. We are dealing not only with the classroom where the teacher is paramount, but with recreation, and individual and family counselling (not in the vocational but in the psychological sense) with wide ramifications.

What has to come is the re-direction of appropriate outside services into the Youth Maturity Institute itself. Social service youth and family counsellors should move their offices and operations into the Institute, be seconded into the Institute, and have their budgets identified as part of the Institute budget, subject to Institute management.

Other organisations which have a bearing on school programmes need to be brought more formally into the Institute budget and field of responsibility. For example, the Youth Maturity Institute, in the running of its theatre programmes, might contract with a theatre company or organisation to do part or all of it, to the benefit of both. Many organisations concerned with the culture of creativity, or the creativity of culture should be more intimately involved with Youth Maturity Institutes, both on premises and off. Such contact would have the additional advantage of introducing children to the hard reality of creation (without putting them off), giving the starry eyes something to focus upon[24].

Since we are proposing an institution which has a holistic view of youth development, it follows that therapeutic and judicial functions[25] should be removed from external organizations and integrated with the Youth Maturity Institutes. This gives the Institutes opportunities to adopt therapeutic and restitutional procedures in the case of violence and delinquency. It enables them, in each case, to focus on the troubled youth and to take as long as it takes, and by whatever means it takes, to reintegrate the youth into peer society. The use of therapy, even of medical knowledge, and of alternative ways of dealing with crime Utopianly come together in one set of coordinated actions which in a formal judicial system is limited by professional bureaucracies and often stymied by the state of the law. Healing circles, psychotherapy, peer group and parental influences will all be part of the considerations as the youth is challenged to recognize the damage heshe has caused, and to make restitution to those who have been hurt. Incarceration or expulsion will not be part of the answer, although indigenous methods of spiritual isolation may well be in some instances. Restitution, recognition, reintegration are the three 'r's.

Clearly parents are intimately involved. Frequently they react defensively, protecting the family boundary, or from the shame of guilt and perplexity. If a child acts aggressively or criminally the cause may not be in the family. Or it may be. We need medical and therapeutic analysis. Parents should not be fingered immediately as the culprits. But they must be brought to understand, helped to deal with the issues and change their habits, and given support, together with the child. Not even "special needs" teachers can do this by themselves. There has to be team work in the Institutes, another reason for stressing the need to use them to replace schools.

Paradoxically, the more such methods succeed the more inner tensions may arise, unless another theme is addressed. For underlying a certain percentage of delinquency is the attraction and excitement of taking risks[26]. Street car racing, experimenting with drugs and sex, toting an AK47, using machetes in moments of hysteria. Logical argument will have only a small effect when such youth drives are paramount. Recognitions of consequences in dramatic form, the experience of devastation, will. But it requires a more widespread policy.

Bronislaw Malinowski's dictum "Let cricket replace warfare" has become a cliché, but deserves attention for all that. For the ills I am addressing it is far too soft. Many—not all—boys and an increasing number of girls want risky challenges, both mental and physical, without which they cannot move knowledgeably into adulthood. Show me a road racer and I will show you a school that is too bland in its challenges. This is an essential part of education, which cannot be completed in the classroom. Youth Maturity Institutes, as do a number of schools, for example in the Duke of Edinburgh's network, need to plan to encourage and support appropriate risk taking. Recently a Canadian private school decided to drop challenging winter skiing because of tragic deaths from an avalanche. On the assumption that all reasonable precautions were taken, the cancellation was a mistake. Risk taking implies just that, risk taking. Mollycoddling so that there are no risks defeats the purpose—and there will be accidents along the way, or the risk will not be there.

Schools are in fact better at devising intellectual risk taking tests—mathematical or chess challenges and competitions for example. But these reach only the elite. Professionals must devise ways in which the youth at whatever level, feels challenged, excited by even small accomplishments, prompted to risk the next stage.

Fear and anxiety are the concomitants of risk taking. Both are normal states even when risk is not at the forefront. Over the decades there have been enormous fears, communicated to school children, about atomic bombs, nuclear war, ecological disaster, poisonous foods. These habe ben communicated by teachers, parents and the media. There is no justification for this. On the other hand fear and anxiety are a normal part of risk and should be accepted as a normal state. Youth must learn to deal with them constructively in order to reach maturity and the Institutes have a major role in developing ways for this to happen.

At the same time there are those for whom various forms of fears and anxieties, phobias. Invade ordinary life in circumstances which may be deemed unwarranted, leading to the serious inhibition of appropriate behaviour. Again, the Institutes will have a pivotal role, not so much through teachers, though they may draw attention to the issue, but for therapists and parents.

Youth Maturity Institutes would accumulate an immense amount of experience and knowledge of direct interest to those dealing with social issues outside the Institutes themselves. Schools in my part of the world seem to have an almost nil impact on the fatally growing use of methadone. They are not equipped to do so. But Youth Maturity Institutes would be. I would find it very difficult to believe that such Institutes, operating effectively, would not know the sources of the drug. They could combine an attack on crystal methadone with risk taking—for example assigning young at-risk victims to accompany police on inner city drug beats. Show them what doctors and nurses have to go through to deal with extreme cases. The synergy that comes from the juxtaposition of professionals with quite different perspectives will lead to many innovative ideas.

The needs of poor countries require special comment. In many of the poor countries' rural areas, despite the trauma of war, and migration disruptions, and the ever present threat of famine, floods, and the depredations of both nature and man, the absence of a sophisticated therapeutic and institutional structure need not hold back a movement to Utopian reform. In some societies there are already male age-specific initiation rituals which can be adapted to go the youth maturity route. This is seldom the case for girls, other than, say, the declaration of puberty. Closely knit communities and kinship bonds do not mean the absence of internal strife, and they are sometimes the very sources of dissatisfaction and emigration. Nevertheless, skilled attention to their positive elements can aid the process.

Despite this, poverty and a natural emphasis on the less personal processes of development create national priorities in which youth maturity may take a back seat. Thus the capability to establish functioning Youth Maturity Institutes will depend on the success of developing countries to gain reasonable levels of living—and hence upon other aspects of the Utopian globe which I approach in later Chapters.

Much the same concerns relate to possible resistances from conservative religions, such as, perhaps, forms of Islam. It is *not* the intention of my discussion to advocate the forcible imposition of a particular form of Youth Maturity Institutes on specific cultures, where a Western model may not be appropriate. It would however be demeaning to assume the contrary, that modern Islam is somehow contrary to the principles of such Institutes. There are many educational practices in some parts of Islam which are contrary to the precepts of the Institutes—in some instances, for political reasons, violence is advocated; in others learning is by submission and rote. But no one can accuse reformist Turkey, pre-Saddam Iraq, or Iran, at least in the cities, of not having educational values and achievements which would be entirely compatible with their own variants on Youth Maturity Institutes.

There is no time to lose. We need the generations which Youth Maturity Institutes will create. Without those generations, the rest of the task of creating Utopia by 2100 will be a rough ride. For we expect the Institutes will minimize human tendencies to violence against and disrespect for others. This is needed to give us the risk taking courage to reform the totality of society. Fortunately, if we have the will, the replacement of schools with Youth Maturity Institutes need not be a long drawn out affair. It could be accomplished in many parts of the world by 2050. Globally, UNESCO (pending the United Nations changes I recommend later in this book) could take a lead role in nudging States to take action, and spreading the word and the message.

That having been said, there are no quick automatic results. There will be trial, error, mistakes. After the introduction of Youth Maturity Institutes, critics and opponents will point out "But there has been no reduction in violence". Of course not, in the short term. It will take a minimum of twelve years for those entering the new system to mature out of it. It will take longer for them to parent new intakes and to find their roles in society. We must learn to be patient and not give in to short term desperation.

V

The Family and the Generations

A problem with schools is often that they exhibit boundaries, with teachers on one side and parents on the other. Children cross the boundaries daily, each time experiencing a little bit of a culture shock. Youth Maturity Institutes will not succeed if the world were to be made up of dysfunctional families. Does Utopia have anything to say about achieving good family functioning?

Today there is a strong tendency in some parts of the West to bemoan the passing of the nuclear family, that relatively unusual residential group of mother, father and children who live together until the children become independent adults; and then consists just of mother and father until one of them dies; and then the survivor until he or she dies or has to be placed in a home. By contrast, Carol James, the Native Indian leader of a political party in British Columbia, openly celebrates her childhood life, during which, because of extended family connections both maternal and paternal, she could never quite predict who was going to be in the house at any one time, a situation which established mobility and flexibility in family relationships, with elders always respected, which gave children a sense of well-being, comfort when needed, and security. "Family was never just immediate family, it was whoever was in the house at the time". By comparison with other types of family around the world, there is something rather bleak, arid, and sterile about the much vaunted nuclear family.

Those who remark on its break up do so thinking of such matters as divorce and what anthropologists now call serial monogamy.

A few years ago there was exactly the same bemoaning of the passing of various forms of extended family, in particular the one most common in the west in which grandparents lived in a three-generational house.

We often also regret the passing of wider extended families—largely under the influence of migration, the example of industrialised societies, and the urbanisation and commercialisation of the Third World. The variety of family structures is still enormous, and the bonds sometimes continue and have utility across oceans, and between town and countryside. To simplify grossly, links in such families frequently involve the common or nearby residence of siblings with their children. Because of rules of exogamy and property, the siblings may be sisters, or they may be brothers, less commonly both. For years analysts linked industrialisation, modernisation, and secularisation with the conversion of extended into nuclear families. Quite often, as in working class East London or the Caribbean, such trends did NOT create nuclear families, but matrilocal and matriarchal families, in which mothers lived in proximity to *their* mothers, gaining support thereby, with perhaps a succession of males producing a family of children with different fathers. Anathema to social workers dedicated to the ideology of the nuclear family, yet under the circumstances highly functional. In technical terms, such structures resemble polyandry, except that the males are serial. Just as we have serial monogamy, here we have serial polyandry.

The nuclear family, with which many right wing politicians so fervently identify, is almost entirely the invention of urban commercial middle classes, with significant differences in aristocracies and both urban and rural working poor. Those social workers who use the nuclear family as the operating model—indeed those therapists who do so—miss significant realities.

Idealised family structures, whatever they may be, are supported by elaborate cultural statements, from myth and religion to rational ideology. Anthropologists are usually trained to look behind such statements to what might be described as the empirical or statistical reality—what actually goes on in life. The myths have a jural, normative, moral function designed to regulate interactions between the partners, and for the socialisation of children and the continuity of culture, and for pressure when aberrations become too obvious and out-of-hand for the rest of society to handle. The myths, the stated norms, constitute texts around which arguments about proper behaviour, and indeed about property, are built. Just as proper church-goers abjure extra-marital sex, but do it, it is quite common for the behavioural reality to be substantially different from the verbal norms, which often become operative only when crisis looms.

One example from my own fieldwork will illustrate. The Fijian societies I worked among (there are many differences between them) presented to the world a strong ideology of a patrilineage, in which men were representative of their lineages and seemed to perform all the primary ceremonial and political functions in the name of their lineages. Ownership of land was invested in such male-dominated lineages. With the coming of formal administration, the system was incorporated into colonial law.

Over time, lineages segmented as there was schism or they grew too large. Or they formed political and military alliances, which sometimes resulted in a form of merger. By contrast to such dynamism, the formal law was static.

Behind the law was a reality, which played havoc, for example, with the system of land registration. The realities were of self-interest and above all the power of women. Whatever the appearance of male domination—and sometimes its stark truth—there is always the possibility of women's power.

Because of the rules of exogamy in Fiji, married women came from different lineages and usually different villages than did their husbands. Frequently lineages grouped together with significant differences from others in their languages, tabooed behaviour, manner of living, rules of courtesy—all those things that are significant in the rearing of children. While men were close to their children, it was the women who bore most of the responsibility of early rearing, and thus of ensuring cultural continuity by teaching children how they should behave.

But most of the women were foreigners to the culture they had married into. Hence at the time of marriage, elaborate women's ceremonies took place, in which the new bride was inducted into the sisterhood, as it were, of foreign wives. Here she found a vigorous and proud support group.

In any society, whatever the norms may appear to be, it is essential to look, as it were, for the opposites and for significantly different parallels. Hence, in Fiji, it became apparent that, despite the patrilinearity, matrilineal and affinal linkages played fundamental roles. The mother's brother played a real part in the upbringing of teen-age male children, complementing the father; and was in a situation in which a young man could demand from him whatever he needed to support his enterprises. Throughout the life cycle there were numerous occasions in which the wife's kindred would support her emotionally, materially and ceremonially, and massively complex and reinforcing exchanges took place between her kin and those of her husband.

There is no doubt that, right up to the most high levels of Fijian chieftainship, women exercised, through such linkages, major powers of influence, often becoming overt in the woman's right. And if this was so, how much more it was in more mundane matters. I traced scores of instances in which a wife, for agricultural, commercial or emotional reasons, decided to move husband and children back to *her* family location. By agreement with her lineage, land would be made available. Over time, the pair's descendants would constitute a new, allied lineage.

Such moves were not formally registered with the government as a change in family land title, so that the official Fijian land registry has little bearing, even today with modifications, on the facts of land use.

Without such modifications to the strict rules, the system would find it difficult to function. At least, it would have much less flexibility. I have grave suspicion of those descriptions of culture and society which are presented as rigid, on the basis of enunciated rules. And what is unorthodox at one time becomes orthodox at another.

Family structures are subject to considerable reality change. Policies which seek to enforce "stability" are doomed and have no place in Utopia, which requires dynamism and flexibility.

Similar considerations suggest that the very definition of what is a marriage is fraught, and, being so, complicates and confuses jural policies based on some definition of "marriage". Is it a union, whatever that is, between and man and a woman? Does "union" imply a common household and/or the procreation of children? Does the "union" imply that only within it is there sexual congress? Is there a necessity for cohabitation, and does that have t to be between a man and a woman? If we look at the world comparatively, searching for *functioning* forms of union, the answer to each of these questions is "No".[27]

A few examples. The Cathars until suppressed by a vicious French crusade, believed that sex was a sin. Ipso facto a union between a man and a woman, a marriage, was sinful. But sinning is human. Only church elders had the strength to be without sexual sin. Other people's sexual activity within AND WITHOUT marriage was indulged as a natural weakness. It was open to women as well as to men, to husbands as well as to wives. But not to the holy

In mediaeval times there was an another institution identified as *celibate* marriage, in which sex and procreation were not to take place.

Numerous societies such as the Ndumba and Sambia in Papua New Guinea, the Mundurucu of the Amazon, and the Hopi in their winter *kiva*, men and women lived apart, the women in individual houses, the men in what some have called club houses.

Islamic societies permit men to take a limited number of wives who cohabit. Polygynous societies[28] abound, in some of which wives live in individual houses, in others cohabiting. The IIRC Human Relations Ethnographic Survey estimates that 75% of human societies practise or tolerate polygyny.[29] Chinese concubinage approximated polygyny.

In several societies it was/is incumbent on the husband's brother to marry and care for the husband's widow.

In aristocratic circles as far apart as Hawai'i and Pharaonic Egypt there was brother-sister union and the marriage of a husband to his wife's sister.

There is some thought that the in-breeding of the royal houses of Europe had detrimental generational effects. Apart from that, all the above instances relate to socially healthy, stable, and well functioning societies. The nuclear family is not necessary for such conditions to apply, and indeed may well be less socially healthy than many of them.

As I write, a journalist in Vancouver, British Columbia has been waging a print attack on the members of a polygynous break-away Mormon community called Bountiful, which she calls polygamous.[30] In this community the people assert a religious duty for men to have multiple wives, with Biblical justification. The journalist points to "the plight" of young men who leave the community, although there is no proscription against them remaining there and seeking to establish extended families. She believes she has uncovered instances of child and female abuse, gathered from women who have quarrelled with the community and moved out. The government has not found cases to prosecute. It continues to recognize the community school. And it does not prosecute on grounds of "polygamous marriage" or bigamy, which is statutorily illegal, apparently since this is likely to run aground against arguments of religious and constitutional freedom.

There is no doubt in my mind that should there be provable cases of abuse they should be handled in terms of the law, according to the Utopian principles I shall describe in the next chapter. However the journalist asserts the equation "Polygamy (a.k.a. polygyny) equals the suppression and exploitation of women and the abuse of the young". As a proposition this is nonsense, both empirically and theoretically. There are no comparative data whatsoever that show abuse to be more prevalent in polygynous communities and families than in monogamous ones. Indeed, there are a priori reasons to believe that children in such families have more protection and flexibility.

There is a major break on the expansion of polygyny in a community. Only "strong" men, as the community identifies them, can maintain multiple wives, many of whom are comparatively young, since it requires a modicum of wealth and senior's ability to handle interpersonal relations. Evolutionary principles have been adduced to suggest the attraction of a polygynous male lies in his success, and that this tendency to success will be genetically and/or socially transmitted. (At a time when it seems that the necessity to have male partners is, for women, slowly eroding, this argument may be due for a revival.)

From a normal woman's point of view, polygyny has some clear advantages. The marital "duty" of being in the husband's bed is no longer a monogamous routine, but shared out. The same remark holds for the tasks of the household, which may in fact become something like a small enterprise with division of labour. There are of course instances of jealousies, rivalries and angers (which could be controlled somewhat by Utopian values) just as there are in monogamous households. As far as children are concerned, as I have already observed in connection with the place of children in a variety of extended families, there are many psychological and supportive advantages in having a bevy of aunts and their progeny toward whom to turn.

Part of the idealisation of the nuclear family is a reaction to the apparent growth of single-parent families since the 'sixties. In some parts of the world, the phenomenon is borne out by statistics, which identify mothers who are single by choice, and young people living alone or with non-familial friends. In my city, Vancouver, there are major sections in which the housing is constructed with residential units for such situations, and those in which two single persons live together with separate bathrooms and bedrooms, sharing expenses. Alarmists raise serious questions, thinking of such a trend as an anomaly, and harmful to children.

On these and similar questions, more perspective is useful. There are in social history many instances in which families have been disrupted by the forced departure of the husband, or of the young, mostly males. One may think of the mines of South Africa, slavery, the indentured labour systems of the South Pacific and elsewhere. Effects on children there must have been, though the existence of wider kinsfolk would mitigate them, unless the adult male population was almost totally absent, as it often was. Extended families however take care. And the role of the mothers is increasingly important

I am reminded of my family arriving at a tiny island off the coast of Papua to camp with the people for a few weeks. The thatch houses were on stilts, next to a very deep channel which separated the house and beach from a reef. My daughter was in her crawling stage. We quickly learned to have no fear. The moment she, or any other, child, wormed her way in the direction of the danger, loving brown arms from some hitherto unseen person swept her up.

In the same community I carried out two household censuses, a few weeks apart. *Almost none of the children*, toddlers or not, were sheltering in the same house in each period. They were cross with their parents, liked the food at the other place, wanted to spend time with someone there, wanted to hear stories—whatever it was, if they felt like it, they upped and moved.

If that happened in a large industrialised city, I can hear the tut-tuts. No discipline. Irresponsible parenting. Certainly no stability. What risks they run. Call in social services quickly.

Yet under certain circumstances this may be precisely the sort of flexibility and experience that both parents and children need and are denied. Though nannies and kindergartens do something institutionally, it is not at all the same. And I have seen instances in which a child of separated parents gained both power and an enlarged horizon by interacting with both households.

Let us return to the structure of the family itself. I have called in question the statistical norms of the nuclear family structure and residence. What about its monogamous base?[31]

There seem to have been two contradictory evolutionary paths at work.

The first probably grew with early hominid division of labour as humans with upright posture were still hunters and gatherers. The human child has a long drawn out non-ambient helplessness, during which time it has to be carried and nurtured by a mother who has herself gone through a restricting pregnancy. The male provided nurture through his freedom of action, his strength, and his continued hunting ability. There was no capital accumulation to give advantage to the amassing of wives. Thus there is a strong emphasis in our bio-cultural heritage towards monogamy as a partnership.

On the other hand, the accumulation of capital, on however modest a scale, made it advantageous to use marriage as part of the creation and maintenance of riches. Settlement, land, agriculture, pastoral herds, trade and the growth of concomitant political powers and structures, all contributed. Marriage created political and commercial alliances. The woman, while maintaining the family and administering the hearth, opened networks of co-dependency with her relatives. Men went about their business earning and increasing wealth.

Under these circumstances it became possible and advantageous to engage in plural marriage. Men could start to afford more wives, and the more they did, on the whole, the more they had, of both women and riches. Furthermore, plural marriage epitomised social status and power.

The phenomenon was mostly in the cultural, rather than the biological domain. Other circumstances arose in which the consolidation of capital was as important as its growth. Here the advantages of polygyny and the choice of brides from "outside" could be cancelled by dangers to the passing on of the estate at inheritance. It became advantageous to seek brides closer to home, and one at a time—even in some ranks of some societies to marry a sister or a brother's widow.

Being cultural, the tendency toward polygyny was affected by ideology and religion. After all, if widespread, it could leave young men unmarried, with disruptive consequences.

The tendency, though, was not simply cultural; it had bio-evolutionary support. Men have a need to make use of their sperm and could not always do so with a single wife. Contraception was there, but difficult. Abstinence after pregnancy was common. There was and is a drive to seek other sexual partners.

For women, who better to couple with than an older man, proven to be successful? An older man had shown that he had the power to survive, significant until the present century. If he were in a position to marry more than one wife, he had status based on personal action—acumen, physical power—or family inheritance. For the survival of society, the marriage of young women to older men had a distinct advantage. Older men continue to beget, and pass on whatever it is in their genes and their social heritage that helped in their success. There are many continuities in this stream of evolution today, as younger women and older men attract each other, though the specific biological advantages are harder to discern.

The danger, as I mentioned above, was in the sexual tensions of younger men who did not have legal access to wives. Usually the incidence of polygyny was not high enough to threaten the social fabric in such a way. But also in practice there were a variety of mechanisms to release sexual energy—pre-marital intercourse, homosexuality, illicit assignations, prostitution, the induction of young men into active "age regiments" for purposes of warfare and political control. As long as the property aspect of marriage was not threatened, the world went on its sex-driven way.

In present-day industrialised society monogamy is the ideological norm which masks the verities. In the 'fifties, men were said to have a forty year itch, and for both women and men "life began at forty". The 'sixties broke open many of the taboos among the young, although most returned to monogamous ideals as they reached adulthood, in or out of formal marriage. Formal marriage became a matter of sacrament or of regulating a property contract, or indeed a ceremony of fun and self-directed thought that publicised a relationship. Maurice Godelier, in his Chapter "What future for what relationships" (my translation) sums up the situation in Western society pithily and accurately—"*Le marriage n'est plus l'acte fondateur du couple*" (Marriage is no longer the founding act of couples—again, my translation) . . . [32].

It has never been a secret that general extra-marital sex has been common over the centuries. Because it breaks the formal rules and involves sex, always a topic of delighted gossip and titillation, it has always been a subject for publicity when public figures are involved, exacerbated nowadays by intense media coverage. Biographies almost always examine sexual behaviour, and usually find something to write about. A novel without some such theme is hardly a novel. We often know what is going on amongst our colleagues, but seldom in our own marriage.

We sneer at the hypocrisy of the Victorians, but even today the phenomenon continues to be surrounded by an inadequate and censorious vocabulary. "Extramarital sex" is so clinical. "Affair" (sometimes with an "e" to make it oh so French, not English at all, you know); "infidelity", "unfaithful", "disloyal", are terms that get thrown about. All, including "affair", which carries the implication that it might be a tough business proposition, carry with them the suggestion of a property right *in one's partner*.

When the terms do arise in a marriage, when emotions get charged by the breach of rights, the consequences are painful, angry and hurtful. Children are caught up in the atmosphere. There may be divorce. Joint property has to be disentangled, a wonderful focus for revenge and passion.

Comparative empirical studies reveal that we are not talking really about a "forty year itch". The behaviour is much more deeply embedded. Helen Fisher has gone so far as to claim that there is a natural cycle from infatuation to seeking another sexual partner in as little as four years. For every man who enjoys sexual revival there is a woman whose own sexual freedom is discovered.[33]

Is it not possible to release ourselves and our spouses from the hypocritical angry passion that is too often the result of a multiple sexual partnership? Can we not admit that at the root is a misplaced and intolerable property right? Can we not see with our own generosity that multiple intimacy can be enriching for all concerned? Can we not recognise that our passionate reactions are the result of insecurity and the need we have for a lie to cover up the truth?

If, as I believe they are, multiple intimacies are the empirical norm, why add to that the sin of lies? If the original intimacy is worth its salt, honesty and the sharing of experience is part of it. *Why should sexual intimacy be the **only** domain of **normal** conduct that has to be lied about?* Why?[34]

It is not necessary and it is uncivilised. It poisons the most precious element in the lives of men and women. It puts the right to one's partner as property, as something owned above the strength of love or even lesser intimacies.

A 2006 report by the Federal Justice Department of Canada and the Status of Women Canada recommended to the Canadian government that "Polygamy be decriminalized" together with an improvement in legislation securing the rights of the partners. Given the unrealistic moral mindset of uninformed politicians, such recommendations are unlikely to be accepted by political parties in the near future.

To move on toward our Utopia is certainly not easy. Yet it is not only possible, but, in many individual famous cases, has been lived. It is lived today by many individuals throughout the industrialised world, and elsewhere. But the idealisation and valuation of such generosity toward and respect for one's partner is far from being admitted into the dominant ideologies. Only the recognition that it is possible and rewarding, incorporated into our own personal behaviour, will eventually bring about the appropriate change. Where one partner is generous and open, and the other possessive and closed, there will be either break-up, or the sacrifice of each persona, most likely by the reduction in generosity and openness.

Unfortunately, that is not the end of the story. Part of the drive toward multiple intimacies derives from the fact that individuals who decide to cohabit change into different personae later in life; and also that the stresses of living together turn out to be intrusive to the sense of personal privacy and integrity.

The world we live in cannot be restricted to family walls. During infatuation we cannot know all there is to know about the object of our emotions. The hormones drive us. They do so with good reason, for the characteristics of the time stay in our memories and emotions. As we get to know more about our partner, we are mostly like adapt.

Our outside worlds pull us apart. There is no help for it. Each of us finds workplace colleagues who irritate or inspire us for at least a third of our time, with another third engaged in sleeping . . . Artists, writers, become absorbed in what they are doing, often excluding families from those times. We correct for these influences by sharing experiences, talking about them, complaining, expressing enthusiasm (for everything except sex . . .) Quite often it works, to the enrichment of both.

But sometimes it turns out that the growing experiences of one partner reveal that he or she is a different person from the one initially imagined. Always, when there is growth, there is change. It may not be the kind of change that you want in a partner. You yourself may not be growing comparably, and may feel inadequate. All of a sudden there is the realisation that the partnership is not there any more, or is minimalized.

So either you move away and try again; or you resign yourself to the intolerable loneliness that marriage can drift into, seeking, if not sex, at least those outside marriage to whom you can talk. This is happening more and more. It is partly that we are a little bit more honest about our feelings, partly that we search for something better. So frequent is it nowadays that anthropologists have coined the term "serial monogamy", though usually there has been some multiple intimacy during the stage of growing disillusion.

There is no way that partners can remain the same during the duration of a lifetime. Whether they can, or want to, or should, adjust to those changes is for individuals to work out. If there are children, what is for the best? Tension or honesty?

There is at least one institutionalized example (apart from polygyny and polyandry) of a method of dealing with this. In Italy there was (is?) a fellow called the *cavaliere intime*. He is known to all and recognized as the wife's boon companion. He was not, as some might think, a toy boy—that was a different game altogether, though I imagine the two roles might merge. In any event he looked after the wife and spoiled her while the husband went about his business, including, no doubt, a mistress. He helped her in her bath, ensured that she had flowers and delicacies, took her to the opera and social functions. In this most Catholic country, marriage, in these circumstances, turned out to be for child bearing and property considerations. Other essential functions in a partnership were handled outside.

Much disillusion is exacerbated by living arrangements. We are finding more and more that the intimate sharing of living space is both richly rewarding and damnably difficult. A greater proportion of adults in the industrialised world are making use of their aesthetic and intellectual capabilities in their home lives, a tendency that has to be reinforced if we are to survive the changes of the present technical revolution. With the advent of TV, multimedia and Internet on the one hand, and the reinforcement of recreational pursuits from handicraft to sport on the other, the possibilities of conflict of interests abound. This is not merely that one partner does one thing while the other does another, which has always been the case, but that the interests compete for space, noise, and attention. Technology may soften the competition, but the Sound of Music can stifle the attempt to write a novel. On a more mundane level, one person's tidiness is another's irritating obsessiveness. Should there not be a space where one can be tidy, and another where junk can prevail?

In theory yes. Although when children come on the scene, one set of conventions seems to have to predominate.

There is another way. It is mostly practised by divorced or separated couples who share children, or when the demands of a profession involve separate locations, or in polygynous societies where individual wives have their own homes.

It is to live separately. There is nothing written in stone which says that a man and a woman living in intimacy have to live under the same roof. By living separately each creates his or her own space without interference. Many of the young individuals who enter the statistics as "one person or one parent households" in fact have "significant others" with whom they sleep and share children.

There are marked advantages to this. The excuse for daily disagreement is reduced. Intimacy is renewed as desire, less as habit. My guess is that the relationship, though in an evolving form, is longer lasting on average. If not two residences, at least adjust the residency to provide a modicum of separate space. It is an expression of generosity and respect.

Of course it is not for everyone. But it appears to be a convention that more are thinking about, or adopting without thought, as natural to them.

I have written about residence as something involving men and women. Nowadays the openness of homosexuality permits the residence of same sex couples, for whom the same considerations apply. But are same sex couples married? The concept of same-sex unions is not as unusual in history as attitudes towards the issue nowadays would make out. They have existed, often openly, throughout European history, sometimes requiring their formal sanctioning. The 1990's were by no means the first period in which the question demanded answers.

Such matters are increasingly the subject of legislation and political and ideological policy. They are thoroughly confused by the ambiguity of the word "marriage" itself. We have already shown that it has no agreed cultural meaning whatsoever. And we could add that if individuals do the things that are to be done in whatever relationship they choose, but decide not to assert that it is "marriage", nobody, least of all the State, really cares.[35]

The Judeo-Christian formal concept of marriage requires the ceremonial recognition of the union. Nowadays unions which are not ceremonially celebrated tend to be treated civilly in Western countries in the same manner as marriage. Yet in any jurisdiction there is usually a requirement of recognition and registration in some form, for example that the couple represents themselves as cohabiting over a reasonable period, and that their associates recognise this also. The cohabitation requirement usually implies common residence, whereas a formally married couple do not have to reside together. Such recognition establishes social boundaries against interference, and may result in public entitlements, and in particular access to property law should there be a break-up. So far it seems that there should be no grounds for opposition to single sex unions, since all that is involved is jural recognition of a partnership, and of the fact that property in partnerships gets intermingled.

Why does the State bother about the regulation of marriage at all? Any rules about marriage can be avoided by people just cohabiting or doing what they want without involving the law. The State gets involved because it needs, or thinks it needs, statistics, and also to regulate the wellbeing of children and the issues of property which arise when a relationship breaks up. A major social purpose of marriage, and the recognition of unceremonialized unions, is to legitimise children, allow them to acquire rights in the family, and to allow rules to be applied with respect to the welfare of children within the family. But surely those issues apply to *any* relationship, whether termed marriage or not.

The next step is more tricky. We are led to the question, in the ideal society, should same-sex unions be thought to have the same relationship to child-bearing as bi-sexual unions?

I think not quite. At the very least, the issue should be addressed in terms of the goals of the culture. If the culture does not care about its continuity and the creation of future generations, there will be one answer. If the culture values that continuity, there will be another.

I shall assume that the culture values its continuity: it is not embarked on a path of self-inflicted ethnocide. In that context the care of children by single sex unions is not to be encouraged or supported. Why?

It is one thing to encourage understanding of single sex unions as a matter of personal choice in a humanist environment. It is another to encourage their spread to become a larger proportion of unions, if not the norm. I think the evidence shows that the example of homosexual teachers in schools and the welcome creation of sympathetic discussion in classes, together with the more open environment, has resulted in increased known homosexuality—although much of the increase is undoubtedly a function of more open living and reporting.

The sources of homosexuality are two-fold: a biologically induced disposition, and the control of one's dispositions by thought and emotions that lead toward homosexuality. In other words, there is both nature and nurture. (Some recent biographies have shown that some individuals who embraced homosexuality through the English public school system turned in later life to vigorous heterosexuality—the dynamics can go in both directions.)

It seems unreasonable to expect same-sex unions to be neutral in such matters in the course of bringing up children. However hard the adoptive parents may try, their example must have a major influence—turning some towards and some against homosexuality. And whether children "need" both men *and* women in their intimate lives is still a matter of debate. In any event it seems highly probable that the caretaking of children in same-sex households is likely to increase the incidence of homosexuality. At first, this may be of little consequence. But in the long run it is surely not to be encouraged by a culture interested in continuity, because procreation is a necessity for that.

I do not consider this to be an argument for *forbidding* same sex couples to have adopted children (there will always be some biological children in such unions). But a culture that values its continued existence should be very cautious about formally arranging adoptions to same sex couples in ways that encourage them to do so.

However, when two people of whatever sex intermingle their daily living, this inevitably involves intermingling property. Little problem—until a break-up or re-arrangement occurs. Then the State is called in to regulate the disentanglement and to take care of progeny, *whether or not there is a formal marriage.*

Similarly, the fact that someone is married or not should have little if any impact on social services. It is the human who counts, not the marital status. Such matters are relevant to my discussion of poverty, and of the universal minimum income concept. In Utopia, forget about marriage as a State concept, and let it lie in the realm of religion, personal belief and practice, and maybe ideology. So it follows—let the State be concerned with relationships and their consequences. Forget the secular use of the term marriage. Leave that to the usage of the Churches and individual beliefs.

And it may turn out that in our Utopia it is decided that artificial procreation is a "good thing". There can be no holding back the advance of artificial procreation. It has many strong humanistically supported advantages, allowing, for example, infertile women to have children. And it *may* be a "good thing" to separate sex from procreation. Procreation is not, culturally speaking, the primary objective of sex, although biologically speaking that is where it all began. Humans in most cultures enjoy sex for it's own sake, for the sensations and intimacies it brings, for its ability to create profound communication. In this respect, humans have evolved along a path in which they take measures to *stop* the procreative elements in sex.

Alas, the issue of artificial procreation does not end there. I find myself in the midst of a paradox. I am preaching choice, the deliberate control of our future. Artificial procreation offers the ultimate in choice. Choice of the sex of offspring, choice of their biological characteristics. Because those choices have been exercised in other domains in horrendously inhumane contexts, we are naturally and rightly suspicious of anything that carries the name eugenics. I do not know how to control these forces, which cannot be ignored. Could it be sufficient to rule that the choices be exercised by the individuals involved, and not by the State or any external authority? Could this be part of the global morality that comes with reformed global government (see Chapter **XVII**).

And now we are already in the era of designer babies. Utopia should resist any intervention of the State or of religious ideology in such matters. In the first case it would be a fruitless attempt to put the clock back, or an unwholesome move toward eugenics. In the second, religions are simply not equipped to handle such issues for total populations. Any such regulation contains the inevitability of creating substantially uniform populations destroying the gene pool and crating an almost robotic society.

On the other hand if individuals, not necessarily in marriage, can choose a child, including its sex, filters for handicaps, and the like, we are pretty sure to get, not uniformity, but variety. And there is the assurance than no choices will be perfect in terms of their outcomes and consequences. Humanity can and will still rule.

Although it is a gross error to assume that potential fathers have, or should have, little or less say than potential mothers in the choice to have children, the fact remains that the sudden enormous increase in the choices available to women is revolutionising their lives. At first the dilemma was restricted to the issue, to work or to have a child? All young women in my experience over the past twenty years or more have had to confront that choice, their answers being as varied as the individuals themselves.

But now, and in Utopia, the choice is even wider. It is when, if at all, how, and with whose sperm? It is no longer improbable that women will have children, themselves or through surrogates, at age sixty; they no longer have to be linked permanently or at all with the sperm donor; they may choose a father and choose not to live with him; they may choose, though not with 100% success, the sex of the child; they may of course adopt. These new facts of life, and many more still to come, are causing much controversy, much of it misplaced.

If a significant number of older women join the small numbers of older men who have new children, the concept of parenting will change. I hope the older parents will be wiser. They will need to make clear arrangements for child care should they die. There may be an evolutionary advantage to having a trend towards older parents, since many very young parents, like first lovers, do not know how to do it properly.

As for choosing the sex of a child, much of the opposition has come from the observation that immigrants to the industrialised world where the choice can be afforded come from cultures in which boy children are more valued than girls. This surely is a temporary phenomenon that is bound to change. If it became more general, which is most unlikely, the unfortunate boys would have few girls to play with. Would this lead to more male homosexuality? Probably. But much more likely is a situation in which the majority of parents choose one boy, one girl, and that's it. There may be an effect on the order of birth between boys and girls. I doubt if that would be catastrophic.

I thus opt for individuals to determine the course of evolution. In Utopia they would have freedom to choose. The State, as I shall affirm later time and again, does not have superior powers of prescience. And my choice is reinforced by the fact that each State will order matters differently, so that the wealthy will be able to find loopholes in any event—at least until we reach a world of Global Government.

In some countries, debates are continuing about whether to give social assistance to adoptive same sex parents. Unless the matter gets out of hand—which is a long way off—the criteria should surely be the welfare of the children. If they are within such a family, the needs of that family should be met. The way of countering such adoptions is not by withholding needed support, but through education and discussion in terms of the public interest.

When I was in my teens and an enthusiastic, idealistic Marxist I tried unsuccessfully to organise youth in my city to stand up and be counted and to express views about what they wanted their lives to be. Not only did I promote the dissolution of marriage, but also advocated its concomitant, the State care of children.

I shudder to think of that now, in the sense that I cannot imagine a worse fate for children. Later experience of the inanities of governments, horrendous bureaucratic chaos in social welfare agencies despite individual officials who are purposeful, well-meaning and sensitive, and the knowledge that State policies are unpredictable in their results, pulls me back from that abyss. And how my parents must have taken my arrogance to heart, for they were caring and supportive and my childhood was in no way painful.

And I have to admit that, despite all the studies as to what happens in child rearing, all the more systematic knowledge that exists about child abuse, the field is chaotic and indeterminate, with public awareness based largely on idiosyncratic information. The ability to disentangle complex strands of influence, let alone causality, is minimal. Perhaps that is as it should be. For both parents and children are individuals, among whom the variety is infinite. Children, as were their parents before them, are genetically programmed (itself a hugely complex consideration), affected in the womb and at the breast, and subject not only to family but external influences such as peer pressure, school interactions, and the media. No one line of causality is dominant—which, thank goodness, is probably why children survive as well as they do. Some children succumb within an ideal family, some survive famously and creatively out of disaster.

The family, writ large, has its happy, jolly times. But it is not over-all a happy jolly place. I doubt if it is meant to be. The socialisation of children is into a tough world where there is no easy ride, and never will be, Utopia or not. Parents do not normally become sadists in order to prepare children for future life; far from it. They are rightfully intending to be protective and caring, and in the best examples, which don't create newspaper headlines or TV documentaries, show their love directly. Today there is stress upon the arts of communicating that love. But in the ordinary life of the family, the recurrence of crises and stresses involving the children, directly or through osmosis, is part of positive upbringing. It is also one of the paths toward ultimate separation, the desire to move away from the family.

We tend to stress the difficulties of the modern age, the problems that confront us immediately, and in so doing perhaps idealise the past. Let us be clear about this, since idealisation of the past will reoccur in later pages.

The past was not ideal. At no time and in no place was the family without its stress and suffering. The common people of rural and urban Britain, and rural Switzerland, in the early nineteenth century had levels of material living that were far below those of the South Seas or many parts of Africa and Asia, to say nothing of North American Indians (at least those beyond the full impact of European invasion), at the same period. In such places as what is now called the Third World there was nevertheless the threat of violence, famine, militarism, sorcery. The life of children and the destitution of families in much of Europe would be, to our eyes if we were to visit, as shocking as are the televised scenes of Darfur or the documentaries about inner city ghettos. Such pains and stresses were much more widespread than they are today. Let us not go backwards. Let us recognise that our concerns about the present are in themselves an improvement over the past, and that if we take hold of ourselves we can do more about them.

For example, we now recognise as never before that child abuse and marital violence are not only vicious but are matters for public intervention. Indeed, that awareness has allowed adults to identify to themselves abuse and violence that under other circumstances they might well not admit. Almost paradoxically, the recognition does not always have positive results. Some men and women dealt with it by ignoring or suppressing it and getting on with their lives. Being forced to face up to it can create fierce pain and self-doubt, increasing the ranks of those who need counselling. We have been given the capacity to repress memories for a biological purpose—behavioural management. Like all biological factors there are complicating side effects, so that the resulting management can fall short of the ideal person concept, and since most of us want to approximate the ideal we identify the management as defective, and seek alternatives, probably through therapy.

The openness and recognition, however, allows us to examine the issues more fully and pragmatically, as long as we do not jump into ideological traps. There has been a major value change, not, I agree, accepted by everyone, and far from even beginning in many parts of the world. Abuse of children, of fathers and of mothers, is no longer tolerated, and sexual harassment between adults is moving fast to the same state, the movement supported by legal procedures in many countries.

There can be no dispute where pain, emotional trauma, and in the case of harassment, fear, anxiety and interference with private lives, are concerned. In the case of adults, even cohabiting adults, no has to mean no. But matters of definition, and impact of ideological wars in place of pragmatic enquiry, are troublesome and suggest that we have not yet put matters in appropriate perspective.

We are sexual animals, in the best sense, with cultures to focus, control, and use, our sexuality. At the same time as we are attacking abuse and trying to get rid of it, we are correctly told that the absence of physical love in a home, of touching, holding, hugging, familial kissing, leads to emotional deprivation, confusion and anger toward parents in later life, to something that has to be dealt with as, even, a form of abuse! As a grandparent, I would resent it very much indeed if I and my grand-daughters were not sufficiently well-balanced for us to hug, to put our arms around each other, or I to stroke their hair. There are many families who, I think rightly, believe that over-puritanical hiding of the body is not only uneducative but leads to unnecessary prudishness in later life: to varying degrees members of such families do not unnecessarily hide their bodies one from another. I think that is the families' right, and expresses what I would regard as a healthy lack of inhibition, just as I would support Scandinavian values on nudity in public places. It is true that in inhibited societies the sight of nudity becomes gross stimulation. It is just this kind of inhibitory result that a civilised society would aim at destroying—by openness. It is inhibition that is the problem, not openness.

What I do feel confident about is that our present political correctness on these issues is far from the last word. For Utopia, I am not concerned with the puritanical morality of the family. I am concerned with the healthy functioning of the relationships between men and women and parents and children. By healthy, I mean relationships that operate in the best possible way to reduce neurosis and provide warmth and confidence in the person.

Children are born, to varying degrees, with marked tactile and sexual drives. When they are infants, we tend to allow these, though we may, wrongly, try to inhibit the self-touching of genitalia. As they get older we introduce the notion of guilt. That varies considerably from culture to culture, and period to period. The very definitions of what is abuse, incest, parental love, individual responsibility for actions, are often indeterminate. Examples.

I should not have been surprised at a documentary aired by ABC television in the United States (on 10th May, 1995). A producer discovered that a certain amount of aggressive sexual activity was going on in grade (primary and kindergarten) school, the clearest example being that of a young boy who made a habit of pinning little girls to the floor under his desk and attempting intercourse. The producer worked with colleagues to test the sexual knowledge and attitudes of young children, from, if my memory serves me correctly, age five to ten or so. They set up a room with television and one way mirrors, and onlookers who consisted, separately, of parents and therapy professionals.

The children were shown raunchy advertisements using supermodels, and parts of progammes that had torrid love scenes.

Parents and professionals were totally shocked at the childrens' attitudes and conversations. *Both* boys and girls enjoyed the shows, laughed in titillated excitement, described clothing or the lack of it as "sexy", used phrases such as "they're having sex", (boys) "I'd like to have sex with her". Some boys were stimulated to touch their genitalia. Girls said they wanted to dress "sexy".

The observers took the word "sex" as having literal meaning, but that was not always true. Sometimes it was little more than repeating what the advertisement said, without further knowledge. However, at the end of the experiment the children were questioned about what the concept meant. Some did indeed have ideas: "When they're naked", "When they're in bed they do things", "When he gets on top of her".

That was what shocked the observers, even the so-called therapists. (I don't know how the latter were chosen . . .)

As far as I could see, the children were totally "normal" happy youngsters. True, the programme was stimulated by the grossly aberrant and aggressive behaviour of a young boy who was not being controlled by his teacher, and by unsubstantiated idiosyncratic reports of an increase in unacceptable sexual behaviour in grade schools.

What was shocking was that the children had "a little knowledge", were interested in matters that adults were interested in, and felt free to express themselves amongst each other, but not to their parents. The show told me more about parental attitudes than about troubled children.

In a previous chapter I mentioned the way young girls danced in a Solomon Islands community, masturbating their genitalia. And note the following from an anthropological discussion group:

Sexual activity directed towards and carried out among prepubescent children is tolerated and even encouraged in some societies. The Sambia, with their male initiation rituals, come immediately to mind, as does the practice of masturbating infants to calm them in some societies. This does raise the issue—which is tangential to my main concern here, but what the heck?—of how widely to define "sexual relations". I doubt we'd describe a Hopi mother quieting a fussing child as having sexual relations with him; likewise, the Sambia ritual[36]

Many of these things go on privately in Western societies, let alone others throughout the world. I know of no studies whatsoever which even hint that such practices create sexually disturbed adults. There is indeed much thought along the lines that minor sexual contact enhances the bonds between parents and children in wholesome ways.

Problems occur, but should not, when such behaviour becomes overt or is discovered in societies embracing Judeo-Christian-Islamic values and is then politically correctly defined as abuse, with surrounding guilt trips, not so much on the adults, as on the children themselves. Then indeed serious disturbances and breakdowns occur. If churches, synagogues and mosques have the health and well being of humanity at heart, it is time they reconsidered their theological, ritualistic, and ethical positions on these matters. Utopia will not be built upon the adages of texts written in the millennial past.

None of this is to excuse in the least the sexual exploitation of minors—or anyone else for that matter—submitted to aggressive sexual practices, often painful and against their will, often by figures who use authority to demand sexual services, and sometimes through the literal enslavement of victims. This Utopian society will not tolerate for one second, and will be dealt with in accord with the juridical precepts outlined in the next chapter.

There is simply no way of escaping the communication of sexual knowledge. The more it is hidden, the more it creates damaging inhibitions, neurosis and crime. It becomes an object of obsessive search instead of a description of a natural world. The problem was with parents trying to hide was real, leaving children with half-baked distorted ideas.

The swings of culture on such matters are the stuff of legends. Remember Michel Angelo's David? A great celebration of the nude body, complete with substantial penis, it was also a metaphor for Florence's then need to stand up to and defeat the larger tyrants which threatened it with death. The followers of Savanorola desecrated a copy of the statue, it was then hidden away, then re-emerged with a fig leaf, and is only now on show in its original form. What, we may ask, is wrong with admitting that the male form has a penis??????????????????????

Utopian culture will not do so, and it will revere the aesthetics and truth in the female form, both in art and alive. That is done as a matter of course in parts of Scandinavia, and was and is done in many parts of Oceania and Africa, save when "Western" culture in its puritan form intervenes. As I asserted in Chapter IV, children in Youth Maturity Institutes—and therefore even doubly more in families—will learn to celebrate sex, and therefore the body

In Utopia, sex will not be a taboo'd subject, but a matter of creative, wholesome, joy.

Next example.

More and more we are discovering the widespread existence of sexual abuse. The phenomenon was improperly hidden until it started coming out of the closet two or three decades ago. Now it is so fashionable a matter for discussion that almost every aberration of the human psyche is being traced to it; the moment a human problem emerges, analysts start looking for abuse. And low and behold they find it. When they find it they stipulate that it was causative.

Of course in a tremendous number of cases they are likely to be right. Yet wait a moment, be cautious.

What happened before abuse became an issue? Many men and women had their lives distorted. They decided they were somehow to blame, and lived with severe guilt and sexual problems of their own. It was a secret. Others lived happy normal lives.

Now the tables have turned. One of the cruellest consequences of the extreme pursuit of cases of abuse is that those who are now made to remember it, to find it in their past, do not in fact escape the anger and guilt. Men and women who did not bother about it suddenly find they must do so, they are expected to do so. Many in fact learn, by public pronouncements amounting almost to propaganda, that if the troubles in their personae cannot be traced to abuse there must be something *really* wrong with them. I need not enter the debates about false memory syndrome. The pressures are real.

The fact of the matter is that some of what may now be called sexual abuse is not necessarily harmful in itself. Some of it is harmful *only* because of the attitudes that surround it in the culture. There is no doubt that sexual abuse is *always* harmful when it is accompanied by pain, exploitation, the use of the child as object, and above all guilt, the knowledge that something was not right.

But some behaviour that now goes by the name of sexual abuse does not have the same characteristics. Consider a child who *enjoys* a light caressing form of sexual contact, even if it involves genitalia, who does not even have guilt until later in life religious or social communication suggests that guilt is appropriate. It is not the caresses that cause the abuse, it is transmitted guilt. When such a child, now an adult, accepts that he or she engaged in guilty behaviour, he or she seeks to identify other aspects of later adult behaviour as also wrong. The two have to be linked. This has the effect of (1) identifying other behaviour (perhaps attitudes toward the other sex) as aberrant when it is perfectly natural, (2) identifying a causative explanation which is quite possibly false and misleading.

The reason child-hood abuse is so significant is clearly that the results can be unknown at the time and nasty in the future. We have made a major advance toward a civilised society in the public recognition of just that. The other reason is that children are defenceless, often not yet aware of judgements about incest and sexual taboo, and are in no position to judge what the experience will mean to them in later life. Some children, enjoying and seeking, needing, the emotional results of physical warmth, often not getting it from parents, may see nothing wrong in the milder forms of sexual contact with non-relatives, may enjoy it and even seek it. Indeed, at a minimal level there may indeed be nothing wrong. The point is the child is not in a position either to know or to control. The child needs protection from the excesses and the disturbances which may result in later life. Yet those problems often arise less from sexual contact than from the culturally imposed guilts that surround it.

In Utopia, guilt about sexual expression in families or between young people would be removed, and the concept of "abuse" limited to those instances where aggression, pain exploitation and/or suffering resulted. But until Utopia is around the corner, it is necessary to protect children from the damaging consequences of guilt and censure and the road of therapy down the line. We are caught between the rock of withdrawing manifestations of natural love and the hard place of implacable social interference.

It is also a paradox that while we seek an end to abuse, at the same time there is a strong school of thought that intimates should not merely say what they think openly, but should let their angers out, shouting the verbal abuse, and hitting, punching and breaking *things* which are sometimes not easily differentiated from the partner! I happen not to believe in this, except as a last resort. It leaves an inevitable bitter taste, can socialise children toward violence or make them cynical about adults just as does viewing violence on TV. Counselling should aim at handling our angers better, not concealing them, but as a reinforcement of self-control.

Just the same, it is inevitable that humans are at times angered or irritated to the point of slapping. Unless it becomes habitual or is used with damaging strength or is a tool of deliberate humiliation, to legislate it out of existence is phoney. We must be self-controlled, but a person who does not lose his or her cool from time to time is hardly human. Furthermore it serves a most significant social purpose. It indicates as in almost no other way that a breaking point has arrived, so severe that it cannot for the moment be put into words. Gesture is communication, and a slap tells an immediate story. In families where that sort of action is almost unknown, it becomes the statement of a boundary, a wake-up call to all parties. It teaches children that other people have breaking points.

We are walking a fine line between love and abuse, between discipline and abuse, and, while we are on the subject, between verbal criticism and verbal abuse. This is not black and white, and wherever an abuse charge is laid, not only must the evidence be squeaky clean, but the general context of family life must be understood.

The case against violence in the family is a nasty part of violence in general since it may be one of the psychological foundations for other violent contexts which constitute perhaps the major manageable challenge for the removal of fear and the acquisition of peace. We must find ways of pursuing peace (NOT the absence of tension) in the family relentlessly until it is totally removed from conduct.

The family is no longer the sole agency devoted to the socialisation of children, and is possibly not even the predominant one. In the long run, that may be useful; it is inevitable as society becomes more and more complex. Families themselves are under scrutiny, from social work agencies, from teachers, from public policy makers. Parents often feel threatened and inhibited by the possible limelight into which an act, justified to them—such as a well placed slap on the buttocks, or a desire to control medical therapy—can reveal and cast shadows upon their behaviour and their "rights". Parents should indeed be put on the defensive against abuses; far too many still regard abuse as normal. But too much reaction to outside norms can relieve parents of their own thinking, their own judgements, their own ideals.

Should it be well intentioned bureaucracies and professionals who create the norms, or parents? Who should be the primary guardians of the continuity of culture, and of democratically, responsibly oriented citizens? At the moment, influenced by many accounts of bureaucratic interventions which have resulted in disaster, I believe that the balance nowadays is tipped in favour of statism and the cop-out of rules and regulations. There are signs of parental revolt, more especially with regard to the educational system, but also in a determination that it is they who are ultimately responsible. Too often professionals move beyond their role as helpers and advisers, as conveyors of knowledge, to become rulers of lives.

Authorities do not "know" perfectly. Those which pretend to do so, whether official, professional, or voluntary, and which translate their knowledge into rules, prescriptions and proscriptions, need to be treated with the utmost caution. Individuals must never be placed in a position in which they cannot say "no" to what is being counselled.

While governments can sometimes legislate effectively, the effectiveness depends on the correspondence between the legislation and individual beliefs and behaviour. Legislation in advance of its time may have an educative role: it may set a standard toward which individuals may decide to aspire. Other organisations are most effective (though not necessarily within their own stated goals) when they indicate options from amongst which individuals may choose in an educated manner. Education, example, discussion, yes. Ready ears in times of crises. Conversations between friends uninhibited by "what others may think". The sum total of individual choices, rather than legislation, will eventually make the difference.

It is a truism that is not necessarily true, in all parts of the world, that "children are not what they were". Of course children are imperfect. They are growing up, seeking their way in a world in which their parents' anxieties are only too readily communicated to them. They can be rude, aggressive especially amongst themselves, lacking in politeness toward their elders, provocative. Adults in contact with children moving around town see much of this frequently. They are pushed aside as children jostle with sharp elbows in stores, on buses. They do not give up their seats to the elderly on public transport. They shout invective and wrestle in your way. They don't seem to know anything. You see bullying, trampling on gardens, and when you tell them off, and perhaps grab one by the sleeve, your are told that their father will get you. A neighbour's seven year old girl, prompted by an eleven year old in the background, came up to me in the courtyard and oh so innocently said "Would you like to stroke my pussy; we'll let you if you give us your balls to play with . . ." Ten year olds (and younger), walking home from school, chaperoned by adults, shout to each other "Fuck off", "You dirty mother fucker", "Shithead", "Arsehole". This in a well-off, bourgeois, genteel, yuppy, area of cultivated adults . . .

Once again, a corrective. Most of the time, and for most children, this does not happen. It strikes the observer because it is more noticeable than well behaviour, which is predominant. And rowdyism has always been there. As children grow older, most of them become aware, and conduct themselves accordingly. Especially with younger children and teen males, the children's sense of space does not forbid body contact, and still needs considerable adjustment. What is different is not its occurrence, but its tolerance. As a boy in short pants I presume I was as rowdy as anybody else, especially in a group on trams. But adults would have no hesitation about intervening if things got a bit too much. Later as a school prefect (in a state school) I was charged, with others, in maintaining courtesy and discipline, outside school (uniforms helped with that) as well as in, handing out detentions right and left.

And parents have never been perfect. There were several sadistic delinquents in my school, some of whom came from families who didn't care. Parents who do care are full of anxieties and frequently feel they cannot cope.

On balance, many of the anxieties are probably with little foundation. There is no one to one relation between childhood experience and the future adult. Even abused children can end up well balanced and caring. Children go through many "stages" in which difficult behaviour is part of growing up. Parents who feel an interior despair but who can maintain a difficult even keel, are justifiably proud of the characters who emerge, their sudden maturity and balance, even when the paths chosen may be alien to an older generation. Children are transformed into what I call "friendren", for they are friends within the family, cannot be called children any longer.

Yet, yet, yet. It is becoming a commonplace that there are more young people, or probably more *visible* young people, engaged in crime and gang-related aggressive behaviour, than we have been accustomed to. This may be true in pockets here and there. As communities change, so do such manifestations. We cannot expect young people in harsh ghettos, in depressed refugee camps, as members of a large unemployed force, to be passive. They will strike out, against their conditions, against themselves, against authority, against the haves. Like the very young Palestinian children who threw stones when I was walking on the hills outside Jerusalem. None of this is new. Gangs of youths roamed European cities in the Middle Ages. Gangs, aggressive or not, and groups are a natural outcome of the search for identity, especially strong amongst youth. Sports teams and initiation rites are part of the same phenomenon.

More than that, young people, boys especially, have an enormous appetite for danger and excitement. I said "boys especially", although there have been many examples of young women with similar urges in the past, and it may well be now that they are discovering similar urges with the same sorts of frequencies, and have greater opportunities to follow them up with physical challenges.

The culturally approved outlets for such urges change with the times. Where wars and dangerous political action are absent, travel, the more adventuresome the better, is filling the role, to the despair of parents who cannot let go. Wisely, it often happens as a break during the endless educational process, an almost indispensable part of self-searching, a rite of initiation into adulthood. After such travelling, it is common for young people who felt lost as to their future, to then more confidently determine their paths with greater confidence.

The need for adventure, for self-assertion, for the active discovery of self has to be tested against the positive results or the dysfunctional anti-social ones. Involvement in discourtesy, and its ultimate form, violence, simply cannot be tolerated in a civilised society. Without courtesy, such a society is a nothing, and is likely to be a threat to neighbours. So that whether current discourtesy and violence amongst youth is greater or less than it was previously; whether it is sufficiently great to cause fear objectively or paranoically, is irrelevant. It must not exist.

Zero tolerance of discourtesy.

I do not want to prejudge that parents, and teachers, can create zero tolerance. I doubt it. In any event they need the support and help of those of us who are not parents and teachers. This does not have to be organised, though I shall turn to that question in the next Chapter. It needs to be part of our cultural response as individuals. It means not turning a blind eye. It means that if I see churlish behaviour I must say so, make my opinion clear. Yes, it can be or can get out of hand. In which case authority has to be called upon.

Adults have considerable difficulty at times in being both responsibly caring and non-patronising. They might start by avoiding the word "kids". The connotations of the word—little goats—have largely disappeared, as have the affectionately patronising overtones. When I was in my childhood it was associated with the wonderful children's matinee programmes, short films that have disappeared as a genre from our screens and cultures, for along with Laurel and Hardy and Charlie Chaplin and wild westerns we had the fun politically incorrect Katzenjammer Kids, children who were alive and laughing in semi-ghetto conditions. My mother was horrified. Don't ever use that word to apply to children. She was right.

The other patronisingly false phrase that adults used to use with great frequency, and which can still be heard, is to pontificate to teens: "Stop complaining. You will never have it so good. This is the best time of your life." It isn't. Certainly, there are wonderful features. The glandular emotions of sexual attraction, of falling in love. The wonderfully naive certainties that you know better than your parents and other adults, whom you can criticise for the state of the world. The discovery of demanding physical activity and intellectual discipline. The ability to talk wonderingly for the first time about the nature of the universe, God, love. Under ideal conditions, these result in experiences that can not be repeated. There is only one time for that kind of self-discovery.

But self-discovery continues well into adulthood. In my own life I have had so many good and totally stimulating times I cannot regret the passing of my childhood. Even the times of intense pain cannot erase the resulting growth. Children must know that their positive lives lie ahead of them, not just in the present. They must understand the wondrous mystery of the future, ignoring hints that the best is all over—if it were, why not, then suicide?

Underlying all the positive features of young adulthood are the disturbances and pains. Sexual discovery is accompanied by sexual doubt, fumbling, emotional hurt, which seems to be arriving earlier and earlier, before children seem to be emotionally or physically ready. Formal teaching puts it into a clinical context, and other kinds of teaching are verboten. There are parent and teacher induced anxieties about the state of the world in which simplicities are turned into, in many instances, paranoia. There are conflicts between learned notions of success criteria, and the likelihood of achievement, as places in universities become tighter and rates of unemployment seem here to stay. There is the continual battering of noise and short attention span entertainment creating artificial highs without which life is a bore. There is the threat of drugs and violence, and the force of peer estimation. None of this is new. But the intensity is increased via the media, and the content changes from one decade to another and one country to another.

Present day parents and some teachers have been through much of this themselves during the permissive 'sixties and 'seventies. Many find it hard to cope, for they are feeling responsible and more conservative, and find the content has moved away into dimensions that are more extreme and threatening. They are more aware of the dangers. They must wrestle with their past ideals as problems emerge.

The advent of the nuclear family and its parallels, and the dispersal of siblings throughout the world, where it has occurred, have dealt a serious blow to inter-generational solidarity. (It is useful to note that the continued weight given to extended family, clan, inter-generational and similar ties by globally widespread cultures, such as Cantonese, Punjabi and Ismaili, have given those families and cultures a major advantage in dealing with issues of present and future.)

There are two notable effects. One is that a force for cultural continuity is threatened by the lack of contact between children and grandparents. Parents, even those who had little contact with grandparents themselves, often place weight on this, and try to make up for it in various ways—recording of the past, diaries, visiting when funds and space allow, stressing family history. At present there is also a vogue for the fashions of the past, and in a deeper sense, young people who come from immigrant families seek to visit their ancestral homes and kin, re-learn half-forgotten languages from their past. It is almost inevitable that other sources must at least partially replace grandparents.

This has to be, at least until attitudes and the realities of work change. Only extended families can cope with the elderly in the home. Otherwise the burden of care and occupying one's self with the fact of elderly boredom is far too much for families who must give priority to work and children to survive.[37] It is seldom now that the elderly and the middle-aged can live together in the kind of harmony and joint usefulness that makes a workable arrangement. Add to that the likelihood of large distances being involved, and major financial burdens can arise. The provision of homes, nursing homes, hospices, is now a major industry, with the best giving thoughtful attention to well-being. But I also know of no country that, as of now, totally avoids the financial, material, psychological and sadistic exploitation of the aged in the worst of such homes, a major scandal in which the lonely have little voice.

The issue is associated with the second effect, just plain boredom. During our adult lives, few of us think of being old. At the age of around 70 events took place in my life that gave me an enormous burst of psychological energy, in which I was able to travel and use my experiences for a fantasy of creativity. At the time I was living on top of a twenty-plus story building, occupied by a mix of young people and the retired. When I mentioned my plans to the manager, she said, more or less, "I'm so glad to see it. Do you know that hardly any of the retired people here have any interests at all? They sit around in front of the TV, bored to tears, or take a motor-home to a trailer site and sit around."

I am sure that these people didn't think of retirement like that when they were working adults. They thought of a happy, peaceful life, occasionally linked to grand-children, with minimal financial needs and worries. But at the moment of retirement they were classified. They were dubbed "seniors", and because they did not have thoughts of a future, or of creativity, they were patronised, jollied along. Those who care try to do something, "seniors caring for seniors", *animateurs* getting the more active to play golf, others square-dancing, learning handcrafts, going on bus tours, going in groups to plays which carry sociological themes with which they are unsympathetic—*anything* for goodness' sake, to keep them occupied.

I am not putting down such activities. I am, rather, horrified at the necessity for them on such a scale. Nothing is more indicative of the fact that the aged (in very general terms) are a burden on the world's finances and consciences. Some of this will always be necessary and desirable; it is important for the elderly to be occupied, and, for some, that they socialise.

But it is tinkering with symptoms, not getting at the root problem. The sources go far far back, to childhood and adulthood, to the near disappearance of the extended family, to good health which makes us last longer. We do not want to reinvent the extended family for the sake of relieving our consciences, or to cut off medical services. We have to get on with what we are doing and improve this part of our lives.

At the same time we may look forward to those Utopian times beyond our grasp. For those who do not fit into the category of the elderly as I have both described and resisted it, there are already major advances. For many, old age is a time to explore, and the increase in travel and demanding educational, even university courses, is becoming widespread. Too often the demands on the mind are not enough: a one-week course at a British university on English art is good for a Canadian tourist, but there is little else to follow up with except another dilettante course. I have ideas for hotels that cater to the retired *who want to think and do*. Hotels which have links to libraries, sources of knowledge, reading rooms, combined study-bedrooms, in places where there are major themes to be explored, and not too expensive long-term stays to permit exploration in depth, and occasionally to make original contributions.

For most of the elderly, such solutions are not feasible if they involve expense and costly travel. They must dig into themselves for their resources. They do not know the interior resources they have, those which have not developed. The solution for future phalanxes of the elderly starts in childhood, as it does for us all. It continues and changes through adulthood as they nurture their potentialities. In short, it relates to education. It is also similar to the problems of unemployed youth. Thus Youth Maturity Institutes hold the long term keys.

The use of the term "seniors" which puts us all together for certain purposes, is ghettoising. The aged should live together, is the incipient message, then we can handle them. Speaking for myself, I resist, I won't have it. I demand more than seniors' discounts, and will force the world, I arrogantly imagine, to give it to me. I have been fortunate, in that being in contact with students for so many years made it possible to imagine I was not in an elderly ghetto; it was true that contact with younger people was revivifying. It still is. (The thoughts in this book could not have emerged had it not been for their stimulus.) I like to be with friends of my own age. We have much to discuss and laugh about. But younger people, from their teens to their 'sixties, teach me more. It is still possible to dine and converse with them, one on one, to flirt and spend time, as friend to friend. Not all younger people accept that. The right has to be earned.

The kind of disadvantaged old age that I have mentioned is, for many of us, the signal that life has ended. Looking around us, we see the state, through our children's taxation, paying for our coming decrepitude. We see kindly volunteers being kind. We see harassed nursing home staff expressing their distaste, irritability and patronisation. We feel it is time to go.

And why shouldn't we, if we feel like it? If we feel that our lives have been lived, that we have done what we can the best we can? If we feel at peace with ourselves? Is this not a good time to go? Why on earth hold on until self-contempt occurs, and depression? Is it not better to go when we can look upon ourselves with dignity, if not pride? Don't make of us an instrument that salves your consciences.

Then stop putting the law in our way. Allow elderly assisted life termination.

In Utopia there needs to be a much more open, flexible, and understanding approach to the family and relationships, removing dysfunctional elements such as jealousies and arguments over jural terms which bear little resemblance to realities. The State should get out of the relationship business as far as possible and be open to every kind of permutation and combination of relationships consistent with the relevant culture. And the more that culture can be flexible and open, finding ways to stop hiding behind the hypocracies of terminology and forbidden subjects, the better.

VI

Of Crime, the Law and Ill-Health

Changes in attitudes towards these phenomena have been dramatic over the centuries, even over the recent decades. We regard crime and ill-health as unhappy disturbances to well-being, something to be reduced to the minimum in Utopia. How?

The juxtaposition of the two problems in this Chapter has nothing to do with the growing phenomenon which seeks to find biological and genetic causes for crime. While there may be significant advances in that field it will, I am reasonably sure, continue to encompass explanations.[38] for only a relatively small number of individuals. Even where it contains an explanation, social measures are necessary. It is these I concentrate on.

At the same time as we are looking again at the problems of crime we are being forced to reconsider our perspectives on ill-health. To be ill is becoming anti-social, a drain on society's resources, and a matter of personal responsibility since we are coming to believe that we can avoid many illnesses if we try. Should we be personally responsible for the consequences of our illnesses? We are also re-thinking, or perhaps redesigning with inadequate thought, the institutions which "deal with" the ill.

Shades of Samuel Butler's *Erewhon*.

The analogies must not be overdone. It is evident that what is crime and what is illness is a matter of contemporary cultural definition. Homicide as revenge for rape or an earlier homicide has not always been a crime. In some cultures today the death penalty is considered morally criminal, in others justified. As to sexual harassment . . . ? The discomforts of some women around menstruation or menopause have been classified at different times as involving spiritual danger, normality, and now a treatable form of ill-health. Some forms of depression are now seen as illness. Chronic urges to sexual aggression mix the definition of criminal and medical. Homosexuality is no longer a crime in many countries. In the United States to bear a woman's breast on television is getting close to being criminal.

On the whole we still have separate institutions for dealing with crime and health, though they have many similarities, such as restriction of movement to institutional cells. I will start with the world known as that of crime.

We would prefer to see in our Utopia a world without crime, for crime is an assault on others or on their interests. The institutions we have to deal with crime do so on behalf of the State, which represents the assaulted individual only indirectly. This is an anachronism based on conceptions of Roman centralised power and authority, carried into modernity by first the assertions of feudal power and then that of the centralised State. Police, criminal law, the criminal courts, prisons and rehabilitation agencies are expensive ways of "bringing order" when the State defines that its peace is threatened by behaviour which takes place against itself or its members.

States have a parallel system of civil law which supports lawyers and civil courts without the vast panoply of supporting institutions. The civil law resolves disputes between legal persons according to rules which define equity and acceptable behaviour that does not involve formal criminality which requires State intervention. The expenses of the disputes are borne mostly by the litigants, which rules out access to civil courts by a large number of aggrieved parties.

This Chapter deals with crime, since that is perceived as one of the major threats to Utopian values, but what I say about crime-fighting institutions will have major implications for an extension of civil law.

Sometimes the relevant institutions are lumped together as "the justice system". Sometimes we hear phrases such as, "There is no justice in this world", or "All I want is justice". When I studied the anthropology of law in the 'fifties I found that both anthropologists and jurists were in agreement. Although "natural justice" is a concept that sometimes, if rarely, has legal expression, there is in fact no such thing in the abstract, standing universally for all people at all times. Justice is an abstract idea which is ambiguous and not universal. The idea of justice, where it exists (and in a vast number of cultures it does not), varies with time and place. It cannot reasonably be referred to as a universal principle against which specific law can be evaluated.

When the words are used they mean in fact that the evaluators believe that at that time and in that context the law does not adequately address specific principles that the evaluators believe to be important. As such the criticisms may be telling and significant. But they are cultural, not natural.

In my view, this is a subject in which we have a great deal to learn from cultures whose law has *not* been derived from Roman or Islamic law. Few will disagree with the observation that the system that deals with criminality is crude and ineffective. A few see the system as a whole in the context of the larger society, as a self-perpetuating growing cancer. I have had the dubious privilege of being embraced by the tentacles of the octopus, wrongly accused of a crime, and living in the world of the incarcerated in France and Switzerland. This was not an anthropologist's "participant observation", but in my unsystematic troubled way my insights were sharpened.

Before that I had seen the way in which some British Columbia Indians, under the influence of drink, social abuse, and severe depression, saw incarceration as a way out, a relief from their desperate world. Some would commit a petty crime, such as breaking a storefront window, to get back in. I had visited prisons as an outsider. The metallic noises were different, but I was impressed by the apparent "normality" of the prisoners. In a vaguely academic way I recognised that prisons constituted cultures in themselves.

As I write, the media, both visual and printed, emphasise the tragedies of the victims of crimes. Persons related to victims find it relatively easy to raise funds for reformist crusades. We see as many relatives with tears running down their faces, their world in chaos, their bitter diatribes, as we do starving African babies. We see women and men expressing their anxieties verging on the paranoid or more aggressively "taking back the dark". The statistics count little. These are individuals, individual cases, made significant by repetition and publicity. Fear stalks the streets, even when we know that it is men more than women who are victims of men, and that, on a population basis, there is in fact less violent crime, and has been, year by year, for at least a decade, in much of industrialised society (including inner cities) where the fears continue to be the greatest.

The reason for the false perception is that the media treat acts of crime as dramatic audience binders, in which the drama is portrayed by people like you and me, with whom we can identify, and in which the story can be followed for several days as in a *Kojak* series, without the payment of actors' and producers' fees . . . The criminal series, because it fills the screen regularly and regularly hits the tabloid headlines, is easily but falsely interpreted as the norm.

Underlying nearly all the media-emphasised public reaction there is one theme: revenge. That is, what "justice" has come to mean in nearly all cases, and in some systems overtly. The system is not working unless the victim's right to revenge is recognised. Relatives of victims often demand harsher penalties, the removal of the young from youth court to adult court, in the United States the rigorous application of the death penalty. It doesn't matter that studies show that such measures are ineffective in reducing crime. That is not important, fundamentally. What is important is that the victim, however defined, be revenged, and that this must be done by the State in the name of the State. The victim does not personally see the judicial murder that he or she has been calling for; except in some Muslim countries, and in communities where reprisal—an eye for an eye and a tooth for a tooth—is sanctioned. The victim is not concerned fundamentally (however much involved in public protest) with the general reduction in crime; rather with the assuagement of anger.

I am more concerned with reducing crime and if possible eliminating it. If revenge stands in the way, revenge must be reduced or eliminated.

Sources of crime are manifold and cannot be lumped together, although I believe one comes through as predominant.

First there is the crime of youth which is an expression of youth. I do not know of a time when this was not a major phenomenon. It seems almost endemic. Some military societies have been able to channel the impulses—Zulu age regiments are an example. In Nazi times youth was mobilized in uniformed gangs, where certain types of thuggery were mandated. In Imperial times youths were enrolled in military cadet corps which disciplined their aggressive tendencies. In medieval times the fortunate young, even noble teen-agers, commanded armies. Present day creative outlets for energy, aggression, competitiveness, group identity and risk taking are there a-plenty: adventure travel, mountaineering, skiing, boating, sports. They are not available for everyone and are mostly costly. The parental desire to reduce risk comes into conflict and leads some into subterfuge. Physical risk-taking, as an aspect of Youth Maturity Institutes, is an essential part of growing up, of putting one's self to the test.

Independent seeking youth often pulls back from organisation unless it is self-directed. A gang in such instances can have more meaning than a school volley-ball team. Organisations, even those such as Outward Bound which use risk as a motive, surround their activities with risk-filtering nets. They have to, or they would be put out of business by law suits and parental vengeance. An essential element in competitive risk is to outdo the others. If schools have controlled-risk sports, there will be a clientele for higher-risk events, with clandestine or grandstanding group behaviour. "Look at me." "Look at what I can get away with."

Mixed in with this is sheer opportunism, the temptation to steal, the imagination of working on a break-in, as on television, and of course alienation. Children who are expressing their anger at parents, at perceived *unfairnesses* at school, at the hypocrisy of church-going, at deprivation—working it out alone, or pulling in accomplices to exercise power. And then the more fundamentally disturbed, who may not see the horrible reality of their acts because the vivid imagination that led to them and the hysterical aggression in the midst of blood and murder has centred their minds in fantasy. One could go on.

One of the marks of growing from infancy to maturity is the increased respect for others. Some individuals are slow to grow up, a small minority never do. Far from allowing the child within to dominate, we must learn to be adult, even if that means sacrificing some of the desirable features of innocence. When youth breaks into crime it is an indicator that respect for others is deficient. It all starts with the lack of courtesy in using elbows to create space on public transit . . .

Hence some of the features of the Youth Maturity Institutes will reduce, but not eliminate, the entry into crime. So will ultimate changes in interpersonal relations, including marriage, some of which I have advocated in earlier chapters. If children too are treated less as property and more as human individuals, without crossing the boundary into lack of parental responsibility, if there is courtesy in the home, the results can only be beneficial. As I write the press is referring to studies which purport to link bullying to "bad" parenting.

It is sometimes pointed out that there is a higher incidence of crime and dysfunctional personalities in "broken homes", by which is meant homes that have been broken by divorce or separation, homes that lack one parent, homes where there is abuse. The point is not that they come from parents who are splitting. There are many well balanced survivors of such events, and many interesting children living with single parents.

It depends partly on the nature of the child's sensibilities. But even more there is a huge difference between "civilised" splits and argumentative property-driven ones, especially when access to the child is a property right; between comfortable splits and those which result in poverty; between amicable splits and those where the cause has been abuse, violence, alcohol or drugs. Optimistically, this is where the Youth Maturity Institutes and their therapy-oriented professionals can make a difference.

In the meantime, and probably for a long time, the fact will remain that juveniles will be apprehended and sentenced, and that many will come from stable, apparently loving, well-off homes. In their late teens, in some jurisdictions earlier, they will be dealt with as adults. Most civilised juvenile courts endeavour to place the child in the context of his or her life, and seek remedies which have a theoretical healing orientation. I do not have the expertise to know the effectiveness of the approaches in practice. I do know that there is a great deal of criticism to the effect that juvenile courts are "too soft" on young violent criminals, especially those who have committed horrendous violent crimes attended with publicity, and on those whose age and sense of responsibility is at the borderline. The criticisms are once again tinged with the cry for revenge. Whatever changes may be regarded as appropriate at the juvenile level, harsher penalties through adult court are the reverse of what is needed.

Further, what is "adult" in this context? The word is being demeaned. It should mean maturity, the practice of responsibility. It has little to do with age. Those who play stupid fantasy games which result in violence are not adult. That is the same sort of demeaning expression as the use of the term "adult movies" for gross pornography; or "adults only" meaning that something is going on in here that is too raunchy or alcoholic for juveniles. Becoming an adult is becoming defined away from what it should mean to "I can now indulge in gross conduct."

In Utopia one would do away with the term adult altogether, as representing a distinction from childhood, recognising that many young are very mature, and some who are old have never grown up. Since I shall argue that the law should deal entirely with individual cases, not classes of people, save in special cultural circumstances, there need be no distinction between juvenile and adult court.

One would also make more use of the term "citizen", and have formal rites of passage that made manifest the transition from the status of "ward" (child) to that of responsibility ("citizen"). The point of transition would not be defined by age, but by meeting requirements of maturity. I know that such a suggestion will be controversial, especially since I have not yet defined in my mind the sort of tests and ceremonies that would be appropriate.[39] It will be controversial since it raises the spectre that authority may use the distinguishing criteria in such a way that perhaps many potential citizens could be kept out for their idiosyncrasies, including political ones.

Perhaps a citizen should become one without challenge, at a time of his or her choosing, with witnesses to maturity, responsibility, rejection of violence, caring. Will you help work it out? The one thing I know is that some such concept is needed.

How can I say talk of civilised ways of handling crime when the crimes are so violent and horrendous, so dangerous and costly to the public?

The reasons are quite simple.

Being caught and punished does not stop crime. It adds to the risk, which, as we have seen, is a potent motivator for the young.

The process of conviction and punishment does not enter into the minds of many young first offenders. They are being dealt with by an establishment and laws which are remote from their respect and experience and abstract rather than reality-based. Almost by definition, they do not see the consequences as real. They have already discounted them. They are already getting respect from certain peers. They are cynical about adult responsibility and the adult world. They are being noted by older adults as possible tools for further crime. In short, the system does not work from their minds to a result, but from the establishment's sense of order down.

From the young person's perspective it can be so *unfair* and it creates even more anger. Remember, most of the young people involved are, in their actions, self-centred with minimal regard for others, at least until Youth Maturity Institutes get to grips with the issue. Now, in addition, many, feel boosted by publicity. Then they are isolated, in their view they are alone, ready for introversion and angry brooding. They deal with lawyers who talk technicalities, who may be provided by the State or by legal aid as a duty rather than a commitment, mitigating circumstances are frequently not taken into account, preventative detention is demeaning. These are psychological assaults that confirm the angers and the oppositions. Almost overnight the dangerous prankster or self-centred ego becomes a criminal, out to show he is at war with the system. And if there were any doubt about this, prison will fix it up and make sure.

For adults who are first time offenders the dynamics can be similar. My information here is going to be tinged by subjectivity; it cannot be otherwise. It is influenced not only by my personal experience, the full story of which is not appropriate here, but also by talking with and observing fellow prisoners, some of whom were acquitted, some already serving sentences. The purpose of my argument is not to set up a temporary set of reforms, but to try to look at the larger scene, raise the long-term issues as we influence our evolution to the Utopian dream.

In summary I am going to argue that criminality is a sub-system within our society that has its own recruitment, demographics, dynamics, rules, boundaries, culture and life. Tinkering with reforms is unlikely to root it out; it may even help to preserve it. Follow the process of dealing with an offender through its stages. We can do this with some confidence, since despite significant variables in various countries there are broad similarities in their criminal sub-cultures and those of the police and authorities who deal with them.

Not every person charged with a criminal act enters into the dynamics in the same way. Some come out of the experience as responsible reliable citizens. To do this they have to have major informal psychological support, faith in themselves, certainty about what they did or did not do, an ability to overcome the trauma in the short or long term, a restructuring of their values. If any one of these features is absent, it is very unlikely that their future lives will be adequately functional.

Mostly, the central system does not address such features. It concentrates on vocational skills and some half-way house adjustment for those who have had long sentences; and there is help from chaplains, some of the social workers, acting as individuals, and of course those relatives and friends who remain loyal and caring—which is often not the case.

It all begins with an event. Police conduct an investigation under various kinds of authority or supervision. In Napoleonic systems they act in the name of an enquiring magistrate, reporting to him. In Anglo-Saxon systems police govern their own investigations, charging on their own initiative or after the agreement of a prosecutor's or public attorney's office. (I am generalising my terminology and descriptions.)

Defence lawyers are continually on guard against police inaccuracy and manipulation, and confirm that sleight-of-hand with regard to truth, while by no means applying to all cases, is widespread indeed. In some instances a conviction or the bringing of a charge would be impossible without it.

I have my own experience, which may be extreme. But I was able to observe in detail similar "methods" being used in connection with accused in Switzerland, and have read numerous press reports about the same kinds of actions in Anglo-Saxon countries. During my enforced confinement I talked with prisoners who had been incarcerated in a wide range of countries—Britain, Netherlands, Switzerland, Germany, Italy, France, African countries, Iran, and so on. Prisoners lie, but they are not necessarily liars. I am confident that there is truth in the regularities.

Once police are confronted with what they believe to be a crime they must do what any other investigator must do, look for evidence, a process which is governed by *theory* and which, ideally, should influence modifications to the emerging theory revision. This is hard to do in any discipline, yes, even in my own of anthropology. For the police the task is much easier if someone with a previous record is somehow connected, or if they can work with some sense of statistical probability. If, for example, there is a murder, they look first for jealousy as a motive, or drugs. If there is a person who might be linked through jealousy or drugs, he immediately becomes a target, unless there is *inescapable and immediate* unavoidably strong alternative evidence. The process is not very different from that used in medical research, for example: use established theory first.

But the police are working in a totally different atmosphere. They are under pressure to solve the crime and bring a charge. To be effective they cannot lose time. The environment is dangerous; often they must react in a split second or their lives could be lost. It is easy to judge in a writing room. Although they did me great harm, I think I understand why they did what they did. Having chosen to become police they do what they believe they have to do to fulfil the mandate *that the public places upon them.*

These are some things that applied in my own case for which I have direct documentary evidence revealed through police documents themselves, some of which were criticised by a supervisory tribunal. Some were admitted into court evidence by the cantonal criminal court in ways that were unlikely to be accepted in most other European or North American jurisdictions. Some of the methods were used by Canadian, some by French, and most by Swiss police in this instance.

Threats were issued against me *sub voce*, but strongly, in circumstances where independent witnesses were not present. Witnesses were influenced by the persuasive statement that the police had all the evidence needed to convict me and all they needed were a few confirming details, when in fact they did not have such evidence. Attempts were made to psychologically undermine witnesses (especially women) through false accusations (in one instance, of incest) and domestic harassment (police calling at the front door with sirens in operation and at awkward times), the presentation of malicious innuendo as truth without independent substantiation, misrepresenting witness statements without securing witness signatures, police signing summaries of witness statements when they also claimed that they did not know the language of the interview, sequestering the accused in a way that prevented him from tracking down supporting evidence, the use of tape recorders without informing the interviewee, using trickery to gain entrance to a residence when a warrant had been refused.

Other methods are often used which were not, so far as I know, applied to my case. They include the planting of evidence, harassing observation, bribing convict witnesses with privilege or reduced sentencing, violence, plea-bargaining.

Now the first objection to this recitation, which could go on, is that in many countries courts would not accept evidence acquired through such behaviour. The court which ultimately acquitted me *did* accept it, and certified, even though a supervisory court did not, that the police behaved impeccably. Just the same, the objection is valid in that in many, probably most, industrialised countries, courts would not. The Swiss cantonal (Vaud) criminal court was an aberration.

Yet in many, perhaps most, criminal cases such methods do not come to light. Police are very aware of the risks they run in working in such ways, and are skilled and collegial when it comes to concealing. Most cases involve repetitive crimes, almost routine, in which no one wants to use up resources in an unequal fight. Criminal lawyers are only human. They will challenge police methods, but what is the point when in other respects the case is cut and dried? When there is, perhaps, a confession? Their task is not to get a declared criminal off, but to see that he is treated according to the rules of the court. There are lawyers who will go the whole way, and do, who challenge every police misdemeanour.

But even that is not my essential point. With individuals who have entered a criminal way of life, police malfeasance is accepted as a reality and shrugged off as part of the conditions of work. The main task is not to get caught in the first place. Some "petty" criminals even take police charges as a way of placating their symbiotic colleagues, and expect to serve time, as long as they can get away with other events. When I exchanged talk of my experience with other prisoners they would laugh. The police always do that. When someone new came into the prison on a charge and I heard, step by step what he was facing, I knew that even the words the police interrogators used were exactly the same as they used with me. "We'll respect you if you tell us all about it, then we'll have a beer. Right?" or "If you don't, we'll turn your life upside down, your friends will leave you even if you're not convicted."

What is much more devastating is the effect on first or early offenders. I met literally scores, mostly non-violent, who had no real defences. Young, naive, sometimes innocent, they become more cynical, angry, betrayed. They had little faith in the lawyers who were assigned to them—usually they had no funds—and were unable to get any other psychological help. There are lawyers and consular officials who act as friends, take on the role of *pater familias*, and spend far more time than their fees would justify. I for one was fortunate in this regard.

I am not setting out the observations in an attempt to excuse young criminals. There are many young people, growing up in similar conditions, who do *not* enter crime. There are those, who, accused and convicted and imprisoned, turn away from crime. It is a question of choice and responsibility, however ill-informed and emotional. Just the same, the majority are vulnerable, weak, poorly supported and allow their experiences to reinforce dormant alienation. The dynamics are deadly and counter-productive.

Prisons for "preventive detention", analogous to "remand", are sometimes in theory independent of police. Again, in theory, such prisons are situated close to relatives. The prison in France in which I was initially confined, a super-modern high-tech city, had no easy public transport access and required an arduous one-hour negotiation of traffic for my lawyer or for consular staff or visitors to get to. Everywhere the undermining was evident and similar. Preventive detention can be used specifically to defeat the accused. The refusal of bail—very common in Europe—is a first weapon, consciously or not. In complicated cases it seriously inhibits the collection of defence evidence, which the accused alone can track down. It drags out imprisonment for months or longer, sometimes in nearly solitary conditions, before a court has had a chance to rule. Remember, some of these people are innocent.

The hurts are deep. A high proportion of prisoners awaiting trial are accused of drug or white collar offences. I met West Africans arrested at airports carrying drugs to finance European studies, credit card sharps, purveyors of stolen art, entrepreneurs accused of fraud. The latter were totally at a loss as to how to conduct themselves in prison. The majority had wives, girl friends, expectant mothers. They were out of their minds with worry. They were not irresponsible within their own worlds. Where they had such affines, their women were working hard to guide defence lawyers, to raise funds. Funds? Yes. For many of the crimes, in France and Switzerland at any rate, involved drug trafficking. The accused negotiated customs duties and concomitant fines, and would not go to a superficial trial until the negotiations were agreed and the funds paid. By which time the accused has in effect served his sentence. Out. We don't want to pay for your cell any more. Now we have our money.

While the accused is in detention, the enquiry proceeds. It has not been completed. In some European countries the accused has a right to the presence of a lawyer during interrogation, an enormous but expensive safeguard, if lawyers take their tasks seriously rather than with a routine shrug of their shoulders. In most industrial countries the police play on anxieties, and try to find weaknesses they can use to more or less bribe the accused. The good cop bad cop routine is real. They try to wear down the accused by taking him to a police cell for interrogation and doing nothing, so that he wonders what is up. They imply that friends are deserting him. Where they have correspondence censorship rights they pick out phrases to use. They attempt to mislead the accused with respect to his juridical position and rights. (Paradoxically in some jurisdictions an accused has the right to lie, to fight back if police use violence, and to escape. In practice, this does not mean much.) When they have no real evidence, they lie that they do.

The reason is simple. It aids the police task inestimably if they can get a confession, whether or not a plea of "not guilty" is entered in court. Indeed, it is quite probable that the majority of court cases, whether successful or not, are brought to court as a result of a confession, direct or implied. This is the object of the psychological warfare between police and accused.

Many accused do not bother to fight back very much. Police pretend to respect this. Police say at least then the accused have the moral strength to pay the price when they are caught. There are typical offers: we have nothing against you as you. We are just doing our job. When you have made our task easier by your admissions we'll be your friend. This is a game the frequent offender knows very well. He understands the hypocrisy involved, although some do in fact, when they are out, have a collegial beer or two.

Police and offenders are in a symbiotic relationship. Without offenders police work would be reduced to that of citizen helpers, directing traffic, giving street directions, reviving the terminology of "sir" and "madam". It is in the police professional interest—as with other professions—to dramatise an admittedly often dramatic role, to build up their undoubtedly courageous image, and to exaggerate crime. Criminals who have been through the system know their "enemy", and, except in the most horrendously violent crimes, play cat and mouse.

Many are so used to the prison system they take it in their stride. One English fellow I knew even published a book about how to survive in prison. For some it is a part of their career, for career it is for many. Many parts of the criminal world have their own professional standards, career decisions and retirement plans. Prison is part of the cost of doing business.

There are others who are so alienated and disturbed that the prison world is their only real world. They cannot survive, emotionally, psychologically, and materially outside of prison. They will commit crimes to get caught and to go back in. For some it is an alternative, however harsh, to sleeping under bridges. For others it is a cocoon, the guards are macho fathers, the rules limit behaviour so that choices do not have to be made any more. They are frightened by choice in the real world.

Periods of prison of a year or more begin to erode the individual's capability of operating in the real world. Vehicular traffic can be anxiety producing, crossing the street a hazard, looking self-satisfied and superior citizens in the eye a challenge.

Imagine what fifteen or twenty years do. Individuals must face the disapprobation of straight citizens, many of whom are in fact not particularly moral. It is unlikely that a spouse will still be there for them, and if so will be a very different person from the one they once knew. They have forgotten how to act heterosexually (although a few prisons try to keep up the practices by allowing wives or prostitutes to visit). Whatever occupational skills they have acquired are treated with suspicion by employers and are not likely to be up-to-date.

Citizens who clamour for longer sentences don't know what they are doing. They are increasing the likelihood of recidivism. Under these circumstances it is remarkable that repeat offences are not much more frequent. *Prison does not cure.* If convicts return to some semblance of non-criminal life, it is by drawing upon their inner strengths, or because they were not leading a criminal way of life in the first place, seldom because "prison has reformed them".

Until the nineteenth century, many punishments were public—the stocks, whipping, hanging. Crime—partly because of definition, partly because of poverty, and partly because of the roughness of life—was more frequent than it is today, even though now we are more worried by it. Prisons were relatively open; it was often possible for the public to enter, to jeer, or to find friends and relatives behind bars.

In the late nineteenth century prison reforms changed these ways. The educated middle class did not like seeing the results of conviction. Their fastidiousness led to reduced, more "civilised" sentences for many crimes. It also led to removing prisons and punishments from the public eye.

There was a general change in the structure of newer prisons, with cells arranged in linear wings with a control and observation post at the point at which the wings joined. The new design was not only to improve the effectiveness of control but, as part of a reformist theory, to enable guards to give the individual prisoners a sense of their own individual space, a responsibility for themselves that close supervisory approximation destroyed. In addition, the efficacy of observation (when doors had see-through properties) was supposed to make it possible to detect individual psychological problems—suicidal or manic, for example—early.

For the philosophy became one of *curing*. The idea, familiar to some modern thought, was that criminal behaviour was an illness. The function of the prison system was to rehabilitate. This was to be achieved by firm but understanding supervision, by in-prison education, and above all by the ethic of work. Trade training became highly significant.

It was an enlightened approach, and there are still many vestiges of it. Minimum security prisons provide opportunities for physical recreation, enlightened educational programmes, creative activities such as theatre and art, discussions and counselling. Sometimes career criminals find their way to such centres. Perhaps they are influenced. The more secure, tougher, prisons also have programmes of this kind, which will speak to individuals.

But in my view there has been a marked deterioration. Neither of the prisons I observed in France and Switzerland had reformist characteristics, even for the long-term convicted. I do know that such prisons do exist in both countries. I also know, from reading, the media, and talking with prisoners, that in France, Britain, Canada and the United States, there are totally dreadful prisons, overcrowded, violent, where the problems of security overshadow most attempts at reform.[40] Prison "work" is frequently minimal wage labour accessed by sharp entrepreneurs, or by charitable organisations who do not recognise what is going on. (In the Swiss prison, prisoners sat in dreadful eye-straining artificial or candle light in their cells, perched on thigh—and back-ruining hunks of wood that served as chairs, hour after hour putting together UNICEF cards on a pitiful piecework arrangement, their hands covered with glue that they often couldn't remove without great difficulty because there was no hot water in the cells, for pitiful "pay" that quickly went on monopoly supplied groceries. You don't have to go to China to find such exploitation. What, may I ask, is reformist about this?)

Why the backsliding? Pressure of funding is one force. The unattractiveness of prison management careers another. The size of the prison population a third. The low priority accorded to prisons among competing demands for public support another.

The very privacy of prisons is the dominant cause. If the public really knew, experienced, the prison culture, opinion would not stand for what goes on. This is not a question of being "soft" on the convicted. It is the degradation of human beings. It is would-be escapees being dragged down iron steps by their heels, heads banging on the iron, step by step. It is screams in the night as adult men have nightmares. It is men going mad spread-eagled against window bars, trying to break their heads and the glass. It is men curled upon an iron cot in a foetal position, unable to respond to food or drink. It is men crying night and day as they think of loved ones. It is being picked out at random, taken to the shower room, stripped naked for the investigation of orifices. It is macho guards who look forward to escape attempts (not illegal in Switzerland) so that they can use their firearms in a hunt. Much more. These I have seen. In the worst prisons, supposedly secure, which I have not seen, drugs, knives, murders, homosexual rapes are frequent. It is a commonplace that within the prison culture there is organisation among the prisoners, especially the long-term ones, with hierarchies and gang rules. This can *only* happen with the connivance of the guards.

These are the toughest prisons, the ones in which security is the dominant priority, everything else coming second. How is it then that drugs and weapons are so frequently encountered? Drugs particularly have to come in from outside. Despite the undoubted ingenuity that convicts evince, which ensure that the prison boundaries will never be 100% secure, I can only come to the conclusion that the drug supply, at least, is condoned, perhaps even unofficially encouraged. The use of medications is frequently abused in prison conditions in order to try to keep individuals tranquillised. The use of drugs may be thought of in a similar way. If so, be open about it. When clandestine it supports corruption among the prison staff and endangers interior security.

So too with interior order. It is not particularly difficult for prisoners to manufacture aggressive weapons. Nor is it difficult—over years, remember—to engage in relationships with officials who turn a blind eye.

Did anyone mention reform of the individual? This is a criminal society and culture. It puts together people who *live* their criminality and continue to do so uninterruptedly in prison, reinforced by their peers. Some are one-time offenders. What a university. It has nothing whatsoever to do with the reduction of crime. Well meaning citizens who advocate longer sentences are in effect advocating the perpetuation of criminality—unless they say, lock them up for good. Then what happens to them is not an issue. Civilised?

It is more than symptomatic that Michael Tonry, possibly the doyen of criminologists in the United States, in his recent publication *Thinking About Crime*, deals almost exclusively with punishment and pours scorn on Dan Kahan's theory of retributive shaming.[41] I support the idea of shame as an essential part of the healing process, though not as part of an idea of punishment. The focus of such writers, and many other criminologists, is on the efficacy or non-efficacy of differing kinds of punishment, measure by the level of recidivism. This is largely folly, for punishment and, especially prison terms, have in themselves very little if any result in reducing crime. The Utopian measures I suggest may do so, but ultimately we will have to mark time until the Youth Maturity Institutes can do their job.

*Is there a Utopian alternative that we can pursue in practical ways? I believe so. And, for once, I do not think it would take expense or decades to bring about. It involves a change of attitudes, a greater weight given to the effectiveness and openness of the processes.

The key I think is this. While we are becoming more and more concerned about the frequency of crime, we also raise ever-more recurrently the plight of victims. Victims are usually quite right, in that the system of criminal "justice", while perhaps listening to their complaints, does nothing for them. Except in "traditional" non-Roman law, here is little or no restitution. The only option is to seek revenge. One cannot criticise victims for this. There seems to be no other way in which to resolve the hurt, trauma and emotional desperation. And in some societies, for example parts of the Balkans and Middle East, the thirst for revenge is such as to threaten the very fabric of inter-ethnic stability and the body politic.

This is no way in which to organise a civilised society when its norms have been breached. Revenge is one of the most destructive forces there is, analogous to jealousy in marital relationships, both to the individual who is expressing deep feelings, and to the social environment. It does nothing to heal the social wounds that a crime has created.

There are other ways. There are older societies from whom we can learn to adapt. They are even, in the midst of this vengeful retributive culture, claiming back some of their older methods.

In a muddled way the United States and Canada are permitting a handful of Indian tribe-nations to exercise juridical processes in the midst of the overwhelming Anglo-Saxon system. In some highly commercialised Indian communities the interests are primarily in administering their own civil law as a method of controlling resources and enterprises, a law which is adapted and borrowed from the mainstream corpus, with little difference.

In other instances mainstream courts allow the representation of tribal authorities when it comes to sentencing. In one example, the court handed over two violent young men to the tribal council. The council and elders banished the young men separately to an island, to live on their own resources for a year, to learn about their inner strengths and contemplate their responsibilities as men, after which they would be placed back in the care of the elders, who would talk with them and ultimately formally reincorporate them into society.

In another example, with the assistance of tribal police, elders and *healers*, an almost totally demoralised community in Canada, riddled with destitution, dependency, sexual abuse and alcoholism, was given the authority to look after its own problems. They did so through treating the abusers and violent alcoholic offenders as individuals who had lost any vestige of self-esteem, any notion of responsibility for their behaviour toward others. The indigenous psychology of respect for lineal elders, meaning respect for extended family connectivity, shame for exhibiting weakness and the hurt of others, acts of contrition and compensation, the examination of self in isolation, the use of traditional psychological healing arts, worked. Transgressors returned to honour in their community, found their self-esteem, understood the harm they had done to others and themselves, and found satisfying pursuits despite the high rate of unemployment.[42]

In some prisons, traditional healing circles are at work.

Such examples are in part helped and made possible by the continuity of tradition which can be recalled, and by the fact that some hitherto demoralised Indian communities have been going through a cultural regeneration. The communities are also, for the most part, small. When they work they are tightly knit, and are still able to reclaim, in crisis, some of their members who have moved into the larger mainstream society, but dysfunctionally. The examples cannot be replicated automatically into the wider culture.

The principles, and others, are nevertheless worthy of closer study. Here are some of them.

The most useful starting point is that the transgressors are socially ill. Their minds have been filled with thoughts and imaginings which are culturally unhealthy. For a healthy man does not damage other members of his community. To be healthy is his own responsibility, a condition of his being a part of the community's network, to which he contributes, and which supports his functioning. He can be sufficiently mad, mentally unhealthy, to reject the community, in which case he goes off and lives as a "wild man", an uncivilised being, on his own. If the methods of healing that are available do not in themselves bring him back into appropriate relationships, then banishment will be the community's answer. Rejection. But this is a last resort.

Prior to the extreme of banishment, the community may work with the following principle: a transgression is an interruption of the social order. The purpose of a judgement is to put that order back in place. This takes priority over the notion of revenge or punishment, though neither element can be discounted in practice.

The kinship orientation of such societies makes the principle workable. If there is violence, even murder, theft, adultery (thought of as criminal), or sexual perversion, the offender is the responsibility of his or her kinsmen, however defined. If the offence is against a member of the offender's own kin group, then that kin group handles it. If it is against a member of another kin group, then, through various mechanisms, including negotiation and ceremonialised warfare, the offended kin group must be satisfied. (Note that, by definitions of exogamy, offences against a spouse may involve *two* kin groups.)

Such systems are also aided by the fact that there are exchanges of wealth at the time of marriage. (In some societies, this is one-sided and can be abused.) If there are problems between spouses, part of a settlement will be restitution or the threat of restitution of at least some of that wealth, depending sometimes on whether divorce is an outcome.

The ultimate settlement will involve such mechanisms as the offending group taking responsibility for controlling the offender, including, perhaps, isolating himer until heshe returns to sociability. There can be ostracism and, yes, punishment. They will apologise for his offence. They will make recompense by transferring wealth or obligations to the damaged group.

The processes are quite similar to those involved in property disputes, for example disputes over land boundaries or failure to maintain ceremonial obligations. In other words, there is little if any distinction between what we regard as civil and criminal law. And it is true that if negotiations fail there could be violence, and that the process does not work well across cultural boundaries.

I must also make it clear that I am not by any means describing "all traditional societies", among whom there is great variation. And that even for the kind of society I have in mind—much of North American Indian, many in Africa and Melanesia—what I have presented is abstract generalisation. The concrete ethnography would show much more complication in detail.

And what can work in small communities will not be suited to mass industrialisation.

Nevertheless there is a great deal here to emulate. For the prime idea is that the social order has been upset, and that the primary task is to restore it. The social order is not considered to be an encompassing state, but a disruption of harmony between individuals which threatens normal interactions between their relatives and friends. To restore the harmony, the victim must be included in the settlement, not left out. Revenge perpetuates the disturbance to the social order. In part, modern state criminal law recognises this, for it does not allow the victim to "take the law into his own hands", that is seek revenge by himself.

We should merge civil and criminal law, and treat crime as a tort. And perhaps at the same time we should consider all crime to involve forms of mental disturbance that require varying kinds of treatment; mental disturbance in the sense that there is defective concern for others and for the social consequences, and there is diminished responsibility. (I am *not* implying that such "illness" is appropriately treated by conventional biomedical models.)

Revenge will not disappear unless we put an alternative effectively in place. My thoughts are of course expressed in great generality; to make progress would require considerable refinement. These are some steps:-

The clearest case for what I am proposing is with respect to juveniles. All families, however dysfunctional, should in principle be made directly responsible for the acts of children and youths, sharing accountability and liability with the offender. That said, the family itself may need major therapeutic attention which may require the removal of the offender to another familial, adoptive, or care home environment. While such alternative home environments may, in practicality, have to have an institutional organisation, the less this is done the better, and, except in very extreme circumstances, the offender should not be removed into an institutionalised prison which abstracts him from direct responsibility for his past acts. The objective is to heal by *re*-socialising through restitution and acceptance of responsibility.

Nor will the juvenile offender be removed from Youth Maturity Institutes, where the healing will take place, though heshe may be enrolled in a specialized Institute suited to hiser needs.

The juvenile offender, to varying degrees, requires special forms of healing. Heshe needs to find hiser inner strength, hiser self-respect, and above all hiser respect for others. The court's task should be to mandate appropriate healing devices.

The primary method is to involve the offender *and the family*, however defined, in acts of restitution toward the victim. I am not talking here about enforced community work that involves an abstraction of public service. I am talking about direct acts in relation to the victim and the victim's relatives. They are not precisely a kind of quid pro quo. They will not mirror the offence. A robbery, yes, will involve restitution of the stolen or damaged material. It can also involve acts like painting a house, garden work, help to an elderly relative or friend of the victim, and so on.

At the same time the offender would undergo direct healing treatment. What it might be would be individualised. It could involve participating in risk-taking adventure groups. (I have been impressed by the principles of a North American organisation called Vision Quest. In lieu of prison, young women with extensive and violent criminal records are sentenced to its care. They heal and find their civilised selves as crew members of a large sailing barque.) It could involve the field study of social issues. It could involve encouragement of creative activity. It could involve therapies of self-awareness, self-testing, aggression control, psychiatry. It could involve, exceptionally, pharmaceutical therapy.

The end of the programme should *not* be determined by a specific time objective. It should be determined by result; when, in the view of qualified assessors, the offender has participated in sufficient restitution to the victim, and when, as a result of this and other activities, heshe is re-socialised.

The end of such a restitutive programme should involve a healing ceremonial in which the victim and the offender, each with their kin, friends or other guarantors, acknowledge that harm has been done, healing has been achieved, and that it was possible now to put the offence away.

How much of this can be adapted for adult offenders? In individualised society, the identification of relevant family (and/or friends) to share responsibility will not be possible in many, perhaps most, cases. In societies where this continues to be possible, that responsibility should be maintained. But we must consider the situation in which the individual is just that, alone and personally responsible.

For the most part the same considerations apply, especially for first time offenders. I make this comment because the majority of first time offenders commit petty crimes, for which the possibility of restitution is practicable.

Courts, in non-confrontational consultation with victims, would not establish coded penalties, although this might come with experience. They would establish the offender's restitutive acts and behaviour, including types of therapy and supervision. In an intermediate period until the system were properly installed, offenders would be held in revised prisons, from which they would be removed to undertake both tasks and therapy. As far as possible, the prison society would be broken up, with minimal contact between the convicted (except in those intriguing cases in which the guarantors would include other offenders). The convicted would in fact continue to live in society, although if needed, an institutional home and its officials would be available primarily for supervision, to ensure that tasks were in fact fulfilled, and keeping him out of further trouble during non-working non-therapy periods.

Especially for "minor" offences, and offences where there is no victim except the general public (motor offences which do not involve accident or injury), including offences where the law is regulatory in nature, some present remedies are likely to continue—fines, withdrawal of driving licences, and so forth. Fines should not go into general revenue coffers, or be considered, as they often are now, a source of general revenue, or, perniciously, income for magistrates. They should be allocated to specific relevant remedies (driver training, alcohol control). Where there is a victim, restitutive acts should take precedence over generalised fines. Where possible, remedial requirements should take precedence over fines—service with an ambulance team, specified hours of controlled driving, for example on major highways at the posted speed.

Certain types of offences would no longer be considered delicts in the present sense. This applies to the remnants of prudish laws (as society permits), such as laws against the baring of breasts. More importantly, offences where *the adult victim is the adult offender himself*, need to be thoroughly reconsidered. Alcoholism laws have mostly, except when the law includes Moslem-style prohibition, reached this point. It is not an offence to drink, or to engage in private and consensual sexual aberration. Why should it be a *criminal* offence to hurt one's self? Drugs and suicide come under this heading. The removal of the use of drugs from the crime list would probably in itself half-empty prisons and reduce court proceedings. More important, it would remove beginning drug users from the spiralling entanglements of the criminal society.

But wait. There are several refinements that derive from our principles. Drug users sometimes *do* harm to others. They sometimes require actions and attention from friends or family, which can be regarded as a form of social stealing. They sometimes engage in criminal activity to earn funds to keep up expensive habits. (So do other addicts). Their personalities change so that they may become aggressive or unable to perform. They require state medical expenditures. The law would be entitled to take such considerations into account for all types of addiction (smoking, alcoholism, gambling).

In short, where there is harm to others, restitutive and therapeutic remedies are in order. Far from solely reducing the field of criminal law, by changing offences to forms of tort one extends the notion of responsibility and remedy to other fields. A smoker would be required to accept his or her responsibility for hiser actions, and undertake some form of recognition, restitution, and healing. As I shall argue below. A person who **becomes** an addict must bear the responsibility of the consequences, including the costs of therapy and of collateral damage to others.

It will immediately be objected to the application of these principles that they will not work for certain kinds of criminal. I agree, especially in the short run.

There are: individuals now so caught up in the present criminal system that they cannot be expected to get out of it, individuals who are so violent or sex-oriented, and of an age, that therapies of whatever kind, as we know them now, are useless, individuals who are so alienated that restitutive acts further internalise alienation, individuals who despite restitution and therapy remain recidivists, individuals whose offences are so large (massive fraud) that restitution (but perhaps not other forms of acknowledgement) is impracticable.

Some of these categories, for example the first, are transitional. We do not expect Utopia to be created over night. It would take considerable time and many intermediary moves, to establish the system I have imagined. Yet boldness is needed, for we are caught in a trap. If we do not posit *what we want to achieve* we will never achieve it. I for one **want** the system I have described to be achieved. Join me; and, since you are younger, work for it.

Some of the categories may respond to more imaginative ideas and to new therapies.

Nevertheless, outside the above categories, the punishing prison system would give way to socially and individually effective healing. The kinds of prisons we use now would be substantially reduced and in time eliminated.

For the above transitional categories, the future will tell how long we will continue to need prisons. The inward-looking structures, reinventing a criminal society, help no one. We should give up on no one within the walls no matter how repulsive he or she may seem. While maintaining maximum security until the public agrees to proven new measures, the alteration in other elements of the prison system should help to create adaptive possibilities. Animal-like cages, decrepit buildings which are insecure inside, crowd behaviour with its threat of numerous kinds of assaults and violence, help no one, least of all "society".

Break up the prison society as we know it now. Smaller prisons, more space, more privacy, programmes with more physical and mental challenge, developing prisoner-based responsibilities for internal order, and the use of at least 50% of time and resources on therapies. That's one way en route to the ideal.

In writing of therapy throughout this discussion, I make no prescriptions, for the data are beyond my command and there are signs that there will be massive advances in knowledge before much of the above is put into effect. Suffice it to say that it includes major reliance on the norms and supports of cultures of which the offenders and victims are members. If these are not taken into account in multi-cultural societies, other methods may be counter-productive. It includes psychological measures, bio-medical measures, alternative therapies, and the use of genetic medicaments in some instances.

I must enter a strong caveat that one must not judge the potentiality of therapies by what is now taking place. There is a major tendency for some therapists who work within the punishment system to adapt their healing techniques and philosophy under the influence of the system and also to claim quick results.

Psychiatrists and psycho-analysts whom I have observed provide one sort of example, as do physicians who deal with problems by the induction of massive tranquillisers. In Switzerland a colleague visited me in prison. She had undertaken considerable controlled examination of the activities of psychiatrists in the context of criminal analysis. What she wrote confirmed my own observations.

Typically, psychiatrists were there consulted during the course of the investigation, after an accused had been apprehended. What they did was to look at the police record as the foundation for their thoughts. Not once in numerous consultations that came to my attention did they question that record. They then conducted perhaps half a dozen short interviews with the prisoner. They came to the conclusions of the police, writing their reports in obfuscating jargon or direct language adding little if anything to what was supposedly known. "A man of violent temperament", "A pathological liar".

In short, they were adding material to the police dossier. This had nothing to do with the act of healing, was indeed contrary to it, and a breach of the Hippocratic Oath. No genuine analysis can be based on that kind of information. Analysis alone, let alone therapy, requires lengthy interviews and "thick data" over months, and, in this context, deep discussion with friends and relatives.

When I returned to life after prison my view of all "holding" institutions changed considerably. Hospitals, mental institutions, nursing homes for the elderly, are literally prisons of a kind.

In these, you are supervised, confined to certain spaces, fed institutional food, taken, if at all, on supervised trips even to a garden, sought after and brought back if you escape, are restricted in the circumstances in which you are permitted to discharge yourself, treated administratively and medically (sometimes) as if your mind did not exist. Facilities are sometimes no better than in minimum security prisons. In some instances, sadism and cruelty are the order, deliberate or unintentional, as rules are instituted with the best of intentions to regularise procedures, or worst of intentions as understaffed over-pressured aides confine people and push them around.

I know of a case when a 90 year old woman with a stroke was moved from intensive care, where she communicated in smiles with smart professional nurses, to a long term ward in which the nurses disguised themselves in informal clothes, addressed everyone by their first names, jollied the patients along with the utmost of patronising equality. The woman gave up immediately, allowing herself to die as quickly as possible, her integrity threatened, probably believing she was no longer in a professional environment.

I know of homes for the elderly in which drugs are mal-administered, and those who cannot express themselves normally are treated brusquely, with contempt, and sometimes violence. I have heard of them screaming with rage and impotent frustration, not in words, but with the keys of a laptop computer, and then having "privileges" withdrawn.

All restrictive institutional settings are potentially subject to abuse.

What is at issue is probably not the doing away with institutions but their revision. In some countries the "problem" is conveniently solved by reducing times spent in hospitals, which is frequently desirable on medical grounds, discharging the non-violent mentally ill, and persuading families and personal homes to care for the elderly.

Mostly, this is escaping collective responsibility, the hidden agenda being presumed financial savings. It is all very well closing psychiatric hospitals, reducing time spent in mammoth city hospitals whose size justifies expenditures on enormous capital and operational equipment, and placing the elderly back in the home. The theory is basically sound *provided* that resources are redistributed to provide alternative support.

The dilemma should be a warning. Utopian dreams will fail, at least in the short term, if the intermediary stages are not well thought out. In care institutions draconian cut-backs necessitated by the bottom line are frequently taking place before the alternatives have been organised, resulting in damage—through homelessness, begging, and family break-up—to public acceptance of the theory.

For alternatives, now and again we can learn from the developing world, and now and again we must innovate from scratch. Entry into a sanitised hospital with its formal activities can be a frightening experience for many people. In tropical countries, where shelters may be erected with space, greenery and informality, it is often the case that special arrangements are made to permit family, friends, visitors to be present, even to supply food, and perhaps to do simple chores like changing beds. The family circle *enters* the hospital.

Similarly the lack of supply of fully trained doctors, especially in rural areas, means that initial first aid, simple supply of routine medicines (e.g. anti-malarial) and preliminary diagnosis, is administered by often highly competent nurses and intermediary medical practitioners with good, short, limited training. They screen and if necessary send patients off to more sophisticated hospitals. They may have a few beds in their charge.

Organisation and therapy often go hand in hand; nowhere is this more evident than in the Third World where circumstances force innovative methods. In Madurai, India Dr. Govindappa Venkataswamy runs charity eye hospitals as businesses. He charges for one-third of its operations, and conducts the rest free. It runs an assembly line style strictly limited to operations for cataracts. Through its methods sight is restored to 250 patients a day, or 65,000 a year. It is planning international expansion as an enterprise to enable it to extend operations in India, and has received considerable international attention.

It may well be that, ancillary to general medical practice, medicine would be more efficient and yield more substantial results if such institutions took care of well defined and open to routine procedures, rather than in general hospitals, and probably through direct patient access as well as referrals.

At the other end of the diagnostic trail, in industrialised countries, in city neighbourhoods as well as in rural districts, local clinics staffed by diagnostic and preliminary aid nurses, male and female, can take much of the burden off the expensive hospitals, and keep patients close to, and possibly in, their homes. Nowadays with computer links to family physicians and specialists, every element of intervention can be recorded and supervised, (a) by a qualified resident doctor in the clinic, and (b) by a patient-chosen family physician.

And bio-medicine is becoming more and more expensive, less and less cost effective. Enormously complex million dollar machines become necessary not only for treatment, but more and more for diagnosis. They wear down, turn out sometimes to be inaccurate, become outdated, so that their shelf life is relatively short and expensive replacement continuous. The simpler, more direct and hands on intuitive approaches of the Third World are often more effective.

And yet the application of technology in aid of the physician's direct contact with the patient is woefully inadequate. What *The Economist* has called the "no computer virus"[43] stalks doctors' surgeries, now in fact offices. Piles and piles of paper records take up the space, each to be hand retrieved. A few savvy doctors have this on immediately searchable computer programmes. A few more have the ability within their own office of pulling up the results of X-rays or eye-scans for immediate careful examination. Most still depend on courier or inadequate fax to move data from one doctor to another. In some geographically challenged places computer connections enable specialists to advise surgeons during operations, but this is rare within urban complexes.

Mobile technology would make it possible even now for a doctor or diagnostic nurse to get out of the office and into a patient's domestic environment, with immediate access to the full record including images, and to specialist advice where necessary. The expense would be substantially offset by the scale of the production of the equipment, the time saved for both therapist and patient, and efficacy of communication. Even the monitoring of the health of those who deliberately choose to be homeless would be feasible.

In the expensive world, the capabilities of nurses are generally under valued. They should be graduated a long way from their traditional role of doctor's helper and medical housekeeper.

Even more to the point, if the clinical nurses can include house visiting, which should be practicable in neighbourhoods, they can introduce a dimension of diagnosis which is now almost totally lacking in "advanced" countries—the first hand contact with the client's domestic environment. It is generally agreed that a "holistic" view of the patient is desirable, though not necessarily as defined by "holistic" practitioners, who themselves deal primarily with body and mind as presented in office discussion, and seldom with total life styles based on observation. How conventional doctors can prescribe treatment for many illnesses without first hand contact with living arrangements, observing daily activities, even knowing more about the workplace, beats me. In developing countries such knowledge is almost inescapable.

Almost everywhere family doctors are under pressure as their colleagues become specialists. Well trained diagnostic nurses, available for both office and house visits, alone or in clinics, can take much of the burden from them.

Similarly in so-called sophisticated countries, the seriously handicapped, pseudonymically dubbed "challenged", are being moved out of institutions back into society. For the physically handicapped the adjustments seem to be largely in place—more awareness in commerce, industry, shopping malls; apartments constructed for their needs; newly formed communities. But for the mentally "challenged" this is not so general. Some, with initial assistance from a social worker, manage quite well. Others are challenged not only by their disability but by sheer poverty (which may be alleviated by the Guaranteed Income advocated in Chapters XVI and XVII. And yet others, in distressing numbers, sleep under bridges, beg, wander the streets confused and in rags, until picked up, with a bit of relief, by the police. That kind of "solution" is sheer cruelty. Thoughtful philanthropists have created villages with stand-in parents for orphaned children. Surely something of the kind can be devised for those who cannot live in our society, through no fault of their own.

The aged who are well off in finance and relatives, can manage through individual choices including well-run homes with maximum independence. But at this time it is unrealistic to expect the indigent and lonely to do the same; they are at the mercy of good and bad operators. And it is, under present circumstances, unrealistic and damaging to expect those families which exist for them to take the aged into their own home, coping with Alzheimer's, seeing mental deterioration day by day, keeping a close watch on wanderers, changing the incontinent. Parents have the responsibility to bring up their own children, and many have to do this while engaged in two or more jobs. Some try very hard, but it can be a recipe for disaster. Institutional arrangements are unavoidable. But they require long-term re-thinking, especially for those who are not able to afford to pay themselves. (Paradoxically, the increased creative non-employment that I advocate, coupled with guaranteed income, may make the home environment more adaptable to the care of the infirm, the unstable, and the elderly.)

Personally, if I were to face such institutionalisation for myself I would favour mixed institutions, composed of units each catering to a different set of circumstances. I would not wish to be segregated into a home "for the aged" (though that may be necessary!), defined as such, and patronised as such. I would miss the mix of individuals who constitute society. I would opt for something like a village, yet close to urban facilities (if I were mobile). Parts of the village for fellows like me, parts for the physically disabled, parts for the mentally disturbed, parts for day to day workers, parts for a community clinic, parts for orphans, parts perhaps for the alienated juveniles. About fifty per cent, let us say, without any noticeable problems, and the other fifty per cent struggling with their handicaps and illnesses. Speaking for myself, I want to be in contact with youth, for I find that rejuvenating and challenging.

Within such a community I would like to see the segmentation modified through service. There are roles to be performed by each of the categories, there are self-improving and self-reinforcing tasks to be done. Almost every single kind of disability can be turned around and redefined to become useful to others. (In the city where I live there are, for example, two private restaurants, one of which trains individuals with mental limitations to work effectively as cooks and waiters and cashiers; and another which trains ex-convicts. Both have a high success rate in occupational placement.[44]) The elderly can help the young, the mentally disabled escort the physically disabled, both young and old can perform work—often as volunteers—in the clinics, library, other services, and so on.

I would like to touch upon an increasingly significant aspect of therapy, which is the role of alternative therapies. In my sceptical mode I see most of them as unproven, possibly of great value, and sometimes dangerous. One of the confusing realities is their sheer number, the confusing array of differing techniques and claims. More and more, individuals resist the biomedical model, psychiatry, and psycho-analysis for therapy, and search for other modes.

Sometimes the search is based on weak ideological premises, uninformed, desperate and dogmatic. In my view, this applies to the proposition, for example, that "natural remedies, because they are natural, are better than manufactured ones." As a general rule, this cannot be. For example, acetasylic acid (A.S.A.) is a compound found in willow bark, the latter frequently used in folk remedies. Scientists discovered that A.S.A. was one of the active ingredients in the bark, and were able to manufacture pure compounds. In the decades that followed, much was learned about A.S.A., including its side effects as well as its benefits.

The difference between swallowing A.S.A. tablets and absorbing willow bark is that with A.S.A. you know much more about what you are getting, and you know that whatever effects it has can be attributed to A.S.A. With willow bark the ingredients are complex and mixed. There is more than just A.S.A. If something goes wrong you do not know for sure what ingredient is responsible; and because there are many compounds involved the chances of something going wrong are increased. This is true of all natural products, save those which are manufactured into purity. So, inherently they are less, not more, controllable than manufactured pills.

The components of reputedly beneficial natural and folk medicines are far from being totally studied. What is it about garlic? ginseng? (I happen to consume both). We know something, but not very much. There are thousand of such remedies available, some still to be brought to the attention of science. It would be foolish either to reject these out of hand or to assume as a matter of faith that they do what we expect them to do without other effects.

The role of alternative therapies is even more complex. Men and women must be in charge of their bodies. They cannot simply hand them over to specialists. It is impossible for them to know all they must know to make decisions, so they must turn to specialists for knowledge, and then try to make their own judgements. In our Utopia, the availability of knowledge would be greater and better communicated, and in Youth Maturity Institutes we would have learned to make more informed data and explanatory judgements. Medical practitioners would not keep their knowledge locked up, and the media would be more careful and accurate in what they report. The Internet changes openness, but we must be able to select the gold from the chaff. That happy state is not here yet.

With exceptions, the more desperate people are, the more they search. The more insoluble their problem is, the more desperate and searching they are likely to be. Handbooks of alternative therapies list hundreds. Some, like acupuncture, have been drawn partly into mainstream medicine, though in my opinion sometimes with modifications (shortness of training time and complexity of analysis) that may detract from its original efficacy. Others have no college of supervision, have their basic premises (e.g. those of chiropractic) challenged and competed for by other schools, or require absolutely no training. It seems easy for practitioners of such arts to skirt the law by not claiming to practice "medicine".

The most dramatic examples are those which deal with the mind and the emotions. Alternative magazines must list thirty to forty competing approaches to emotional, spiritual, personal healing, disguised as "counselling", including family, marriage, and personal counselling. The "success rate" is seldom if ever reliably measured by controlled methods. Some unethical clinics create dependencies and use mind control. Individuals in this kind of trouble are extremely vulnerable and open to suggestion. With exceptions that are unfortunately difficult to identify, they can reinforce the very problems they tackle and create others. There is nothing so dangerous to the persona as the half-knowledgeable interference with the mind. And such therapies, even the most established, are not even half-knowledgeable.

Yet the need is clearly there. If they are working from a massive data base of ignorance, so too, when it comes to the mind, does conventional medical science. It is not surprising that individuals, coached by the media and by the cultural climate of problem reinforcement, are anxious, depressed, hurt, and desperate to find both remedies and *explanations,* turning from one school to another in an endless quest.

Meanwhile, poor Utopia. It may be that the Youth Maturity Institutes will enable individuals to be more secure in their judgements, and that knowledge will, most probably, improve dramatically. In the meantime, however, the clinics I have proposed above might very well open their doors to selected alternative approaches. This would at least give an opportunity to relate differing approaches one to another, to monitor, and to learn, as well as giving patients more freedom of choice.

It is now evident that in this Chapter I am bringing crime and illness together. There are three strands to this exercise.

Both crime and illness are culturally defined. Neither are defined by nature, although we have been accustomed to thinking of illness as a natural pathology. An illness, disease, has to be identified (however unscientifically), named, and culturally recognised as requiring some remedial action, from isolation or banishment of the victim to therapy. Each decade brings the recognition of new constellations of symptoms which were there all the time but which hitherto did not come into this category. Repetitive Movement Disability Syndrome (have I got the name right?) is one of the latest. Some forms of aberrant behaviour are regarded as eccentricities, some as illnesses, some as misdemeanours if not crimes. There is a great deal of variation amongst the populace as to what fits what categories. Sometimes the definition is therapy-driven. For example, new drugs such as Prozac make it possible to define non-extreme depressions as remediable illnesses.

There has always been a cross-over between crime and illness. The long and the short of it is that some would say that *any* anti-social act is evidence of a disturbance that can be thought of as illness. The issue then becomes, can it, ought it, to be treated, and how, and with what chance of success? Not very different from the way we try to deal with AIDS.

Then there are those illnesses that are brought about by deliberate risk-taking—smoking, drugs, alcohol in excess—until they become addictions. Insofar as they start out deliberately as a matter of choice, they can be fingered as having a criminal component. And are not some criminals *addicted* to their crimes, like a drunk or a smoker?

It seems as though the definitions may be in process of merging. If this results in better attention to therapy for offenders, so much the better. Smokers, who, knowing the consequences, start smoking, are sick criminals. So are those who *start* taking drugs, robbing, gambling, using violence.

Even now, and the more so as the merging proceeds, there are major similarities in the handling of defined crime and defined illness, of which the most notable is institutionalisation. The amelioration of institutional approaches and the treatment of "crime" as a tort, and repetitive "crime" as an illness will bring the two sets of remedies even more closely together.

Crime and illness are destined to coalesce. That, indeed, is the civilised, Utopian way. Let us hasten the process.

VII

Community and Diversity

In contemporary large-scale societies it is common for the individual to feel "lost", little more than a tiny atom in a global universe over which he or she has no control. Just as worrying, there is a feeling of helplessness, an inability to influence the course of events. This is a relative matter. Someone in much smaller sixteenth century London, especially if arriving from the countryside, had to find a way, to adjust, and without doubt felt a small spoke whose task it was to attach himself to the large wheel.

It is this feeling which inhibits conscious moves towards Utopia. We leave it to the politicians. But we have already noted that individuals *do* have power. Time and again in this argument I will be referring to ways to identify that power, and to make it count.

The human psyche has ways of counter-balancing such impersonalisation. In North American culture, and increasingly in other large scale conurbations, therapists lead the way in demanding that we "know ourselves", that we try to understand who we are and how we as individuals got there. As a result of therapy, or because of their own inner strengths (which were in culture before most modern therapy was invented), many individuals do find their way to a personal balance. They use their inner tensions to spur them to action, whether that be politics, warfare, entrepreneurship, intellectual activity, loving or isolated meditation. These and similar values enter into the profiles of culture and their individual demand schedules.

The other methods of "finding one's self" and counterbalancing the alienating effects of atomisation existed long before contemporary therapy, which mostly ignores them. In parenthesis it may be observed that traditional societies have been rich in therapies that are oriented to the most powerful of the everlasting methods, namely identification with community. Humans place so much value on identification with others that it may be regarded as biologically induced and culturally defined. Individuals who are so self-reliant or so troubled that they do not want to associate with others we regard as aberrant, eccentric, driven, or emotionally disturbed, states sometimes justified by resultant religious fervour or worldly success.[45]

Two methods I distinguish are the reinforcement of links within a specific culture, and the entry into group-associations. (I use the phrase "group-association" because the groups are not necessarily formally organised. A regular bridge party may serve the purpose as well as a Rotary Club meeting.)

The neglect of much therapy to take this into account is curious and only partly explained by another phenomenon. Throughout known history, but very much increasing in scale nowadays, is the drive to *escape* the group or culture of origin. Individuals express their maturity, adult independence, risk taking, and curiosity by moving away from the parental family, more and more into paths that are strange territories to the mother and father. While some children opt for some form of continuity today, most do not. The phenomenon is a well known source of strain amongst, for example, Asian families with children growing up in Europe or the Americas, though some Asian families are most adept at redefining and retaining old ties with new practical functions.

Early students of development suggested that the breakdown of the family and traditional culture (particularly in its religious aspects) was not merely a concomitant but a *necessary* condition for urbanisation, globalisation, industrialisation and economic maturity. They may be forgiven for being wrong. Such breakdowns were at most temporary results of those processes. Where individuals had the psychological and cultural means, they took steps to *re-invent* affinities and groups.

Nevertheless perhaps therapy is recognising or suggesting, by concentrating on the individual persona, that individualisation is an evolutionary trend. I cannot be sure that this is wrong. But for my part I suggest two things: if we are to influence the direction of evolution, we do not want that trend to be a total outcome. We do not want such a trend because in its extreme position it is the epitome of selfishness and of the denial of the validity of the other. There is also considerable evidence that the opposite is occurring. As many people become better off, they devote increasing proportions of their income to group identity and to ceremonial.

Paradoxically we do not want a society in which individuals have to feel uncomfortable in themselves when they decide to be isolated for positive reasons, to be loners. And we do wish to place a value on the adaptability of individuals to move from one culture or sub-culture to another. One of my earliest strong impressions of the United States was the flexibility and adaptability of individuals moving from one kind of work to another, and from one part of the country to another, and the way in which society and employers sometimes tried (not always with success) to smooth such transitions. At one time it was also a characteristic of the British Commonwealth, at least for its white citizens who could move almost seamlessly from one country to another, a characteristic that I personally felt was destroyed with the growth of the trappings of nationalism and the realization that to be a New Zealander in Canada was no longer a smooth transition.[46]

The purpose of this Chapter, however, is to look more directly at the issues of community and association in themselves.

Humanity is characterised by the fact that its communities, brought together by descent, then reinforced by the needs of material survival and defence, were and are never totally self-bounded. The earliest boundaries, and those of the most isolated tribes, were marked by distrust of strangers, but also, as sophistication increased, by elementary exchange, and the capture of territory, land, humans—in other words, contact that implied some movement across the boundary. This led early anthropologists to seek for information about the relative force of internal evolutionary innovation on the one hand, and diffusion on the other. The diffusionists tended to win the day

In the present context diffusion is inescapable. Community is still defined by boundaries, but those boundaries are permeable, highly variable one to another and over time. Today, one can even be a member of more than one community, through marriage and migration.

It is worth noting for a moment the nature of the movement across boundaries. First there is marriage. The endogamy inherent in many communities is breaking down, and some communities, such as some Swiss communes, were by preference exogamous (the in-marrying woman retaining her family name and rights to the property of her commune of origin). In other words, there is now more movement of people across the boundaries.

Migration reinforces that movement. It does not necessarily mean a break with the community of origin; that is a matter of choice. East Indians often travel "home" to India or Uganda or Fiji, just as early British migrants travelled "home" to England, Wales or Scotland. Young immigrant children re-discover the forgotten language of their parents, and travel to meet unknown relatives; adults keep in contact with their parents and villages. Many Chinese migrants have family lineal ties all over the world—it is not uncommon to have contacts established in Hong Kong or Taiwan, Peru, Canada, Britain, contacts that can be used for purposes of commerce, education, migrant support. Swiss abroad maintain their required military service, do not lose their communal rights, and have rights of elected representation and social security.

A recent Canadian Broadcasting Corporation documentary exemplified the dynamic adjustment of boundaries. It as about Rankin Inlet, a largely isolated Northern Arctic town. Third World immigrants, finding it difficult in the cities, are sometimes encouraged to use their skills in such places. Such was the case with a Filipino woman nurse and a Somali male teacher. From almost opposite ends of the earth they created a nucleus of friendship based on the discovery and daily application of shared values derived from their native cultures and their experiences in the alien, becoming normal, frigid land. A new cultural ethnogenesis?

Across the boundaries flow exchanges, commerce, and above all ideas. The religious innovations in Melanesian communities (both traditional and prophetic) owe much to adapting what is observed elsewhere. We need not spend time on the obvious force of the principle in modern-world communities.

Modern communications, when present, facilitate movement across the boundaries. Much commentary has stressed that this moves in the direction of a single global culture (perhaps American dominated). Yes and no; not quite.[47] Ease of communication permits several things. There is a certain core of ideas which becomes global. Slowly but surely all parts of the world arrive at inter-communication. That is, one may communicate from or to a culture without leaving the home culture. As communication becomes faster and less expensive, there is a move towards equalisation; there is no *technical* reason even now why a village in the depths of Burkina-Faso cannot be in touch with the World Wide Web or the Paris stock exchange. Funds for the infrastructure are not sufficiently there now, but that is only a matter of time. The technique and matériel of communication will be global; so no doubt will be the language. The village in Burkina-Faso will have its culture dramatically changed. On the other hand it will have the resources, the education, to reinforce and protect those elements in its way of life that it values, and to call on other communities with like-minded priorities.

Wealth and communication change culture, there is no doubt of that. But whether it is to the detriment or in reinforcement of culture is a matter of choices. Take note.

British Columbia Indian communities, mostly destitute and thoroughly demoralised during the 'twenties to 'fifties, have revived their traditional spirituality and expanded ceremonial. They are in fact exporting and diffusing elements of their ideas to others, through art and spirituality. There has been an explosion of innovative art based on traditional ideas, far beyond tourist junk, such as major art collectibles with adaptations into high style clothing and jewellery. Political skills have been honed, languages re-learned, education adapted, all with pride in community, expressed as nation-hood.

In Europe, think of the re-invention and restitution of community reinforcing ceremonials. Medieval football in Florence, the horse races of Siena, carnival in Basle, bull fighting in the South of France, Romany lore, all at one time forbidden or predicted to die. The list can be extended throughout the world, wherever people have resources to expand what they believe in, and the choice to direct their energies. Some activities spread. The dragon boats of Hong Kong, which are community-oriented there, have given rise to associations and international tourneys from Vancouver to Germany, in each case with its own community roots as well as the global spread.

At another level, sociologists have long measured associations and participation in them. Every major centre of population has a myriad. It is a major sociological task to map the cross-hatching of individual membership, relating it to other cross-hatching themes such as income, religion, cultures, professions, education, and the like. Thnk of the groups to which you in some way belong or with which you identify; and think of the additional ones you could belong to or identify with. This is an urbanisation, modernisation, phenomenon, applicable in all dynamic parts of the world.

Behind these phenomena are straight-forward principles. People value association with others and gain reinforcement of their own values and self-identity by doing so. The personal linkages created give some force to the otherwise helpless. In the massive-scale world, they provide small-scale fields of activity.

The individual plays within a set of rules, dealing with limited possibilities, rather than the hugeness of infinite choice. Those who like to follow can follow, those who like to lead have the chance to do so. One can be influential instead of kow-towing to the boss. Perhaps, even, ideas are welcome. And one, usually, can get out at will.

Many do. They change their loyalties. Even communities find this. Loyalty to community is being re-defined. More and more, where it is retained, it is a matter of choice. In the mobile flexible world of the present, even in hitherto untouched areas of the Third World, communities cannot *bind* their young people. There was once a dictatorial, authoritarian aspect to communities, a restrictive approach to norms, morality, and activity that is no longer appropriate in this world of choice. Many, especially in rural areas, are finding that their existence is threatened as their economies are no longer viable in the older way.

But communities are far from dead. They are being redefined. The old parishes and communes of Europe continue, notably in Italy, Germany and Switzerland.

In modern cities without centuries of history, neighbourhoods begin to have community meaning. Such a city is Vancouver, only about 150 years in age, where geography creates scores of niches, separated by microclimates, ravines, coastline, mountains, highways, ethnicity and lifestyle. Developers and planners touch such neighbourhoods at their peril, defensive associations lobby and protest; where neighbourhood and ethnicity coalesce festivals and celebrations turn into newly formed tradition. In older cities such as London or Paris immigrant populations add to the mix of identities, with strong definition. In rural areas, small towns and villages, afraid of dying, turn their creative thoughts to new ways of establishing continued viability. Sometimes they are at least temporarily destroyed by incorporation into suburbia—the Netherlands seem like one huge suburb, with commuters criss-crossing like tribes of ants, yet I doubt if what are in effect suburban neighbourhoods entirely lose touch with their historical individuality. The United States and France, both considered to be "melting-pot" nations, are honeycombed with definably different communities and neighbourhoods.

Modern technology does not necessarily interfere with their creation. There are small communities in the United States literally built around the reality of cyberspace. Though small as communities they are the location of firms engaged in computer hardware and software production. The homes, local government, hospitals, emergency services, library and schools are linked by fibre optic cable and e-mail, binding them.

Per Norback, in his contribution to the 2004 World Utopian Competition, describes his initiative in binding together the youth of the small community of Vallentuna in Sweden through e-mail. The focus was to use the tool as a way of discussing local policy issues. E-mail bound together young people who found they had a common interest in their community, an interest that was merely dormant before. In discussing issues they formulated policies and created a "non-political" political party which elected a member to the local council.[48]

The sense of belonging may affect only a small proportion of the community/neighbourhood population in normal times; indeed another characteristic of many is internal divisiveness, fighting over what the community means, arguments over policy and definition. When it comes to cultural self-expression, thinking about the future, communities of the new kinds have major creative impulses. Cultural events used as identifiers, or perhaps there is the revitalisation of a declining neighbourhood. They are not necessarily organised into formal local government. There is a spontaneity which brings the notions of community and association together. There is also a perfect opportunity for power trips, the kind of domination and argumentation that the involved individuals could not express in large firms or major government.

Such developments are not necessarily progressive. Many are the communities which resist, for example, the placement of therapeutic institutions in their midst—half-way houses, homes for the mentally disturbed, "social housing" for the poor, drug rehabilitation centres, abortion clinics. Communities, however, are not all-powerful, and should not be. There needs to be a counter-balance to the potential of communities to insist on total conformity. One of these, of course, is the existence of higher levels of government, about which more later. Another is the increasing ability of individuals to move to and live in the communities of choice, and to leave those they find unpleasant. A third is, to some extent, the growth of varying democratic practices, though these can create rigidities and do not always ensure liberty, and may exclude newcomers from participation. (Witness the urban Swiss commune which insisted that a building, ten centimetres higher than code allowed, be restructured or torn down . . .)

At present many parts of the world are going through a revival of the bane of ethnic intolerance. This is not a part of my personal Utopia. My personal delight in ethnic variation is tempered by my realisation that there are limits to my own tolerance, and reinforced by the functional value of ethnic difference under appropriate conditions. Ethnic difference is the most visible indicator of cultural difference. It is an indicator that is grossly misleading, in that cultural differences that are just as strong exist in modern societies without ethnicity, in its popular sense, being a factor at all. The lumberjack and the doctor, the fisherman and the rock musician, the academic and the money market trader, each have ideas, symbols, values, modes of behaviour—that is aspects of culture—which are unique to their colleagues, which they do not share easily with the wider world. In any given society they constitute at least sub-cultures. In some instances they have more in common with similar professionals in other countries than they have with many of their own fellow-citizens.[49] In other words, cultural differences permeate society, often without consciousness of what those differences are. Ethnicity in its full sense is only one such cultural binding and differentiating force.

Furthermore, nowadays, none of the cultures are bounded within nation States. Patterns of migration and ex-colonial boundaries have resulted in kaleidoscopic patchworks, international travel and communication link members of most sub-cultures together in world-wide webs. Jazz, "world", and symphonic music are spoken almost world-wide.

Within the patchworks and the global networks, differences continue in modified forms. An anthropologist cannot assume that Sicilians in London, New York and Toronto have the same culture and patterns of behaviour as their forebears in Sicily, or indeed as each other. Each experience brings about a cultural variant. If one were to count cultures one would find that, along these lines, the number of cultures is growing fast, possibly exponentially.

Contrary to popular belief and ideology, political nationalism in the nineteenth century was less a liberation of "national cultures" than a centralising move to control variation. Centralising France, Italy, the Netherlands, England, Prussian Germany, forced in varying ways the adoption of a single language upon culturally and linguistically different communities. In France, Italy, Spain, Canada (even excluding the Québec issue) and Britain, to name just five countries, there are enormous resentments which continue, and sometimes grow, to this day. Only in the early 1990's did Alsace gain the right to teach Alsatian dialect in schools, or expand the teaching of High German, rights which are still fiscally restricted by the centralised organisation of French education. In all countries where nationalism was the rallying cry there are wondrous literatures, often comic and satirical, about the ways in which the dominant elites reinforce their arrogance with blindness.[50]

Indeed, I would go so far as to say that the difference between a State and a tribe is that the latter is culturally uniform, whereas the former gains its character through the ways in which it includes within itself populations of *different* culture. Anthropologists who look for the processes that created States from tribes identify economo-technical factors, such as the administrative requirements of irrigation or of settled agriculture. My theory is complementary rather than competitive with such explanations. It states that, for whatever other cause, tribes found themselves in the position of having to handle other kinds of people in sufficient numbers so that an administration was forced upon them. Bantu "kingdoms" are a case in point since they were historically observed in a phase of large land expansion, driven by northern forces to move onto land already settled by others. Their military organisation had to deal with the original settlers as part of their society, and used regimental outposts for control, defence, aggression, keeping rambunctious young men occupied, and cultural inter-dependence. The increasing scale and demands on wealth gave rise to forms of taxation and fiscal organisation.

To the extent that I am right, ethnic cleansing is a return to tribalism, a nasty glitch compromising our move to Utopia. And of course if effective it slows the rate of dynamism and innovation, as I advocated in Chapter II.

The events of the 1990's, continuing into the present century, have shown us the serious dangers that cultural intolerance can produce. We may have partially overcome the extreme excesses that typified Nazism. But catastrophes in Rwanda, Darfur, ex-Yugoslavia, and the former Soviet Union show that we cannot be complacent; that where ethnic difference is kept in control by central government alone, chaos follows its collapse.

In all instances the fierceness that has erupted is fuelled by geographical confusion and land claims, and the historically false notion that ethnic difference justifies a new national State. In the countries I have mentioned, such purity is impossible to achieve without repressive and horrendous ethnic cleansing. The ideology the leaders have used is historically and socially false. Nation States gain their identity and strength *from the ways they handle the reality of differing cultures within their borders*. The United States is "American" in large part because of the way it handles large populations of ethnically differentiated immigrants and centuries-old settlers. France is French because of the way it handles language and the Alsatians, Bretons, Languedociens within its borders. Britain is Great Britain, largely because of the Welsh, Irish and Scots, and even more, the Cornish and Yorkshiremen, and now the waves of immigrants. Switzerland is Switzerland because . . . Canada is Canadian . . . And so on.

Extreme ethnic hostility used to be blamed on poverty. It is still a major factor, for example in the Middle East. But it has a great deal to do with land claims and with the mind. Land claims mix with centuries old history, and intersect with family relationships. It is noteworthy that in the most dangerous parts of Europe, the Balkans, social rivalries, competitiveness, and strict views about "honour" were and are expressed, not through the consensual problem-solving I have referred to in Chapter VI, but through continued hostility and the institutionalised idea of vengeance. Blood feud, in other words. Land, sex as property, and violence constitute a potent explosive. Ethnicity becomes an excuse, not a cause. It is an excuse in which violence breeds violence, allowing the unscrupulous to attain power, to exercise brutality and repression, through the smokescreen of defending their own people by punishing the others.

The 2005 riots in France seemed initially to be ethnicity driven. But it turned out that the mostly young people involved were frustrated and devastated by their inability to rise in the socio-economic order. (*They were mostly NOT immigrants*). Significantly they were the *children* of immigrants, their parents often successful. But French society did not accept them as such, so there was a mixture of poverty, high expectations, and ethnic bias discrimination. It is the same kind of frustration and denied expectation that is part of the classic model of the dynamics of messianic cults in other contexts.

It shows that forms of multiculturalism are highly varied and not in themselves enough to be functional. I say again, there must be cross boundary communication and socio-economic-cultural exchanges to make a variant successful. The patronising stance of French political and cultural elites does not contribute well to this within their own country, although there is more success in welcoming cultural exchanges with persons who may still be counted as representing the "other". Singers, dancers and artists and writers find interaction, especially if they were born elsewhere. The exotic is praised. This is true not only of France, but of England, Italy, Germany, Toronto and Montreal.

But for other kinds of people, and especially for the young who wish to be accepted as were their parents, the same societies preach, if they notice at all, "tough luck'. And a result is ghettoiation of the different young, driven almost mad by boredom and frustration and (relative) poverty. It is not accidental that it took a major hurricane to reveal this soft under-belly of poverty and prejudice in surface-happy Louisiana. The Blues are paeans to despair, not to joy, ultimately a way out and up for the creators.

Significantly, this is not new, but seems to be more intense because of legitimately higher expectations. The Blues are matched by the heart-plucking passions of fado, tango and flamenco, rooted in centuries past cultural deprivations. Spain and Portugal provided contrasts, the one with Castilian superiority over Moors and Indians (the latter not invading the metropolis), the other mass converting slaves and patronising democratic sex and miscegenation. In Britain peoples from the Caribbean, South Asia and other Commonwealth countries rioted, if at all, as part of the distressed countryside or urban workers. Nearly all European countries, to say nothing of the former Anglo colonies, established ghettos not only for Jews but for skilled immigrants practising trades. By the late twentieth century the descendants of such people had achieved upward mobility and contributed to all ranks of life. The ghetto did not stop external communication in such instances, but it took a long time to have a total effect. Utopia can learn from history, and should.

Two differences between much of the past and much of the present stand out. One is that many of the ghettos used their own resources and skills to create not only expectations but success and respect. A clear case has been the long term success of Chinese abroad, with their supportive networks, now, in places like Vancouver, no longer ghetto-ised. Much the same can be said for Ismailis escaping Uganda, Armenians, Scots, Welsh and Irish. Can those from the Middle East, Africa and Latin America create a similar fate and use cross-ethnic and inter-ethnic communication to innovate and prosper? It is not generally recognized that the upper echelons of Swiss success, which is historically quite recent, made use of a high number of key immigrants interacting with a Swiss diaspora. If Switzerland were more open to an influx from the world, it might regain that dynamic,.

Religion, and the fables of the mind are just as potent. Serbs, Croatians, and Muslims in ex-Yugoslavia, as well as other peoples, are, depending on your criteria, themselves an ethnic hodge-podge of numerous smaller units. They also have unities of culture—the Serbian and Croatian languages differ mostly in the alphabet used and primary religious adherence. Those differences have historical roots. The central European plains were from prehistoric times the routes of invaders, who left behind them patchworks of ethnically different populations. The latest Grand Invasion was that of the Turks[51], who introduced coffee, much of Balkan cooking, a little religion (Muslims in those days were largely tolerant and non-proselytising.) Where the Turks administered, Eastern religions and the Cyrillic alphabet prospered; where they did not there was Roman Catholicism.

Again, religion is a rallying cry. It is a magnificent tool to organise the masses, and sometimes it can be regarded as causative. But in ex-Yugoslavia, a country which in recent years has been characterised by inter-marriage and religious tolerance, I doubt if religion and language would have established the current rule of force had it not been for land and the culture, especially in Bosnia, of blood-feud.

What then of Utopia? In counteracting the excesses it is necessary to make a choice. If we believe that such excesses are an inherent part of ethnic and cultural difference, we might be well advised to do everything in our power to limit, even destroy, it and create a homogeneous, every-one-the-same global melting pot. This, at least locally, is the rallying cry of many majority ethnic populations who feel that their dominance is threatened by immigration and difference. (It is interesting to note that such populations do not use the word "ethnic" to refer to themselves, but only to minorities. In Canada we have "ethnic" restaurants, which means "of a different style", not recognising that the dominant Canadian cultures are also "ethnic".)

But if we believe that cultural difference is valuable, as I do, we must make clear wherein that value resides.

Cultural diversity is necessarily valuable to the global Utopia in itself. When cultures turn in upon themselves they become a source of prejudice, false information about the value of others, dogmatism, and static control of individuals, even brainwashing. They can become fanatic and potentially aggressive if the inward turning changes to external action.

Once again, the indicators are at the boundary. To what degree and in what ways are there movements of ideas, values, matériel and individuals across the boundaries? If such movements are infinite, we can hardly talk about a discrete culture; it would not exist. A culture implies some limitation of cross-boundary movement in practice, if not in ideology. A culture, or sub-culture, suggests that there is more movement in the networks within the boundary than across it. As I have pointed out, professions and similar value—and network—centred groups have such characteristics, and can be called non-ethnic sub-cultures. From this it follows that individuals can, in this world, belong to several cultures or sub-cultures at once.

That phenomenon establishes different boundaries for individuals for different purposes. What may be restrictive in one context may be opened up to communication in another. A Muslim woman's purdah may be modified by her membership in a medical professional sub-culture. It is next to impossible for a culture to have unmodified boundaries in the modern world.

Such modifications, which still allow a culture to retain its integrity, its sense of unity and of difference with respect to others, are worthwhile. They permit ideas and symbols to flow across the boundaries. They enrich the cultural pool that is available to mankind as a whole.

A major primary benefit comes when we consider cultures to be experiments in living. No culture has all the answers to life, and never will. (The last statement follows from my premise in Chapter XIV knowledge, by its nature, is imperfect.) Varying cultures give us an opportunity to note how others approach problems we ourselves have. We may not like what we see. But even then we are challenged to think about, to reappraise, what we ourselves do, and to evaluate alternatives. There is a sense in which the excitement and stimulus of travel can be replicated in our own cities. The enquiring mind can seek explanations for differences in norms, and perhaps learn from them. My discussion of crime learned from the way it is handled in some other cultures.

Another fundamental benefit comes from the fact that, by definition, more cultures mean more ideas, more concepts, a greater variety of activity. To the extent that knowledge of this increased pool circulates, that is crosses cultural boundaries, the greater the rate of innovation. As I pointed out in Chapter II, the more ideas there are, the more they interact, the more they combine to create new ones.

Cultural diversity contributes to the process. You don't believe me? Here is a hodge-podge of examples. The Swiss chemical industry received its inaugural jump start out of the observations of Swiss in India (dyes); the watch industry from the movement of Huguenots from France; the chocolate industry from a combination of Swiss and American ideas; the metallurgical and heavy engineering from Swiss and German; early banking through inputs from Germany and France; aesthetics from the interplay of individuals and resources rooted in the varied Swiss cultures. How could British textiles in the nineteenth century have evolved if Britain had been an island in isolation? Diasporas, in which individuals and families have been forced into contact with other dominant cultures, created commerce that provided inter-cultural links. Asian students, driven by family values and respect for thought, outbid their less-driven North American co-students for places at computer terminals, often in their early twenties establishing new enterprises or moving on to scientific research. There is nothing automatic about such relationships and results. That is not the point. The point is that the *chances* of innovative results are higher when inter-cultural contacts take place. Once again, it is not always ethnic. Interactions and synergies between professional and discipline sub-cultures have similar effects.

Under appropriate circumstance, then, cultural diversity is to be welcomed. It is appropriate for our Utopia. Furthermore, cultural diversity constitutes a kind of data base out of which our thoughts about Utopia itself, and about how to get there, will emerge.

It is important to stress and encourage the functional rather than the dysfunctional aspects of such variance. We must not be starry-eyed. If we close our eyes to the strains of some immigration, for example, we will be disappointed and damaged. The right wing French politician Le Pen, building his career on fear and hate, is evidence of damage. Yet we must recognise that behind that fear and hate there are real problems, of which they are the symptoms.

Some of the North Africans who move from the rigid, sexually disturbed and pathological niches of their societies into the free-wheeling self-expression of France naturally have difficulty handling their frustrations in acceptable ways. The following is merely one of many such incidents I observed in Paris. A North African fruit and vegetable store. A beautiful and openly attractive French woman is a customer, from her point of view, on friendly terms with the North Africans. She discusses the produce, smiles at them, her body revealing, for she comes here often and feels natural. The North Africans serve her with polite but embarrassed energy. As they do so, they talk amongst themselves in their language, and when she leaves they burst out into lively comment, hands and eyes suggestively moving. They turn to me and tell me how they would love to fuck her and put their hands on explicit parts of her body. Their frustrated sexual tension is enormous. It seemed far greater than the ribald jocularity, more openly offensive than macho men might employ when a pretty woman walks past a work site.

That sort of thing, intensely frustrating, is potentially explosive. Two cultures touching, neither understanding the other, poles apart in their mix of values. Stereotypes emerge. Just as men's locker rooms are stereotyped as places of ribald jocularity that are totally offensive in other contexts, so many French—and others—stereotype North Africans—and others.

There is a strong obligation for immigrants to understand the source of stereotypes. For this they need help. Tired, exhausted, traumatised refugees cannot be expected to absorb the theory of adjustment. Other immigrants seek the support of being with members of their own culture, a support that is often essential for survival, but thereby losing some adjusting contact with the wider society. It is not simply a matter of understanding the mechanics of shopping and dealing with authority. It is learning what words, gestures, attitudes, points of view will be interpreted as offensive—a difficult line to convey in adjustment education, since the integrity of viewpoint of the immigrant must also be understood and respected.

By the same token, it is essential for receiving cultures to avoid a static view of what they are. Intolerant anti-immigrants, racist or not, in Britain, France, Germany, Italy, Canada, the United States . . . make much of the "threat to our traditional values." To do this they must ignore history. Late twentieth century Britain does not have the same spectrum of values that applied in the nineteenth or even the early twentieth century. The values of Canada and the United States, whatever they are, emerged out of differing experiences of immigrant interplay. Americans often, rightly, puzzle over why Canadians should feel different from them. In North America, to follow the traditionalist anti-immigrant line would logically imply accepting pre-Columbian Indian cultural values and ways of life . . .

Too often the majority way of acknowledging respect of other cultures in their midst is to encourage "harmless cultural expression" by way of folkloric dances, costumes and foods. This again can be stereotypical. Quaint. It avoids the deeper questions. What do people want in their lives? It is never just money. Money is merely an expression for something else. What do they love? How do families enjoy themselves? What do they think of as being creative? What do they think of as being bad? What are their hopes and their nostalgias? What is it that develops pride in themselves, accomplishment, a sense of failure? How do they perceive the socialisation of children? What is the place of religion, alternative medicine, fear, in their lives? So much more.

Utopia will make the utmost use of differing values and cultures, seeking not tolerance but *understanding*, preaching not one solution to the structures of multi-cultural society, but many.

Whatever we say, increased communication will induce cross-cultural knowledge. Youth Maturity Institutes will have to encourage understandings, without preaching the adoption of different cultures; and to reveal the nature of stereotypes and the difficult realities that lie behind them. Utopia will also be frank about difficulties of adjustments, identifying inner tensions, and the conflicts of values that contain the seeds of danger. Management of danger with minimal interference, sometimes a tricky balance, especially when it is tempting for politicians and other leaders to on the dangers for simplistic solutions that bring them unthinking support in the polls. The last phrases do not describe the Utopia towards which we struggle.

VIII

Language, Media and Communication

Never in history has it been possible for Authority, not even the government of France let alone the Académie Française, not even schools, to dictate the practice of language. As a bit of a purist, part of me wishes it could be so, in the interests of clarity and stability. Yet I must recognise that, however grammatical rules, censorship, and courteous customs may sometimes dominate, language consists in the sum total of what individuals actually do. It is the ultimate People Power. With thought, it is the first and last bastion of human freedom.

I sit here with a relatively new Pentium 60 computer, a beautifully clear screen. One of its benefits is that, as I write, my eyes peripherally note a large clear text. Some mistakes jump out at me and I correct them immediately in a manner quite impossible with a typewriter.

In the opening paragraph I had written "some total", an error which prompts me to correct, and also to modify the sequence of topics designed for this Chapter. I use the incident to point out that I could leave it as "some". Publisher's editors, proof-readers, and reviewers would be onto me like a horde of midges. No one, except non-English speakers, would mistake what was meant, although "some" and "sum" are indeed opposed in meaning. Some people could perhaps puzzle for a moment, thinking that it was a different kind of mistake, that I meant "some of the total". They would then have to wonder about the reality the statement was meant to convey.

Such mistakes are frequent in the English language, and frequently result in new practices. Should we, Utopianly, worry? Yes, I think we should, at least from one point of view.

For in Utopia, clarity of communication is required. For clarity of communication we need the meaning of words to be understood by both the speaker (or writer) and the hearer (or reader). And in written work, in which the mind converts the words into interior speech, the use of punctuations gives not only cadence but in doing so can change meaning.[52] This is *not* the *only* requirement of language.

We also need ambiguity. This is achieved in part because every statement has to be interpreted, and there is always slippage. When a sentence is read, the reader places it in the context of others in the same book, in other writings, and that part of his consciousness which is currently prepotent. Certain elements in a sentence or a paragraph stand out, are retained, are used in the mind, others are clouded or slip away. This takes place during the act of reading. After the act or reading we intensify the filtering through the operation of memory. Save for some individuals who have enormous retention powers, most of us find it difficult to re-quote what has just been read, still less an oral or television statement. Discussion with others further modifies our perceptions.

The phenomenon is infuriating to pernickety scholars like myself, to writers and journalists, to public speakers. Never have journalists ever quoted me 100% correctly, and they probably never will, despite the use of recorders.

Ambiguity is also achieved through imprecision in the meanings of words, meanings which change in context, and through the flow of dynamics in which people make mistakes, thus inventing new words or new meanings. (In the sentence above I initially wrote "unfuriating". Not a bad word. I like it. I must find a way of using it.) That ambiguity is, as we know, at the heart of English poetry. The French claim that their language is less ambiguous. I do not agree. It is often more so. *Baiser?* (To kiss or to have sexual intercourse?) *Disparu?* (Disappeared or died?) *Femme?* (Woman or wife?) In these instances, for example, English has clearer distinctions.

The positive side of ambiguity is that it can lead to new thoughts and linguistic enrichment, and that the ambiguities make us think creatively about what is said. If that were not so, we Utopians would be better off creating a totally logical language of mathematical style symbols. There is an aesthetic quality to ambiguity as well, which, when used and received sensitively has the artistic merit of even more ambiguous painting. The use of language is artistic, even in technical reports which have need of more precision. (I feel I do not need to go into minute detail to explain technically what lies behind the preceding sentence. If you do not immediately recognise its validity or otherwise, think about the fact that technical reports are acts of persuasion. I do not want to set up a maze of puzzling statements, but sometimes the provocation of puzzlement is useful to my purpose.) Unfortunately technical reports, and their derivatives, often use imprecise jargon to give a false impression of non-ambiguity, which creates obfuscation or interferes with analytical thought—the dysfunctional extreme of ambiguity. (In my own field, post-modern, neo-colonial, globalisation, economic, are among the many nuisances.)

Aesthetic judgement is a major part of our reaction to a presentation. Flat dull words from a speaker send us to sleep. Each of us reacts differently to the varied styles of novelists or other writers. There will be some—I hope not too many—who will intensely dislike the way I write.

Some of the changes now going on in language I want to resist. Ultimately it will be the users who decide. Yet in a future Utopia I hope that those who have *influence* through teaching, criticism, and the like will make more noise about the significance of dynamics which honour clarity and aesthetic purpose. As individuals, we should support those innovations which enrich, and shudder at the barbaric distortions, just as we shudder openly when a smoker on the street blows fumes into our faces.

I shudder and send a note to the pilot when I hear the announcement "We will be landing momentarily". He is telling me that he is going to touch the ground for a moment and then do something else (take off again?) fast. There is no advantage whatsoever in replacing "in a moment" with a word that means something quite different. There are disadvantages, both aesthetically ("momentarily" is at best jargon-sounding) and, by fusing two inconsistent meanings confusingly onto one word, in terms of clarity.

Similarly, although perhaps with a very small modicum of excuse, the North American rediscovery of the old meaning of "alternate" is too bad to be acceptable. There are two opposing ideas based on the same root. One means that two different events occur in sequence one after the other. The other means that there are two different possibilities, such that either one could be adopted in the *given* interval of time. A confusion arises because "alternate" used to mean the second and "alternative" the first, whereas in recent history "alternate" means the first, as in alternator, and "alternative" means there is a choice. Recently there has been a huge, in my view mischievous, slippage in North America toward the adoption of "alternate" to mean the choice, without at the same time changing the meaning of "alternative". The result is the worst of the whole world of words—confusion as to the meaning of "alternate" without adding any aesthetic ambiguity and the failure to reserve a word for the meaning "one after the other". When I hear such usage I immediately brand the user as an insensitive illiterate, which doesn't do his or her message any good.

In the course of an argument the fepeson child accidentally sat on the chair who happened to be a worperson. "Ms ms ms" (it) cried out, "I am gender-challenged and require more respect. The question is, may I remind you, do we or do we not admit into our caucus our age-challenged brothers and sisters?" "No point in fucking around" said the feperson child, "The Caucus of Pre-schoolers is demanding to be heard. They consider their name to be discriminatory and age-biased, and they demand Class 5 certificates because they are just much huperchildren as them in Class 5." "The international imperialist-colonialist capitalists call intimacy between brothers and siblings incestuous," intervened a male displaying minimalist clothing, "but I think it is overdue and we need compensation for parents' responsibility for child abuse." "Ho, ho, here we go" the audience chanted enthusiastically. "Hold on," cautioned another, "Can we be sure the pigs won't inmate us? If they do, mightn't we get to be co-opted?"

The jargon of political correctness is anti-Utopian. Its worst offence is to deliberately replace thought with slogans, examination with jargon. It is aesthetically crude with no linguistic sensitivity and a simplistic approach to the socio-cultural context of language. It is thoroughly inconsistent both within its terminology and in the use of words to achieve its aims. "Chairwoman" recognises gender equality with "chairman"; "Chairperson" denies the existence of women as well as men, and "chair" reduces the function to an object to be sat upon (which it often is) while "son" in person carries a masculine connotation that so far has been permitted. There is a tendency to use "male" and "female" instead of "man" and "woman", that is to replace social terminology with the biological. Surely this is the opposite of appropriate politico-social goals? Men and women rise above their biological differences, converting them to social use. Males and females, it seems, are differentiated because of their inescapable biological makeup, driven not even by their cultural sexuality but by their genitals.

I resent the appropriation—for that is the fact—of the word "gay" by homosexuals. I do not mind at all if they say they are happy in themselves, that their spirit is gay. After all, that is what we all want. But as a synonym for homosexual it means that I cannot use the word for the most natural, innocent, and pleasurable of states. I cannot happily announce to the world "God I feel so gay today, isn't it wonderful?" I cannot forgive homosexuals for that debasement, especially since I suspect (without evidence) that its origin was probably bitter and ironic.

The reaction to such linguistic abuses, as I have said, is not in the hands of centralised authority, nor should it be. Nor am I saying that my view should necessarily prevail. Perhaps in Utopia such language will be thought to be beautiful and to express thought accurately. However that may be, my conclusion is that Utopians should stress that language should have aesthetic qualities and be clear. That will come about only by example and by education, by discussion and examination of language by reference to the importance of aesthetics and clarity of thought in a well-balanced life and for effective communication. It will then inevitably be up to individuals to make their choices in their personal use of language. The mobility and flexibility of language will continue. But at least let us state that such sensitivities are part and parcel of the values of our ultimate Utopia.

Most linguists nowadays argue for a kind of linguistic relativism and an anti-grammatical and anti-standard reality based upon what people actually do, especially when they talk. This I can understand, because what people do is close to their hearts, is part of their identity, and it is the breaking of the "rules" which gives language its ability to adapt to ever-changing cultural and societal needs, even those of literary expression.

At the same time, there has to be a balance. Language is shared. If each individual has an extreme form of his or her own personal language there will be no communication. Most of those who find it easy to learn new languages, but who have only the written word to guide them, try to understand the structure before they fit in the vocabulary, in other words, pay attention to the grammar. Only after that can they become sensitive to anti-grammatical usages. (It may be different if they are learning orally.)

There is a good reason for editors to impose conventions on their writers, and to check their expressions. They are concerned with communication, and they want their readers to know what to expect in their magazines or newspapers. When it comes to books, there is now a tendency to impose a structure and style on the author, tearing the text apart and re-writing it to fit a model. That is not accidental. It is what the marketing people know the public will buy and perhaps read. The process has gone furthest in the United States, where "how to" books, especially dealing with healing, spirituality, and interpersonal relations often contain about half a chapter of "message", the rest being easy-to-read padding. Editors who deal with other topics and with literature must draw a finer line, allowing novelty and idiosyncrasy—a "voice"—while keeping an eye open for the possibility of better impact and comprehension. In and out of this, writers emerge who use variations only when they are for effect and verisimilitude, their originality emerging from the refined, apparently easy, style with which they make "the rules" their own effective medium. When we find such books, we hold onto them as things of beauty.

Language is not only communication, but a badge of identity and a symbol of belonging. Societies or cultures which imagine themselves to be under attack, to be in danger of disappearing, hold on to their language. In times of cultural or political regeneration, language, with art, ceremonial, and religion, is among the first aspects of group life to be emphasised. This is why autocratic and centralised regimes attempt to suppress or restrict minority languages, counter-productively adding to their importance.

Apart from political correctness, massive changes are under way that make purists such as myself frown.

One is the emphasis on the short attention span. While psychologists, medical practitioners, therapists, teachers and others are identifying more and more groups of behavioural symptoms as disorder syndromes, and developing treatments for them, culture, almost deliberately, is sometimes negating their efforts. It is difficult to tell, for example, whether the notice being given to Attention Deficit Disorder results from more perceptive analysis, or from increased incidence among both children and adults. I rather suspect the latter. [Note the politically sensitive language. Not "Deficiency", not "Syndrome". Does that succeed in removing suggestions in the terminology that something is humanly wrong? The fact of the matter is that ADD *is* dysfunctional. It requires remedies. Why fudge it?]

Consider what has been happening to young people for about the past forty years. From the advent of rock music, rhythm and louder and louder noise have impinged on their lives in more extreme forms than ever before. Alongside some gentle, sophisticated poetry and angry lamentation, there are messages of incredible despair, naiveté and crudity. Very few, even if they wanted to, can escape the impact, though there are choices as to the style they prefer.

Youth Maturity Institutes have a major task in engendering an appropriately critical view of the data and messages contained in the media. This seems easier to do with respect to print, where there is a long and lively tradition of debate, and a certain cynicism with regard to newspaper agendas. It is much more difficult with television, and now film (which is entering into the politicized debates). Living images contain a drama and persuasiveness which print has never had. "The camera never lies" is an absurd cliché, a lie in itself. Youth must be aware of the ways in which the lies and errors occur.

One problem is that there is no room for rebuttal. I have a great deal of sympathy for the message of the film *The Corporation* and for many of the "documentaries" which are becoming every more popular. But where can I or anyone else insert our modifications, our doubts, our debate? Yet to my mind only if there is an open dialogue will the thesis of the film have legitimacy—and that has to take place in other media. In the meantime, viewer beware. Propaganda is propaganda, whatever the motive.

There is another class of film which requires even more subtle attention, that of the "Docudrama".[53] Here the producers inform the viewer that parts of the story are fiction, but that it is based on fact, and attempts to convey some truth. So far, this is legitimate. What is not said is that the approach *inevitably distorts the truth*. I use the word "inevitably" with great deliberation.

Let us leave aside the accuracy of the facts, which will vary according to the seriousness of the research and the motives of the producer. A docudrama is work of art and as such implies interpretation—by script writer, and above all the actors. They are not automatons. They may do their own research, and try hard, but they are not historians. They give, and must give or it would not be art, their own interpretations. Just as a Museum departs from the original reality, so does a docudrama. This is not to denounce docudramas as an art form. But they should eschew the claim to mirror events, and youth need to learn to approach them cautiously and objectively.

Television and, to a lesser extent newspapers, condense "stories" into two minute, five minute, fifteen minute clips, even when the topic is "educational" or "documentary". There are of course longer series; but these require commitment and attention. Story and speed of presentation are the operative concepts. Stories are not fairy tales. They are episodes in which the dramatic impact is deliberately exaggerated. When I watch or listen to the commentator, my eye always goes into the background, sometimes because this is the only way in which I can determine a cultural context, sometimes because the background scenes are revealing. BBC World News, as received in North America, frequently uses file scenes without identifying them as such. Others use scenes to keep some kind of visual dimension on screen, without the slightest logical or intellectual linkage to the story. The commentator could just as well be on radio, for all the irrelevance of the background images—except for the fact that television recognises, and creates, communication by icon. The face must be seen.

The two motifs are brought together in music videos. In the videos split second scenes follow one upon another like an old movie badly projected. The band, the singer, appear in sequences of opposing mood, clothing, even story-line and degrees of aggression, the speed and unpredictability of the changes violating the mind. Everything is designed to hit the viewer hard, to present the greatest degree of contrast without the opportunity to reflect. Life as represented by videos is one of brutal incompatibilities, without resolution. If there is hope in one of the messages, it is destroyed by the violent rapidity with which the scenes alternate.

There is an assumption in communication psychology that people are capable of and interested in only short attentions spans. To some extent this is true. Are not all of us put off by long-winded television advertisements that go on and on? Do we not start to nod in overly long lectures? It depends largely on our interests. If we *are* interested we are prepared to stay with the topic much longer. Television sports summary clips give brief shots of someone scoring or failing to score. Or of a fight. The rest is ignored, though it may contain the greatest beauty of the game. But those who *are* interested in the sport tune into the channel that broadcasts the whole game, and will put up with much boredom in the process for the overall interest.

What the video industry is doing is to imply that popular music buffs are *not* interested in paying attention. Other methods must be used to create the sensory hook. In doing so they develop, emphasise, place a value upon, the short attention span, and use the iconographic approach to communication. By reinforcing these elements of psychology as recruiting devices for a cult they damage those who are most susceptible and in greatest need of help in becoming accustomed to *long* attention spans.

Some educators don't help. They say, this is a fact of life. Most young people have short attention spans. Therefore design our techniques around that, introduce short attention span methods into the classroom. This is simply not right.

Longer attention spans will come with motivation and interest. Youth Maturity Institutes must cultivate them. If education does not—and the competition is tough—the population will be divided into two—those who can pay attention and give their energies, as a result, to creative pursuits; and those who cannot and who are psychologically distressed as a result, and, worse, cannot communicate or be communicated with in any serious form.

Not in my Utopia . . .

Now that I have one of these multimedia computer systems with drag around icons and drop-down menus and lots of cascading windows and the capacity to import graphics, I have become aware of the way in which television screens are responding to computer methods—those little notes that appear at the bottom of the screen, the way in which messages or icons are placed somewhere or other and moved around.

In their desire to become user friendly, most software is using somewhat standardised messaging techniques to allow the operator to communicate with the machine to tell it what to do. The dreadful manuals, though still not written in comprehensible English, are better than they used to be. But the operator's main help is on the screen. The software people assumed that operators don't like the written word. So they have introduced icons, an icon-based language.

Curiously, if you just look at the icons you have to scratch your head to figure out what they represent. There is a whole library of them waiting to be put on your screen one by one if you decide you are going to use the operation they represent. If you *do* decide to use an operation that is not completely familiar to you and semi-automatic, you must click your mouse on the appropriate icon—but first you must identify it. And how do you do that? You run the mouse over the range of icons, and as it touches each one, guess what, *words appear*. It is words which identify the icon, tell you what it means . . . not the other way around.

I do have to admit that the icons have a use. They decorate the screen (unless you chase the mouse and make them disappear), which is also decorated with the pretty colours you have chosen for background, borders, and so on. It is indeed much more pleasurable to work in that environment than chewing a pencil or clunking a typewriter.

On the other hand some software push the icon idea further. Microsoft, for example, produced a simplified home programme called Bob, in which the commands were represented by cartoon type characters and objects. This may simply be an over-reaction to the illiteracy of earlier manuals. It may be that Microsoft believes that there are illiterate customers they have not yet reached. Interestingly, Bob has not earned popularity—is there a limit to dumbing down?

Or, more worrying, perhaps they have come to the conclusion that their clients of the future will have been brought up on computer games, prefer comics to books, have short attention spans, choose the superficial over the substantive.

The language of computers and Internet is developing rapidly into a global dialect. E-mail uses pictographs formed from combinations of keyboard characters, called "smileys". For example "B-)" [I wear horn-rimmed glasses], ":-)" [the next statement is a joke], ":-[" [vampire], ":-E" [buck-toothed vampire]. Some require even more by way of translation. The following appeared recently in a university computer magazine:

☐ _☐

/ <

` [ ]

^^^^^^ (I've taken up swimming)

Acronyms stand for phrases, e.g. AFAIK=As far as I know; CU=Good bye for now, flame=a message that is inflammatory; HHOK=Ha Ha only kidding; ROTFL=rolling on the floor laughing. Everyday words acquire new specific connotations. "Quit" usually means I am leaving the present menu (which now means a list of alternative commands) and wish to return to the main or previous menu. "Bye" means "I'm hanging up and leaving all you guys." "Menu" means a list of goodies, from which you select commands that move you along in your work or search. "Directory" or "Folder" means a grouping of files, as in a storage drawer. It is not, as you might have expected, a list, although you may entice the screen to produce a list of what is in it. The list of directories that you have created and the files within them is located in a "File Manager". This is because almost anything that comes up on the screen is there to be handled, managed, changed, organised. Thus you not merely see the list but can delete, add, re-arrange, call up. "File" means the selected bunch of data that has a name and pops up on your screen when you name it. It is a "file" because, for example, you can place several documents such as letters within it. Terms such as "upload" and "download" ("up" and "down" having horizontal rather than vertical connotations), "client-server" (on the Internet) are not to be interpreted in common sense ways, but understood only through use.

Now and again newspapers and computer magazines print mini-dictionaries of some common terms. These, however, deal with the basic elements of computer jargon that you might wish to understand before buying or using. They tell you what DOS, Windows, RAM are—they might give you some other words to be equivalent to "cache memory" but seldom explain what its function is. The time has come, however, for a dictionary of computer language, that is, the language you tap out or select with your mouse. Classes in computerese, in my observation, are very poorly set-up. They deal with bits of what is out there, making you progress from one to another, and learn things you don't need to know. It is like teaching you to drive by making you master the mechanics of the engine, the exhaust system, and the car's electronic controls. As a self-taught user I want to operate things, and I find it much more relevant and comprehensible to master one task at a time, according to immediate motivation.

The reason for this is simply the language. There are so many choices, so many routes to follow, and you are quite lost if you do not work out what the language implies by way of specific actions. When you begin computer operations you are putting your toe gingerly into the waters of a sub-culture, a vast international lake of words, sounds, symbols, pictographs, music, moving pictures. It is as much an international sub-culture as the life of musicians or of immigrant Haitians in an Anglophone country.

It seems as though smaller languages which serve as cultural identifiers are strengthening, which is all to the good in Utopia, as long as they do not involve impenetrable boundaries, that is turn their speakers in upon themselves. For them to work as a source of stimulation and of innovation, to be counted in the global culture, their speakers must be able to convey their ideas across the boundaries. Thus there has to be a hierarchy of languages, with regional and global acceptance. Even English, which is dominant as a lingua franca in so many fields, is far from universal. To work globally, it often has to be connected to other major intermediate languages, such as French, German, Russian, Spanish and so on; or else you need an interpreter. Esperanto, mostly because it was artificial, did not gain acceptance as a rival to English. Language, as we have noted, is quintessentially natural and evolutionary.

Cybertalk" though initially coming out of the needs of computer laboratories and the minds of people who discarded their humanism for binary discussion, is now moving fast with a natural and evolutionary impetus. Although word processors exist in scores of languages, and you can work on your screen and printer in several languages at once, the root language is American English. The words of Cybertalk will, I believe, enter into United States dictionaries faster than into others.

In the English speaking world Americanese is getting a major boost. In English Canada, word processors automatically supply me with U.S. dictionaries, thesauruses, grammar checkers. Were I French Canadian I could get a parallel programme which gives me the choice of French French or French Canadian. There is an Australian English version. It happens that the best for me is English (UK). Otherwise I must enter my own versions of spelling into the US or UK dictionaries, a boring process. Since Canadian school children use the US dominated spell checkers, we can expect a destruction of Canadian linguistic identity.[54]

Not only are the grammar checkers incomplete—that is only to be expected—but they can be erroneous, misleading and anti-aesthetic. My recent English (UK) spell checker from Microsoft refuses to recognise plurals, turning them all into possessives. My French grammar checker refuses to recognise

Y-a-t'il, and doesn't like question marks. The *Economist* recently used the Grammatik grammar checker to work on Jefferson's Declaration of Independence.

The original reads:

> "When, in the course of human events, it becomes necessary for one people to dissolve the political bonds which have connected them with another, and to assume among the powers of the earth, the separate and equal station to which the laws of nature and nature's God entitle them, a decent respect to the opinions of mankind requires that they should declare the causes which impel them to the separation."

'Corrected' (!) for grammar it reads, according to the *Economist*:

> "During human events, it becomes necessary for one person to dissolve the political bonds that have connected them with another. They take among the powers of the earth, the separate and equal station to which the laws of nature and of nature's God entitle them. A decent respect to the opinions of humankind requires that they should declare the causes that impel them to the separation."

The resulting translation contains at least two grammatical errors in itself. The main point, however, is that, otherwise, you can deduce the clear and sound grammatical rules that have resulted in the changes, rules or principles that many editors apply in their improving work without the use of electronics. Jefferson's "powerful" prose (the *Economist's* term) uses the rules and rhythms of the ear. (I do have to admit that Jefferson's constructions were more common in his day than they are today.)

Computers and word processors are in, for example, Canadian schools and businesses. Not very often do they choose to change the Americanese dictionaries that they are supplied with. The worst effect is that school children of all ages, in their insecurities, are likely to go to grammar checkers before they hand in their assignments. To the extent they do, their originality will be suppressed, their voices lost, in the name of conformist turgidity They are submitting without much thought about it to a major cultural invasion, probably more potent than some of the other cultural invasions about which intellectuals protest. I sometimes wonder if this is why Canadian newspapers use "theater" when the actors and stage companies and cinemas all use "theatre", even in their advertisements in those same newspapers.

This is an instance in which a global language competes by destroying dialects and aesthetic variation. It is destructive of individuality. It is no use laying down the law about it. It *is* useful, however, indeed indispensable, to draw the dynamics and the value considerations to the attention of those who influence the use of language—newspapers, teachers, television—so that they in turn can inform readers, school children, university students, who, ultimately, are those who decide. That, I believe is what the French should do, rather than issuing cabinet decrees, which mostly have to be withdrawn . . . I do not believe that anyone is in a position to *dictate* the use of language.

Influence is another matter, since all of us should be concerned about the efficacy of language as both identifier and communicator, and about its aesthetic qualities. And it seems that Cybertalk, as a dialect of Americanese, will compete in the future with other versions of print and oral English. Perhaps, just as print and oral English differ and are reserved for their own environments, Cybertalk will be in parallel. In any event, major changes are happening with astonishing speed. Cybertalk in European languages tends to be distinct from that in Americanese, which contains the largest data-bases and chat-lines.

The other feature of Cybertalk, resulting from the technology, is the ability of individuals to communicate in multimedia formats, and to do that with minimal censorship and governmental interference. In my presentation, the implications reach both backwards and forwards, so that we Utopians will have some serious issues to ponder.

We reach back into the school and the lives of children. Already there are Cybertalk "locations" which young children have designed themselves, or which adults have created. Some have elaborate screening devices which make sure that only children participate. Otherwise there is the danger of adult predation and the obscuration of the content by adult nitwits. Children themselves are not inhibited by such matters. They can set up Cybertalk conversations without such controls. Already they are using the World Wide Web as an exciting place in which they can exchange messages with children in fascinating places, send them drawings, even music. Schools have joint projects internationally through Internet linkages. It costs money for the equipment, and for log-on time, though there are numerous ways in which the latter can be next to nothing, and the cost of the former, with more and more power (multimedia swallows available computer memory), is tumbling. North American homes are spending more on computers than on any other communications devices, including newspapers and television.

We debate the social influence of the media, which are mostly controlled by commercial, seldom educational, objectives. It is less my task to elucidate the causes and effects of media messages at present than to think about what I would like them to be. The study of causes and effects is not yet producing very useable results, so laden with difficulty and confusion is the subject.

We hear the similar indeterminate discussions, with similar implications, when the questions are, for example, does violence on television create crime; does it increase sexuality and violence in the young? Does television distort political action by focusing on the idiosyncratic dramatic event as if it were typical and all-important? Do media discussions of problems such as the appearance of a fatal virus in Africa or an earthquake in Los Angeles create anxiety states that are, on the one hand, too extreme, and on the other, too ephemeral?

Not even Utopia will be able to control the flow of images that reaches those who are unable to manage their absorption, nor, as I shall argue later, should it. Remove images that show skin and torsos, and you simply return eroticism into other more dubious channels. As a young boy my erotic feelings were stimulated by pictures of fully clothed women, because there was little else, except pictures of female statues. Then as an impressionable young man I was in an environment in which all women, young and old, beautiful and not so beautiful, bared their breasts and thighs twenty-four hours a day. Because I came from a culture where this was not so I was stimulated—but I couldn't remain in a state of continuous erotic stimulation for twenty-four hours three hundred and sixty five days a year! The men who belonged to those women appreciated beauty, had affairs, were slapped down if they were out of line, and had no greater incidence of perversion than anywhere else.

I am more concerned about violence and exploitation of the weak than I am about eroticism as such. Again, Utopia cannot stop the portrayal of violence. It *can* affect individuals' reactions to perverted sex (however we want to define that), and violence. Back again we go to broad education. "Healthy" citizens do not need protection, and will view or not view, interpret or not interpret, in accordance with their values. I would not object if Utopia were libidinous. I would object if Utopia were violent, and if individuals could not handle violent scenes without copycat violence or an increase in aggression. This is not a matter of available images, but of the maturity of individuals to deal with them. Back once again to Youth Maturity Institutes.

If that balance and maturity is unformed (as with children) or weak (as with unbalanced adults) corruption or hurtful behaviour is likely. Children will grow stronger if the issues are not brushed like vermin under the mat, but are the subject of education. The unbalanced adults who behave in predatory or violent ways are, it is true, stimulated by what they see; but that does not have to be media images. It can be children in a playground, the possession of a gun or a knife, a macho challenge, a woman in a secluded place.

Am I then arguing for an unbridled media free-for-all? Absolutely not. I am saying that nothing will stop the flow of images and ideas, however perverse, once they are formulated, a different proposition. *And that we must prepare ourselves for that.* If we accept such a fact of life instead of denying it we will better prepare our children to deal with the impact. This will be better achieved, on the whole, by recognising, at the same time, the sexuality, angers, frustrations and violence that lurks inside children's beings, rather than pretending they are not there.

And I am also saying that those who present images and ideas must be prepared to face the consequences of their presentations. This, in my view, is known as responsibility.

I have no sympathy whatsoever when a media organisation demands access to information and the right to print or show whatever it wants as an expression of unfettered and absolute freedom of speech. There is little if anything to add to the interminable debates on the subject. They need addressing here only for completeness, and because the subject intersects with every other characteristic which constitutes Utopia. We know that no "rights" are absolute—they are culturally defined and in competition. The "right" to a free press is, for example, to be balanced against the "rights" of individuals to, for example, privacy, and to discussion that does not damage unless there is an overwhelmingly sufficient cause.

First, let me address the remedies for irresponsibility in the media. Under present arrangements, self-policing works only in a few extreme cases. There are civil and criminal remedies in most countries for such things as libel, slander, damages, sometimes in a very weak way for invasion of privacy and in many others for criticism of the State. In democratic countries, ironically, individual access to the law is extremely expensive and painful, achieved mainly by the rich and famous. In totalitarian countries the criminal law is overly available, but individuals have little access unless they are politically connected.

Utopian remedies are quite different. They depend on the existence of a system of law in which infractions are regarded as torts against the individual rather than crimes against the State, and in which the objective is of recompensative reconciliation. They also depend on equal access to the law, in accordance with which aid would be in place to compensate for the financial power of the media barons.

Professional ethics are not matters solely for the professions concerned. Statements of ethics need to consider the public role of the profession, and hence require at least a minority of public representatives (I do not mean politicians) on the group that draws them up and approves them. I have seen a variety of statements of journalistic ethics drawn up by self-serving media groups. Some are excellent and all-encompassing. Some are weak and obfuscating, avoiding the issues of public importance.

In the present context we are concerned with damages. Statements drawn up in the way I have suggested and incorporated into the law should, as a minimum, require remedies when damage results from such events as:

- o invasion of privacy
- o false statements
- o true statements which prevent fair trials
- o misleading dramatisation
- o omission of relevant known facts
- o prevention or inadequate emphasis of a reply to allegations
- o unsubstantiated allegations
- o implying guilt prior to a judgement
- o implying guilt by association without other substantiation
- o hurtful behaviour (e.g. violence) which can be traced to specific media stimulation

The above criteria will not be agreed upon by all, let alone media representatives themselves. Probably most debate will surround the last one.

If a father instructs his minor son in the art of bomb making, and preaches racial hatred, and the son goes off on a rampage against school and fellow pupils, it is likely that the parent will be held responsible. He should be. And he should be part of the remedial reconciliation. If he does the same with an adult son, the son's responsibility for choice is increased. But the father is a contributor. The father should be held as partly responsible, and should be part of the remedial reconciliation. The father has freedom of speech just as do the media, but not without responsibility.

If the media do the same, and consequent acts occur, their responsibility should be similar. They must have responsibility, and accept that the results stemmed from their actions. There is no right without responsibility.

The right to individual free speech is similar. It must be possible for anyone to state his or her opinions, set out his or her analysis, however ugly or irrational or contrary to mores, politically incorrect or repulsive to majority opinion, *provided the speaker takes responsibility for consequences*. To fail to accept freedom of speech leads the way to political authoritarianism, the equal danger of conventional community authoritarianism, the creation of nasty underground movements, and the suppression of nodes of ideas buried in the unpalatable talk, which, through opposition or adaptation can lead to advances in thought. In addition, that which is suppressed today sometimes becomes conventional wisdom in the future.

Responsibility is trickier. There exist laws against hate literature and speech in a number of countries. To me, both the messages of hate in western democracies and the laws are anathema. I do not with to see laws against ideas, thoughts, speech which are considered anathema in Utopia.

What I *do* wish to see is that those who speak accept responsibility for consequences. I do not agree that an author is not to be held to account for the ways in which his book is used. If his book is being used detrimentally, he has an obligation to try to make his position clear. The dilemma is not unknown in anthropology. Anthropologists must be on continuous guard against the possibility that writing will be taken out of context and used to support a political action that is inconsistent with what we are in fact saying. We must be sure that, although we are writing about living contemporary people, our material built up from individuals, we do not identify individuals who may be damaged or embarrassed, perhaps even pursued by the law as a result of what we write. (These conventions were not applied as recently as the 'fifties, and have developed slowly, sometimes embodying ridiculous extremes.) On the other hand, our work is not value free, and if we have a political position, it is obligatory for us to reveal it. As individuals, though not in the name of anthropology, we can adopt personal political stances that may even put our lives in danger. Journalists will understand.

The hate monger is not to be pursued for his reprehensible statements of hate. He is to be pursued for advocating hate, if it can be shown that he has influenced others to involve themselves in damaging action, and on the assumption that the hatred of groups is something that Utopian civilisation will not tolerate. He is to be pursued if it can be shown that his message has resulted in another's individual act of violence.

Similarly, the media should be pursued. If a television station shows violence which can be linked to a copy cat crime, it must bear part of the responsibility, taking into account the susceptibility and character of the offender. It should be part of the solution, entering into the procedures which bring about restitutional reconciliation. Of course, this would reduce, perhaps to some over-reduce, the appearance of violent crime on the screen. It would be a more effective mode of creating self-control than weak-kneed press councils trying to minimise confrontation and punishment in the name of unlimited freedom. There might be fewer paparazzi and scandal sheets.

Remember to place these notions in the context of Utopianly reformed law. Offenders do not go to jail. They are not fined. They engage in restitution. For the media in particular, that could be a highly salutary and educational experience.

Given this point of view, media representatives will be involved in Youth Maturity Institutes where they will take responsibility for the effect of their actions on youths.

It is common nowadays, particularly in the richer countries,[55] to deplore the ways in which media barons work to monopolize their control of combinations of newspapers, advertising papers, television radio and even entertainment. While stories of political control in such monopolies are often speculative, editorial slants and political spins have their effect on what they present to the public. It is what I call top-down media control.

So at one point I set about attempting to reverse this through a bottoms up approach, beginning with the internet. Many have attempted this, sometimes with success—the journalistic control of *Le Monde* is one famous example. But I think my idea went further.

I took the city of Vancouver as my starting point, and created a working template of an internet magazine. Since I had exactly no resources, the editorial line represented myself. But I used multi-media approaches to try to document the life of the city, from dance to music, from public festivals to night clubs, from theatre to dining. Many helpers contributed, but all were volunteers, none professionals.

The result was technically inferior but the content indicated that it could be expanded almost ad infinitum into every corner of city life, a living ethnography of its world. And it had the potential to become a permanent data bank of that life.

The plan had further ambitions. If it proved workable— and that at least I was able to demonstrate to myself and my collaborators—then why not in other cities? Why not in Barcelona, Valparaiso, Nairobi, Beirut, Geneva, Bangkok, Delhi? And then why not pull all these initiatives, disparate but with related templates, into one global multimedia web magazine?

This would ideally reflect the priorities of the grass roots local cyber-journalists, rather than commissioning editors. It would be an alternative to the monoliths of CNN, the BBC, even Al-Jazeera.

Of course, despite proving that at least locally it *could* work, the major ambition didn't, for reasons I have outlined in the chapter on innovation. I personally did not have the time, the connections or the business experience to pull the operation together. When I did approach media powers to take an interest I found the ideas came up against their own, to my mind destructively inferior, ones. The idea was competitive and offended the sense of hierarchy. Their own efforts in some cases foundered because they continued to make use of inadequate outmoded models, and in no case did their productions approach the model I had in mind.

IX

Humans in Nature

Humans are natural beings. They have been created by and are subject to the same processes and evolutionary patterns as the rest of nature. They are not above nature, they are part of it.

Each species has its own role and characteristic in the natural world.[56] *Homo sapiens* is different from other species in many respects, but one stands out as relevant to this discussion.

Humanity has more culture, some would say civilization, than other species. It is uniquely equipped to think about consequences including its relations with the other species. This is part of its culture, what some would call civilization.

Decades ago Clive Bell[57] defined civilization, or culture, as humanity's control of nature, a point that most anthropologists and ecologists seem to have ignored. Think about it. If we include humanity within nature, as we must, then every bit of our thought and creativity zeroes in on adapting nature, including ourselves, to our wishes. We can't avoid it. That is our nature as part of nature.

So the cry "Leave nature alone" is a non-starter.

It behoves us however to be acutely conscious of this symbiosis, and in accord with our Utopian goals to be conscious of the consequences and to choose to determine which consequences we want and which we do not want.

In my first draft I did not include this chapter, largely because my thought was focused on humanity's environment and on the large debate on climate change, and I felt it was redundant to enter the fray. But it seems necessary to make some points.

Many humans are choosing to protect species, which is their right. They do so because otherwise species will disappear, and there will be a reduction in the gene pool, which they can argue persuasively is not what we want in Utopia. Fair enough.

But wait. Throughout the history of the world species have disappeared, been wiped out. Other species have evolved to take their place. The desire to save species from extinction is a human intervention in the processes of nature, even when the threatened disappearance is attributable to human actions. It is a *cultural* phenomenon and thus a part of humanity's behaviour in attempting to control nature, just as is humanity's action leading to the specie disappearance. And by no means all the disappearances are the result of human action *per se*.

An interesting and challenging thesis appears in the course of a novel by Martin Cruz Smith.[58] Drawing upon rapid species changes in the area of the Chernobyl disaster it speculates that one way of "saving nature" from humanity would be to cover the globe with high radiation atom bombs, leading to massive species adaptation.

This may be no more than a fictional notion, but the history of the earth has been one of impacts from extra-terrestrial objects which have had profound effects on species. The import for human thinking will be addressed further in the next Chapter.

A more disciplined argument for the disappearance and adaptation of species may be found in the work of S.R. Reice, who writes "catastrophes can ultimately have positive effects on natural communities. The core idea is that disturbances foster increases in biodiversity . . . and these in turn provide . . . nutrient cycling, decomposition and the increase in production of plants and animals . . ."

The upshot is that general ideological positions will not be accurate enough to help us properly. We cannot escape the fact that humans are in control and thus bear ultimate responsibility for what happens in the natural world, even if that control is both deficient and often muddled. To the extent that it is possible, each decision affecting the environment and even nature outside the immediate human environment, requires careful study and analysis. Consequences are specific to the case in hand, not derived from a generalised global axiom.

These matters involve value judgements, about which Utopian society will need to make up its mind.

Half a century ago the great worry was that humanity would unleash a devastating nuclear war. That concern has now lessened but it is still there as a consequence of nuclear competition, lack of security in the handling of dangerous stock piles, and terrorist possibilities. The Utopian solution will take place through the joint creation of Youth Maturity Institutes and an effective Global Government.

But what has replaced that worry is fear of the consequences of climate change, which are seen as a challenge to humanity's ability to control the rest of nature. And that is proper worry, confused by emotion though it may be.

The first point to make is that the global climate has always changed dramatically as a result of forces beyond humanity's control. We know of past ice ages and global warming. What are now tropical animals used to roam Europe. At the time of the initial overseas expansions of Dutch, British and French maritime empires, the fleets, both commercial and navy, were manned in part by refugees from the farm lands of Northern Europe, ruined by a descending mini-ice-age. Greenhouse gases and other human interventions had nothing to do with such phenomena.

It appears that in the next century or so we can expect to have a non-human initiated warming globe as a predecessor to a bounce back to at least a mini ice period, *whatever humanity decides to do about it*. At this stage in human evolution there are some parts of nature that remain beyond our control.

That of course does not let humanity off the hook. We are bound by our cultures to seek to control, and we do have a responsibility. What I have written above does not in the slightest remove our notable effects on the cycles. We know that human engendered changes overlay the natural timing. We know that changes in our behaviour will lessen the impact, even if we stopped such effects immediately, it could take a decade or two for results to be seriously noticeable.

The conclusion? Humanity owes it to itself to mitigate the current warming cycle. But that in itself will not prevent warming. Utopian governments will need—and it appears to be urgent—to take action to protect shorelines, move communities, and prepare for major changes to agriculture and pastoralism. The idea that the control of greenhouse gases in itself will be enough is fantasy, and dangerously inhibits action in response to the inevitable natural cycles.[59]

The impact of warming is most dramatic and obvious with respect to the oceans and shorelines. But, more subtly but nevertheless just as strongly, it will affect the land mass, and with it human food supply.

A report by the Royal Society[60] in 2005 examines what we know about the role of agriculture in climate change and the effects of climate change on agriculture. While there is much that is unknown many trends are clear. Climate change will affect yields, protein and toxin levels of crops. It was thought that there were major benefits from the effects of CO_2 in the atmosphere, but this is less than was thought. Some crops will have their yields reduced by 30% as a result of near surface ozone.

The report urges more research in tropical areas (see next Chapter), but the most practical recommendation is for the rapid development of new cultivars. One wonders what the impact of this thought will be on genetic modification. However, it seems that every advance carries its costs. Thus crops using water more efficiently will reduce rainfall levels, with effects on the water supply.

Already water shortages are appearing in parts of the world where water was recently treated almost as freely as if it were air, and such shortages are affecting electrical power supply, once considered the most eco-friendly way of creating power.

For decades, one of the few genuine interactions between Israeli and Arab scholarship has been devoted to desertification studies, for the increasing spread of deserts is noticeable and is amenable to concerted human reaction, especially in the tapping of underground aquifers and improved vegetation—even as I saw near Beersheba the use of re-circulated liquids for fish farming and the production of commercial and vegetable crops. Much of the present day desert areas were once lands of milk and honey, and can, at a price, be returned to something like that state.

Shortages, such as those of oil and water, are not necessarily disastrous, leading as they do to innovations and changes in cost benefit ratios. Utopians will undoubtedly be placing more emphasis on wind and, less obtrusively, solar power, and ultimately desalinisation and the more efficient natural recycling of water.

Agriculture and pastoralism use up soil attributes. In some parts of the world they are at least in part replenished by nature—the flooding of the Nile Delta is a case in point. Farmers have long learnt the benefits of crop rotation. Some traditional methods such as transhumance and East African cattle usage appear to have modifying effects.[61] But overall, whether the inputs are chemical or organic, the problem of soil deterioration remains, with dire warnings of effects on food supply from, for example, the European Union.

The same dynamics affect our approach to fisheries and oceans, increasingly polluted, and fish farming, which requires massive inputs of feed obtained somewhere along the food chain.

The year 2005 was something of a record for natural disasters—the South Asian tsunami, the devastating hurricane season in the Caribbean, Mexico and the United States. The human response has been to deal with the effects through massive national and international relief aid. It is most unlikely that we can do much if anything to stop such events, but improvements in forecasting are under way, and there is talk of creating a permanent revolving disaster fund under UN auspices that will provide the money, if not the people on the ground, for immediate instead of delayed responses. The relief efforts are bedevilled by national interests and rivalries (which affect our analysis of dysfunctional government and ideas for Global Government), and also by an unwillingness to give the UN the powers and authority to fully coordinate both governmental and private efforts.

But the problem and its mitigation run deeper. Disaster and human settlement authorities have long pointed out that, for example, housing construction in many of the threatened areas are dangerous in earthquakes—it is seldom the tremors that kill, but sub-standard buildings. This is not so dangerous in tropical areas where homes are made of thatch, but is lethal in areas where heavier materials are normal. There exist in the United Nations system specifications for non-lethal construction, which countries such as Pakistan and India ignore.

And what about a further moral dilemma. To what extent should populations be encouraged, even allowed, to remain in seriously threatened areas, in inaccessible mountain areas or tsunami threatened coastlines? The disaster of New Orleans in 2005 could have been mostly averted by heeding warnings of floods waiting to happen as a result of poor engineering, and even better by relocating the city away from the water tap.

Relocation however runs against a deep rooted and almost universal rule. Populations return to areas of disaster like lemmings. The psychology of this phenomenon has not been adequately studied—the natural drive of poor populations to avoid the unknown, in direct opposition to the migratory tendencies of others. Both "solutions" involve the assessment of risk, about which it is the role of governments to advise, perhaps not to enforce. And probability falsely advises "It has happened now. It will be generations before it happens again."

We must take note of the effects of ever increasing urban sprawl and invasions of productive land for tourism, industry and other purposes. The macadamization of productive land. Multi million cities with their square kilometres of heat inducing macadam and housing that replace vegetation create centres of natural destruction. But humans in their civilisation are supposed to be able to control nature for the globe's benefit.

In cities like Kinshasa smart city workers emerge from simple huts, but those huts are located on small plots of land, with fruit trees, shrubs and vegetables. That is one kind of suburbia, common to Europe and North America. It is at the expense of intensive agriculture or forestation, and in the largest cities does not survive population pressure. In an attempt to soften the effects of expanding residential land use, cities like Vancouver opt to use air space instead, thrusting apartments into the sky, with major effects on urban living and working.

Whether suburban or towering urban, insufficient attention has been given to greening criteria. There are movements afoot to persuade city planners to insist that roof tops be green and even food productive, though so far with insufficient effect. Tailored parks do not do the job. And to convert the dysfunctional capital of buildings into structures that are not only eco-friendly in themselves, but contribute to the vegetation stock of the world, is a mammoth task. But Utopia requires it to be undertaken. We cannot sit back in the lethargy of defeat.

What should we say about population control? It may be that the globe as at present constituted cannot support very much more by way of increased population. This has been said since the nineteenth century and almost nothing has been done about it. Direct population control measures (China and India) have mostly failed. Improvement in wealth and education reduce the propensity of women to have children. This can be carried further as women experience a reduced need for male sexual partners. That however is speculation. But Innovation will improve the carrying capacity of the world in as yet unknown ways.

Paradoxically social evolution may be moving in this direction. Increased awareness of the rights and role of women does not necessarily reduce the birth rate, unless accompanied by birth control facilities and access to abortion. Despite my remarks about homosexuality in Chapter V, perhaps this could be nature's way of controlling the birth rate. And so could the increased empowerment of women, who, as I pointed out in that Chapter, no longer need men for biological purposes in the traditional ways. Utopia will need to devote attention to removing any brakes which exist on the spread of women's empowerment throughout global cultures.

Humanity's involvement with nature including itself of course involves many other priority issues, such as, for example, the application of genetic engineering. Some of these I will refer to in the next Chapter on Knowledge. For there is no doubt that we need to know more, and urgently, if Utopia is to be able to control its future. And that may require more and more reliance on effective Global Government.

X

The Pursuit of Knowledge

In every section thus far we have touched upon imperfect knowledge. I opened with the assertion that knowledge, not even in Utopia, can be a certain thing. We must live with fuzzy logic and uncertainty, take pleasure in them for they represent excitement and human challenge, not be afraid of them.

If a little knowledge is a dangerous thing, the danger is necessary. Since uncertainty surrounds us, we cannot wait for certainty in order to act. We must get on with the job.

A merit of democracy is that it implicitly recognises that technocrats and scientists are limited; that the little knowledge of each individual adds up to great principles—freedom, understanding—that since no one individual has superior knowledge about all of life's affairs, the ignorance of one is more than counterbalanced by the sum total of the wisdom of many. Provided, of course, that the many are not swayed out of their strongly felt reason by the more than strongly felt hype and hysteria of inflamed rhetoric or crowd drive. That, once again, is where the central importance of logic and rhetoric in Youth Maturity Institutes' comes in.

There are degrees of littleness. While we cannot wait for knowledge to be perfect, while commissions of enquiry and statements of uncertainty are often used to inhibit action, it is nevertheless appropriate that we should improve the pool of knowledge, support investigations of strategic questions, and distribute that knowledge as widely as practicable.

But what is knowledge? Are there such things as truths and lies? Is knowledge simply that which someone believes to be true?

I see three primary kinds of knowledge, and two apparent dichotomies. As I mentioned before, there is knowledge based upon faith, which we can call religious. I believe, therefore it is. There is knowledge based upon and communicated by art in its manifold forms. I express and you receive that which your own spirit tells you to receive, amending the message as you do so. And there is knowledge based upon sceptical questioning, with answers provided by attempts at control, and the tests of logic and falsity, namely science, in which the object of communication is an unambiguous message.

All three deal with concepts of more or less, even when the assertions are couched as absolutes or aesthetic values. More sin or less sin. Total renunciation or none. Great beauty, less beauty, or great ugliness. The harmony of form or its disharmony. High probability or low. Warmth or cold. For each, differences of degree are possible and stated. Differences of degree can, theoretically, be translated into at least ordinal quantification, though the specific method of acquiring knowledge may, at least for now, abjure that.

"Subjectivity" and "objectivity" are always mixed. Once the assumptions of a faith are disclosed, logic may be applied to the consequences and implications of those assumptions. Theology, political philosophy, exposition of values follow. Initial faith may be challenged by logical attack, but if the faith is deep, it is impervious. That does not mean it is a lie. Even if "disproven" by some investigation, it is true to believers, and must be counted within the pool of knowledge with which people use for action. Intuition is arriving at conclusions without evidence or reasoning, conclusions which may in fact be supported by other methods. Those of us, like myself, who believe in scepticism have a form of faith—commitment to scepticism; so have the rationalists. Ultimately we have no means of proving beyond doubt that rationality and scepticism are the way the natural universe intends us to think. We can, however, argue about it.

There is a sense in which art differs from science mainly in the fact that art addresses individual phenomena, teasing out implications, instead of grouping phenomena and testing the significance of variables. It is just as empirical as science. Even when the art is embodied in words, in poetry or literature, its message cannot fully be agreed upon by verbal criticism, which in itself is a subjective art. The message is between the artist and the viewer, the hearer, the reader. Again, the difference between art and science is not the sensory base of the communication, for all communication is sensory. Scientific and mathematical judgement is full of terms such as "elegance", "simplicity". Attempts to objectify the terms do not remove the fundamental subjectivity on which they rest. And the choice of the scientific enquiry, however much bolstered by argument and rational justification, is totally subjective. I *choose* to be a mathematical biologist or an astronomer and try to answer such and such a specific question.

We must therefore not separate specific forms of knowledge too certainly in a hierarchy of method and truth, though there are major differences in the central types of communication. Faith asserts, art seduces, science is expository. But here again faith can result in exposition and can use seductive methods; some art is programmatic; and scientists love to seduce through simplistic but dramatic exhibits.

Knowledge is communicated for it depends on innovation. It is often the case that the root of a piece of knowledge is indeed not directly communicated, other than to those who share that knowledge. Those who have the faith share it with others of the same mind. We seem to be going through a temporary phase in which some artists club together with other artists and feel purposeful in so doing. Scientists often look down on those who try to communicate beyond the sacred walls. Knowledge leads, then, to monastic orders; but at least within those there is communication. Knowledge, as I asserted in Chapter II, grows from that communication, and could not do so without it. The isolated person who has in his sensibility some truth or innovation is not dealing with knowledge but an interior emotion.

Knowledge, then, is communicated insight.

And that insight deals with generalised relationships. "It is a beautiful sunset" has little to do with nature. It compares the phenomenon to other sunsets. It tests the insight against ideas of beauty. Those ideas relate, for example, to the shape, intensity and spectrum of colour, all of which are in a particular relationship, comparable to and differentiated from the relationships set out in other sunsets—and indeed other phenomena, such as dawn, reflections on water, a painting. They may relate the sunset to emotional experience, to love, to romantic opportunity. That the judgement is made in a split second does not remove that characteristic. That is why abstract thinking and rationality, which attempt to reveal relationships, have a special influence in the way we think about knowledge.

I suggested above that the great methods of acquiring knowledge are mixed together and not to be put into some sort of absolute hierarchy. In my usual contrary way, however, I now assert that not all bearers of knowledge are equal, and that they never will be. Indeed, as we have noted, an amazing defect in some theory and practice of childhood education is the assertion in the classroom that anybody's idea, however arrived at, is as valid as the next child's, especially in matters of the "humanities". Democratically, that may be so. It may even be that a child is nursing an idea that, when he or she comes to maturity, turns out to be revolutionary in its implications. But ideas are not at all equal. Those ideas which influence other ideas have greater significance than those which stay isolated.

Standards of enquiry are inevitable and necessary. Genius may be hidden, but most of us, though capable of more than we let on, are not Genius. Genius takes a swathe of contemporary knowledge, combines it with some other swathe of knowledge, and turns everything topsy turvy. But to do that Genius has first to find the swathes of knowledge that pre-exist. It has to choose what elements to master, but mastered they must be, so that they may be changed and developed.

By mastery I do not mean that the school or university has a monopoly of the swathes of knowledge that Genius or lesser mortals will eventually play with. Much will come from outside.

But the school and university do have the responsibility to show how knowledge is gained, and what devices we have for testing knowledge in its various forms, how it is communicated within and without the monastic halls, and how people go about making their judgements about what is valid and what is not. A child has to learn to put his thoughts to tests, yet ultimately not to be constrained by those tests; to accept disagreement, yet be strong enough not to be disheartened by it—nor even necessarily to agree with the disagreement.

In the population at large we are going through a time in which democratisation of knowledge, that is the widespread sharing of it, is being exponentially expanded by communication methods. The time and space constraints of the media, to say nothing of their commercialisation, insist on reducing complexity and uncertainty to simplicity and certainty. The time frame of television documentaries requires enormous skill to convey complex questions, a skill and an aim which is most frequently not there. The space and structure of newspaper "stories", though able to complement these with longer, more analytical treatments, stress a dominant theme at the expense of other themes which are just as significant for interpretation. At the same time sources and counter-sources are usually not adequately revealed. The World Wide Web and internet constitute an enormous and democratically available fund of information, with little by way of quality control. The viewer must depend on hiser own resources to determine the likelihood that the message has truth or is a false scam.

There are millions of examples every day. I shall take two to illustrate.

A doctor conducts a major study of the use of temoxisen, a drug that is effective in the prevention of the spread of breast cancer under certain conditions. The object is to try to quantify the risks of numerous side effects which previous studies had reported. In medical research there are large numbers of statistical studies which are not definitive because numbers are too small for the control of variables, or the statistical tools are simplistic. These are widely reported in the media as if they were truth, or definitive break-throughs, whereas they should be interpreted only as presenting possibilities or hypotheses for further enquiry.

This study was, however, thorough. It traced large numbers of side effects, among which was an increased risk of cervical cancer. The press seized on the last point, trumpeting the danger, and creating considerable anxiety in patients, with which no amount of reasoned discussion could compete. The facts revealed (as probabilities only) that without temoxisen there is a 2% likelihood of a breast cancer patient acquiring cervical cancer. With temoxisen there is a 6% likelihood. Further studies will most likely show why, and perhaps which women are most likely to be at risk.

The figures show that in the meantime caution is required and that women should be informed of the risk. If they opt to take temoxisen they should watch for the first signs of cervical cancer, which, I am informed, is, relative to breast cancer, a low risk and a treatable disease. The discovery, which was not new but was properly evaluated in the study, did not justify the kind of fear promoted by some of the U.S. national press. (In fairness, I have to say that I heard the "balanced" approach during a discussion by a woman doctor on television. But for that I would not have had my information modified.) In other words the media, in reporting the study, exaggerated one of its elements for dramatic impact, corrupting the implications of its results.

The Canadian Broadcasting Corporation has built up a reputation for being stolid. Perhaps to make up for this it sometimes goes overboard in trying to be at the forefront of scandal mongering. In 1995 it decided, for what reasons are not yet apparent, to follow through on allegations that Care Canada, a non-governmental aid agency, had wasted monies raised from the public to provide relief to Somalia. They alleged that "not a penny" of what had been raised had gone to Somalian food or medical relief; that instead money had been spent on security guards in Kenya and a public relations officer in Mogadishu; that air tickets were at full economy rates instead of bargain basement rates; that officials had stayed at a $225 a night hotel in Sydney, Australia during a conference. Before the telecast Care Canada officials had declined responding to what had been put to them as a general problem of allocating money, since they believed the untruth would be apparent and the programme would not air, at least in that way.

It did, causing an immediate stir amongst all Canadian aid agencies, since there was a strong likelihood that the public, believing the stories, would become disenchanted with giving to anyone.

There are indeed private fund raisers, even some who harp on religion, who are open to suspicion, and who are more concerned with maintaining their competitive advantage than with delivering help. But Care Canada is one of those with a fifty year record, and one which is regularly audited in various ways, including by government agencies who provide some of the funds.

A reliable account would have approached the matter differently. It would have placed the complaints in the context of the dynamics of aid delivery. That would have shown, for example, that in Mogadishu at the time journalists from all over the world were harassing aid workers and preventing them from getting on with the job. A public relations officer was a defence to enable the agencies to meet the emergency.

It would have shown that to allocate money in advance too rigidly would prevent aid agencies from adapting to unforeseen and rapidly changing emergencies. Thousands of Somalis needing help were in Kenya; Care Canada, in coordination and consultation with other agencies, was mandated to focus on them. The complaint that private donors thought the money was going to Somalia (which, incidentally, no donor had then been able to do) was splitting hairs in a damaging way—it was going to Somalis. The charge that the money was in part being used for security guards instead of for food shows extraordinary naiveté. Massive looting, unrest, violence, interference with convoys, if not checked, would have prevented *any* food reaching the sufferers. As I know to my cost, full economy air tickets are necessary if travellers are to be able to change their plans to meet emergencies at a moment's notice—and in this case, travel agents gave rebates. As for hotel charges, the "investigators" quoted the published full tariff rate at the hotel, not the amount actually paid. That amount was at a reduced conference rate. It *might* have been possible to get a room at even less, though that would have to be demonstrated under the conditions of the case. But staying at the conference appointed hotel is part of the cost of doing business; not staying there indeed raises ethical questions, since if those who attend do not stay there, if the guaranteed rooms are not occupied, then the conference is liable to pay for meeting rooms that it otherwise gets free or at a nominal charge. The hotel booking is in fact a subsidy to the conference, without which it could not take place.

If a television producer and writer did not have the knowledge of the principles underlying these statements they would not be qualified to undertake such a documentary, and would be doing so simply out of muckraking hubris. But, ethics apart, it shows how dangerous a little misleading information can be.

The CBC presentation was, in my opinion, anti-knowledge. As I have said, no knowledge is perfect. But there are degrees of imperfection. Misleading statements are all the more serious when they come from media outlets that the public is trying to trust.

In this context, the point of both examples is that it is not just the media who are responsible for interpretation. The public is responsible too. It is almost *only* through the media that the public gets information, if we include books and the Internet in the definition. In our Utopia the public will not tolerate deliberate or careless mis-information. It will demand accuracy. It will demand that scientific journalists do not depend solely on the press handouts of scientists, but go to the original sources, and to the scientific debates. It will demand that muckraking is not enough, that information revealed be put in context, for only then does it become possible for individuals to make their own interpretations. Knowledge is not something hidden in universities or research labs—it is something every one of us amasses every day.

One of the most troubling aspects of the knowledge industry is the way in which it is forced to depend on probability statistics, and at the same time regards something counted as being necessarily objective. In the social sciences and in medical research statistical correlations are frequently mishandled or misinterpreted. It is quite common, in situations of great complexity, for a correlation which is stronger than chance to be interpreted not as revealing a causative hypothesis, but as demonstrating a cause. The public—and other investigators—needs to be on guard.

A statistical correlation is nothing more than that unless it feeds directly into a theory which is supported by other evidence. Furthermore, in areas such as medicine and much of the social sciences, degrees of probability reveal usually ignored hypotheses as to why the correlation is not universal. It is as important to know *why* some patients do *not* fit the pattern as to know that they are exceptions to the rule.

Fortunately, in medicine at least, a corrective appears to be on the way. In October 2005 the International HapMap Consortium published[62] the results of its "completion" of the map of human genetic variation. It found that 99.9% of humans have the same genetic information, regardless of "race". The remainder (which sounds small but is pretty large in content) they consider to be the result of medical, environmental and other non-biological factors. According to some this opens the door to individual gene mapping, or the identification of genes specific to individuals and having an effect on their health, the effectiveness of drugs, and other medical interventions. As with any technical advance, this is open to unethical manipulation. But it also opens the Utopian possibility that will be able to carry their individual genetic chart into the consulting room, and avoid being lumped into a statistical pool.

So far I have treated the media as purveyors and creators of knowledge. Behind them is the panoply of research institutions, artists, private investigators, universities, technical schools, inventors, corporate research facilities.

Amongst these I shall focus on universities.

I would define a university as an adult institution with the central objectives of: generating enquiry and creativity through teaching and research, expanding cultural resources, including knowledge in the sciences and the humanities and arts, developing powers of scientific, aesthetic and moral judgement, *using the technique of rational enquiry*.

A university is by no means the *only* location in which such activities take place. Indeed, artistic endeavour, for example, is best located outside a university, since the constraints of rational scholarship and of other demands inhibit artistic freedom. The reason for this is that a university distinguishes itself, ideally, from other institutions by its use of rationality to advance knowledge. It criticises and explains rather than writes novels. It explores the historical genesis of art movements, rather than paints.

Immediately I must make the point that once again terminology is likely to be thoroughly misleading. First, not all institutions which name themselves universities concentrate on these functions. Some, in many parts of the world, are more concerned with learning outcomes defined as packages of facts, rote instruction, and the control and use of knowledge as a service to industry, rather than because it is in itself creative.

Other institutions might well be considered of a university kind, especially some of the great Institutes of Technology, Schools of Art, Colleges and so forth. Elements of universities are in many places. And even universities which meet the definition are seldom "pure": They balance budgets through military and industrial contracts; they have to teach the elements of languages by drill and exercise; some of the non-creative things that universities do are but a means to a creative end. They cannot afford to lose a good mind because it can not put words on paper properly, hence they may dip into coaching techniques to reach the constructive goal. If they do this too much they may find themselves, as do most North American universities, including a component that is little more than a high school, and not even a good one at that.

The last statement points to a tricky balance. To create, there must be a basis for creation. As I have pointed out, the basis consists of at least some of what has gone before. So the university, in order to do its job, must take part in the preservation of what has gone before, retaining and communicating the pool of culture. It does not have to communicate solely to formal students and scholars. Communicating to *anyone* who wants to listen is surely part of its mandate.

It is beyond my task here to go into the terrible dysfunctions and anti-creativity processes that go on in most named universities, except to plead that in Utopia we can make them go away, or transfer them to other places where they are not damaging. One such dysfunction is the North American obsession with course-work, comprehensive examinations and the like in Ph.D. programmes, course-work which is either not needed or more properly insisted upon at the M.A. stage, comprehensive examinations which, if needed at all, should be part of the student entry and selection process; both dulling, sometimes for ever, the enthusiastic creative mind.

Knowledge is not to be neatly packaged. Though organisation of knowledge is essential to the rational mind—and, remember, universities are involved with rationality—those who are searching, both students and those who have passed the degree test, must be free to wander. The tricky balance is to draw the attention of students to the rigours of argument and areas of subject matter that the student is not aware of, on the one hand, and to encourage his or her freedom to search for associations, synergies, anywhere. And to demand that assertions reveal their locus in scholarship, their relevance for enquiry and for further thought.

Furthermore *anything* is open to challenge. Professional schools, by definition, have at least tiny places where challenge is seldom open—I refer to the statement of conduct that defines the ethics of the profession. Such Faculties have to watch that this central orthodoxy does not permeate, and, if they call themselves universities, to be open to challenge even here.

Since anything is open to challenge, there is no room for blind faith, except in rationality, though that may rationally be challenged. (I am NOT saying that rationality is the only, or even the best, way to knowledge. I AM saying that it is the special tool of universities, and that there is as yet nothing of equal merit for the effective and relatively precise communication of ideas. Faith and ambiguity are primarily elsewhere. Universities do not have a monopoly in the modes of searching.)

This means that those who cannot stand up to such challenges, who are disturbed rather than stimulated by them, who are liable to suffer psychologically if their faith or aesthetic intuitions are hurt, should avoid universities. The point means that students, to understand their position, to act appropriately, must be capable of reasonably mature judgement and know rather specifically what universities are about. Secondary school counsellors too frequently limit their talk to careers and job hunts. Although universities indubitably affect, even create, careers, that is a by-product of their primary concerns. It is not the contemporary university's fundamental job to train skilled doctors; that can be done in independently accredited medical schools. It *is* the university's job to assist enquiring minds, whether they belong to doctors or philosophers, to think about medical matters, to be a locus for medical research and debate, and to educate those would-be doctors who wish to think creatively about their profession, its human context, its science.

Too often so-called universities allow parts of themselves to be training schools, rather than horizon-wideners.

The "pure" university will be rare until Utopia is achieved. Most universities, even if dedicated to the goals and methods I have in mind, will have elements that are service-oriented. Institutions outside of "universities" will have elements that are consistent with the objectives. Thus being a university is a matter of degree—an institution is "more" of a university or "less" of a university.

The social role of the university is not to provide *technology* for tomorrow. Since it is dedicated to discovery, that will happen as a by-product. The many forms of rational creativity to which the university is devoted are valued now and will be even more so in Utopia for additional reasons. Youth Maturity Institutes are more directly instrumental. They, as we have seen, must be concerned more and more with the non-vocational aspects of living. Universities do not do this directly. But the emphasis on rational creativity, on discovery, on searching, on finding out, will be of immense benefit to those millions who, in the future, will be released from day-to-day other-directed work.[63] Universities will attract the increasing numbers of non-gainfully employed, free to follow their creative impulses. To handle this, universities must reverse the unthinking surrender that is taking place, surrender to pressures to make them directly vocational, directly subservient to industrial and commercial needs. Let there be other types of programmed research or technical institutes to do that.

It might be thought that I am advocating ivory towers divorced from their communities. Not at all. There is a pent-up demand for thought, intellectual exploration, knowledge in communities—the movement of the elderly into the realm of educational tours, short courses of higher education, even degrees, is noticeable. Unfortunately, a great deal of this is "talking down". Universities will have an increasing role to play in opening doors to those who are interested in learning, not just for "it's own sake", but as a means to a creative adult life;

and designing methods, uninhibited by the swaddling of degree rules and regulations, to respond to the intellectual potentialities of the population.

Furthermore I have advocated, and still advocate, community involvement where it matters—not so much in the university Board rooms, not in academic decision-making as such, but in talking with staff about the intellectual and community issues of concern to them. In other words, faculties and colleges might well have liaison and consultative committees drawn from the community to discuss such matters as the possibility of stimulating courses addressing new questions of interest or the techniques of discussion and dissemination. University staff naturally tend to address issues, especially in the sciences, which are determined by their peers. As a result a large number of matters of concern to the public are not on the priority list for investigation (see later). Remember, I am suggesting *consultation*, not problem-oriented control. There are many factors involved in making decisions about priorities for enquiry—funding, aptitudes and capacities of personnel, the unfettered passion to solve a problem, among others. The consultative groups must learn to understand these, to stimulate, not to demand; to be useful through stimulation.

And I am not abjuring applied research. Indeed I feel that in the social sciences, for example, applied research is not accorded the intellectual status that should be accorded to it—largely the responsibility of the practitioners. In these subjects it is through applied research that we may address matters of great significance—for example the testing of hypotheses, the investigation of ethno-social science (the hypotheses about cause and effect with which every manager and politician, counsellor and lover, operate), the elucidation of the values and goals into which technology should be fitted, and the discovery of new questions. In making the point I am readily aware that this is a part of knowledge that is in its infancy.

I cannot foresee the structure of research in Utopia. Ideas I may have about the organisation of enquiry on the whole, changes in the communication of data and knowledge, the relevance of such buzz-words as "interdisciplinarity", about funding—these are matters of technical detail which are changing rapidly and profoundly. There is no one right way. May many flowers bloom. Let them be wild as well as cultivated. Let them invade the desert spaces that men and women have been cruelly fashioning for themselves, desert spaces called the emptying of the spirit.

But I do not want to leave this topic without indicating the vastness of our ignorance, the infinite terrain that is there to be explored. We are accustomed to the idea that knowledge is increasing at an exponential rate, that the number of enquirers living now is more than equal to the sum total of all those who lived before. That the output of data is getting beyond control, creating difficulties of management, access, quality control, and absorption.

If this is so now, what may it be like soon, let alone in Utopia? Democratisation is an inevitable and welcome feature. With democratisation will come even greater magnitudes. Even greater difficulties is finding the diamonds in the sand, the need for even huger data-managing machines. But also there may come a breaking away from the constraints, not of mental discipline, but of artificial disciplinarity. Academics will potentially be in much greater contact with non-academic creators. Academics will be challenged as never before. The amateur, as in the first days of science, may well find his or her niche. The hidden minds of the third world will come to the forefront. If only we learn to turn the electronic age toward its rightful purposes . . .

Many years ago I suggested to fellow-anthropologists that we should stop the print publication of heavily subsidised primary journals—those concerned with data reporting and initial interpretation—leaving the print field only to those which were concerned with synthesising and theorising. I suggested also that we should try to develop electronic intercommunication through the nascent Internet in such a way that workers in the field could transmit their data and papers openly, and access library resources as needed. This, I argued, could be of immense benefit to third world anthropologists, whose ideas are rejected by referees because they are not embedded in the literature for the simple reason the literature is not available to them, even in libraries in their country. I saw this as potentially being a heaven-sent equaliser.[64]

It was of course quite impracticable as an immediate goal. Portable field computers did not have the power. Telephone lines were missing, and telephone systems unreliable.

This is just about not so any more. Technology is available so that phone sets will not require wires. While the memory demands for the software that can make such a system work are growing day by day, the packaging of memory and devices into portable computers is keeping pace; costs are tumbling; power sources—longer batteries, solar power—are becoming available more slowly. It is considerably cheaper to put rural and poor communities onto the Internet than to build physical libraries. To the extent that this becomes so, it can be exploited as The Great Equaliser.

This does not mean the loss of books, smaller demand for paper, or the disappearance of printed journals. Although it is far more effective to write to a modern computer screen than on paper (if one is settled), it is still more appropriate to use hard copy printouts for most reading and many reference purposes. Most scholarly journals—as many already are—should become "on demand" journals, available to everyone who can electronically skim tables of contents and summaries, and then read selected material and order printouts or store on disc. Journals and books will be in a limited number of central libraries and data centres. The most valuable will be those which synthesise out of the chaos, the imaginative rather than the descriptive.

For the Internet, as it is now, will be swamped with junk. I do not believe this will go on in the present form. It is now possible to determine in advance which home pages and chats are serious, though there are a tremendous number of home pages which are little more than publicity brochures and most of the chatting is hardly intellectual. Users can learn ways of escaping from cyberbabble. The relatively new Google service for scholars which restricts searches to primary papers and documents is in fact a major initiative, as is Google's programme to digitalize and make available the contents of five of the world's great libraries.

But note. The origins of the Internet go back less than two decades; its widespread use in academia less than one decade; its democratisation perhaps five years; its sudden popularity and the beginnings of its vast expansion and growing commercialisation only since about 1994. As a communicator of knowledge it is in its infancy. As a generator of knowledge, it has hardly yet begun.

An essential condition for the proper operation of universities, and of the knowledgeable world outside of universities, is freedom of ideas and communication. I abhor the entry of politicized racism into scholarship, but I defend the right of such thinkers to express their thoughts. The only university remedy is the confrontation of reasoned argument. To me it is a shocking that there have been incidents of de facto censorship, including the cancellation of scholarly visits, at such venerable institutions as Harvard and Oxford, let alone dozens of minor players.

Much of this has to do with the power of "political correctness", a phenomenon which has no place in true universities.

In the Muslim world, in particular, different forms of political correctness prevail.

The International Union of Anthropological and Ethnological Sciences, of which I was then president, accepted an invitation from Egyptian colleagues to hold an international meeting in Alexandria close to Christmas. Egypt then had diplomatic ties with Israel. In accordance with policy the IUAES had received assurances that no person would be excluded on the grounds of citizenship or religion. A few days before the meeting we received word that the meeting was cancelled—because students at the American University in Cairo were threatening mayhem if Israelis were permitted.[65]

In 2005 an international academic historians conference was to be held in Istanbul, examining the issue of the slaughter of Armenians in the wake of World War I, a slaughter which outside critics dub "genocide", an appellation the Turkish government refuses to acknowledge, describing the victims as traitors. The Turkish government heavy handedly proscribed the meeting. This from a country that is seeking to join the European Union.

There must be many instances of meetings in Muslim universities which do not involve such censorship. And there are many Muslim calls for the opening of freer internal discussions. But until such issues are addressed frankly and firmly the Muslim intellectual world will be unable to become a full participant in Utopia, and will be unable to make its creative voice heard the way it should be heard.

Let me turn now to set out a number of subjects which I believe are under-investigated by contemporary science and scholarship. This not intended as an exhaustive trip into the unknown, but rather as a demonstration that the unknown is very much still out there, despite the fact that we now have the tools, if not the will, to create a socio-political Utopia. In some respects, scientific knowledge now is to knowledge by the end of the twenty-first century as scientific knowledge in Ancient Greece is to scientific knowledge now. The ability of the human mind to keep up with such a vast leap forward will be sorely tested, as will the capacity of scientists to create intelligible interpretations of what they explore. I anticipate that demands on the mind will prompt its evolution in ways that draw upon as yet unused mental powers. Science, all knowledge, is, when it all boils down, a matter of imagining and transforming rules of the universe into terms that the human mind recognises. Perhaps the universe has no rules; those little dangling bits of probability that are unaccounted for may, one way or another, remain dangling for ever. But as long as we can use the mind's predispositions, and yet be prepared to accept uncertainty, we seem to be able to find enough by way of regularity to function.

Everything we have by way of perception, knowledge and feeling is organised and made conscious within what we call the mind. We believe that the mind is the activity of the brain made conscious. (There are of course a host of other meanings, from soul to memory.) It would seem that if we are to understand knowledge, we must understand the mind. Most of the knowledge about the mind has come from internal reflection, observing what happens when we are conscious of thinking and meditating, and from uncontrolled inferences that come from asserted probing into the subconscious, to which we add the body of psychology and the analysis of culture and of behaviour. It is a huge amount, but, curiously, gives us very little data (comparatively speaking) about how the physiological body interacts with what seems to be known from these approaches, (even though psychology began with attempts to understand the senses and to relate these to perceptions and thought through philosophy).

As the major working hypothesis we locate the physiological processes of the mind in the brain. It is notoriously difficult to study living brains.[66] Yet to understand them, to be able to account for what happens within them, is the major missing factor in the comprehension of the mind, and hence of knowledge. The more we understand those processes, the more we will understand how it is we know and believe what we do. The more that understanding progresses, the more we will understand how the rules of knowledge link with the rules of nature, or depart from them.

Thus I place enquiry into the brain and the mind at the top of my priorities in research. The challenge is indeed being taken seriously within the constraints of contemporary science. As a layman, it seems to me that neurological and physiological studies are proceeding at a rate far exceeding that of the past— but that the data are still not ready to lead us beyond speculative models. The development of mood changing drugs such as Prozac, with some understanding of why chemical intervention affects the brain's processes, and the location of areas of the brain linked to behaviour and emotions, indicate increasing interest and success. Some of the studies provide a physiological basis for understanding ways in which the *total* bodily system, including the senses and organic malfunctions, affect the brain and its consciousness. But by comparison with what we don't know, this is as yet picayune.

Consideration of the brain opens up the can of worms that the current methods of science are probably not enough, indeed may well be epistemologically insufficient. Innovation, remember, is linked to what is already known. Epistemologically, this means reliance on modifying, or tinkering, with what is already tried and true. We advance with analogies and depart from them at our risk. When they are departed from, it requires others to recognise that the departure has use. The history of science is populated by those who reversed a known principle (Galileo), linked hitherto unlinked observations (some new) together (Newton, Darwin, Freud), and so on. Recall the resistances, not based on criticism of what was proposed but on ideology and on the conservatism that results from the inevitable dependency on what has gone on before.

It may be that we are awaiting more such revolutions in the investigation of the brain. Those who suggest that there are phenomena connected to the functioning of the brain that the epistemology of contemporary science is not equipped to reveal are frequently dubbed as cranks. In some sense many are at least confusing science and faith. But behind the confusion lie some real questions.

The term paranormal is indicative. Science on the whole deals with the normal world, a world of tested methods and the predictability of their usefulness. In that body of concepts there are primary notions of energy. Never mind that these notions are being revised almost continuously as atomic physicists and astrophysicists and brain researchers learn more. There is a set of concepts that are organised in such away that the kind of energy represented in nature is consistent and coherent. We sort of know what we mean by magnetism, light, sound, radio waves, electrical charges, gravity, and the ways in which particles play with each other. We know that scientists observe and measure these things. And that as they do so problems keep cropping up requiring more refined measurements and observations and new loci of energy. We also know that three hundred years ago some of the types of energy that are talked of today were not known as such.

Let us start with the kinds of energy we know about. If you place a suitable designed receiver at any spot in the world that is not shielded you will be able to receive and translate radio signals from thousands of transmitters. Any amateur can do this, as I did as a boy. The basic premise has to be that all the thousands of signals are *simultaneously* passing through the one place where the receiver sorts them out.

If the brain is not shielded, the signals must be passing through the brains of each of us. Each of us is a potential radio and television receiver. Sci-fi apart, that is not my point. The point is that we are not conscious that this is happening to us. The waves exist in nature, so that to some extent the brain during its evolution had to deal with such invasions. What do we know about this? I understand that there is a considerable literature on, for example, microwaves. Most issues that are argued about in the press deal with potential associations with physiological disrupture such as anaemia or cancer. And I apologise (as I must do through the discussion here) if there is a major body of knowledge of which I am unaware. I would expect that the passage of such waves through the body would have some effects. This does not mean that they cause anaemia or cancer. The relationship between energy waves and bodily functioning seems to me to be likely to be subtle and undramatic, but nevertheless there, just as the effects of food intake are there. It may even be that the body has defence mechanisms to inhibit such invasions from having effects, from, for example, disturbing its internal electrical impulses. Existing scientific methods should be able to tell us something.

On the other hand, are there other energy systems, or other energy sources which are consistent with the current paradigm, that a study of the brain may reveal? I most certainly do not believe everything I hear about the paranormal. But I regard the fantasies as the expectable outcome when humans are trying to deal with, and manipulate, that which is *not* understood. Is this not a portrait of alchemy dealing with the unknowns of chemistry? And, as with alchemy, there are those who, in limited ways, try to investigate paranormal phenomena. They find fraud, trickery and hypnotism. But they also find indications that "there is something unexplained".

I do not have to provide a comprehensive list. Human auras captured on photograph. Close-to-death experiences. The transmission of feeling between persons in physical proximity. A part of what in anthropology is called "mana", exuding power and charisma. The capturing of thought across space. Faith healing. *Déja vu.* The consciousness of events, such as the death of a loved one, which occur far beyond immediate perception.

My scepticism extends to the dismissal of such reports as nonsense. Many are not. It may turn out that there are as yet unknown psychological processes of an ordinary kind which explain them. It does not seem likely that such explanations will be valid for all instances. My scepticism suggests that dismissal is based upon the unquestioning belief in present scientific paradigms, at least to the extent that they cannot be revolutionised.

It may well be that existing energy concepts will be capable of handling such questions; but not if they remain relatively uninvestigated. If they are so capable, much that we do not know about the brain will be revealed; including, in the extreme, ways in which the brain constructs fantasies and communicates them to others. But in my view the investigations are unlikely to be fully revelatory unless the investigators are prepared to use as hypothesis that there may be kinds of energy linked to the human body that we do *not* know about, and which may not be measurable with the kinds of instruments at our disposal. *The energies of contemporary physics may not be the only kinds.* Perhaps we need a concept of the transmission of force, or power, that uses quite different metaphors.

We cannot talk of the mind without raising problems in psychoanalysis. It has been shown on many occasions that Freudian and Jungian procedures, for example, are based on faith, that curative claims for the procedures are defective, and that there have been very few attempts at controlled studies of outcomes, a process that is foreign to the movements. I am not concerned with those charges, which are common to almost the whole body of alternative therapies, partly because the practitioners have been driven, at various times, into self-defence cults through opposition (itself failing to set up controlled studies). I am instead concerned with the basic underlying concepts as subjects for investigation.

These are the subconscious, almost universally accepted as a concept nowadays, the collective unconscious, and, by extension, archetypes and the place of dreams in what I am calling the mind. I find the concepts so chillingly lacking in accuracy, yet adhered to in their psychoanalytic form by so many respected intelligences, that I wonder what I must be missing. That in itself doesn't matter: the reader will be able to correct. But the *issue* matters because I have asserted that a precise knowledge of the mind-as-brain is essential to us in so many ways.

There can be no doubt at all that there is a subconscious. If that were not true, the brain, in order to function as a memory bank would be flooding us with millions of images, in a totally chaotic way. They have to be stored away, ready to come forward on call.

But we know that most of our memories are not literally true, or are true only to some degree. We only have to think back and check against realities, such as diaries of the time. I have done this and am surprised at what my memory of my youth is and at the discrepancy with diaries. Psychoanalysts would argue that this is because we are suppressing. That suppression takes place is also correct. The connotations of suppression and forgetfulness are different. Is an Alzheimer's sufferer suppressing? I think not. Suppression implies a deliberate act, sometimes of the conscious mind, and unconsciously through biases, some would say distortions, of the psyche, especially when troubled. Forgetfulness and inaccuracy of memory are different.

Two points immediately arise. If it is in our nature as humans to suppress in the more deliberate sense, or even to forget, the questions are how and why? A functional and evolutionary approach would suggest that there is good reason, that we are *meant* to do these things for the good functioning of the socio-biological unit. If so, to pull these out of the subconscious could be a dangerous game, and may account for therapy failure. Forgetfulness may of course result from the need to clear the brain's storage capacity of space, rather like clearing a document from a hard drive. The address to the location is wiped, but it remains around somewhere and may be retrieved by appropriate searches that do not depend on the address unless it has been over-written. A troubling feature of a psychoanalytical approach is that it is directed not only at those who declare themselves to be sick and who seek help, but at those who in normal society are considered healthy. Freudian-based psychoanalysis demands that a qualified analyst be analysed to know himself or herself. The process—apart from its secret society overtones—implies that what the organism spontaneously does is not organically sound. Psychoanalysis is somehow God's gift to make up for the mistakes of nature, and can only be understood through immediate subjective experience of it.

The other point is that retrieved memory is not necessarily accurate—in fact it won't be, for memory never is. There will be errors, trivial or significant. To base remedial action on memory, spontaneous or retrieved, has to be the case. Memory, it has been pointed out, is a *living thing*, a part of a living, ever-changing, ever-renewing body. To assume that what is retrieved through analysis is any more accurate, without independent verification, than spontaneous memory is too big a jump.

Thus we need vastly more research on how this all happens within the brain. And in parenthesis we may remark that discrimination in memory has positive effects (in addition to avoiding the unpleasant), since as a result we put our knowledge together in various new shapes and forms, in other words we are predisposed to create. It might well be that if we had complete and accurate memories of our past we could not function.

The search for the collective unconscious, and of archetypes, is a different matter, for the issue here becomes one of nature versus nurture. It is distressing that both Freud and Jung necessarily drew upon an anthropology that was in its infancy for their stimulation and claims of universality. It would nowadays be argued, for example, that the interpretations that Jung made on the basis of short-term African experience must by their nature be flawed. No one, it would be argued, could reasonably interpret myth, religious and spiritual concepts, psychological orientations, dreams, or any sensitive materials in which ideas require contextual interpretation, without extensive participatory enquiry into the depths of culture, which in turn requires the mastery of language. Which does not necessarily mean that Jung was wrong; rather that he could not know if he was correct or not.

Probably because of his training as a doctor, his theological and paranormal interests, and the climate of the time, some of Jung's concepts of the sources of the collective unconscious leant toward the biological, and/or theological. (This is innovative synergy at its best.) The collective unconscious, it seems, was independent of the processes of *cultural* transmission, especially conscious socialisation. The themes of myths and dreams are composed of elements which have localised cultural content and application, but which are embedded in the nature of humanity. This explains why some of the themes crop up pretty well universally, everywhere from prehistory to the present.

For such an interpretation to be true, in the present arrangement of our concepts, it seems to me that one of three processes must be involved (or some mix of them). Most closely linked to Jung's thinking would be the genetic or the spiritual. The genetic implies that archetypes are somehow carried from one generation to another biologically, that is through genes. If genes were not the source, then the soul must somehow be involved. There must be a spiritual entity that contains the regularities of the archetypes, embodied in the collective unconscious. I am not sure how this would link with free will.

The third view is cultural. Archetypes and their equivalents (present in the work of Kroeber and Kluckhohn, and Gorer's national character) do not exist in the Jungian sense. They do exist in the sense that one can find similar patterns of thought, dreaming, and myth-making in differing cultures, but then the term would have to discard its Jungian features. The processes that result in such replication are several.

The most fundamental is that humans in different contexts ask similar questions, and have similar intellectual resources with which to answer them. How did the first humans come into existence? Without the contemporary data-base of science or the intellectual prop of evolution, one imagines on the basis of what one knows. What one knows is the behaviour of humans and the immediate phenomena of the natural world. Myths of origin are bound to have similarities that can be abstracted out. Anthropomorphism comes naturally out of experience. There are quasi-universal features of sex, of the relationships between men, women and children, out of which images and metaphors emerge. The mind can easily make connections between crises in the natural world—eruptions, lava flows, hurricanes, floods—and crises in imagined human history or in the story of the individual persona. This is embodied in the nature of art, story telling, myth making, imagining, philosophising, dreaming, in other words creative thought.

A further problem I have is with the interpretations of dreams, not in themselves, but as being a special kind of revelation of the unconscious. By definition they are *not* unconscious or even uncontrolled, any more than waking thoughts are. We are acutely conscious of them, often worried by them. A dream that is truly unconscious, if there be any such thing, does not count until it becomes conscious. There exist techniques for increasing the control over them, both in terms of calling them up and in content.

In our more wakeful hours our imaginations work in similar ways; we sit by the lakeshore than let our minds wander, day-dreaming. Thoughts come into our consciousness unbidden. Several trains of thought are sometimes in our conscious minds simultaneously. Just as with dreams, when a waking image comes, if we want to hold on to it we rush for a piece of paper. If we don't we may lose it, perhaps for ever, just as we do with dreams. Those who put analytical prepotence on dreams and are asking for their recall are in fact further removing the dream from the subconscious, denying in practice the theoretical premise of their work. They are in fact asking the mind to deliberate on the dream, to hold it, and thus to influence its content. It is like an anthropologist who, by over-insisting on his or her questions, encourages an informant to re-think what is being communicated—which is why the main schools of field anthropology distrust verbal information on its own, always trying to compare with observation of real behaviour.

I believe there *is* a difference in kind between two sorts of thinking. One kind consists of images, which can be intense pattern and colour combinations as in painting, or, more commonly, sequences of dramatic events. The other consists in series of words without the images—what language do you think in?—sometimes with two or more discussions going on in the head simultaneously. Neither are easy to recapture, to hold on to. But the former seems to come to consciousness more frequently at the time of the onset of sleep or awakening or during "day-dreaming" when the biological system is, as it were, in neutral, just turning over. And the latter is more typical of the alert moments. And the two may be intertwined.

Both manners of thinking are highly creative, reveal characteristics of their author, and appear to be located in the brain.

Although my opinion and bias will be obvious, I am not saying "this is so". I am saying let's check it out. This is another reason to work hard on knowing the brain.

Another field of enquiry which Utopia requires, perhaps more urgently, is in the field of pedagogy.

Utopian plans for Youth Maturity Institutes can so easily be watered down, trivialized and made ineffective by weak pedagogical instruments. Colleges of Education have been derided in the past, especially in North America, for insignificant, frivolous and inept research activities. This is unfair to those individuals who have maintained high standards on serious issues and I am sure that the research ambience is changing.

But in part it is caused by time spent on looking into marginal or logistical questions rather than fundamental ones. What we desperately need to know is answers to such problems as: How, and with what approaches, can Youth Maturity Institutes, with their anticipated resources, most effectively counteract violent tendencies in youth? Classroom exhortation is clearly not enough. How can prejudice and charity be turned into understanding? What classroom methods can be devised to ensure the effectiveness of the Youth Maturity Institute goals? How do these intersect with non-classroom activities? What indicators can be made available, or developed, to enable observers to detect the emergence of individual stresses and psychological issues in the children?

Another subject of major concern for Utopian enquiry is the potential capability of humankind to live elsewhere than on this planet. Humankind discounts the future in terrible ways. We turn our backs on doing anything about volcanic eruptions or earthquakes or even global warming because it seems to be not here today but maybe decades later. Astronomers are good at noticing alien bodies about to impact the earth. The sighting and tracking of a significantly damaging body can start when it is many years away. Research is taking place to attempt to destroy many of the lesser bodies before they hit ground. But a truly cataclysmic body capable of destroying the earth's surface would surely, by its very destruction if that were possible, have other devastating effects which would threaten life on earth as we know it. We cannot wait to know how to evacuate the earth until just the moment the danger is sighted, long though our warning might be. For the answer to where do we go has not even begun and is hugely complex. So, rather than waste money on huge earthly missile defence systems (when the answer to that danger lies in Global Government) we must start knowing about a future homeland and how to get there. This is for the 21st century to start, not the fiftieth.

We have knowledge as yet of how to organise a mass evacuation of earth. Nor do we know where such an evacuation should end up. While we are continuously looking for signs of life comparable to humanity elsewhere, there is very little we know on that subject with reasonable degrees of certainty, given the vastness of the universe. And we definitely don't know how much time we have got. Because cataclysm is unlikely to hit the living generation in any but critically manageable form, we assign relatively low priority to such studies. In Utopia, enquiry of long-term, very long-term, significance should be more than equal to the resolution of the immediate.

Quite possibly linked to our future fates is the controversial domain of hyperspace, the theoretical and applied study of multi-dimensions—I am told up to ten dimensional space as it exists now. Such words raise science fiction thoughts of parallel universes, of the possibility that living beings can arrive on earth in dimensions we cannot or can only partially, detect. I say "raise thoughts" because the understanding of ten or so dimensions is totally beyond me, and in truth I have no idea whether the concepts have any relationship at all to what science fiction writers imagine.

The point is, however, worth making because of the innovative dynamics outlined in Chapter II. However unimaginable are the imagined worlds of science fiction, they consist of weaving together conceptual strands that are already in our pool of culture, so that the whole cloth, consisting of newly imagined relationships between existing culture-facts, is like a magic carpet transported from another, yes, dimension, to float within our minds. Quite often, elements in science fiction are not far ahead of what scientists are already addressing. Sometimes the imagined cultures consist of the present, satirised to be sure, with existing phenomena exaggerated and extended toward the impossible, which later turns out to be real. It is false to think of such imaginings as minor. Electronic tracking devices for humans, communication from any human body to any other located anywhere on the globe (or even in space), video surveillance, robotic domestic services, semi-intelligence devices working with fuzzy logic, instant data banks on everyone, electronic identity cards containing one's personal history, surveillance cameras tracking every movement—these, the stuff of science fiction's paraphernalia that underlie imagined social and political systems, these are already here, awaiting refinement which is coming at a pace not seriously believed to be likely (save for a few) forty years ago.

Imagination is the stuff of knowledge, and, in whatever form it is presented to us, sparks disciplined thought, which, I believe, will increase in intensity the more human beings are released from drudgery so that they may, each in their own way, live creatively. Remember, our Utopia is a creative society.

Thinking about ecosystems has become indeed a major preoccupation for those who enquire conventionally, those who manage commercially and politically, for those who show their concerns by joining with others and attempting to influence outcomes, by schoolchildren. The remaining issues of ecology are still, not only serious, but on a scale that requires much more disciplined attention.

The natural world on earth is so enormously complex, with so many trillions of interacting elements, that I am confident that what we believe to be sound knowledge today (sound knowledge that is seldom agreed to by all) will look quite different in the future.

The study of minimal eco-systems can embrace for simple manpower reasons only a tiny proportion of what could be known. (Question: could not many of the creatively non-employed become para-ecologists, trained to undertake much of this work?) Another set of studies, interacting with the former, deals with wider eco-systems. The task of integrating all these, and other forces, into global models is, literally, in its adolescence. Data on global warming are capable of several interpretations. When one seems to be prepotent, other sets of data, themselves necessarily imperfect, call for a re-arrangement of the factors, another set of explanations. This is necessary, will go on possibly *ad infinitum*, but surely clearer knowledge will emerge. (It strikes me that the identification of an eco-system is a little like the identification of a society—an arbitrary creation of a boundary within which a system can be abstracted by leaving out of consideration external factors. Thus a neighbourhood as a social system, an ethnic community as a society, a country is one. The only true society that corresponds with nature, the only true eco-system that corresponds with nature, is global. And even that, particularly with nature, can be extended to include extra-terrestrial events.)

But many of the consequences of global warming, and of the large cycles of natural warming and freezing, are inadequately studied. These include protection issues—defences against rising waters, conditions in which population shifts may be necessary, and, as I pointed out in the previous chapter, the adjustment of food supplies through modifications in the food chain to fit new climatic conditions. In previous tropical or ice ages mankind did not have the tools to undertake such studies or modifications. Now, once again, we do, but do we have the determination and the will to do so?

Which question leads immediately in to the issue of genetic modification . . .

Genetic modification has become a portmanteau word buzz phrase carrying ideological premises as if every form of genetic modification equated every other. There are dangers in slap dash, careless, not considering the consequences, genetic modification because all such activities carry consequences, not all of which may be known. There are other acts of genetic modification which are as well controlled as is humanly possible, and the controls continue to be improved. In other words it is false to tar each act of genetic modification with the same brush. Each action must be judged on its individual merit, weighing the costs and benefits, just as is done with new pharmaceuticals.

Furthermore, genetic modification has been with us since the invention of breeding animals and cross fertilizing crops, and very often the results have been the reverse of what was wanted. But the crosses which persist have been invaluable—new strains of wheat and rive increased yields in the Third World, relieving some poverty. And even a new animal, the mule, came into being, to say nothing of specialist wool bearing or flesh enhanced sheep, and quite different strains of horses and cattle. It is my contention that the difference between this and laboratory genetic manipulation is that there are more controls with the latter, and that there is no reason in principle to ban it, or to ban the use of the results. There is every reason to insist on maximum investigation of consequences before any product is released to the public.

Indeed this is a field which demands major priorities in research, for the simple reason that it holds one of the answers to the effects of phenomena such as global warming. Humanity needs, in very short order, to adjust its crops and animal husbandry to the swings of climate change—of global warming in the now future, and of at least a mini ice age further down the centuries. Genetic modification is probably the fastest way of doing this—and given the huge diversity of domesticated species, no time should be lost. Ironically, a form of genetic modification is already normal in human therapeutics—the identification of genes responsible for certain illnesses, leading to the use of this knowledge to create gene-suppressing medication.

So much work is going on in the world of medical science, with exponential growth in research and its costs, and in its results that it may seem redundant to stress it. However the balance seems awry. The profit motive, which I do not deride, has the consequence of making drugs out of reach even for governments. New and more technical machines arrive and after all their absence are suddenly deemed to be essential at the cost of millions, and perhaps of advances in other medical fields. There is no simple Utopian answer to this.

One of the despairing features of medical and pharmaceutical research is the way its priorities are governed by national immediacies and the attendant commercial priorities. Scholarly associations in various countries do try to draw attention to imbalances, but governments are chary of listening. Despite the sometimes successful efforts of the World Health Organisation, global issues get little attention unless, like influenza, there is a probability of direct impact of a country's population. All too rarely, it takes the initiative of a major private donor to break through the confines.

Thus it has taken the private initiative of Bill Gates to start to address one of the major imbalances. Profit-oriented research focuses to a major degree on the ills of financially advanced countries. Would the scourge of AIDS in the poor world have received attention if it had not also devastated the West? I think not. But malaria, disease of the poor, kills as many in the countries where it is present. Europe and North America got rid of it only a couple of centuries ago, but they did. Bill Gates, noting the few resources available for the study of anti-malarial vaccines, drugs and therapies, established a well endowed Foundation to concentrate on the issues. He has also created a specific fund to endow researchers in areas of medical study that are inadequately supported by conventional funding sources.

There are few benefactors with the wealth or sensitivity to do the same for the other scourges—ebola, the tsetse fly, locusts (for a different branch of science), sleeping sickness. Hepatitis, schistosomiasis, and many others.

And once again governments, until the problem jumps over borders, sit on their figurative hands. They tend to put it off until it really does start to become or to threaten a pandemic. Dangerous short-sightedness and selfishness. A case in point is germane as I write—so-called bird flu. The WHO has issued its warning of a possible pandemic if the flu jumps from human to human. I have no idea whether this is justified. But the point is that this sort of dramatisation is directed to stimulate not only protective measures, but the fundamental research necessary to deal with it. When it was thought of simply as bird to an Asian peasant or poultry farmer, the monied world took little notice. Another argument for Global Government which transcends selfish national interests and balances the needs of health and medical research against those of armaments.

The only governmental organisation capable of taking a world view is the World Health Organisation (or its Utopian successor forecast in the chapter on Global Government). It needs a massive injection of research funds by the Utopian Global Government—Bill Gates multiplied by ten. If my call for the concentration of military power in the hands of Global Government, for the criminalisation of national armed forces and for the suppression of the arms trade were to be heeded, the sums needed would be readily available. Turn arms manufacturers and their research establishments into medical and pharmaceutical companies. It is a matter of direction, priority and will, rather than of resources.

And a word about anthropology. Like economics used to be, anthropology is not a discipline but consists of points of view that make use of varying disciplines. I do not hold a brief for anthropology in its present state. But if we are to examine the potential paths toward Utopia, to trace them, and if Utopia is to be recognisant of and based upon sound knowledge of the ways in which societies and cultures work, then what anthropology, somewhat unknowingly, stands for, is essential, even if by some other name. In its underlying but imperfectly applied philosophy anthropology is in fact the nub from which a holistic, synthesising interpretation of the world can emerge.

The statement rests upon the fact that anthropology draws into itself theories, methods, perspectives and sometimes data from all other disciplines (and some others in addition) which bear upon the nature of human behaviour. The most effective anthropologist, from this point of view, is one who has been trained to the graduate level in another subject (once a mandatory requirement, in effect, at the London School of Economics). Obviously, no scholar can encompass the whole of what has been achieved in other subjects. But his or her knowledge of at least one of history, biology, psychology, economics, some sociology, music, art, mathematics, political science, will inevitably enter into his or her methodology, question-formulation and theoretical constructions.

This is necessary to anthropology, a central part of its system. To construct explanations, it must try to put the phenomena it examines *in context*. It is clearly, at this point, extremely difficult if not impossible to achieve totality in accounting for a context. But that is the aim, whether the problem be connected with incest, the money market, or the ways in which illnesses are recognised.

After the contextualisation comes the simplification, the reduction of the data to abstract principles. To do this we need data bases, some of which are known as "thick ethnography", of great detail, of many dimensions, and at a relatively low level of abstraction. Unfortunately, the creation of thick ethnography is often thought of as a goal in itself. It cannot be, if the powers of anthropology are to be released. Anthropology needs many more abstracting minds at work, if its answers are to be applicable to humankind.

My examples in the penultimate paragraph hint at another feature. There is literally no subject area of human existence, at any time or place, which is beyond anthropological study, in which questions of anthropological relevance are not embedded. This is a point that most non-anthropological social scientists do not at present realise.

In part, they do not realise it because anthropology lacks the enormous man and woman power to obtain not only its data base but to emphasise its links with colleagues in other subjects. This is reflected in the conservative organisation of scholarship. Ph.D's do the work, often alone. In my view they need to be supplemented by hosts of simply trained data gatherers, whom we may call para-anthropologists—recruited from professionals like teachers, nurses, agricultural officers in the field. And also, why not, some of the Utopian army of the non-employed who will emerge from the Utopian employment conditions and guaranteed income proposals to be outlined in later chapters.

And it is also a reflection of the fact that the weight of anthropological enquiry moves with fashion, and that very few specialties within anthropology have enough critical mass to meet their goals, let alone make them known outside the profession. To make its rightful impact, for example, economic anthropology would need to have almost as many practitioners as the whole of anthropology now. How else can it cover the territory? All times, places and questions? And that is the same for several score of anthropology's other interacting parts.

I have tried to give examples of long term, very long term issues that come to mind, and I do so as a corrective to the current intense preoccupation with immediate and even payable results. Readers will identify other domains of knowledge which in their view are equally, perhaps more, significant, to our future. Good.

For what it all adds up to is that Utopia is knowledge-based, and that to get there we need expanding understandings. Other Chapters have brought forward the notion that humankind, the individuals who make it up, seldom have the challenge or opportunity to use their creative minds to the fullest. There are vast mental energies which are underused. This, rather than in wage-earning, is the true unemployment we face.

It is here that the venture lies. This will be the location of human contentment, growing out of grappling with challenges. It will be through these kinds of activities, or never at all, that we reach Utopia.

XI

Terrorism and Freedom

If this were war, then current terrorists have won these skirmishes. At least temporarily. Nevertheless they represent but a tiny proportion of the world's activity, drawing disproportionate media attention to their barbaric acts. They are driven by extreme doctrines, some clearly political, some fervently religious. Their bloodthirsty consequences alone require that they be stopped. More fundamentally, they represent an adulation of violence which, as we have seen, is totally in opposition to the peaceful world we envisage as our goal. They represent the antithesis of civilisation.

The shock of 9-11 in the United States sent the world into a tizzy and, in the U.S., into paranoia. 9-11 was not the first, the largest, the most brutal, or the last of the massacres. It was pitifully small by comparison with the official wars of the last century, and does not compare with what is going on as I write in Darfur[67] or the Congo, or recently in Rwanda. And especially Iraq. Che Guevara got away with murder and became a hero in the process.

Terrorism has been with humanity in one form or another for centuries—remember the Assassins?[68] They were a branch of Ismaili Shi'as, a group who once ruled Egypt, had castles on the offensive and defensive in Sunni and Mongol Mesopotamia, and whose swirling dervish rituals and food practices[69] had a significant though peaceful hold in Turkey. Certainly present day followers of the Aga Khan cannot be accused of bloodthirsty intentions, which give hope for peaceful segmentation and evolution.

Criminal murder is often a form of terrorism. Suicide often has similarities. Violent death takes place in order to dramatise a grievance and cause fear in relatives. Contemporary terrorism is distinguishable in that it targets the innocent. The Assassins and the anarchists of the nineteenth and early twentieth centuries targeted those they believed to be guilty, thus taking the law into their own bloody hands, although other terrorists and, yes, official armies, have been guilty of indiscriminate massacres over the centuries.

Why have terrorists won this stage? The Western world, largely following the United States, put the defeat of terrorism at the top of its policy agendas, making all other policies subservient to it, although there are signs that Britain and Europe are stepping up other priorities, such as dealing with world hunger. That perhaps natural reaction is just what current terrorists want—it is their best public relations.

President Bush characterized the defence against terror as a "war", with huge consequences for the deployment of arms, the demonization of opponents, and the disposition of treasure. By doing so he used the identical public relations strategy as the terrorists—jihad and war both become justifications. This has diverted funds from the handling of social ills in his own country and undermined the United States' ability to act as the wise leader of the world.

That is only a small part of the current terrorist victory. In embracing war, the United States leads the way in its attack on freedoms, freedoms which most of the world believed it cherished as a founding principle. The Patriot Act, the dismissal of the Geneva Convention, the extreme controls over the movement of visitors to the country, the detention of suspects without trial or access to legal support or time limit, the intrusion of racial profiling, represent a major step backwards from the strange and imperfect liberty that the French statue in New York harbour upholds as a beacon to the oppressed of the world.

The assault on due process is mirrored in other countries, even Britain, that supposed bastion of freedom, and France, the land of liberty, equality and fraternity. It is like a nasty virus which has escaped the control of the WHO.

Justified by war? In this case the word is a mere slip of the tongue insofar as terrorists are concerned. If war, then where is the Geneva Convention?

Justified by 9-11? Only by paranoids, however understandable is the reaction to the horror and tragedy. The trouble is that the paranoia has persisted, dragged out by the freedom of the presumed Al Qaeda leader, of which more below, and the failures of policy in Iraq. Thus the attack on liberty not only prevails but has become routine in the practices of governments, which some suspect to be politically motivated in order to control public opinion.

Over the centuries men and women fought for the acquisition of liberty and the rule of balanced law. It is symptomatic of the state of affairs that I feel the need to remind fellow citizens of this, of the huge sacrifices made, often in vain, of the way the Second World War was fought for freedom, of the wave of populist determination to turn autocracy and nepotism into freedom in Georgia, Ukraine, hopefully in Afghanistan and Iraq, and against an occupying force in both Lebanon and Iraq.

There has been no acquisition of liberty without pain and sacrifice. The deaths at 9-11 were not an excuse for war and more violence. The correct memorial is that the country becomes more than ever determined to stand up for its liberties, not giving an inch of them away. Reaffirming and celebrating them. But we are a long way from this. Vengeance, the vengeance of the terrorist, has gripped the United States, giving the terrorists the tactical victory. An eye for an eye and a tooth for a tooth has be-devilled domestic life and politics in the Balkans and the Middle East. Has it now arrived in the West?

Military abuses in Guantanamo Bay, Afghanistan, and Abu Ghaira should surprise no one. Canadians in Somalia. British in Iraq, have been caught in the same way. They go unnoticed in full scale war. If we want to stop them the first thing to do is to stop war. But they also reveal a gun toting macho mentality which has deep roots, and a culture of abuse and shame in U.S. prisons which is part of U.S. culture and spreads amongst its young unarmed men, as do the sloppy trigger happy lethal reactions of a small minority of frightened soldiers.

In such a context the boast of the U.S. President that he will support liberty and defend it in every part of the world is hollow, naïve and hypocritical. In countries where it counts, as perhaps in Lebanon, it is hollow and even counter-productive, giving strength to the nationalist opponents of liberty and U.S. interference. The demand for liberty comes from within. Outsiders can help but not impose it. President Bush, too often is the cry, put your own house in order, a cry the Chinese use with effect, and undermines genuine moves towards democracy.

Terrorism at the present time[70] is mostly Islamist, though others join the fray for psychological, pillaging or other motives. As in Darfur[71] it can be openly organised, even State supported but this is not the global form. It therefore behoves the Islamic world to support the basic premise—the removal of the cult of violence. Islamic Youth Maturity Institutes. Only when the ideological power of Islam focuses on reform, and takes responsibility for the disaffected young, will this kind of terrorism, perhaps to be replaced by some other until Youth Maturity Institutes take hold. This will not happen over night.

First, the Muslim world needs time to embrace the Youth Maturity Institute concept, then it requires practical organising, and then it will be years before the first full graduates reach adult citizenship and influence. In the meantime Muslim, Christian and Jewish schools must be prevented from preaching, approving, let alone sanctifying, violence.

Acts of terrorism are justified as part of a war against evil, defined by the group.[72] The Utopian perspective argues that evil is best countered by persuasion and example, and that violence is never justified.

There are good signs in such a direction. Influential mullahs in Saudi Arabia on both sides of the action have been meeting together for public theological debates. May their influence spread. Following the London bombings, for the first time Imams globally issued *fatwahs* condemning terrorist violence as un-Islamic and inexcusable. And Pakistan is taking draconian measures in an attempt to root out terrorist indoctrination from religious schools. It is minds and hearts which count. And that works the other way too. The increasing persecution of both Arabs and Jews in Europe not only contributes to terrorism but is ugly and anti-Utopian in its own character.

Terrorisms root causes? There are many, not just one.

Poverty is often cited. Based on the history of peasant and messianic movements, this is too simplistic. People who are in the depths of poverty do not usually engage in terrorist martyrdom. Instead, there must be a relationship between the level of poverty and expectations. Usually this occurs when the level of poverty is decreasing or has decreased, but all around there is wealth, and the poverty population asks why us?

To poverty must be added claustrophobia. This is particularly relevant in Palestine, but there is also a kind of psychological claustrophobia in Afghanistan and Iraq.[73] Not only is there poverty and unemployment, but there seems to be no way out. It takes little imagination to emphasize with Palestinian teenagers, growing up already in an atmosphere of repressive hostility, of rock throwing and aggression, with communication by graffiti, with the presence of troops ready to kill, to impose curfews (however justified). Live in a society in which for hours on end you are confined in your homes, with no power or water and no news and inadequate food, totally against your will. That is what terrorism has invited and the occupying power falls into the trap with more repression.

We have seen in earlier chapters the major importance of risk-taking in the lives of growing energetic youths. In such conditions, and the lesser ones of Afghanistan and Iraq, risk-taking means breaking curfews, jeering at occupying soldiers, establishing enemies whom you can taunt, risking your life by painting a graffiti. This adolescent extremism, an equivalent of Western road racing, obtains justification and extension as adult "responsibility" grows and finds the religious justification of terrorism congruent and appealing. The adolescent adopts the beard of the converted religious activist and finds that risk taking has its serious rewards.

In certain societies for lack of education and knowledge there is no clear secular answer. This does not lead to individual terrorism but contributes to messianic movements, led by a religious figure supported by organisers. European leaders, explorers and armies and navies, throughout history, have assumed that for every unknown but definable group of people there must be a leader. Western naval expeditions and labour recruiters alike in the South Pacific sought out "the chief" with whom to talk.

The United States approach to terrorism had been bedevilled by the same archaic and ignorant expectations. As soon as the notion of Al Qaeda appeared the cry was, find it's leader and exterminate him, and all will be well. At least policy did recognize that Osama bin Laden could not operate without a team of executives, so they too appear on the hunt list.

Much the same attitude applied in Iraq. The villain was clearly Saddam Hussein. Get him and all will be well. The occupying forces got him. All is not well

What is missing is that all leaders, even those who turn out to be the most despotic, require freely given popular support in order to rise to power. The removal of the leader may merely turn him or her into a martyr. Or he or she may become the object of revolutionary anger. Once power is achieved, however, the resources of the state are in the hands of the leader who can readily become a despot—Hitler, Idi Amin, Stalin, Mao are obvious examples, and Hussein is another. Therein lies one of the strongest cases for the removal of armaments from individual State control, and for the international tracking of arms supplies, to be discussed in chapter XII.

What we have here, then, is a mismatch between the level of living on the one hand and aspirations, whether material or ideological, or religious on the other. We also have an ideological leadership supported by an executive of ability.

In both instances a driving supportive force, from which the ideology takes its message is in the Christian/Islamic extension of Judaism with its beliefs in the Messiah, prophets, and martyrdom. It is no accident that a considerable degree of education and religious knowledge is required to justify and act upon the terrorist message. Osama bin Laden is neither a fool nor dumb and those around him have considerable education. Che Guevara and the Bader-Meinhoff gang represented varieties of terrorism with more secular ideologies, unless we count Marxism as being the Judeo-Christian-Islamic tradition.

On the basis of this theory in 1976 I published a prediction that the Palestinian diaspora and particularly the refugee camps were ripe for a fully blown messianic movement.[74] I was wrong. But on reflection not as wrong as all that. By focusing on the Palestinian diaspora I completely neglected, or was ignorant of, the widespread disaffection of millions in the Arab Islamic world outside of Palestine.

The Islamist phenomenon differs from the conventional messianic and millennial templates in several respects, yet may be considered to be an extension of such phenomena into the modern Islamic world. The first is the very size of the populations that are open to the relevant dynamics. From Palestine and Iraq to Iran and Afghanistan to say nothing of the North African littoral the forces are at work. This is a huge population which dwarfs those of the medieval peasant revolts and even more so the localized millennial movements of Asia Africa and the South Seas in the nineteenth and twentieth centuries.

Allied to this is the efficacy of modern communications which are open in principle to everyone. Television and the internet are powerful unifying forces which supplement the effectiveness of localized graffiti which carry sub rosa details.

The leaders of millennial movements seldom proclaim that they are messiahs, but in effect they carry a holy message. In Palestine the words of the crippled imam Abdullah Azzam are, in the words of one observer, treated "almost as if they were holy writ".[75] Sometimes, though not in Islam, there is indeed a messianic claim, as with the Lord's Liberation Army in Uganda, which also used abducted children to reinforce its vague message.

Another factor with Islam is the absence of a religious hierarchy in the normal meaning of the term. There are leaders who, because of their positions, hold important doctrinal sway. But in addition to the natural sectarian divisions, imams essentially are responsible to their individual mosques, though of course they are open to pressure from other religious leaders. On the one hand they are localized, but on the other their message an influence penetrates far more widely because of the velocity of circulation of ideas that the modern world brings with it.

Al Qaeda is the most notorious and clear example. I do not know that Osama bin Laden has ever claimed to be a messiah, and he mixes the political with the religious in his messages to carry them to a different even more potent level. And with many such movements, his failures to achieve his results (apart of frightening the West) do not undermine faith in his calls to arms.

We do not have to posit some kind of spider web global organisation. Clever organisers he has, but the culture of revenge and violence is at the fingertips of any would be follower, not necessarily with clear organisational links beyond inspiration and encouragement. By no means all of the events in Iraq are attributed to al-Qaeda, but enough are, and they provide a model for other acts of terrorism with sometimes quite different motives.

The underlying characteristic of conventional millennial movements is also missing, though one could argue that it is present in a different but analogous form. Millennial movements are typically social-community based—a village or a region. In this case the unifying ideology is that of a set of religious ideas which impact on the life story of individuals. The martyrs are individuals, not communities. They are not bringing the millennium to their fellows here on earth. All the evidence is that they truly believe in the reality of Paradise with its carnal and other-worldly. Pleasures, a joyous relief from the horrors of the earth, and a powerful and real reward for martyrdom, which asserts that the secular life is unworthy by comparison.

It is difficult for secular minded politicians, or those like George W Bush from different religions, to imagine the appeal of such martyrdom, even though Bush uses a great deal of religious hyperbole in his discourses, hyperbole which falls on completely deaf ears because in a contest with committed martyrdom there is no contest. For the individual involved, a suicidal attack has an almost automatic scenario, a state that approaches that of an active trance. Nothing matters accept the planned action. The mind and body are impervious to outside influence, to the environment except as it is a part of the scenario, and certainly to reason. In the successful events there has been a long build-up, not only of ideology and religious reference, but in something approaching ecstasy.

The current style of terrorism stresses martyrdom rather than the Messiah. Bin Laden may be a prophet but I have not seen information which suggests that he is messianic.

I may be well off base in my analysis of how individuals are open to such influences in Islamic society because my imperfect knowledge of the Middle Eastern. But I suspect much lies in family life and resultant psychosis, exacerbated by Palestinian like claustrophobia. It is common, though variable, in Arabic Muslim societies for children to be brought up by the women of the family, with fathers initially more remote figures. Then all of a sudden around the age of puberty the fathers take charge of the boys and introduce them to a male society from which women are excluded and strictly separated, unless they be women deemed to have low virtue and thus open to sexual exploitation. Or in the diaspora and many refugee camps the boys are let loose, with little fatherly guidance. I can imagine little that would be more dysfunctional, confusing the sexual stresses of puberty.

Thus in the mix we have young people dealing with deep sexual frustration and malfunction, a domain of sub-conscious psychological trouble to add to all their other disappointments, angers and frustrations. We do not have to go far to find sources of fanaticism.

That this perpetuates men's view of women there can be little doubt. However by no means all men become terrorists as a result. Far from it. The human child is highly malleable and survives the worst of horrors, amongst which this can hardly be counted. But an impressionable and sensitive and intelligent boy, and now girl, with a predisposition to psychosis would find the need for extreme outlets, into which the ideology of violence and terror fits like a glove. And what better than Paradise?

This does not quite account for girls becoming martyrs. The West expresses surprise that women martyrs turn out to be well educated often from prosperous families. Therein lies the rub. But consider. Such women must have deep personal grudges against the society from which they come. Their mothers did not have the same chance. The girls are striking out, becoming different, professionals while all around them are other girls destined to be mothers only. Their internal anger must be very deep and religion provides them with a way to demonstrate their determination and their power. The final step.

Once again I remark that the authoritarian response is to use force, and to go for the leader, the figurehead, who is deemed to be responsible. If only Bin Laden had not appeared the world would be alright. Let's get him. What rubbish.

No. It will take a long time to resolve the issues, but it can be done within this century. It is a battle of ideas, not guns. And the debates must, will, be undertaken within the Arab and Muslim communities themselves. The ideas of non-violence, courtesy, understanding and empathy are needed on both sides of the struggle. These are Muslim, Christian and secular values to which by far the majority of the population adhere.

Let them be stressed in Youth Maturity Institutes in the Middle East as everywhere else, and let those Institutes be equipped to understand and help with emergent psychoses and extreme social grievances.

At the beginning of this Chapter I proclaimed that the terrorists have won. They have undermined liberty and created a climate of distrust and nervousness. The defence against terrorism has avoided the primary causes and concentrated on violence and counter-violence.

A main theme running through Utopian society is that of responsible liberty in its most creative forms. Events following 9-11 have set that principle back perhaps for a decade of more. Armies and anti-missile defence systems have diverted thought, energy and money from the real issues. Current policies sacrifice liberty, are not Utopian, are not even good *realpolitik*.

As I write this, individuals suspected of the July 2005 bomb attacks in London are arrested in what seems to me to be brilliant police work. But, as with the Iraq invasion, what of the aftermath? It appears to me that there will be trials, in accordance with current judicial thinking. I imagine that, if found guilty, the result will be long prison sentences. With what result? Unless the guilty are in solitary confinement for the rest of their lives—cruel and unusual punishment—they will mix with other prisoners in the world's most effective school for crime.

Does Utopia have a better solution? Back to Chapter VI, following the principle of restitution. Confine the guilty until other conditions have been completed. Obtain the services of mullahs who will conduct discussions with them individually and as a group to relate their thinking to the holy Q'ran. Set them, individually, to maintenance cleaning in the underground and on buses and other forms of shaming and demeaning and ideologically restitutive services. Have them meet with the victims (especially but not only Muslims and poor immigrants) of the first blast to help with the victims' healing. Have them undergo appropriate therapeutic treatment. If and when it seems that remorse is present and genuine, have them appear in mosques and youth organisations to explain themselves and their changed perspectives.

The trial of Saddam Hussein provides another example. If and when he is found guilty, imprisonment in itself or death is inappropriate. He should be required to perform menial restitutive tasks in the communities he has damaged. He should face the individuals he has tortured. He should receive the scorn of the survivors of his depredations and, under judicial supervision to move the events from mere revenge, work out what amends he as a man can make. Shame is the greatest of deterrents.

The furore over the 2006 publication in Denmark of satirical and very pointed caricatures of Mohammed is highly revealing of the issues the world faces when confronted with Muslim frustrations angers and hostilities We must respect the religions of others, goes one well meaning cry, which verges on "we should censure the caricaturists". This kind of reaction is not only dangerously simplistic but in my view contrary to the holistic approach to deciding our future. It would mean sacrificing the central value of open freedom of expression to fanaticism, however deeply the fanaticism is held. Religious figures of other faiths are regularly criticized and caricatured, sometimes giving rise to constructive debates: there should be no exception for Islam. And, even more importantly, the conception of society for which I have been arguing is one in which violence is not excusable and is to be eradicated. Youth Maturity Institutes are part of that reform. But in the meantime the world owes it to its own future to utterly condemn those, of whatever faith, allow themselves to have their emotions and beliefs directed into violence. About this there can be no compromise whatsoever.

If the United States were seriously putting the protection of innocent civilians as its top priority it would divert the billions it is spending on northern missile defence on (a) making *global government,* as in Chapter XVII, work to control rogue states, and (b) putting protective measures around shopping malls, rock concerts, trains and buses for the length of their journeys. Ferries, wherever crowds congregate. But the latter is ineffective, contributes to paranoia, undermines the quality of life, and is a waste. Israel, which has the most experience in such matters and a supremely efficient protective service, has been quite unable to stop suicide bombers. No amount of protection or limitations on freedom will stop a determined and clever terrorist group. And the damage such groups can do, even given 9-11, Spain and London, is tiny given the huge life of human activity. It is a price worth paying.

Over the centuries men and women have died in the cause of freedom and liberty. They have kept up their vigil, improving its state in the Western world, refusing to countenance the idea that crime is a justification for its emasculation. We do not, and will not in Utopia, consider that murder is a justification for the destruction or erosion of liberty. We have created courts to deal with that.

Terrorism is a form of crime, murder and kidnapping and blackmail. If some innocent people die during terrorist acts, they die in the name of freedom. Do not destroy freedom in their name. However tragically, they are paying its price. Let the courts, as described in Chapter VI, decide.

XII

Of Work and Poverty

Contradictions and paradoxes abound. I do not seek them out; it would be easier if they were not there. They present themselves.

Perhaps the most troubling of all is that of striking a balance between work for payment and spending time without payment. Even our vocabulary fails us. The differences are usually expressed as between employment and unemployment, work and leisure, work and play—or free time, recreation, spare time. Reflect upon each, and you will notice immediately that none correspond even approximately to the realities denoted by the phrases work for payment and spending time without payment.

The distinction between work and enjoyment-implying phrases does not apply. While, for many, paid work is drudgery, for many others, and at many times, work is enjoyment. Writing this book is work. It is not employment, but, I hope, it will result in payment. When I finish writing in the late morning I feel a sense of accomplishment. Whether what I write turns out to be drivel or otherwise, it feels good.

Retirees often regret the pleasure that going to work gave them—despite its annoyances and hassles it kept them on their toes, alive.

The explosive entry of women into the "work force" is mostly determined first by their *desire* to work, because working brings them into contact with a world that being a housewife does not; it provides them with a stimulating challenge, the ability to do things that once were men's preserve. It enables them to earn their own income, to be more equal. Then they find perhaps that they are trapped, just as men are, by the need to balance income and expenditure. Before they know it, two incomes become a necessity for a family. Nevertheless, for both men and women the workplace is an *escape* from domesticity. If they are lucky they enjoy parts of their paid work and would not want to give those parts up. The pains are a price to pay.

Agricultural advisers in developing countries sometimes endeavour to introduce what, to them, are more efficient instruments, for example a spade instead of a digging stick, and are surprised as its rejection. What appears to them as an innate conservatism that rejects the new is not conservatism as such but a judgement about the wider context of efficiency. The digging stick may or may not have some technical advantages, but more importantly it requires the use of quite different muscles, and often a different kind of rapport with fellow workers. The discomfort of using different muscles is a cost; so is the loss of enjoyable rhythms and banter.

Work is not to be equated with employment. In my city Italian, Hungarian and Chinese suburban residents grow luscious vegetables in back gardens. They tend to specialise in one or two crops, growing much more than they need. They then exchange "over the garden fence" tomatoes for corn or peppers, apples for pears.

Probably to the detriment of the monetary system, there is an upsurge of unpaid voluntary work, in charities, ecological movements, struggling little printed papers, neighbourhood television—wherever you look it is there. It is not employment in the financial sense; it is carried out because the workers feel it to be right, that is, they gain a sense of value from it. Many are driven to it for the same reason that others are driven to seek employment—the *need to do* something, to contribute, to gain self-worth, and enjoy human contact. Work around the house—carpentry, sewing—is driven as much by enjoyment as by duty. In any cost benefit analysis, this must be recognised.

I wrote that such work may be to the detriment of the monetary system. That system depends for the generation of wealth on the velocity of circulation of money. If money is not moving around fast, the opportunities for profit taking and the re-investment of profits is missed. This was as true of socialist countries as of capitalist ones. The exchanges in kind can be regarded as a sort of circulation, but the speed and efficiency is much less than with the intermediation of money. If a large portion of the gross domestic product is outside the monetary system, with volunteers, it is contributing only to direct production, with few spin-offs that come from multiplying effects.

The point relates to one of the weaknesses of community development in non-industrialised countries. The movement relies largely on do-it-yourself techniques. These can be extremely valuable in getting things done when money is not available, but by the same token they inhibit the growth of specialist enterprises—house construction, well boring, brick making—and the division of labour, without which the circulation of money is restricted. If community development moves from a valuable innovation to a dogma or entrenched habit, it will have provided merely one step along the path of change, not a dynamic. It must transcend itself and create specialized work to evolve into a dynamic force.

Yet it is possible that the return to voluntarism and self-help in the new 21st century ways is indicative of an evolution. If my notions are correct, the benefits of the monetary system need somehow to be extended beyond employment in much more significant ways than they are now. Those who are not working for gain will need to be compensated. The old communist adage "from whom according to his ability, to whom according to his need" describes in fact where we are headed. But it needs to be seriously redefined, and it needs to be blended with the mechanics of capitalism.

To some extent this has already been done, for wealthy countries have created expensive social safety nets. Capitalism almost "with a heart" made this possible, without, it seemed at first, restricting the economy. Now we know that in almost every country the form in which social security became established required growing indebtedness that the fiscal systems could not handle. And there is a backlash against high taxation which restricts freedom of expenditure and creates a situation in which individual discretionary real expenditures are often falling. Since my argument implies more, not less, by way of public expenditure on what may be built in to social security, we will have to deal with this issue head on in Chapter XIII on fiscal responsibility.

At present there is an extraordinary resistance in the public mind to facing up to some obvious realities. Governments, both conservative and social democratic, are gaining public approbation for facing up to the short-term reality of reducing debt, demanding more efficiency from social services, and embracing slogans such as "Get people into employment, make them get off welfare." We have proposals to force single mothers whose babies reach six months of age into the full time work force. There is talk of moving the age of retirement upwards, from, say, 65 to 67, or 60 to 63—for fiscal reasons. (All that does is to increase negative pressure on the entry of the young into the work force.)

Stop a moment or two. What is this? What is the objective of living? Where do we want to go? Will it next be child labour? Is that the answer to youthful alienation? Do we not *care*?

Ironically, every major economic ideology in theory looks forward to a time when there will need to be *less* work, imagined as *less* employment, *less* drudgery, and *more* leisure. Read Marx for the communist ideal. Capitalism is justified by the steady increase in capital, which is competitive to labour. For decades, governments heeded. They attacked child labour, slavery, and destructive work weeks.

Now puritanism has returned. Paid labour seems to have regained its position as a moral force. If you are not in employment, or self-employed for gain, there is something wrong with you.

Levels of unemployment, so defined, are at the highest since the Great Depression, and have remained so steadily now for a good decade. Minuscule reductions are greeted as political triumphs. It is a mistake to extrapolate the present into the distant future. "Downsizing" is the buzz word, and downsizing means reducing the work force in particular enterprises—including governments, which are trying to reduce the civil service at rates not seen before. That creates unemployment as a matter of policy, by governments who are sworn to reduce it.

The policies of governments and of private enterprises are not likely to change quickly or drastically, since the major restructurings are responses to realities, financial truth, and technical change. It may well be that technical change often creates new employment, just as computers increase rather than decrease the use of paper. Thus policy makers can argue that the unemployment which is being created is temporary, a blip, a friction, in the process of adjustment. To some extent they are right, and I cannot claim for sure that they are wrong: I remain sceptical.

We are in fact living in the midst of a change, the knowledge revolution, which is as great as that of the industrial revolution. Knowledge has always been an (unrecognised) prime commodity, but now it dominates. It translates into rapidity of communication, management of vast data, exponential growth of innovation, and electronic marvels. Many marvels reduce the need for large work forces, whether of management or on the production line, and make it desirable for companies to spread activities more evenly across the globe. New countries sometimes have an advantage not only in labour costs but in not having to write off or destroy or rebuild old capital investments to make way for the temporarily modern.

The social effects of the knowledge revolution are just as great, if not greater. The application of medical knowledge increases the supply of potential workers at both ends of the age spectrum. Education reaches further and further into the global population, rapid communication puts almost everyone with a computer in touch with the world. Individuals force education onto themselves, whether they are aware of it or not, enjoying the new technologies and challenged by them, and absorbing all sorts of data, whether reliable or not. So strong is this that it is likely to be beyond the ability of national governments to control or censor. The effects on political movements and organisation will be profound.

The distinction between workplace and home is becoming blurred. Perhaps we should say rediscovered, since the home as workplace is still typical of agriculture and activities in developing countries, and was normal for artisans and many others during past centuries—the separation seems to have been a recent phenomenon. From the point of view of efficient synergy there are pros and cons to working at home rather than in a main office or workplace. Just the same it is often feasible. Electronic communication strongly affects and loosens up the location of the knowledge industries. Pleasant working environments and synergetic communities and data bases are becoming more significant than locating in a downtown core or industrial park.

Unemployment, coupled with the necessity to earn income, has sparked more innovation. Individuals turn to entrepreneurship, self-employment. Many have done so with innovative fervour, adding to the supply of services, small industries, and employment which still does not provide work for all. I have also noticed that there has been a semi-explosion of artistic activity. If you can't get employment, do something you like and feel are good at, and get some cash for it in the process. Pottery, crafts, bands, specialist foods, art, even busking. There are creative impulses on which to build. Alas, many do not cover the bills.

There are several ways in which national policies could solve the paradox. The one that seems to be uppermost is, create jobs at any price. Governments force unemployed into re-training programmes. That is all very fine and might be worthwhile, but training implies a decision as to what for and it takes time. Most training programmes create competition with individuals who are trained by other means. When training is finished, there is no guarantee of employment. The requirements of commerce and industry may also have changed overnight. Effects on employment are minimal, though they could be extended if training were to be on-site for specific jobs in specific enterprises. Pushing newly trained people into hunts for non-existent jobs is alienating, and damaging to the spirit.

Another is to enter into a command economy or to heavily subsidise unprofitable enterprises, that is pay people to pay others. Both are destructive of production. I do not have to demonstrate the point at this moment in the history of Eastern Europe. Because effective production is limited, they create more and more demand for more and more unproductive jobs, viciously spiralling downwards.

The unbridled single-minded search for greater employment could have disastrous side-effects. In "under-developed" countries the danger is already expressed. Ecologically sound policies cannot be afforded; employment has to come first. This could be the case in industrialised countries. Although environmentally protective industries themselves create employment, there are many voices to be heard resisting eco-friendly measures if they affect an industry that is already an employer.

We could also encourage the production of any and all "widgets" (to borrow *The Economist's* evocative word) irrespective of their social value. More dangerous toys. More drugs. More useless souvenirs. Subsidise the production and distribution of pornography. More and more armaments. A jolly good world war. In effect, we do much of this now. Certainly we could achieve full employment. Do as India does and former communists did—enrol the unemployed in the civil service, whether they have anything to do or not.

We shouldn't want to. That is not Utopia. Stop pretending.

As a matter of fact, I do guess that the richer industrialised countries could possibly achieve near full employment for themselves by globally free commercial policies, although it including income tax, have been clumsy attempts to redistribute income. The greater their level, more especially with income tax, the greater the interference with individual choice. Income tax is the most direct form of indicating to the public that the State knows best how to use your money, and that the vote is less powerful than the internal revenue office.

To finance Utopia through income tax would essentially mean little individual income. This is obviously a contradiction in terms, since spending is one of the few ways in which individuals exercise their choices. To have no income is not to spend, not to exercise choice.

If corporate taxes can in some fundamental sense be equalised so that there is a level playing field, it might not matter if they were raised to the roof. We would simply be in a world in which the prices were denominated at a higher percentage overall. But I do not see it as a level playing field. For example, a good may pass through, say, ten companies or twenty as it moves from a raw state to the consumer. Corporate taxes reflected in the ultimate price run a risk of being very much higher in the second case than in the first, however they are levied. To the extent that this is true, it would be more in tune with the Utopian idea that the individual is sovereign to keep corporate taxation to the minimum, with one exception.

But corporate taxes are a tax on initiative. The more successful the company, the more, at present, it pays. The more workers it employs the more it pays in employment taxes. This is no way to run an economy.

The exception is to require corporations to pay for goods and services they now get freely, and to pay the full costs to society of their doing business. If they pollute, they pay for it, is the prime example. If they use roads, they pay for the use. If they employ educated people, they contribute to education. If they cause illness, they pay for the cures. If they move people from one location to another, they pay the full costs of such an operation. If they destroy forests, they pay. If they fish, they pay for the maintenance of the fishery. They are not subsidised from the public purse; nor do they get loans of public money. They pay their way, and charge accordingly. The public then knows the true costs of that which it is choosing to buy and can make its choices accordingly.

If present corporate taxes are removed and replaced by payments for social services and social costs, one can assume that corporations are paying directly for those things they choose to use. While this would cover a substantial amount of social services and costs (which have become the primary item in State expenditure) there would still be a major proportion of public expenditures not yet covered. I imagine—and it is not a calculation—that perhaps fifty per cent of public expenditure would be met by this revenue item, reflected in costs to consumers.

Income tax is also a tax on initiative. The more you earn the more you pay and in most countries the rate of tax can increase.[77] Customs duties are a small proportion of revenues in most countries. But again they increase the costs of production when the goods are destined for industry, can be protective in defiance of free trade; and are costly to collect. Time to remove both of them, and examine the roots of taxation with a clean slate.

So I turn to the direct consumption taxes mostly in the form of Sales tax or Value Added Tax.

There are two contradictory principles at work. On the one hand, much consumption is apparently wasteful of resources. I object to creating employment for employment's sake, since this can, among other objections, lead to the production of useless widgets, using up scarce resources, and made available to consumers by artificial means. My position is somewhat snobbish. The tourists who line up from buses to buy junk are exercising their choices. Who am I to say them nay? If corporate taxation is amended as suggested above the social costs will be reflected in price.

The other principle extends the recognition of freedom of choice. This does not mean no taxation on consumption. It means equal taxation on different forms of consumption (it again being assumed that social costs have been reflected in the course of production itself). Alcohol might be taxed at the production level to cover costs of alcoholism, a tax reflected in wholesale price; at the consumption level it is taxed at the same level as bread. The consumer chooses.

If this is so, the effects on the individual consumer will be at the margins of his expenditures. The pattern of expenditure will be modified, but freedom of choice will remain. The individual will still control what happens with his income. This is not the case with income tax, in which choice is removed. If consumption tax moves from 5% to 100% the choice still remains. I would far prefer to pay even 100% on consumption than 40 or 60% on income, *provided the consumption tax was universal* and the revenue went into social services and guaranteed income rather than the military. On that assumption, a consumption tax feels less like State robbery and control, *and it enables me to determine how much tax I shall pay.* By consuming less I pay less. By consuming more I pay more. To a much larger degree it is in my control. The public's choices totally control consumption tax revenue.

Unlike a flat income tax, the consumption tax is progressive, even though it is the same for all categories of consumption. Taking the extreme of a 100% rate, the millionaire may buy a Ferrari now priced at $200,000 for the new price of $400,000, of which $200,000 goes to the State. The starving student or artist buys a jalopy now priced at $100 for $200 of which only $100 goes to the State. Heshe is also helped by guaranteed income.

Further, the relief from corporate and employment taxation, though partially balanced by charges for environmental and social costs, enables firms to pay higher wages and salaries.

Admittedly, an extreme 100% consumption tax (a figure that would be unlikely) would overnight create a one time halving of the value of money. However, it is again unlikely that such a tax would be introduced overnight (though it could be). Fiscal authorities would have a major task to perform in adjusting the supply of money, and ensuring its spread to the population. Draconian measures of this sort have indeed been applied from time to time in the history of States, some successful, some not. The adjustment is not beyond the bounds of our imagination. And once achieved, particularly on a global scale, the major crisis of adjustment would be over.

In other words I consider that society as a whole will reflect individual values better with equalised consumption taxes than with income taxes, whatever the rate of the consumption taxes. The individual also knows that there will be no fiscal penalty attached to earning more, only on spending more. This will keep motivated individuals in the work place as needed, rather than holding on to the guaranteed income floor because work is no longer taxed away. Once again, the combination of guaranteed income and no income tax allows individuals to make reasonable choices.

Furthermore, consumption taxes, in making the consumer think more about how heshe spends, could have important effects on the quality of life, reducing spending on widgets and giving an opportunity for consumers to think about such maters as the ecological or fair trade implications of their choices. *And, once again, the individual is in control over how much tax heshe pays.* If I purchase that Ferrari, think of the tax I would be paying to a government I don't like. But if I *do* like government expenditure policies, buying the Ferrari would not only satisfy me, but be a political statement.

The ideal, especially with free trade, is that such taxes be at the same level throughout the world, perhaps even set by Global Government instead of State government, collected by State governments to be placed in Global accounts, and shared. However at the point at which this becomes practicable, regional disparities and differences will continue, for ethnological and geographical reasons. We are not talking about uniformity of life. It is for this reason that attempts to put low or no tax rates on some goods and high ones on others (necessities as against luxuries, for example) would be next to impossible to administer globally, so different are the cultural definitions. While one would thus argue for global uniformity in tax rates, State governments, in agreement with the Global Government, would have the right to influence the level of income at which the consumption tax kicks in or is rebated for special considerations.

For example, State government could rebate the consumption tax on necessities of life for those on the guaranteed minimum income, as defined by the culture applicable in the State. (A rebate is preferable to giving a card authorising non-payment, on grounds of social equity.)

Customs would not disappear. Officials would now be trained not only to prevent the entry of contraband, but to make sure that taxes on imported consumption goods are included in the price, this to make cross border shopping equitable. And it would be necessary to have a tax refund system for non-residents returning to their homes, as is the case with sales taxes and VAT now.

So here we have it. No corporate, individual or customs taxes. All revenues based on consumption.

On the expenditure side, no or minimal military spending. No subventions to individual corporations. Removal of all current social service payments, which now vary according to the power base of segments of the disadvantaged. Introduce guaranteed income for all at a liveable rate which does away with special funds for segments of the poor—the unemployed, the halt and the lame. Guaranteed income for all removes the competitive disparities in handouts to the disadvantaged—the unemployed, the sick, the destitute, returned service men and women, first time job seekers, artists.

I wonder which country will be the first to translate this argument into reality? All products of changes adopted after the second world war, though many, such as the dole, existed previously. Graduated income taxes have not existed for all time. It took innovation to establish them. We need to make a start—and in this as in so many other facets of Utopian reform, half measures are troublemaking.

XIV

A Note on Organisation, especially of capitalism

Do the remarks of the last Chapter imply some such revolution as the end of capitalism? Not at all. Fiscal change removes a major burden on corporations as well as individuals. But corporations would be channelled into thinking about their place in life, about the effects of their actions in the wider culture and society. For too many centuries they have ignored such responsibilities because they did not enter into their balance sheets. With fiscal change they would have to watch their steps much more carefully, for a mis-step could mean ruin.

The population may be conceived as having three parts: (a) those who are part of organisations which use money for accounting purposes but whose purpose is not to make a profit—universities, schools, voluntary and charitable groups, public service, military, hospitals; (b) those who are part of organisations whose intent and legal status require that profits be made; and (c) those who are not part of either (retired, unemployed, youth). There are overlaps: individuals who are in (b) may also participate in (a). Some whose time is mostly spent in (c) may nevertheless participate in (a). For individuals, the distinctions are not watertight in their daily living; there are matters of degree of commitment here. Some university professors (a) operate entrepreneurial enterprises (b).

Even though there are overlaps, nevertheless the distinctions are real. The three categories represent, broadly, three differing cultures, each with their sub-cultures, which carry over from the centres of operation into family life and social interactions and discourses. Between the cultures there are many fundamental misunderstandings and lacks of knowledge. Most entrepreneurs and workers, white collar or blue collar, in category (b) have little understanding of, and indeed often an antipathy to, workers in category (a), especially, for example, teachers, university professors, doctors and nurses. The reverse is true also. Most university professors and civil servants, many adherents of single cause organisations such as those dealing with the ecosystem, have little or no knowledge of the decisions, the risks and the manipulation of factors of production that managers have to deal with every day. Yet it is what managers decide, with all the insecurities involved, that governs the material world in which we live, from the food on the table to television programmes. How much of the artistic world—plays, for instance—apart from some popular literature, is rooted in management themes that have such a major influence on who we are? Why is the culture of management such a tiny (perhaps growing) part of contemporary social anthropology?

Meanwhile, let us note that ideological preoccupations with the simplicity of social class categories, from left and right, have diverted our attention from these other, more dividing and troublesome, cleavages. Class as a descriptive category indicating a number of people who are positioned close together on a scale measuring a given criterion (wealth, education), helps scholars analyse relationships between criteria. Other than that it has no reality: it is an arbitrary academic construct. Class in the Marxist sense goes further, arguing that broad categories (workers, peasants, bourgeois) had so many conditions, objectives and interests in common that they constituted organic entities with historical roles. That, as I have argued elsewhere, is simply not true, save for brief periods in history when members of one group brought themselves together for action. Peasant revolts might be an instance. It is intriguing to me that, particularly amongst those trying to challenge authority, leadership more often than not came from outside the group concerned, and that such groups did not embrace the totality of the assigned class, among whom considerable difference of opinion, even opposition, existed. Significant numbers of the British "working class" have consistently voted Conservative. As we struggle toward Utopia, class concepts, in this second sense, are of no use.

What may be of more use is to think of various kinds of organisations, not only in terms of their conventional effectiveness, but in terms of their interactions and overall norms within society as a whole. As a short-hand I shall use the categories I proposed at the beginning, and the divisions within them. However, just as I point out the limitations of assigning an individual to a class according to his or her position on a given scale, because on other criteria the position changes, so too I caution against using my broad categories to define the characteristics of an organisation *a priori*.

It is now customary to have individuals who are familiar with profit and the bottom line in board, management or consultancy positions in category (a) organisations, and to try to borrow management techniques from (b) to (a). I am not opposing this, but consider it to be inadequate as a tool in itself, and possibly damaging if other tools are not developed.

What *are* the objectives of a university or a hospital or a military unit? What are they there to do? Financial efficiency and not getting into bankruptcy; the greatest economy of material or personnel resources, as measured in profit-making institutions, may simply not be relevant. If not profit, what is the output that should be selected against which to make the measurements? Are the true costs monetary? What about the destruction of an individual assigned to work in ways he or she can't handle, because he or she can't be let go? What about children who are mistaught social studies because a teacher, counted as doing the job, has no knowledge of history, sociology, political science, or anthropology? What about hospitals which refuse to allow nurses to handle procedures of which they are capable? How do you measure the efficiency of a military unit which is up to strength, has all its assigned equipment, is well field-trained, but is racist or is personally loyal to a dissident commander? Is a policeman's efficiency to be measured by his salary divided by the number of arrests?

Such conundrums put enormous complications into judgements about how well organisations in category (a) are doing their job. Just because the judgements are complicated, such organisations must not be left off the hook. The judgements have important uses—by funding donors, by taxpayers, by patrons buying tickets at a certain price. I do not have nice easy answers, but there are alternatives awaiting development.

Once upon a time economists (do they still?) pointed out that their subject was the study of the ways in which scarce means were administered in order to fulfil competing ends in the most satisfying manner. For obvious reasons, of which analytical manageability was the main one, this became mixed up with the use of money as a *scientific* measuring rod, instead of a means and an end mixed together in real life, competing with other means and ends. If money doesn't come into it, the main schools of thought in practice believed, we can't handle the dynamics or the judgements. And if we can't nobody can. Not many challenged this canard.

The original propositions of economics posited the balancing of different ends to achieve the optimum result, the latter determined not by the observer but by the subject. No use buying a Maserati if that meant going without a combination of food and opera and dressing the children properly. But if resources change one might do all those things. Or, once confronted with the fact, one might effectively decide it would be more satisfying to redo the kitchen, pay for John's university, and have annual holidays in East Africa. The potential ideas floating in one's head do not necessarily become prepotent when the chips are down.

There are many models in the various disciplines that play with these kinds of issues, and their complements, the varying choices which individuals make in the task of combining different kinds of resources to produce the result.

With some limitations, for individuals read organisations. Organisations in category (a) need goal plans, a statement of objectives. But those goals, at least Utopianly speaking, are not simply things like graduating so many students in so many fields, undertaking so many heart transplants a year, or making sure that we can raise so many millions to redistribute to yet other organisations, or reducing the income tax defaults to such a percentage of potential revenue. The *quality* of what is done is at least as significant.

Statements of objectives in such organisations require qualitative assessments. In category (b) organisations it may be assumed, though probably inaccurately, that the qualitative issues are reflected in competitive advantage, and hence the bottom line, at least insofar as customers and clients value them. This is not so in category (a) organisations. One needs to adjust the easily quantifiable factors for the less precise but nevertheless paramount ones. One needs comparative data on the quality of learning and initiative in graduating students, on long-term health of discharged hospital patients, on the quality of life of aged clients in long-term care facilities, on the re-insertion into society of prisoners, on the accuracy of analysis and capacity to provide effective services by charities, and so on.

Of course such examinations and analyses do take place. But I consider we have a long way to go before they meet the standards of Utopian analysis. In part, we are bemused by cardinal measurement. Ordinal measurement usually implies comparison, for example, very much happier, quite a lot happier, happier, about the same, less happy, a bit miserable, very miserable, desperate, by comparison with some standard. We already know that vested interests hate such measurements and comparisons, even if less subjective than the extreme example I have chosen. School teachers jump onto the attack if the quality of schools are compared. Doctors and lawyers resist any public comparison of their results. Very few studies are done comparing charitable or lobbying organisations, except in terms of fiscal honorability. Academics hate it when objective criteria of scholarly or teaching value are applied to their proposals for new courses of study.

But we must be in a position to make judgements about organisational objectives and efficacy, just as we try to do when such organisations apply for grants. The more we can refine our tools for doing so the better. For the most part, this involves being clearer about the *whole mix* of organisational goals—the schedule of ends, material and other, or of the wants they are there to satisfy if you will.

In fact similar principles apply, with differing tools, to organisations in category (b). I am not arguing against profitability or the use of money in exchange. Far from it. Whether it is easily apparent or not, all societies have standards of exchange value. Inefficient standards exist in barter, and in some so-called "non-monetary" societies which have different measures of value for different purposes. There is no escaping the reality and efficacy of the principle that the more rapid the circulation of money the more opportunities there are for profits to be taken; that those profits can be summed as a large quantity of profit in society as a whole; which means a greater opportunity for capital accumulation and its investment. Utopia must be monetary, for even in Utopia I do not see the day, nor desire it, when all wants can be satisfied without exchange, or when there is no possibility for the improvement of anything (which implies investment). How utterly boring. A pox on communitarian non-monetarists.

However that is a *very* different thing from saying high-riding capitalism, as we know it today, is the most effective and desirable way of satisfying human goals. It is not.

The reason it is not is straightforward. In present capitalism money-based profit-taking enterprises usually define their goals as narrowly as they can, and make manipulative use of public services that are provided to them free of cost.

If I want to make widgets or provide internet services I will do my best to economise on costs. In doing so I do not pay for the air I breathe, and it is very unlikely that I pay my share of my polluting effects or the development costs that have been incurred in placing technologies in the public domain. If I lay off workers so that I can down-size or move to a less costly country, I may, or may not as the case may be, pay the costs incurred by the dismissed people.

In other words, the goals are defined in such a simple way that the true costs are hidden. Neither the individual enterprises, nor the consumers in buying the products, count or pay the full cost. In one sense, the consumers do, through current modes of taxation, which in effect subsidise industry and commerce.

Such a reality is not particularly difficult to grasp. But what do Utopians *do* about it?

Legislation can sometimes ensure that companies take a spectrum of goals into account, translated into their financial bottom line. Thus certain payments to laid-off workers can be legislated, and protection of an eco-system can be mandated. (Why do executives get generous termination packages, but not workers???)

But there are two problems that modify and corrupt such legislation, and put the brakes on it.

If strict ecological rules are enforced for the hewers of wood, but not legislated for formers of concrete or developers of housing estates, the market is improperly distorted. Developers will cut down the trees and there will be a move toward concrete instead of wooden houses. This might be desirable, but it can only be assessed if *all* enterprises have to meet the same social objectives, writ broadly, but interpreted in detail for each industry.

Similarly, if one country adopts stringent objectives and rules, there is a financial temptation for industry to move elsewhere. It is argued that this imbalance will correct itself in the long run, and that developing countries will never catch up if they are charged costs that the rich countries did not have to bear when they were creating their strengths. In the middle term, there is no point and much danger in being too harsh and rigorously inflexible.

But in the long run, Utopia must require near universality, modified by cultural differences, in its approach to identifying and charging for social costs. Only universality will establish the beloved "level playing field". We are rapidly reaching the point at which "national" governments cannot do the job required of them; only a global approach will ultimately do. There will still be major differences because of cultural variations which will effect the location of enterprise; I am not saying that the level playing field does away with, or ought to do away with, comparative advantage. But the principle of the obligation to meet social costs should not be a matter of difference between countries.

The universality of the imposition of social costs and the inclusion of social goals in enterprises will indeed mean a rise in prices. This is another argument for across the board standards: we do not want to reward industries which are excused or which avoid paying their social costs. There will still be differences. Those enterprises which legitimately incur fewer social costs will have a cost-price advantage over those which have more. This is as it should be. If you want things that have high social costs, jolly well pay for them directly, not indirectly through taxes. Then you may understand the meaning of what you consume.

Such changes will of course mean considerable changes in management, including the criteria of successful management. Social costs will be a factor of production, to be analysed as such.

There are other elements of present capitalist structure which derive from history and have become entrenched, but should be questioned.

For example, there is the relationship between owners, management, lenders, and workers.

Financial capital is a factor of production which in large part underwrites other factors of production—labour, capital equipment, knowledge, etc.—insofar as costs cannot immediately be met out of current revenue. There are three main ways of raising financial capital: by government grant, by interest paying loans, and by the selling of shares. By now so many techniques of raising capital have been invented that there are all sorts of permutations in the implications of particular arrangements. For example, shares may or may not involve rights of ownership which influence management; they may be issued with varying degrees of priority when it comes to rights to income or assets. Thus it is necessary for me to simplify down to the typical prime essentials.

Each of these may imply a legal seat on the management board, which acts as executive supervisor for the owners. Who gets to be on the board varies according to the laws of countries, and, within those laws, the practices of specific firms. One major variant typical of Germany is that worker representatives sit on the board. This is, however, extremely rare. Usually the board consists of representatives of, that is persons elected by, those shareholders who are accorded such rights, that is the initial providers of financial capital plus others who buy-in later. (In Switzerland, for example, foreign shareholders may be excluded from such rights.) In Europe and some other countries it is common for banks which have provided finance to acquire ownership and/or management rights as a result. Occasionally, depending on circumstances and political philosophy, governments insist on board representation as partial security for their financial involvement. In the remnants of communist countries, such control can be still dominant and politically motivated, but they have been giving way to the other forms. Private firms, usually led by families or close partnerships, do their best to avoid giving up control when they raise capital.

Whatever the variants, one thing is clear. Capital is the primary factor of production which carries with it ownership privileges, and the power to control the destiny of firms. In this sense, certainly, we are in the midst of the capitalist age.

Is this what is needed and desirable for Utopia? I don't believe so, not quite. Capitalism is needed, but capital controls need modification.

The reason capital, with private entrepreneurship, has been the main factor of production to be recognised in this way is that it has been, historically, the most difficult thing to put together. It is mistakenly held that price is the determinant of the supply of capital. This is only partially true. Interest rates are mainly governed by the ratio of supply and demand for money, true. But in this new century the entry of funds into both the stock markets and the international exchange markets is largely influenced by speculative considerations, as much as by the need for enterprise capital. In other words, motivations which create the flow of money into such markets are based upon *guesses* about the future rise or fall in relevant prices. [I do not know of any well supported and publicised anthropological studies of the culture of stock and money trading.] Even the acquisition or sale of firms is governed largely by financial considerations—the desire to raise cash, pay off debt, or acquire a money-making opportunity, the last being a speculative judgement about the future.

The fact of the matter is that when it comes to a firm raising capital, especially to get started, subjective matters come to the fore; interest rates will even be adjusted to take these factors into account. The lender *judges* the track record of the borrower. It has become somewhat scandalous that money is often not available *at any price* to women, to those such as Indians living on common reserves who have no individual security, to new would-be entrepreneurs. It is just as common that if you are in a social relationship with those who control the flow of finance, you will find it easier to raise millions. The downfall of many a great entrepreneurial holding company has come about when, in time of sudden difficulty, the lenders realised that their connection was too optimistic; it was time to look behind the man to the reality—and then, often, as in the case of the initial Canary Wharf fiasco or the Conrad Black empire, not look enough forward to see the conception ultimately come into reality. Risk is serious. The judgement of risk, despite all the charts, is ultimately subjective. The market deals with it only partially by a manipulation of interest rates. It can say absolutely no to $1,000 at desperately punitive interest rates, and absolutely yes to $1 billion at preferred interest rates, based on little more than friendly or unfriendly eye-contact, golf games, or earlier business deals. The formal papers are not irrelevant for most routine transactions. But they are little more than background for negotiation in many significant instances.

The relevance of such considerations is increased by the custom of appointing or electing to boards members who have "connections". The appointment of representatives of external lenders onto boards is seldom a matter of tighter supervision—such companies are usually very well run in any event—but a pipeline to further capital should it be needed, and a possible exclusion of other lenders.

Why should capital be the primary, if not the only, factor of production (apart from initial entrepreneurship), to be represented in ownership and the government of firms? Historical power has to be the answer.

The only other influences on factors of production which conceivably could have had such power, historically, have been labour and government. (Government policy has not usually been listed among factors of production. But in some form it is a variable which is highly influential on the conduct of business, whose managers manipulate its powers as their possible resource.) Government has indeed used its power to influence and dominate enterprise, often with disastrous and distorting results, of which both fascism and communism represent examples I do not need to examine.

Labour is a more puzzling story. I suggest that labour's failure to enter into ownership derives from its organised origins in the nineteenth century, in which labour unions literally had to fight for almost every decency in the workplace that we now take for granted in the major countries. Save for a few enlightened employers, the typical response to requests for decency was to deny them, to use ownership by the entrepreneurs and stockholders, and the socio-political relationships with the lawmakers, to fight them down every inch of the way.

No wonder Marx talked of socio-political classes. More to the point, no wonder that unions, fighting for their very existence, learned the hard way that the only way forward was for confrontation, not only with the management but with the politicians. They had to search for, fight for, power, and after many decades, with many ups and downs, they eventually got most of it.

In Switzerland, in the 1930s, the conflict reached such a point of violence, and the threats from outside were so intense, that in an abrupt *volte face*, all those involved knew that the confrontations were about to destroy the country, literally. The idea of Switzerland as a genetically peaceful country is totally false. To the extent it is peaceful, it is a matter of deliberate decision translated into policy, because the alternatives don't work. Certainly confrontation continues in many aspects of Swiss life. But in labour-management issues confrontation changed dramatically into consultation and consensus. To achieve this, both sides had to change their methods and their modes of thinking enormously, to work on the premise that the health of the firms required frank openness and the joint working out of the firms' objectives and methods. Since such solutions, and those of Germany in which workers' representatives sit on boards, depend on the state of trust, openness, and the external socio-economic-political climate, they cannot be regarded as permanent or fixed, especially in a world where, for the most part, confrontation between unions and management is still the convention.

What does Utopia want in this arena? Why should the capital providers have priority in ownership over the workers? Is there any logic to this at all? History perhaps, but logic? Efficacy? The logic might say that workers, by reason of their background, point of view, and education, are not fit to make management policy decisions, whereas moneylenders are. Perhaps moneylenders are indeed, at least insofar as financial manipulation is concerned. But perhaps one might argue that enterprises are driven far too much by financial wheeling and dealing. That issues like spinning off companies or parts of an enterprise, or merging and acquisition, while sometimes driven by supposed "synergy" or the lack of it, by desires to broaden a holding company's portfolio and spread risk—or to do the opposite by retrenching so that a company can concentrate on its core business, are far too often driven by management's personal pocketbook or effects on share prices rather than productivity.

I see no compelling reason, other than that they are risk-takers, why shareholders should have the sole say in choosing and "controlling" management. Except for the larger shareholders, whose interests may not coincide with those of the smaller ones, the majority of shareholders take very little interest in the specifics of management. They may express disapproval by selling shares, but give their proxies for annual meetings. Further, workers, suppliers, dependent customers, anyone who enters into a contract with the firm, are exposed to the firm's risk. For the workers the risk is the greatest of all, for if the firm goes belly-up they are without their livelihood. Period.

For most of the industrial world except perhaps Switzerland and Germany, the risk to workers, and their selfish interest in the success of the company, have been obscured by the union convention of confrontation. The nineteenth century ethos that the boss is the enemy is built into the activity and ideology of the most powerful unions, whose leadership, that is management, lives on aggressive stances. Certainly, under these circumstances, the boss *is* the enemy, for he feels he has to fight back to save his company. There is still an attitude of union-bashing, if the boss can find ways to do it.

Unions were necessary, at least until World War II, and in the short run may become necessary again. They are necessary in many parts of the world where conditions of employment are dreadful. But in most of the industrialised world, in most occupations, unions are the workers' worst enemies, or at least as much so as are the bosses.

Some unions are so large and powerful, and so monopolistic in their areas of activity, that they are in fact entrepreneurial businesses, sellers of labour. In these, no one can get a job without holding a union card and being nominated in union controlled labour exchanges. In others strict rules of seniority rather than ability apply. Inter-union agreements, forced into labour contracts, govern, sometimes in minute and anti-efficiency detail, the division of labour.

Thus my experience the other day when a trolley-bus came off its wires with trivial damage such that the bus could not proceed. On board was an off-duty driver who had the skills necessary to effect the repair on the spot. "Don't touch it," said the duty driver, "or the union will get you." Instead of proceeding on its way, the bus stood still waiting the arrival of a union-certified electrician from the other side of town. Rules of this kind create feather-bedding, inflexibility in the allocation of work, idleness in some workers while they wait for a call, and gross inefficiency and extra costs.

Unions are run as businesses in themselves. The capital raised through membership fees, the need to invest strike emergency funds and pension plans, makes some of them among the largest corporate investors in the market. A few can make or break industries through their investment decisions.

The management-shareholder-union scenario, (coupled with large business bureaucracy, which is another story) must be one of the most inefficient and socially damaging patterns of organisation one could imagine for a sophisticated economy. Despite itself, it has great achievements to its credit. I do not dispute that—how could I, looking around at my world? The mind in fact boggles at the way management and workers, together, have used knowledge and innovation and organisational skills to bring food to the table, clothing and shelter, and a range of technological marvels requiring ever-more complex lines of supply from nature to the user. This is not to be sneered at in some high and mighty way, or despised because of some ideological *a priori* principle.

But I am not writing about that; I am writing about the best of all possible worlds. And, for Utopia, there is still room for improvement. I shall set out a model.

I have already argued that firms should bear the social costs of their activities.

To be interpreted in similar context is the curious distinction between salaried and non-salaried employees. Once again, this is an archaic socially disruptive historical distinction, deriving from the days in which it was expected and accepted that humans be treated as disposable factors of production like any other. They are not. When firms get into a bad patch, the easiest target for retrenchment to pay for management's errors consists of the non-salaried employees. It is true that of recent years salaried employees are being dismissed during cut-backs, but this is done usually through such devices as early retirement, severance packages, and the like. By contrast, non-salaried employees are treated as completely disposable. This is most dramatically evident in large-scale industries where demand changes have immediate effects on supply—forestry, automobile manufacture, construction and so on.

It cannot be argued that retrenchment cannot occur. Of course it must. But, in equity and for social values, the distinction between blue collar and white collar, between salaried and non-salaried, is an anachronism and improper. Put the blue collars on salary. Management can then certainly find other ways of smoothing out the ups and downs of demand than making the workforce pay through a cycle of hiring and layoff; and where dismissals have to take place blue collar workers have similar needs to those of white collar ones. Indeed technology is rapidly reducing the distinction.

I now argue that it is no longer necessary or desirable for the suppliers of finance to hold ownership and management rights. True, it will be necessary to post the assets of a company as security for finance. Given that, there are, except for small start-up enterprises, sufficient methods of supplying funds through ordinary borrowing techniques. (I have already argued that government lending and subsidy is normally a distortion of the market.)

Close down the stock exchanges. Figure out the implications. Number one is the removal of gambling, the speculative drives which, rather than rationality (for the future is unpredictable and what knowledge there is, is unevenly distributed) determine the fate of companies and the state of currencies.

Utopianly speaking, the start-up entrepreneur and his partners will usually place their own funds in the company to get it going, supplemented by borrowing. Ownership resides in those who register the company as owners, and who operate it as partners, not in relatives or institutions from whom they may borrow. Applying to the stock exchange for an IPO usually comes much later.

Since we are no longer talking of joint-stock companies, the structure of management is open. There is no longer a need for a board to act as a tame watchdog for shareholders. We are talking management, pure and simple. Remember, also, that Utopia has created more effective education, and that guaranteed incomes ensure that workers can live reasonably outside the workforce. Under these conditions, employees from sales staff to production line have the intelligence, imagination and self-interest to identify with the future of the enterprise as partners in it; otherwise they are unlikely to be there. Wise and efficient firms will make the utmost use of this, placing workers on management boards and consultative committees, and inducting them into ownership, depending on the size and structure of the firm and the nature of its work.

The firm is part and parcel of culture and society. It is not neutral. Its present arrangements do not have to be taken as holy. The firm has served society in its present forms very well indeed. But society in its present forms is defective. So is the firm. As society adjusts, so too must the firm, or instead of being the valuable provider it will be the liability working *against* the lives we want to lead.

To sum up, Utopian society will raise capital through loans, not the stock market. Firms will take social costs into account as factors of production. They will not be supported by government funds. Workers will be partners, salaried. And, drawing from other chapters, firms will be relieved of corporate taxes.

XV

The Poorer World

The reference to countries which have not shared in the industrialisation and commercialisation of the Western and "advancing" Asian worlds has changed over the decades from under-developed to developing to emerging, to Third World (the Second being communist and the Fourth the inner city poverty) and so on, each reflecting the analytic presuppositions of the writers. For the present, I prefer to use the descriptive term "the Poorer World" which I think makes no assumptions about developing dynamics or other processes. It is there, there are many causes, many movements, and a tumultuous range of conditions. And it is a part of the richer countries also.

The very term "poverty" disguises many significant variations and is open to interpretation. The displaced agricultural workers of Europe and their surviving villagers of the eighteenth century and those affected by the disastrous famine of the potato (an introduced staple) crop in Ireland later, had much in common with those living in the disaster areas of Africa today. I do not recall any of the great explorers of the South Pacific using the term poverty in describing the level of living of the South Sea Islanders (though they often despised the cultures). Had they done so they would have been treated with ridicule because of a potential comparison with the conditions of their seamen, or with the country folk of their homes, where destitution was forcing men to go to sea and flock to unemployment in the cities.

Today we have measures. A great deal of intelligence has gone into the construction of international definitions of poverty, such is our passion for quantification, and the attempt to capture misery in figures. We don't really need to do this, except as a justification for bureaucratic and charitable intervention. Images on television, selective though they be, do the job for us. And further the very scale of the figures is disheartening, whereas the one image can make us angry. Half a billion? A billion? True, figures sometimes tell us whether it is getting worse or better. But even here there are so many assumptions and inaccuracies in the compilations—just as there are in assessing the death rate in Darfur. If poverty were at one tenth of the scale posited, it is still unacceptable today and in Utopia.

There are cross cultural implications in the idea of poverty. Many populations are in fact dying out as the result of poverty induced disease, malnutrition, and migration. These are not always in Africa or Asia. There are Italian, French, German, and Swiss mountain villages, to say nothing of those in the new EU countries of Eastern Europe, which fit the bill. But in those places there are State initiatives of partial help which are not available in many other parts of the world.

Quite often we read reports that such and such an area is living on less than, say, ten dollars or less a month. To Westerners this is shocking, and in many conditions so it should be. But such figures and their implications need a dash of scepticism. To the extent that it is true of urban poverty and depressed labour, it is indicative of severe pain. But it can also ignore the subsidisation of urban life by family goods flowing in freely from the countryside. And it can often ignore the miracle of self-help. Intimate studies of shanty towns in Latin America (admittedly higher on the income scale than many) reveal initiatives, a *joie de vivre*, and creative energy that has material results in improved physical conditions, noticeable if you visit them from decade to decade. This often in the midst of drugs and violence.

The qualifications are even more of a problem when assessments are made of the level of rural living. Is the help of kin or community in the building of a home, however simple, or in parts of agricultural or forestry labour counted as income? Are stories, music and laughter quantified? Is the Western observer distressed at the "wastage" of marriage ceremonies, failing to take into account the reciprocal activities between kinsfolk over time, the cancellation of debts and the creation of new obligations, and the social benefit of marital stability—in short, the notional income derived from the social organisation of which it is the evidence?[78]

Such international measures ignore cross-cultural definitions of poverty. They imply Western standards of health, education, above all material income, and similar factors. The measures, being international, are imposed from outside with little reference to the specific goals and wishes of the people in question. Increased material wealth may go into ceremonial or non-material events, from Carnaval to bride price, from mosques to moving into exciting urban slums. This is not just a poorer country issue. It happens in Europe.

Indeed it is false to talk of poverty and wealth in simplistic terms. Economists by and large fail to take into account the non-material values that always compete with the material. Indeed a better term, though still containing ambiguities, is "societal progress". By this we mean a state of affairs that moves from one set of conditions to another *in accordance with the total values of the people in question*. This is not easy to do with precision, the only ultimate indicator at present being *what people actually choose to achieve given changing costs and benefits*, material and non-material alike. Unless academics and policy makers investigate actual and potential changes in such demand schedules, their policies are as likely to be off as much as on target.[79] I will however continue to use "poverty" as an easier-to-read shorthand.

Oh my, you are going to think, the man is justifying poverty.

Not at all. There are parts of the poorer world where these observations do not apply, where children are dying and parents starving or too stricken by disease to function. No, this is not a suggestion that we turn a blind eye.

Quite the opposite. I am saying that in the very depths of the poorest world there is hope. Given a chance, the people everywhere are showing that they have resilience and are determined to improve their lot by increasing their energies devoted to traditional culture or by seeking new lives. Given a chance, free of guns, free of disease, managing climatic traumas.

The societies of which the poor are a part are organic networks which even have extremely rich and often corrupt individuals. They are also organically part of the global community. Changes in politics, power rivalries, entrepreneurial conditions, the approach to tradition, access to markets, between men and women, taxation, education, health services, power supply, and so often overlooked, physical infrastructure, have profound consequences. Not all of them are welcomed. But a change in one can have deep effects which ripple throughout the society, polity and economy. The opening of a road to a hitherto unserviced community can have major multiplying effects on every single one of the factors I have listed. Whether it does or not will depend on the points of view of everyone involved, from State departments to village elders and individuals who decide whether they intend to take advantage or not. The poor are not just passive recipients of hand outs, and we must avoid that dogma.

Poverty is a function of societal conditions. Development economists have pointed out two sets of these. First, there is the situation in which the lack of one or more elements in a functional economy vitiates the ability of the system to work. The list is well known—inappropriate education, ill health, malnutrition, corruption, inadequate distribution system, frictions in access to markets, poor transport, social mores weakening the role of women,[80] lack of capital. The work of Utopia is to assist in the filling of such gaps.

But sometimes the imbalance in the social conditions will stimulate further growth and innovation. An educational stride ahead may stimulate demand for better health services, for more employment, for better adult knowledge. The entry of internet centres into villages may increase the velocity of circulation of information in circumstances where post and telephone are lacking. It may even put cities in poor countries in active touch with the stock market. The eradication of malaria may revolutionise agricultural practice, and vice versa, through the replacement of wet by dry framing.

What is the role of the Utopian world in bringing Utopia to the poor? Aid? Technical assistance? Charity and crisis relief? Military intervention? Sanctions for improper government conduct? Free trade? Improving national government?

None of these are simple.

The most dramatic of these is international charitable aid in times of crisis—tsunami, violence, drought, earthquakes. The popularity of giving direct aid under such circumstances is unquestionable and represents the best of Utopian values. However, despite the skills of many of the charitable NGOs, it is seldom directed towards the dynamic substitution of wealth increase for poverty, that is of dynamic social progress for stasis. Nor is it often directed toward the movement of populations away from locations of potential natural disaster. We cannot as yet control all such disasters, though we can alleviate them.[81]

Man made disaster, and particularly the use of violence and of autocratic corruption, is a different matter. We expect Youth Maturity Institutes to play a major role in the correction of such causes; this will take time. Global Government, with the monopolisation of weapons and the use of rapid intervention will be needed. Criteria for controlling or replacing governments under Global Trusteeship can be arrived at quite rapidly, though the mechanisms for enforcing this will be inefficient until Global Government is reformed. What is without doubt is that the situation in such countries as the Congo, Myanmar, Sudan and formerly Rwanda cannot be allowed to continue in a modern Utopian world. The growth of international morality puts limits on the destructive independence of States.

Non-crisis technical assistance and international aid are the quiet undramatic and effective methods of transferring the knowledge and practices that transform static communities and economies into dynamic ones, capable of slowly changing the poverty spectrum. Despite its good intentions, however, such aid is often limited in its objectivity. The limitations are legion.

The early attempts to design aid often had naïve expectations of indigenous societies in the poorer world. Two of the most important movements were to stimulate the formation of cooperatives and a movement known as Community Development. There have been some excellent results which however, globally speaking, have been patchy. And there have been movements, such as the poverty bank system in

Bangladesh, where tiny amounts of individual deposits amount to sums that provide loans for capital purposes, which have something in common and have been imitated elsewhere with success. (There have even been copies in the richer countries, such as the community development movement in Saskatchewan, which came from experiences in India, and a people's bank in Vancouver—which failed). I myself urged the formation of cooperatives, seeing these as consistent with indigenous values and social structure, when an administrative officer in the Solomon Islands in the 1940's.

But a review of United Nations supported community development[82] and field work in Fiji[83] convinced me that, given the high percentage of failures in some countries, this was no panacea. The naïve view of indigenous culture is that the natural thing to do is for everyone to work together—and indeed there is a great deal of truth in that.

But this hides dysfunctional tendencies and individual interest. It works best when the material conditions of life are limited, and collegial help is essential, for example, to build a traditional house. The moment it goes beyond that to the point where, theoretical, wants become unlimited (as happens when money takes hold and a people can witness the ways in which riches can help both material and non-material ambitions) internal rivalries and competition start to take hold. Defections occur, quarrels ensue, rival camps emerge, and individualistic entrepreneurs seize their chance. This is not to deny that, sufficiently motivated, groups will combine for specific purposes—reforestation, irrigation, public health installations, or, as with many North American Indians, the use of collective resources for commercial enterprises supported by politically organized income, including taxes.

Nor is it wiser to come to the conclusion that society must break up into a mass of individual entrepreneurs for societal progress to take place. Especially in their start up stage, but even if they become wealthy, entrepreneurs in most poorer countries still must observe the socio-cultural norms of generosity, social responsibility and familial distribution. (Ironically, the Sicilian mafia "families" provide a case study of this kind of motivation.) Western observers often consider this phenomenon to be a brake on growth, diverting liquid and capital resources into non-material objectives. But for many an entrepreneur this is part of his/her motivation. To destroy it is in fact to destroy enterprise.

Indeed, in my critique of Community Development mentioned above I argued that it could often hold back growth. The reason is based on a simple economics principle. Accumulation depends upon "taking in other people's washing". Community Development is most frequently and puristically based on everybody doing the same thing for everybody else. We all get together to build everyone a better house. We combine to build latrines. In theory it is the obverse of the division of labour, based on the fact that there is little or no money to do otherwise. That's all very well, and is sometimes the only way forward. But as a principle of dynamics it is flawed.

"Taking in each other's washing" is a better principle. It means that numerous transactions take place, and that each transaction creates a profit, however miniscule. Those miniscule amounts add up, and while much may go in consumption or ceremonial support, bits accumulate for capital improvement. The sum of those bits create monetary wealth. Just ask the women traders of West Africa. Let there be a specialist washerwoman in the village, and see what happens—if there are other specialists such as a village carpenter, water purveyor, thatcher, goat herder. After all, when it comes to ceremonial affairs there are likely to be numerous specialists in various stages of the proceedings, so the concept is not completely unknown.

In the 'nineties aid donors, tired of the weaknesses of governmental practices, moved almost in concert to transfer much of their support to local non-governmental organisations, hoping to avoid corruption and to tap into the very sense of community that characterized the theory of Community Development. The decade was characterized by a jump in progress and enthusiasm, followed by disillusion and despair as so many of the hopeful organisations yielded to corruption, mismanagement, bureaucratic interference,[84] argument, personal rivalry, power broking, and segmentation.[85, 86]

Governments which give direct aid are more than likely to be motivated by political strategy, choosing countries in accordance with the donor's global interests. This was particularly the case during the Cold War, but is still practised. Sometimes strictures and conditions in the use of aid by one country are negated by the offer of aid without such strictures by another donor. Donor countries frequently insist that their money be spent on their own products or technical experts, even though cheaper or more effective sources are available (which is why channelling aid through the United Nations is preferable and more effective). The effectiveness of Canadian aid, for example, is limited by the requirement that wherever possible the aid be furnished by Canadian suppliers, whether these are or are not the most economical and effective. In the case of some more sophisticated recipients government departments can be rewarded in their national budgets if they succeed in attracting aid, at the expense of departments that do not do so: and the "experts" find that their task is simply to evaluate and perhaps rubber stamp proposals which equally competent national civil servants have already formulated.

As well, country donors frequently assess aid requirements in terms of meeting a static goal. Increase rice production by x%. Provide the funds for more school buildings. Dig how many water wells. Treat a thousand AIDS victims. Useful. But not *development* aid unless the process not only continues when the donors have left, but establishes multiplying effects throughout the society with static rather than dynamic effects.[87] This is a waste of money and more like charity than aid.

For the dangers of charity must be avoided. Poor people are not objects to be patronised. They are men and women with brains and feelings and potential skills. They can be creative, and indeed are. Not many citizens of the rich world could survive under their conditions, but survive they do. They must not be turned into mendiants, but given the chance to better achieve their own goals.

Thus in the meantime aid must become more objective, more dynamic. This is by no means to decry the self-sacrificing efforts of the most effective donors and especially the United Nations and the NGOs, who know these lessons and these facts and take care of them. International aid must move from bilateral to multilateral, including the use of the effective NGOs.[88]

But ultimately we speak of Utopia. Can we remove the extremes of poverty? Yes. Absolutely. Let's get on with it.

Economists—and I—have long preached the mantra of DEVELOPMENT. But this buzz-word can mean so many different things in practice. Jeffrey Sachs, on of the most vigorous and influential proponents implies the conversion of economic systems into the Western free market model.[89] I am a free marketer myself, in that I abhor the dead hand of bureaucratic intervention and distortions. But we must recognize that nowhere in the world has the free market, or even State management of the economic system, resulted in the abolition of poverty. They both create the rich and the poor, the advantaged and the disadvantaged.

There must be some form of redistribution, and there should be recognition that for some of communities, development does

NOT equate with social progress—in fact possibly the reverse. Believe it or not, some people are becoming disenchanted with the consumer society, which is what an uninhibited free market entails. Insofar as redistribution is concerned, as I pointed out in Chapters XII and XIII ways must be invented to create systems of guaranteed minimum income that take into account, where necessary, the realities of subsistence farming and similar institutions.

But development in one form or another is still an operative concept and we must keep returning to it.

The record of the international community with respect to the creation of appropriate tools is patchy to say the least. Bilateral aid is driven too much by country interests—tempted to pressure the people to, for example, build a specific number of latrines, the marketing of commerce, political influence. Multinational aid sometimes runs up against rivalries between aid donors, inexpert experts, crisis resolution. Both have high costs, and are limited in the way they learn from experience.

Again, the last phrase I use advisedly. Aid projects have frequently achieved excellent results, even where side effects have not been known. The improvement of rice strains, the monitoring of locust explosions, fish harvesting techniques, some eradication of disease, some educational advance, are only a few in a long list.

Yet very seldom are projects submitted to what I would call *developmental* evaluation. While there is now more attention given to hitherto unsuspected side effects—on the ecosystem or the socio-cultural system—objectives are almost always given in static terms rather than in the dynamic ones that genuine movement embraces. We need to *judge projects on their multiplier effects*, not on the way they reach a single target. It is as though we are content if we know that A moves to B, even if the world stops at B. We do not often ask what happens after B, whether C and D will follow *ad infinitum*.

And it is not as if we have not been told that the objective, both to be valid and to be successful, should be defined in ways that meet the people's own concepts of their aspirations. We have. And many grass roots "developers" do just that—the more "grass roots" they are, the more likely the development. But government ministries, many regional officials, most official aid experts, avoid such disturbing problems by retreating into the position that "they know best". Only now are pastoral officers in East Africa beginning to understand that there are values to the cattle complexes and the indigenous uses of camels amongst the populations that they, the experts, were not cognizant of.[90]

What do people want improvement for? What price in values are they prepared to pay to get there? What happens when the aid project comes to an end? Does it just die on the vine because it ignored the reality of the people? Or perhaps it is renewed as permanent subsidised aid *ad infinitum*? These are among the most often overlooked beginning questions.

There are many more such conceptual difficulties involved in the aid process. When is aid designed to stimulate a dynamic, and when is it merely self-satisfying charity or power-based intellectualism? There are answers already in the literature and in experience, but they are too often disregarded.[91]

The correction of inequities will be necessary every step of the way toward Utopia. It is not to be done in ways that remove decision-making from the populace. In fact one of the most important principles that community development tried to grapple with (mostly unsuccessfully, as the movement became bureaucratised) was to give people the right to say "No, no, and no again." A further problem is that often so-called self-help, correctly drawing on local resources in lieu of currency, inhibits the growth of entrepreneurship, since it inhibits the circulation of money.

These remarks are not intended to advocate the reduction of resources allocated for aid; far from it. The world is considerably below agreed targets, as minimal as 1% of G.D.P. At the 1985 G8 summit not all members agreed to raise their contributions to 0.7 % by 2012. At the 2005 G8 summit they did exactly the same, and it was touted as a revolutionary breakthrough!

As the poorer countries begin to solve their problems, to create increased levels of living and better qualities of life, so too will their expectations grow. New dangers then develop; dangers of aggression because the pace of improvement is too slow; and more determined and experienced demands for a better life. The objects are legitimate and part of the Utopian dream for everyone.

Similar remarks apply to migration, the movement of populations. The pitifully tragic mass migration that is the response to violence and natural disaster cannot adequately be handled by international refugee organisations, however hard and selflessly they try. The scale in the 1990s was and now in the 21st century is enormous. According to the World Watch Institute, about 125 million people live elsewhere than where they were born (most legally and by choice). In the 'seventies there were about 2.5 million new refugees a year. In the 'nineties the figure rose to four million. There are 27 million internal refugees, whose plight is more serious than most of those who flee their country, and an estimated 10 million illegal migrants. Ten million people are removed from their homes by public works projects, such as dams or roads, usually with insufficient attempts to soften the blow of a change of living.[92]

Too often men and women in the field have to stand by, confronting massacres, unreasoning panic, mass death by disease, the distortion of humanity by starvation, psychological trauma. In the twenty-first century? In the age of Internet?

The unremitting tragedies have given rise to commerce similar to that of slavery in the last century. The illegal trade in population movement has the status of a massive industry, comparable to that of trade in some drugs. Thousands of dollars change hands in individual cases. Unlucky victims often find themselves literally in conditions of slavery, from Germany to California.

Global Government has to be able to respond quickly and to interfere if States refuse to admit help or to give help. It has to be able to declare such situations to be disasters as great as those of natural cataclysms, to be totally unacceptable to civilisation. It has to be able to act effectively.

Even more troubling are certain situations where, it seems, no amount of intervention, no amount of development-directed change, will help. I refer to regions of endemic disaster and poverty of resources. Here we must be careful once again to respect the values of the population that lives in such conditions. We must not assume that because life, to our eyes, is unbelievabley hard, that it is therefore non-valued; that the population would be happier tucked in bed with television. *It is up to the people to decide.* If they don't want change, if they can manage, leave them alone.

But if they do want change, as a result of suffering, persecution, or wider horizons, they are right to seek it, and we are right, have a duty even, to help them on the way.

In some instances it can be argued that cases which are otherwise hopeless can, with education and communication, carve out niches in the world economy. Hong Kong, investment havens, resorts. It is unrealistic, however, to expect every difficult situation to be resolved like that, or that all such cases can support the subsequent population level.

Richer countries are still having trouble learning that is it is not usually effective to revive dying industries. Populations cannot always be kept in place when industries die or are replaced. Adjustment includes population movement. If richer countries try to create artificial population stability within their own borders they subsidise ineffectively.

If this is true nationally, it is also true internationally. The population level in a few countries will simply not be viable, not because of high birth rates but because of lack or destruction of productive possibilities coupled with the inability to finance education that will make under-employed life acceptable.

The world as we know it today is the result of continuous migrations. Mankind has never been without them. Many were the result of military force, a process that we have nearly overcome. Others were the result of poverty, nomadism, the search for better pastures, and the restlessness of the human spirit which we can never do without. Diasporas are universally present, even in Japan. Even though many have been politically and culturally persecuted, that has been because of their very effectiveness, creating jealousy and envy. Their world linkages have promoted enterprise and trade. There is no reason to believe that their positive effects will not continue. Not only do they contribute to the dynamics of the host country, but they frequently re-invest in their countries of origin.

Thus a major tool for the reduction of inequities is steady migration, even if host countries initially pay a price that may not be returned until the next generation. To have optimal effects, migration should be spared the ups and downs of welcoming and hostility, and should be within the capacity of host countries to manage, provided the concept of management is long-term rather than in response to short-term costs and prejudices.

Much has been made, correctly, of the stranglehold of debt that kills off positive movement in many of the poorer countries.[93] To reduce or even eradicate past indebtedness from the poorest countries was indeed one of the new promises of the 2005 G8 summit. It sounds very good, but is it much more than public relations? Will it happen? And why just the poorest countries? Is this not discriminating against those poor countries that have in fact pulled themselves out of the quagmire—in effect saying "Do well according to *our* standards, and we will refuse to countenance debt relief."?

This is topsy-turvy aid, especially when much of the indebtedness has been wasted on corruption, military expenditures and gross inefficiency. And may it not simply start the cycle of indebtedness once again?

Of course international finance is needed, and of course special considerations by way of repayment schedules and interest rates are necessary. But discipline is needed. Cut off the tap if the funds are going into private pockets (though see my later analysis of corruption) or into excessive military or similar hardware. Under Global Government supervision freeze and sequester overseas bank accounts of leaders and officials which do not correspond to their legal incomes.

In the long term we hope that much of this will be beside the point. More fundamentally, poorer countries need to be able to *earn their own living* on a level playing field. Open international trade is not a complete answer, but it is the major plank. There are poorer countries which resist this, because they wish to protect inefficient industries. That is like post-war Britain, which blindly tried to prop up dying industries, even towns, delaying recovery by perhaps a decade. There are industries in the poorer world which must be allowed to die, with charitable help and adjustment.

But at the same time they might even sometimes survive if poorer countries, particularly in Africa, eliminated tariffs between themselves. Way back in the 'forties, as a graduate student, I had two articles accepted by a "Special Correspondent" for *The Economist*. One of these suggested that too much attention was being given to trade between African countries and their colonial metropoles. More attention should be given to within-continent trade, and for this to happen massive investment in infrastructure connecting the countries through trade channels—roads and railways particularly—ways one of the ways forward. Sixty years later, although there have been some notable improvements, *the need is still there.*

That does not let the richer world off the hook. Once again the 2005 G8 summit made good noises, about reducing, even eliminating the protective barriers that they have set up to protect their agriculture, particularly, from poorer world competition. At least, at this meeting President Bush announced that protection of cotton would be phased out. That is but a small beginning. Where are you Europe?

Quite often this is not a matter of bold strategic sweeps, but of little, almost unnoticed adjustments. Canada permits raw Thai silk without duty, but Thai silk clothing gets whammied. Obviously this is on the theory that to import the raw material creates Canadian manufacturing jobs—yet Canadian manufacturing hardly uses the stuff. To remove the tariff would create more jobs in Thailand. Isn't that what we should be aiming for, to the benefit of both countries? We will not create wealthier workers in the poorer countries, with income to spare to spend on richer country goods, if we deny them some competitive advantage.

Now it will become apparent that this kind of trade is dependent on the existence of appropriate resources in the relevant countries, resources that are not at this moment being used to everyone's advantage. And some countries just don't have those kinds of resources.

Or so it is thought. But they do have people. It may of course be the case that those populations do not want to bear the inevitable costs of development. Fine, let them alone. But for the others there is an answer, and India has shown part of the way. The people are the resource, but un-nurtured, their capacities unfulfilled.

So hear we go. Massive investment in education as the number one priority, regardless. Within a decade, good high schools, if necessary to begin with imported teachers. Instruction in English, French or Spanish as a second but fully functioning language. Universities and technical institutes.[94] Education in commerce, engineering, architecture, agriculture, applied science, social sciences, computer science, the arts. Make it possible for the people to become creative on the world stage.[95]

Although India is a very different country, starting with the advantage of good education in English up to the highest level for at least a corpus of innovative people, much can be learned from its experience. What has been noteworthy in less than the past decade is the application of skills and knowledge to jump over slow evolution into the revolution of internet technology. (This is but one field—engineering, pharmaceuticals, textiles are others, but it is the most relevant for this discussion.) Most of us know of Bangalore, the Silicon Valley of the country because of its success in capturing a proportion of the world's internet service work . . . The people who are responsible are not village communitarians but advanced entrepreneurs, often in partnership with the world's largest firms. And Bangalore is now significant not just for services but as a location for creative software and hardware development of a world standard.

But the important point is that it is not limited to Bangalore. There is a significant trickle down effect as the process of innovation is leading to the creation of new systems of both hardware and services to the poor. On such is an enterprise called Hole in the Wall. This is the brain child of NIIT created as long ago as 1981 to bring computers and people together—at a time when computers were a long, long way from their commonplace now. In 2001 it began a project called Minimal Invasive Education which how has operations in scores of slum locations, and conceived as an alternative to the expensive and elitist provision of computers in formal classrooms.

The operation is simplicity itself, but to be successful required innovative skills in bringing known elements into focus as solutions for unexpected problems. Computer screens are typically located in series along a slum street where children are at play. Behind the wall is supply equipment and technology to gather information about the use of the monitors. To each monitor is attached the equivalent of a mouse—but that had to be completely redesigned to withstand the roughness of the children's enthusiastic hands and fingers. It was also discovered that the children opened too many screens for the computers to handle so that they crashed. Hence devices have to be invented to limit the number of screens open at one time. And so on.

The children are left alone to get on with it. They quickly learn searching skills and move from games to information as they wish in self-directed education.

Another type of computer extension into the countryside is offered by an organisation which puts computers into villages for anybody to use. The computers are in a sense old fashioned, going back to software basics, but in another sense are highly advanced since they must be protected against rough handling, pollution and dust and shut down automatically when the temperature is too high. These are not high street models. They must also face interruptions of power supply, so that they come equipped with a backup battery charged with solar panels. To supplant poor telephone connections, plans are being formed to find ways to make use of large area wireless technology. Indeed the demands of this kind of countryside may make advances in that technology more economical and practical than its attempted applications in the richer world.

But once the system is working it has numerous applications. Farmers can check market prices in various nearby locations before thy decided which one they should take their produce to. They seek immediate advice on cropping problems. The computer may be linked to an electronic bulletin board with community information. In short the rural village changes its character and enterprise is supported. Knowledge is power over one's destiny, and computer is its messenger.

Perhaps too much attention is being focussed on free trade for existing products. But what about new ones? Much of this is dependent on richer world policies too. Here is but one example.

Sugar has bedevilled the economies of many countries. Like bananas, it has often emerged as the major product earning overseas revenues (apart from tourism) in tropical countries. There is a global over-supply to present markets. Former colonial powers protect the supply from former colonies.

At the same time the richer countries are gas guzzlers and at the same time over-consumption of sugar is known to have negative effects on weight and diet. An alternative fuel (used with success in Brasil) is ethanol. Poorer countries could in theory contribute to both these issues by manufacturing at home— ethanol and sucralose, a sugar alcohol suitable for diabetics and other dieters. Inexpensive and readily available ethanol would remove the excuses which lead to the manufacture of petrol powered vehicles and to human induced global warming.

Richer countries will need to help the poorer establish Youth Maturity Institutes and eliminate aggression from their lives. It is my belief that there are inherent courtesies in the poorer countries, and that except where there is critical racial or religious intolerance, the tasks of establishing their values will not be as difficult as in some Western locales. In other countries where passions run deep, it will take a major mobilisation of public opinion to say enough is enough, we need understanding not continued violence.

And the issue of guaranteed income is still to be addressed. We need to introduce it globally, initially with regional variations to take cultural and material goals into account—and this will need global analysis and financing.

XVI

Bureaucracies and the Archaic State[96]

What is a State today? It is the highest political unit, short of a regional or global authority, which co-ordinates the affairs of a country. This seems to give it geographical boundaries, which are indeed there for certain purposes. The boundaries enable scholars, arbitrarily, to simplify the world by denoting the activities within them as societies, by abstracting the values and symbols within them and calling them cultures, by counting the transactions that take place within them, and summing them as economies. The boundaries are indeed real, but the only sociological reality that coincides with them is the polity with its clearly defined and hierarchical authority; and even there the independence and power of such a polity is severely modified through external forces and internal pressures.

As for matters deemed sociological, cultural, economic, the political boundaries constitute frictions in the mobility of people, goods and ideas but do not eliminate such mobility. Cross boundary movements imply that the only full society, culture and economy are that of the globe itself, and that analyses limited to what occurs within polities are by their nature artefacts of scholars and politicians which do not fully reflect reality. These considerations will affect the notion of Global Government. and the issues discussed in Chapter XVII.

Although there are States based, for example, on religion, and although in the Soviet era some emphasised the disorganisation of production and distribution in an effort to prop up the system, it still remains that nationalism is the ideological principle, carried further into the notion of self-determination of peoples, that States use to justify their existence. Seldom has there been a more cynical, yet effective, rallying cry. It is a slogan, like so many others, that is manipulated to legitimate the most blatant and naked assumptions of power.

The nineteenth century politicised the principle, as radical heroes across Europe, and especially from Britain—already an amalgam of Scots, Welsh, Irish, Cornish, and others, certainly not Britons—carried the flag for assumed ethnic uprisings against tyrants—Italians (who were they?) against Hapsburgs, Greeks (despite the absorption of almost a total cuisine from their masters and centuries of miscegenation) against their cousins the Turks, who themselves had been affected deeply by Greek influences), and Germans of considerable variety whose populations were inextricably mixed with those of other ethnicities.

Once the movements achieved centralised government, *internal* variants of nationalism were put to bed, became traitorous. England ensured the dominance of English, and received Irish resistance and lesser centrifugal movements for its self-righteousness. France seemed to do better, but merely, with arrogance, swept nationalisms under the rug. Anger, often satirical, and long historical memories, sometimes of religious massacre, affected many of the attitudes in Brittany, the Langued'Oc, Provence and Alsace. Italians seem to accept Italian as a *lingua franca*, as Germans do High German, but some citizens of those countries have difficulty speaking beyond dialect, and ethnicity and regionalisation grow rather than disappear.

In Canada, and possibly elsewhere, part of the *dialogue des sourds* which characterises argument between centre and region, is reinforced by geography and by linguistic misunderstanding— in the sense of using key political words in differing senses. For

French Canadians, nation retains the meanings of its Latin roots—tribe, if you will. Tribe is defined as a group having a distinct way of life, a culture, and paramountly a language. The English cannot be tribes in the plural because they speak the same language. When it suits French Canadians they can lump English Canadians in with Americans, although most do admit there is some sort of distinction. Their debate becomes English nation in partnership on equal terms with French-Quebec nation.

The English nation sees it differently. First, "nation" means the Nation State, whatever its origins. Canada, including Quebec, is the nation. However, if you must insist on tribal-cultural criteria of difference, English Canada is not one. Apart from some dialect, the commonality of English is misleading and irrelevant. Toronto, Montreal and Vancouver are not the same is spirit, ethos, culture. British Columbia is distinct in everything that makes up culture from the Prairies, from Ontario, from Newfoundland, from the Maritimes. The differences are based on geography and history, and the patterns if immigration. Quebeckers have difficulty understanding that if Quebec is to be regarded as different, so too are the regions of so-called Anglo-Canada. If the population of Quebec is one people, then English Canada has at least five peoples, to say nothing of Indian First Nations.

As a matter of fact I cannot think of any Nation States—except perhaps Andorra and Niue—which are ethnically "pure". Ideologically speaking, the idea of the Nation State is a double-edged sword. Quebec separatists are already discovering that First Nations Indians and Inuit within Quebec want their own separatism; and that immigrants are less than enchanted with the idea of being compelled into a uniform French-Canadian culture; that Anglophones can be a dangerous bloc. Not Turkey, not Iran, not the international community which speaks of the "inviolability of borders" will recognise that the ideology of the Nation State demands that millions of Kurds at last look forward to their own polity. The idea of the Nation State, of nationalism, is there to be used and manipulated, like all sacred texts, when it suits those in power or wishing to be in power.

In the nineteenth and first half of the twentieth century, aided by the appeal of self-determination (which Hitler soon made use of for his own purposes), nationalism justified boundaries. Certainly, maps were not drawn puristically. In the former colonial world, colonial boundaries were mostly maintained, cutting through the middle of ethnically homogeneous peoples—European State nationalism was afraid of African national tribalism. Amazingly and curiously, national identity in Africa began to be identified with the artificial creations; peasants showed allegiance to central governments. In Europe, Sicilians think of themselves secondarily as Italians, in Britain Scots and Welsh feel themselves secondarily, surely not as Englishmen, but part of Britain. Languedociens. Alsaciens, Bretons, Provençals are French; Corsicans less so. But all have complaints about the centralisation of French cultural power, affecting as it does education, literature, and feelings of identity. The issues are clearer in Spain with the overt dynamics, politicised, of Catalan and Basque insistence on autonomy.

Press another button, and the spin-off forces win. The principle seems to have a relationship to authoritarianism. Yugoslavia, to the outsider, seemed to be working. My visits to Croatia revealed the strong nationalist rivalries between Zagreb and Belgrade, even in scholarly matters. But within Croatia personal relationships, inter-marriage, burial in the same cemetery, laughter, regional restaurants, seemed to indicate that religious difference, blood feud and hatred were not realities, were overcome by an over-layer of respect and friendship. That over-layer was definitely there, and not only in Croatia: in Sarajevo for example. But its fragility, surprising to the West, was open to manipulation by the power hungry, macho spirits with vicious guns. Using nationalism as the myth of cohesion carries dangerous messages. Since no set of State boundaries encloses uniform ethnicity, the myth enables minorities to claim the right to separation—strongly exercised after the break-up of the Soviet Union.

The problem with authoritarian regimes is that one does not know how much volatility is there because the stopper is in the bottle. How many genies remain to sneak out. In the 21st century we began to find out.

The whole matter is tied in with boundaries. Let us examine them once again. The boundaries of polities are supposed to be neat and tidy, binding together a coherent population of individuals inter-acting with each other much more than they do with others outside the boundary.

Boundaries define the geographical territory within which the State exerts its control and power over individuals and their activities. State boundaries are the location at which the authority is exerted over individuals, goods, services, even bacteria and viruses who would enter or leave. Within the boundaries it is normal but not universal that individuals may move freely. Authoritarian states frequently control such movements with internal passports, residence permits, and the like. Even democratic states like Switzerland require commune permission for permanent residence. The provinces of Canada restrict the flow between them of, for example, liquor, and supplies directed to the public service.

The myth that States have full control over their destiny and what goes on within their boundaries continues to flourish. But as a description of fact it is wrong, and as the fundamental normative principle that applies to the global system it is, to put it mildly, debatable.

As to fact. Without any recourse to world government States are subject to the international environment in which they live. What they do is limited, as even Hitler discovered, by the reactions of other States. They are also a part of a global eco-system, so that pollution, water flows, air flows, the spontaneous and man-induced migrations of natural life, impinge upon their internal affairs. While even democratic States try to do so through cultural policies, in the long run ideas cannot successfully be forbidden at the boundary.

States have also entered freely into alliances and treaties which place obligations on them and guide their behaviour in restricted fields. More and more, bilateral agreements are being replaced by multilateral ones. International agreements governing fishing are a mix of global and bilateral conventions, with the weight moving toward global understandings. In particular fields, global organisations stand above regional and bilateral moves, working out treaties and conventions to which all or nearly all States subscribe. The United Nations "family of organisations" is the obvious example.

The State has in fact given up many of its powers, a fact which is reinforced by the many regional arrangements and organisations, from river basin management to military matters. States have inputs and influence, through delegations and representatives. They initiate policy ideas and undertake lobbying and back-room deals. They administer their responsibilities under the policy meticulously or with obfuscation. But they must persuade the other members of the organisation if policies are to change. They can opt out, though usually, as with the World Trade Organisation, the results could be very damaging both to them and to others. Paradoxically, self-interest binds them to others.

States can only inhibit the movement of ideas, not stop them. Even patent and copyright laws have limited effect. The time comes when they run out. The advances in technology are such that similar results can be achieved by other methods, by-passing the patents. Prozac was followed by half a dozen related drugs within a few years. Microsoft created Windows to produce similar easy-to-use software hitherto dominated by Apple Computer. Authors know how next to impossible it is to gain their rightful income from reprography or to have their interests respected in China. Reproduction of materials on tape or CDs is now so easy that there are major industries doing just that in India, China and elsewhere, without compensation, and it is often difficult to tell whether you are buying an authorised version or a pirated one. The full policing of micro-satellite dishes and availability of unauthorised decoders is next to impossible.

In many fields prohibition may inhibit consumption but at the same time create added-value, increased interest, even addiction. This is obvious with drugs. Remember samizdat in the Soviet Union? Putting a quota on foreign (usually U.S.) films suggests they have greater value to the consumer than local films, increases demand for what is available, encourages local film producers to copycat, and magnifies the demand for authorised or unauthorised videos. Television reception moves to international satellite. Culture, despite its national and ethnic value, is quintessentially made up of individual decisions and preferences. It is not easy, and not desirable, for official policy to do more than make sure the options are open, from which people may choose. Restriction has the danger of turning individuals to the very options the State wishes to discourage. The emphasis should be positive, on encouragement not discouragement.

The State is the "internal administrator" of countries in this modern world. To do so, our Utopia will be democratic for the setting of policy. Alas, the word "democratic" has so many meanings as to be useless in itself. One-party States call themselves democratic, even if so-called elections are rigged. British style representative democracy is in effect autocratic rule by the majority party, or its coalition, until the next election, or until the coalition breaks apart. In British style democracies, the prime minister, during this period, wields immense personal power through various devices such as the party whip and the threat to call an election if his cabinet does not stay in line. In most parliamentary democracies the mode of discussion is oppositional. Loyal oppositions consider it their duty to oppose everything that can be opposed, even though, if returned to power, they find it expedient to put into effect the very policies they derided.

Constitutions are usually conceived from the top down instead of from the bottom up. The primary exception is Switzerland, which is a *con*federation of sovereign States of which more later, in which all power not allocated by agreement to the central government is exercised by the cantons. In the United States, constitutional amendment requires both popular and internal-state support. However, the usual approach to constitutions, except in Switzerland, is one in which the central government is defined, and other levels of government are adapted to it.

It is this characteristic of government that makes a mess of ethnic and regional diversity and aspirations. Centralisation usually means that, in democracies, all individuals are equal—that is, they each have a vote and the law applies equally and in the same way to each. Policy, with a few exceptions such as in illness or disability, and now racial opportunity, assumes that all persons are the same as each other. The constitutional structure, then, should be the same for Cornishmen as for Yorkshiremen, for Parisians as for Bretons, for Newfoundlanders as for Quebeckers, for Los Angeleños as for Bostonians. And differences, which must be consistent with the overall constitution, will be expressed by the content of policies created by "lower" levels of government. Rednecks in Canada object to the modernisation and rectification of Indian treaty provisions, or Sikhs wearing turbans in ex-servicemen clubs, or Muslim girls wearing head scarves in some Toronto schools, on the grounds that equality means that everyone should subscribe to Anglo-Canadian practices.

Britain has modestly and unwillingly accorded variation to Scotland—again by the "top" deciding this should be so. Despite Quebec arguments that the policy has not gone far enough, Canada has been forced to accord constitutional and quasi-constitutional variation not only to Quebec, but to Indian First Nations. The ability to do this in a limited way is now part of the Canadian political structure. But it is still the top approving the design, which must not upset the overall constitution.

The nationalist myth helped create another; that significance accrues only to what happens inside political-geographical borders. This latter myth has never corresponded with reality, yet is so well entrenched that we speak of the British, or French, or Russian economy in those terms, to say nothing of their respective polities, cultures and societies. Scholars and journalists do of course pay attention to cross boundary phenomena, and governments secure rights of extra-territoriality to administer issues concerning their citizens abroad. And in unpublished study I have asserted that the stimulus for industrial and commercial growth in, say, Britain, the Netherlands, or Switzerland, was caused in part by (a) the diaspora of their citizens who paid their country back by importing and adapting techniques and ideas from abroad, and (b) the acceptance into the functional life of the country of foreigners who brought new ideas and methods, and adapted them to local conditions.

Thus the model should be that British society should include all those within the geographical bounds plus all contacts and interactions across those boundaries. The concept of the permeable boundary with variable phenomena is all important to the notion, and is ignored to our peril.[97] The United States is probably the most aggressive in its conscious assertion of extra-territorial jurisdiction.

So far so good. But herein lies the danger. When circumstances warrant, State policies obvert the proposition and assert not only protectionism but a truly unholy competitive jostling for supremacy in matters from the cultural to the commercial.

Thus in such events as World Trade Forums and the like, and in the journalism of economics, we find worried attention being given to changes in the distribution of production. There are significant signs that China, India and Brasil are competing effectively in certain industries with the European Union and the United States, and may even become leaders in GDP. Horrors! So we have the introduction of trade quotas to "protect" local industries and their workers, and the spectacle of millions of dollars worth of inexpensive Chinese clothing held up in warehouses because they are above quota, and then the Ministers scurrying to find a way to withdraw the finger from the dyke. Because China is a potential major market for Western goods, including armaments.

What is missing in this analysis is the Globe, *tout court*. Governments of course have a right to look after displaced workers, and should be shifting the country's production to work where there is a comparative advantage, and by the use of guaranteed income. Competitive State protectionism is always at the expense of the consumer, and when that happens it is the poor who are most deprived. Those held up Chinese garments could have helped the cost of living of the very workers the States supposedly were concerned about, to say nothing of the homeless of New Orleans.

So, economists and business tycoons and politicians, when you meet in World Trade Forums or influence the policies of the World Trade Organisation, take the welfare of the Globe as your unit. Do not be blind-sided by selfish and mistaken State protective competitiveness.

State policy is executed, and sometimes created, by the bureaucracy. At this point I must clarify that bureaucracies are by no means limited to political organisations such as the State. Bureaucracies are present in any large organisations, including corporations and universities. Hence this part of my analysis will cross-refer between these institutions.

There is an enormous tension between the conservative and innovatory sides of a bureaucracy, an extreme example being the difficulties with former apparatchniks in Russia. The British system of an a-political bureaucracy, advanced on merit, has been, with little doubt, together with the constitutional role of royalty, a force limiting the temptation of politicians, not only in Britain but in similar parts of the Commonwealth, to use their powers dishonestly or autocratically. On the other hand, a bureaucracy can become entrenched in its ways, too independent-minded, so that the politicians find it resistant to their mandate, and sometimes even paranoically suspect wise advice to be opposition motivated.

Two results then occur. One, endemic in the United States, increasingly used in Canada, France, Britain and present elsewhere, is to by-pass the bureaucracy with political appointments and outside consultants, selected to give the "right" answers. The next government sacks them all and appoints a fresh contingent. Long term civil servants are then less "ideas" men and women but guardians of the archives, designers of forms, helpers to fill out forms, collectors of statistics and fees.

Another is corruption. Bureaucrats are then controlled by payments. They have power, not to influence policy, but to manipulate its administration in their personal interest. They are not in the seats of so-called political power, but exercise power, instead, in their day to day relationship with individuals. They corruptly do what individual ministers tell them or bribe them to do, sharing in the profits. They charge fees, often exorbitant, for services rendered. When they are in uniform, armed with a high powered gun, they put tolls on the roads, and demand recompense for allowing you to go home at night. This kind of bureaucracy is usually to be found in ex-colonies and in totalitarian regimes where the authority of the centre is invested in the lowliest of bureaucrats.

One of the least admired features of bureaucracies is to be found in corporations as will as in polities. Whether the organisation consults with its membership (employees) or not during the formulation of policy, it is necessary that the execution be co-ordinated between the different sub-divisions and that employees, in exercising any initiative they may have, do so in conformity with the overall objectives and methods. I am here less concerned with the internal smooth running of the enterprise or the government department, than with the manner in which it articulates with the outside world—customers, clients, John Q. Public, suppliers, other organisations.

Sophisticated government bureaucracies used to be castigated for their insensitivities and defects, and denigrated by comparison with private companies. While I can understand annoyance at those insensitivities and defects, I cannot understand why the comparison should be made in this way. I do not know of controlled comparative studies. My own experience, coupled with anecdotal evidence from friends and people in private companies suggests to me that the latter have as many problems in their public interface, even when their profits suffer as a result, as do governmental bureaucracies. Some companies do much better, as do some government departments.

But here is a list of the kinds of things that occur.

Passing the buck. This is not my responsibility, it belongs elsewhere in the system. Or it belongs in another department or firm. Go there. The new contact sends you to another, or back to the first one. Mail is missing. The Post office sends you to a central complaints office. They give you a form that requires impossible to remember detail. Back to the post office to check on some of the information. You understand of course that it is not the mailman at fault, it's the contracted courier. It couldn't have happened here, it must have happened at the point of mailing. But I had all my summer clothes in the parcel. Sorry, you didn't insure, we can take no responsibility. But **You You You** lost **My Summer CLOTHES** . . . Not our fault, we accept no claim unless insured. But I paid for it to be delivered, it was in your hands, you lost my property . . .

Remote registration of the problem. You want your computer repaired. Instead of dealing directly with a technician, you are made to phone long distance to a central sorting office which takes your complaint (often without the necessary technical knowledge), sends authorisation to the technician, who then contacts you when you are out.

Middlemen and warehouses. In smaller countries such as Switzerland, this is less of a problem in the private sector, since distribution is so good that, for example, auto parts can reach any part of the country in a few hours. It does become a problem when auto parts are not stocked in Switzerland, but in France, Germany or Italy. In a vast country such as Canada, parts, CDs, books are likely to be warehoused as far from the retailer as the original manufacturer or publisher. Warehouses run out of supplies, or distribute with priority to the nearby retailers, letting the distant ones wait. I have searched for parts for national and international brands in vain, phoned the national office, been put on hold until they find someone who knows the wholesaler list, approached the wholesalers to hear they can only sell to "resellers", gone back to a retailer on the wholesaler's list, find he doesn't stock the part, but will make a special order, with an additional charge, then finding the wholesaler has to back-order the part from the manufacturer ... In the public sector, this sort of thing is less relevant, but it still crops up. Postage rates change, but the stamps aren't in the post offices. At income tax deadline specialised forms are not available. Explanation? It's not my fault, it's someone up the ladder.

Failure to address complaints or observations. You are passed over to a public relations or consumer relations office, whose expertise is to draft replies that show they have not read your letter, since they address other issues; or they send out a form letter which simply summarises the policy that is giving you trouble. You point this out. You get the same document back again. When you do get to someone in real authority, a lawyer drafts the letter and again talks past you, not with you.

Refusing to make a precise appointment, or not honouring it. Result, queues in doctor's offices where the patient's time is worth less than the doctor's. Waiting for a plumber all day when you have other work to do and then he doesn't arrive. (In England, where I found this to be dreadful—but other countries have caught up—I used to read about queues and tradesmen's surliness in the Soviet Union. Add to that the unavailability of parts, and I felt the accounts could have been written about Britain or Canada.) Agreeing to phone an income tax auditor at a specified time, only to find he's gone off on a course, no-one knows when he will be back, and, no, nobody else can deal with your file. Thank you very much.

There's no point in going on and on. My meaning is clear. I include the private sector in my diatribe, since by doing so I indicate that the problems are inherent in insensitive organisation of any kind (including charitable organisations and universities). Remedies start with the acceptance that public relations is not simply an exercise undertaken by specialists who make a profession out of common sense. It is elementary courtesy. True democracy is based on courtesy. Utopia is based on courtesy.

But real courtesy, not the pro forma kind. Not civil *servants* whose imagination stops at making sure that you, the citizen, fill out the forms correctly and obey the rules minutely. Who do not have the will or the power to guide you to the place at which the rule might be reconsidered, changed, or deemed not applicable.

Once the civil service letters I wrote and received ended with something like, "I have the honour to be, sir, your most obedient and faithful servant." Let that archaic formula return—but let it have *meaning*. Let employees who deal with the public be trained so that they know they are like body cells on the skin, an essential component which draws substance and information into the organism, returns information to the environment, at the same time protecting the organism, not by aggression, but by exchanges that allow the organism to adapt. They are not there simply to do the routine tasks, but to send signals to wherever the brain might be when there is a problem. The brain can then react to deal with it, rather than ignore it at its peril.

Ironically, in the much maligned colonial service, I was counselled that my job was not to push aside people with problems, *but to find solutions*, not to work by the rules (though God help me if my accounts showed a half-penny that shouldn't be there; it was worse than a loss, since it meant I had short-changed someone) but to find acceptable ways around them; not to deny that a problem existed, but to deal with it constructively.

Can Utopia manage this? Are humans innately predisposed to be rude by offence or by default—like the Australian post office clerk, when I was a boy, who grumpily said "What do *you* want stamps for?" and refused to serve me for ten minutes . . . I don't believe so. Much is cultural—the Aussie's gruffness, the stereotypical French equivalent which expects you to know what you want but can't be bothered explaining what you might need, the Italian caffe lady who takes your money at the till when you are still trying to figure out what you want and how much it might cost . . . And much is due to the low status and remuneration and long repetitive tasks accorded to those in the front line; or to too few tradesmen or specialists in a niche.

Rules provide small men with power. Rather than saying "I am using my judgement, and I find it appropriate that you do such and such, or that you don't do it" the rule-administrator points to a section in regulations. If he is in private enterprise, he says "it is not our policy". (I was, for example, denied knowledge of the timing and contents of a television docudrama about an episode in my life, because "it was against the broadcaster's policy".) The only recourse then is to go to the top and try to get the policy changed, even on the most trivial of issues. To be able to point to rules impersonalises the judgement, puts the appellant in a class along with all other people with the same problem, abstracts the issue. The rule-administrator can present himself as an unwilling pawn; he does not to have to confront the act of thinking or of standing up to another's argument.

Frequently rules exist because the rule maker works with a different set of assumptions from those used by those to whom the rules apply. Sometimes the challenge to those assumptions, coupled with some sort of outcry, makes it possible to change or ignore the rules. I remember a time when good hotels had to ensure, sometimes with proof, that a couple were man and wife. I doubt if it took a formal change in a written rule to set that aside: no doubt some hotels still have that in their regulations.

In Montreal—and I know this has happened in other cities—public health inspectors have tried to apply rules defining the safe and acceptable temperatures at which Chinese glazed ducks would be cooked, displayed and stored—the high-tech methods the inspectors require dry out the meat unacceptably. They have told sausage makers to use preservatives if they insist on hanging their dried meats in the air. Perfectly safe tandoori ovens were attacked by fire inspectors because they did not conform to an unnecessary technicality, even though the inspectors could not prove that they were a fire hazard. In none of the above cases had there ever been a customer complaint about the "objectionable" procedure or a health or fire crisis, and the safety history of age-old cooking methods was simply not addressed. Public outcry forced Ottawa to reverse a decision to ban the importation of unpasteurised cheese:

similarly it forced the Vancouver health inspector to reverse his ban on Chinese poultry cooked slowly in restaurant windows, as had been the custom for decades (and still is).

The main trouble with rules, however, is that they become everlasting. It is harder to get a rule off the books than it is to put it on. When the public objects to rules or they become out of date, the public, when it does not have to negotiate an outcome such as a successful application, ignores the rule, making a mockery of that part of the law, until it is no longer applied. In Vancouver there are rules about beach dress on city beaches, which are enforced. But nudists adopted a relatively secluded area where they disrobed. After a time the police, who regularly patrol, gave their attention to drugs and theft rather than to absent clothing and a vibrant self-governing community, even with gardens and food suppliers, evolved.

Such a reaction to rule by pettiness is not always feasible. At my university a group of colleagues joined to try to empower a Senate committee to review all rules and regulations to determine which could be discarded. They failed.

Bureaucracies almost always think inside the box. Otherwise they disturb their political masters. It takes a cataclysm such as World War II to enable thinkers such as Lord Beveridge to touch the political nerve of a nation with his plan for universal social security, a plan modified in other countries as it in turn became bureaucratised in Britain. When thinking outside the box, which usually means thinking outside bureaucracy, happens, miracles can follow.

Once again (see Chapters VI and XV) think of the failure of State bureaucracies to address health epidemics in the poorer world, where private corporations are notoriously unwilling to invet. A private individual, thinking outside the box, has established a way of beating patents and developing drugs to target devastating illnesses. Victoria Hale has established created the Institute for One World Health, which searches for promising medications protected by patent but never developed. With the help of the World Health Organisation, and financial support (once again) from the capitalist rooted Bill and Melinda Gates Foundation the Institute is testing and arranging for the development and applications of drugs for major diseases which have so far resisted treatment—and therapeutic support (because no one else has been sufficiently interested). This is the kind of initiative that will create immense benefits for poorer countries in a truly Utopian spirit, that archaic States. Fail to address.

Does that not strike your Utopian conscience? If it does not make you angry, it should. States, however necessary, are letting their peoples and the world down. They are not living up to Utopian ideals. One day issues of this kind will bring feeling and thinking people out onto the streets, just like Orange Revolution.

The above is not Utopia. In the colonial service I was told that all rules existed to be broken. I believe almost that. With enough ingenuity you can find circumstances in which the strict application of a rule results in dysfunction or is an assault on common sense or public interest. Rules replace human judgement, which, while imperfect, is the better for its exercise. *If we wish to be civilised, we will replace rules by judgement whenever we can.*

Because these things are cultural, they can change. The public interface roles can be redefined to allow more creative participation of front-line workers in the organisation. If other aspects of Utopia are in place, we can expect more courtesy to be natural. We can also expect that those who are working will know in a sense that they are in an environment in which paid work cannot be taken for granted, that, in fact, they are dependent on their clients who deserve respect and answers. More importantly—and perhaps this is the most difficult part of all—we must find ways to ensure that managers are not artificially shielded from what is going on at the boundaries, on the skin, of their organisation.

Therefore in Utopia I hope there will be minimal, or no, rules. This does not mean chaos or anarchy. Rules may need to be posted to *guide* individuals in the most effective procedures, to ensure co-ordination in complex co-operative activities, and to help define a legal situation such as an adoption or a binding contract. As a first step along this path, I would like to see all rule-making authorities, from social service agencies to State governments, from universities to corporations, review their library of rules (regulations, laws, by-laws, operational guidelines), subject each one to the test "can we do without it, and if not why not", and jettison all those which can be deleted. Then there must be escape clauses which empower trusted employees to by-pass any rule if there is justification. One must ensure that every individual who asserts that a rule is in some way improper in his case can have his representations reviewed without delay by an authority empowered to by-pass the rule, and to review whether the rule can be deleted or amended.

After all this, what is the justification for the State? A common answer is that it protects and defends the individuals living within its boundaries. But it regulates them in minute detail, even in democracies, in ways that only in the most indirect sense have to do with protection. It can be said that taxes are needed to provide a social security network and a military force and police. Enormously ponderous regulations govern income tax, corporate tax, sales tax, customs and excise. Ignorance of such laws is not a defence, yet they often puzzle specialists. But not all taxes go to such concerns. There are immense bail-outs of failing private and semi-public enterprises. How do State-run airlines meet the criteria? Could not infrastructure projects be financed and operated outside the public sector, with public supervision? Military defence, in the defence of boundary, or defence of interests, sense, is becoming less relevant and indeed must go with the creation of Global Government.

More and more it seems, States endeavour openly or under-handedly to divert tax payer's money to propping up failing industry. This is most noticeably dramatic in the aircraft industry—Canadian Bombardier v. Brasil's Embraer; U.S. Boeing v. Europe's Airbus, supported by massive taxpayer funds, and spending enormous sums in vicious battles before the World Trade Organisation—but it affects and distorts all industries and agriculture. To my knowledge, only Switzerland has this under control—and it subsidises its alpine farmers. The control is effected by writing into the constitution the principles and programmes that govern the use of taxpayers' money, *a feature which should be inserted into all State constitutitonds.* It is extremely difficult to get a constitutional amendment passed that would permit expenditures on such handouts. Perhaps also Global Government could strengthen WTP legislation on such matters with binding force.

The United States government calls itself an administration. It is a very political one, with politics running deep into every petty function, so that the word seems a misnomer. Yet if we look at the situation in global terms, the State apparatus of decision making and policy execution in all countries is indeed mostly administrative. The more global concerns increase in weight, the more States will appear to be just one more level of administration between the community and the whole world. The more we can look forward to an effective world government, the more States will be concerned with variations, mostly cultural, within the world order. They will be concerned with maintaining and supporting differences in ethos and style rather than determining pollution standards or trade procedures, which will be global. States will be less sovereign competitive entities than country administrators

Except in the smallest countries, and to some extent in Switzerland, central State government seems remote to its citizens. To show that the centre is in fact concerned with communities, politicians are driven to establish projects, particularly in identifiable buildings and transport links, which enable them to say "we are looking after you". There is an inherently corrupt and patronising attitude that creeps in. The visibility of the central government becomes a matter of major importance, influencing otherwise technical judgements.

Relationships are topsy-turvy. The reality of life, for individuals, is highly selective and relatively localised. Culturally speaking, there is a cross-hatch of international connections and local residential roots. While the international, horizontal, connections are rapidly increasing, it is a geographical fact that, simultaneously, the individual is in a primarily limited space at any one time. There are connective sequences—home to work to play to home; London to Los Angeles to Cannes—but in each of the locations there is a set of perceptions, communications, interests which help to define political and policy interests. In each place there is a combination of very local everyday housekeeping and style concerns, and broader country-wide and international ones. They influence one another, but when it comes to public action representing those concerns they must, for practical reasons, be applied at different contextual-geographical levels.

What this means is that political structures should influence the individual from the world down, and be responsive to the individual from the home and community up. Present political structures do neither very effectively. Utopia must do better. How?

Some years ago I undertook a study comparing the Swiss and Canadian structures,[98] with passing glances elsewhere. I have personally been hurt and damaged by some Swiss practices, so have no incentive to idealise the Swiss or their institutions. I do believe however, that both are improperly caricatured outside the country, and that they have mastered extremely difficult issues, not because of misleading tradition (William Tell and all that), but through sheer determination to do so, as a result of relatively recent crises, which at various times threatened the very survival of the country.[99]

The Canadian federation, I opened, is built and conceived from the top down; the Swiss from the bottom up. Canadian linguistic and multi-cultural policy, which helps to define the "nation", is almost the reverse of the Swiss. What elements of each, and of others, are best suited to Utopia?

In making my choice I acknowledge that in Utopia the mode of linking individual and community to the State will vary in accord with the rich diversity of cultures. Relatively homogeneous Japan may stay that way. If it is by choice, and if it does not attempt to influence other countries that homogeneity is best, Utopians will simply record that State, individual, and community are in Japanese harmony. My guess is that one century hence, however, the Ainu will have asserted their own sense of community, and that regional-occupational differences (as now between rice growers and urban dwellers) will emphasise community differences within the State. As for the United States, China, and Russia, the powerful forces of national identity will, I believe, have to come to terms more seriously with growing regional-community difference some time in the future.

However that may be, let me propose for debate that the community is worth emphasis in the global political picture. I do not believe my proposal is that of the communitarian movement, as I understand it. I call for recognition of community as *one* basic building block, but not the only one, and not as dominant. This is neither a romantic return to the past, nor a revival of the autocracy of community. The reinforcing and humanistic values of community provide many forms of security, which need to be countered by outlandish creativity, freedom to move to other forms of community, and shaking off the burdens of conformity.

In the past, and in most regions today, community, land, production, religion and language go together. These are mostly the poorest and most conservative parts of the world, though poverty and community are by no means correlated. The poorer ones will either disappear, as with some mountain communities of Europe, or grow richer and more vibrant with changes in technology, with the loss of some population and the gaining of newcomers. In some rich cities with a lively cultural tradition, parishes, communes, neighbourhoods are finding new roles, even though they may not be recognised in the political process, and even though residence may not be tied to property ownership or occupations.

One of the weaknesses of Swiss communes is that their conservative political tendencies often predominate, so that newcomers are not fully incorporated in the political process save in special circumstances. There are two sorts of excuses for this. One is land and property, some of which belongs to the commune, whose members are also traditional land-owners in their own individual right. To accord rights to newcomers means the danger of diluting the concentrations of land, and modifying lineage and other kin structures. Linked to this is religion and language. Contrary to much popular belief, Switzerland does not accord equal rights to the four main languages under all circumstances. It is expected that immigrants will adapt to the language of their new residence, whether or not they are accorded membership in the commune. Italian speakers do not expect Italian language schools in francophone Switzerland. (There is also considerable evidence that individual families and total communes have changed language over time: my examples are from German dialect to French in parts of Valais (Wallis).)

The positive part of commune organisation as a fundamental building block is that it can be used to define the nature of the community. In Switzerland, you must be accepted as a member of a commune before you can attain Swiss citizenship. This is extremely difficult, though perhaps easier in some of the larger cities.

In Utopia I would like to see something like the Swiss arrangement, but with modifications to make it less restrictive and autocratic. The commune should have the power to be the major influence in its cultural and political identity.

In most parts of the rural world, this would not be difficult to design because the communities are already there. In cities it would require more thought and ingenuity, and the powers accorded to the communes (or neighbourhoods) would be more directly modified in the interests of providing large-scale services, and even large-scale character.

The powers of communes to control residence and to be the first step in the citizenship process require modification. It is inconsistent to build a global polity with respect for societal dynamics, minimal rules, and individual freedom if nationals are stopped from residing where they wish. The communes are not intended to be monuments to stasis. They are intended to be places which represent differing life styles within the larger mass, to be one of the loci of identity and sharing with others, and to change as society changes.

The commune should be bound to accept newcomers as residents without property restriction (save for a share in possible communal property). But then they should expect newcomers *to accept the language of the commune* in practice, and the commune should decide, say after two years' residency, whether to accept the newcomer as commune member. Nationals immigrating would already be members their former commune or commune of birth, and foreigners would, on becoming commune members, be recommended for citizenship.

In this world, in-migration would change the nature of the commune. Even the language, conceived as the local language, would change. Cities would have locations where different languages would be regarded as local. In much of Canada's prairies German, rather than English or French, would be the recognised local language; Punjabi, Cantonese, Portuguese, Vietnamese, Spanish, Italian, to say nothing of First Nations languages elsewhere.[100]

Migration into the country would be handled by discussion, agreement, negotiation between central authority and communes, constituting the sum total of what the communes agreed to in terms of numbers, occupations, refugees. It will be argued that the communes will be restrictive and negative by nature. In the years prior to the achievement of Utopia, this may well be the case. Such communes, in my view, will suffer. They will lose the dynamic that immigrants bring. Many communes will see that immigration is in their own self-interest, especially if they have a say in who goes where; there are communities with considerable openness to refugees, more so than that of the State (opposition usually revolves around a feeling of helplessness, lack of control); the sense of public responsibility will grow. Just the same, the short run counts, and this principle will need to be adjusted considerably in the light of international inequities.

If there are levels of government between commune and central authority—metropolitan, regional, state, province, canton—they too will need to be structured to reflect the concerns of the communes which make them up.

The Swiss example has more to say about the structure of the higher authorities and their modes of decision making.

The constitution is such that it defines the principles of government as well as the powers of authorities. If a law includes a new or a changed principle, it must be confirmed by constitutional amendment. This involves approval in parliament, and a referendum. The referendum is preceded by major consultations with cantons representing communes, and with the major identity-locating organisations—trade unions, employers' associations, churches, co-operative groups, and the like. To pass, the referendum must be approved by a vote in which the majority of all citizens in the country is tallied, together with another tally in which they are counted by canton to determine whether the majority of cantons also agree. Thus there is further force given to regional concerns.

In the central parliament, the upper chamber consists of cantonal representatives, much like the Senate in the United States. The lower chamber is by electorate. Several parties are represented. *Groups of individuals* may propose laws and constitutional amendments, which, if sufficiently supported, must go through the same process of discussion and decision.

Although the cabinet is by no means powerless, and in fact initiates the bulk of policy, its method of operation is strikingly different from that of other democracies. Because of the power of the constitution, and the difference between principle and application, the day-to-day work of the government is administration. On principle, the cabinet may propose, the electorate disposes. And the cabinet is constructed to make administration happen. The cabinet may not change the principles of government without referendum; it applies those principles in detail.

The cabinet is restricted to five members, one of whom acts as President-chairperson, a position that rotates once a year among the members. He is by no means a Prime Minister or a French or U.S. President. He is usually hardly known to the public. The cabinet itself is consensual. In practice (I do not think by law, and as ratified by Parliament) it consists of members belonging to political parties, distributed as far as possible according to the representation of those parties in the legislature, and including at least one German, French and Italian speaker (not necessarily Romansch). That means in effect that opposition parties are members of the cabinet. This is not rule by majority; it is not rule by gaining a majority through intraparty negotiation. Each member of the cabinet is elected by the legislature, which respects these principles.

It is said that Switzerland operates through consensus because of its long democratic tradition and the hand-raising of the Canton of Appenzell. Maybe. I doubt it very much. Switzerland was the only country to reject Napoleonic reforms, fighting an internal war against his occupation because the reforms were *too democratic* for an oligarchic society. It is said that women were politically suppressed. No more, but it was true until very recently.

No. Political debates, especially in referendums, are as strong and as viciously vigorous as anywhere. It is only a few decades since bombs were used to gain the "rights" of Jura as a canton. There are extreme radical movements, both left and right.

The system as we know it today evolved as a result of a crisis in the desperate Great Depression days of the 'thirties. Horrified Swiss citizens saw worker demonstrations dispersed with brutality, horsepower and fire power. On the other side of their borders Hitler, Mussolini and French étatism were a visible threat. The pragmatists of Switzerland decided, consciously and deliberately, that if they fought like this amongst themselves, Switzerland would no longer exist. They needed each other to resist the outsiders. They opted *consciously and deliberately* for consensus, as recently as the 1930s.

Since that was a deliberate decision by men and women with opposing interests, languages and philosophies, I have good hopes that our way to Utopia will be marked by similar deliberate decisions. At the same time I fear that it may take disaster and crises to knock our silly heads together. We have to decide to start on the way. Isn't the fear of terrorism, nuclear proliferation, international crime, eco-devastation, poverty, enough?

For Utopia, I prefer the Swiss cabinet. I prefer referendums. I prefer the linkage of community to State. I dislike the histrionics of oppositional parties, and the almost unbridled powers of a majority. I do not like powerful executive Presidents, although executive decisiveness is essential. It is a matter of judging values as well as mechanisms.

And to that I add elements of cabinet-ministry operations which have been introduced in Sweden—the use of electronic technology to make ministers able to carry out duties with less of a disturbance to their private lives—thus humanising the operation and drawing on a wider group of candidates for the job. A minister may live out of the capital for most of the time, visiting only where the ministerial presence is physically necessary. For the rest, the minister may talk to bureaucrats on screen, deal with documents and data electronically, from a home office. This is the kind of contact that minimises family disruption, appealing to child carers, and to those for whom nature, perhaps quiet, is more stimulating for good work than the hurly burly of a lobby-filled capital.

And now the accountability of elected representatives. Theoretically, in representative government the member of parliament is free, and perhaps obliged, to act and vote in accordance with his best judgement. In practice, he is restrained and guided by party politics, enforced by whips, and various threats that the cabinet and prime minister can apply. Revolts within the party are not infrequent, but their consequences can be dire—the fall of the government, sanctions against the revoltees, even new elections. This is not so in the United States, where party discipline is next to non-existent. However the benefits of the legislator's mature individual judgement on the issues is there grossly compromised by powerful lobbying, the voices of constituents heard over his shoulder, and in some legislative instances, the power of electoral groups to try to force a recall. Since elections are set by the calendar rather than by the ability of a government to command a legislative majority, the member does not have to worry about a governmental failure;

he is more concerned about his own electability. The cabinet, and many high ranking bureaucrats, report to the President rather than to the legislature, which then has to devise many a trick to assert its influence, with the temptation of confrontation competing with the practical need for consensus.

I see little in these systems that is of benefit to Utopia. It strikes me as autocratic for a ruling party or coalition to restrict the free judgement of parliamentarians. It strikes me as corrupt for lobbies to have private influence. Rather than go through the farce of registering lobbyists, we should demand that their representations to individuals, parties, governments, be open and public, as part of the data on which individuals in and out of government make their judgements. If lobbies have something to say, say it openly and publicly.

Similarly, the closeness of the legislator to his constituency, which is essential in the systems I am proposing, should be safeguarded but not complete. He is elected as a person who stands for certain things, a person whose *judgement* the electorate can trust. He is not a cipher, going back time and again to the local opinion polls to tell him what to do. If that were the case, get rid of legislatures and set up computerised polling booths. Polls do not allow for full information, full reflection, and the balancing of a local issue against wider, even global, ones. There should be no recall on the basis that the representative voted contrary to popular opinion. He is there to lead, as well as represent; if that balancing act is tampered with, there will be no political change except through the demagoguery of those outside parliament who catch the public ear.

The primacy of the individuals who make up the legislature is nowadays being eroded by other forces. The privilege of legislators to be free of constraint and hassle, which as a schoolboy I naively thought was enshrined in Magna Carta, has already gone. The power of the Fourth Estate, conceived as the epitome and representation of the individual's freedom of speech, modified as a non-elected power to counterbalance monarchy and parliament, can be muck-rakingly unholy. Would-be legislators must think a dozen times before they put themselves in a position in which their every private move can be open to denigrating constructions. What journalists themselves do by way of sex and money changing is almost never reported; from their glass office towers or sleazy basements they are content to shatter the images and the public service of able individuals.

In support of such investigations, sometimes in competition, stand police forces. In countries such as France, Canada, even the United States through the FBI, possibly Italy, the power of the State police forces over legislators is low-key and distressingly seldom questioned. When their investigations reach the public, the individual is already tarnished, and the police become heroes because they have presumably uncovered yet another case of political corruption or misdemeanour. Distressingly frequently, prime ministers or their equivalents get rid of an embarrassing office holder before the matter comes to trial, on the basis of private police reports—which, as any criminal lawyer knows are not to be trusted. The phrase Star Chamber quickly comes to mind, even if the event is followed by a court case.

Police in democracies do not yet use such destructive procedures to bring down a government, but the power is there to do so. It is getting quite close to that in Canada, where the Royal Canadian Mounted Police maintain continuous observations of numbers of legislators at all levels of government, where puritanism in public life is an excessive preoccupation, where the morality of legislators is treated cynically, and where the rewards of public service do not compensate for the risks.

Utopia will need to get back to the basics. Bribery to affect the political judgement of legislators should be an offence. Sexual habits should not be, in themselves. Endangering the public security should be (and sex can sometimes create that danger). Excessive alcoholism or other compulsions should be only when the public interest is affected through judgements or anti-security behaviour. And so on. The legislator should not escape judicial proceedings, for example for murder or non-payment of child support, when other private individuals have been victims.

The criteria for sanctions involve political attitudes. What is a security breach may involve a political principle rather than a weakness. An external judicial suit may be brought for political reasons and be with little or minimal foundation: the act of it being brought has done the job of ruining the target.[101]

Legislatures, not in their own defence but in the defence of democracy, should get this house in order. They are afraid to do so because superficially it looks like the protection of an undeserving, self-serving group. If they are afraid on this basis, they are indeed unworthy of public trust; they play straight into the hands of the cynics.

In Utopia, no police force whatsoever would be permitted to investigate a duly elected legislator without the prior approval of the legislature through such processes as the legislature would determine. If the police had reason to suspect an offence, they could, for example, bring the information that would lead them to investigate to a judicial committee of the legislature. The committee would give or deny the authority, and would do so only if the judgmental powers of the suspect to perform legislative duties was likely to be affected, or if there were reason to believe that a criminal investigation was significant. The suspect would be informed.

If the investigation continued, the judicial committee would decide whether or not parliamentary immunity would be lifted so that charges could be made. Perhaps that recommendation would require the vote of the assembly, as it does in a few, not enough, countries.

The trial, in the case of misconduct affecting the judgement of the individual in the performance of duty, or security matters, would go before a specially constituted open court consisting of judges independent of the legislature but acting in its name. The lifting of immunity for criminal or civil offences would result in the trial going before the normal courts, with the normal (revised along the lines of our earlier discussion in Chapter VI) sanctions. *Only in the case of specified offences of extreme gravity* would the individual lose his elected seat, although conviction would more flexibly result in loss of formal positions, such as member of the cabinet, for a specific period. (Alternatively, his right to retain the seat could be subject to a yes or no poll in his constituency.)

Let us return for a moment to an aspect of democratic State constitutions. I am writing from the Kingdom of Canada which follows British parliamentary principles. Next to Canada is the United States, a world leading Republic.

The following are among the *constitutional* monarchies: United Kingdom, Canada, Australia, New Zealand, Japan, Netherlands, Sweden, Spain, Denmark, Thailand. I leave out of consideration absolute monarchies, and monarchies of the past, even into the twentieth century, in which modern constitutional principles were not at work. I also leave out non-constitutional monarchies, such as Nepal.

The prime characteristic of constitutional monarchies (even in Britain, paradoxically without a written constitution) is that, although the monarchs sign law into effect and justice is administered in the name of the Crown, the monarch has no legal authority over such matters. That authority is in the hands of parliaments and Ministers.

Except. Except the signature is necessary, *and in dire circumstances could be withheld.* Usually, the monarch dismisses parliament and authorises elections on the advice of the Prime Minister (who has been defeated in Parliament).

But wait. A constitutional monarch can, in very dire circumstances, dismiss parliament and call for new elections without the Prime Minister's say so. This power has been used very infrequently indeed, on evidence of serious corruption or autocratic instead of parliamentary behaviour. But it is there, and a useful reminder to democrats gown awry.

A more immediate power is that the monarch appoints the Prime Minister. Usually this is symbolic, for the obvious candidate is he or she who commands the Parliament.

But if the Prime Minister loses that confidence in a motion of Parliament, or if he does not command an automatic party majority. The monarch may, for example, invite another parliamentarian to try to form a government, or indeed call a fresh election. This power for instance has been of major importance during the Martin Liberal 2005 minority government of Canada. That government was defeated by a motion on a minor matter which included the word "confidence". The Governor-General, the Queen's representative, after much studying of constitutional precedents, did not rule, leaving the government in power, because the matter was too trivial and the public was not in the mood for an election. However a few days later a full confidence motion took place on a budget bill in which the government just scraped by. If it had lost, the Queen's representative could either have called on another party leader to attempt to form a cabinet with confidence or have called an election.

The monarch does not run the government and does not interfere in the country's affairs. But the monarch is an important independent unelected automatically-acting safety valve which no republican system can emulate.[102]

Republics vary in structure. In some, like Germany, the President is Head of State with powers vary similar to those of a constitutional monarch. In others, such as the United States and France, he is both Head of State and Chief Executive. In others, which we need not examine, he is dictator.

The problem with such Heads of State is often that they are in fact the political masters of the country. Balance of powers theoretically intended to keep them in line look good on paper but in practice they are extremely unwieldy and depend upon other politicians, with their own agendas, to operate. In the United States elections are for fixed terms (using antediluvian techniques), so that, apart from individual recall provisions, there is no mechanism for a fall of or dismissal of government.

It is true that most other republican systems, such as Germany and Italy, operate with parliaments where the government can be defeated leading to an election and the President has similar options to those of a monarch. But the President is a politician and cannot be above the fray, immune to political rather than constitutional pressures. Note the re-appointment of Berlusconi in 2005 after his parliamentary defeat.

If indeed we compare monarchies with republics, it is evident that constitutional monarchies are stable[103] and less open to political corruption (though not entirely without it).

This is not to say that republics cannot achieve similar standards, as Ireland and perhaps the Baltic States, bear witness. But they are few.

Under the revised political system of the Utopian world, Global Government and its auxiliaries (treaties, conventions and the like) will stimulate what are now State governments to evolve their roles. No longer competitive military powers, they will be able to innovate and concentrate on and be responsible for the cultural and social implications of the new world, within their countries. They will humanize their relations with their citizens, listening as it were with ground placed antennas, ensuring that localized Utopian requirements will be met, rethinking their fiscal operations, creating Youth Maturity Institutes.

They will not at first change willingly. For this to happen we much mobilize public pressures.[104]

XVII

Global Government

The major, but not the only, causes of strife between States and armed struggle within them, consist in a parcel of inequities which lead to competition for power. The excuse is to relieve the inequities. (I say "excuse" because it is by no means unknown for the leadership to be motivated as much by personal aggrandisement.)

In past history the *creation and reinforcement* of inequities through imperialist and expansionist dominance was a major driving force. It was as though the struggle for survival required such dominance and aggression; otherwise the would-be aggressor would itself succumb to others. In the nineteenth century, architects of dominion defined powerful "civilised" States as those which could defend themselves against the assumed aggression of competitors. The aggression might in fact be turned against weaker peoples or against neighbours. The competitor saw that as jostling for dominance.

The Cold War may have been the last major vestige of such drives on a world scale, though suspicion and armed competition are still there. Relatively new States (Indonesia, the Balkans) have adopted similar imperialist methods and the United States has not yet learned to use its power in a non-domineering manner and the effects of the resurgence of Chinese dynamism have yet to be seen.

One inequity is that of sheer size. When coupled with wealth, size lends itself to a non-democratic imbalance of military and diplomatic power between peoples. In the absence of an effective global government, the United States today stands out alone, although China, India Brasil and the European Union may provide counter balances in almost every dimension possibly except for that of technological armaments. Its potential power is weakened by ambiguities in the will to pay the price of such responsibility and by foreign policies directed by the opinions and interests of the single country population (not the global one), especially but not only at election time. This is not global government; nor is it legitimized policing, especially since in many respects the United States refuses to ratify or observe some international laws and courts. It is possible that the United States will change, gaining confidence and experience as a global policeman, enforcing United Nations laws. In the immediate future that does not seem likely. Furthermore, the dominance of any one major power does not last for ever.

Is that what we want for Utopia? To depend on one or more Powers for this function would inevitably mean the imposition of that Power's values and perspectives on others. Global stability might come, but at the cost of diversity and democracy.

I will later be arguing that Utopian Global Government is better achieved through the association of political units which are closer to being equal. A Global Government of a few elephants surrounded by jackals and midges will achieve decisions only at the cost of great resentment, angers, jealousies, and frustrations which lead to distrust and the ignoring of inconvenient policies. The United States has been a front runner in undermining the United Nations family, frequently condemning the organisations for undoubted inefficiencies, trying to impose its own idea of efficiency, and at times withholding its legally agreed financial obligations without which the United Nations cannot be effective.

Apart from the United Nations, what Global Government there is consists of a spider's web of thousands of international agreements. Some are brought together in a substantive global grouping, as with the World Trade Organisation, nuclear non-proliferation and the painfully growing Law of the Sea. Others are regional in scope, with greater or lesser binding arrangements, from the European Union, to Nato, ASEAN, NAFTA, and all the other diplomatic acronyms. They have evolved rapidly in the past thirty years, demonstrating that behind the sabre rattling that has been going on, there is a trend towards settling differences by binding agreement.

In addition there are scores of multilateral contacts affecting the ways in which bureaucracies and professions evolve. As Anne-Marie Slaughter[105] has pointed out, the network of bureaucrats and experts continuously communicate and develop policies behind the scenes. Musical, bureaucratic, professional and academic international communication, conferences, exchange of data and views create global influences on national cultures and official behaviour. Note the representatives of national governments, elements in their populations which try to influence the policies, and international non-governmental organisations and multinational companies which have become lobbyists for their own positions, as well as acting in parallel with governments in the international sphere. Add in the United Nations family of organisations, and regional agreements, organisations, and laws.

This is a diverse, competitive "organisation" which in another context I am examining as the culture of *Wemovagla*—the name derived from an acronym for the Web of Moral Values Globally Approved. Wemovagla is a global tribe, an ethnos, which in the last two centuries has been struggling to find its identity through ethnogenesis.[106] Wemovagla strives to create a global system of values which comes in conflict with and struggles to amend local values. It deals with such matters as women's and children's rights, labour codes, educational goals, corruption, liberty and human rights, nutritional standards.

The gross inequalities between States govern the power structure when it comes to decision making and action. The larger States are as self-serving as any and are no slouches when it comes to bullying the smaller or weaker, as the recent disgrace of the failure of the World Trade Organisation to remedy the effects of nationalist subsidies, tariffs and trade barriers on Africa, Latin America and Asia clearly demonstrates.[107]

Plans for a Global government must take into account such realities and overcome them.

Why should there be Global Government at all? Most observers would agree that the United Nations has not fully lived up to expectations. The operative word is "fully". The United Nations was set up with the primary task of preventing further wars between States. Its key instrument is the Security Council which gives a veto to the main victors of World War II, with little reference to current power positions. There is no doubt that the Council, with its vetoes, clarified the relationships between those States even as they were embroiled in the Cold War, and was the locus and inspiration for diplomacy which prevented a further world war.

Since the *de facto* peace that has ended the Cold War, the role of the Security Council in *preventing* war between States has been diminished. The United States, with Britain, exercised their "right" to go to pre-emptive war against Iraq, an action which the United Nations charter forbids, save with Security Council authority. As many predicted, other signatories to the Charter may now feel justified in following suit—as with Israel's U.S-approved raid into Syria in 2003.

Through its Social and Economic Council and related bodies the United Nations has mounted vast campaigns of famine relief, refugee help and technical assistance with awe-inspiring success, both directly and through international NGOs. It resists nationalist strings being attached to such help, which endears it to recipient countries. As I have noted many donor countries, however, prefer bilateral aid which enables the donors to give contracts to their own citizens, whether or not such contracts are in the best interests of the recipients.

Failure is therefore not an operative word. Not doing everything its evolving mandates demand and achieving both dramatic and little known successes is a more just description.

And when that happens, despite some of its administrative inadequacies, it is not the United Nations *per se* that is at fault.

The United Nations is a creature of its member States. If they do not want it to work, it can't. Although the United States is by far the largest financial contributor and has been generous with voluntary contributions, it tries very hard to turn the organisation into a fief, even to the withholding of contractual or agreed contributions when it is miffed.

Even when the Security Council gives its mandate and direction, the co-operation of willing States is in fact voluntary. The United Nations has no permanent military force, which makes logistics, communication, and scheduling a nightmare with slow reaction times as each contributing State places its own interpretations on the role of each contingent in a peace-making operation.

Although it is the creature of States, whose responsibility it is for any of its defects, in theory it stands above them all.[108] It is the only available coordinated and authoritative body to speak *on behalf of the world community*. We may not like its resolutions or concordats, but, theoretically, the world community has spoken. In the context of the war and occupation of Iraq the United States, in its actions, did not share the concept, frequently treating the United Nations as an organisation in parallel, rather than a superior organisation, both morally and legally.

"Theoretically, the world community has spoken". In practice this is not so. The resolutions, whether of the Security Council or the General Assembly, are the result of negotiations *between States*. It is the States who are responsible for any deficiencies which occur, including chronic under funding.

But an effective Global Government there simply has to be. We have to find a way to create a world order which will *dominate, discipline and co-ordinate States*, rather than the other way round, in the interests of the *peoples* of the world community. We must tease out the weaknesses, and create new instruments which will have the kind of strengths we need. This is not in order to sanctify Global Government. It is because if we do not have an effective Global Government the world is headed for man-made disaster. And then Utopian society will be further away than ever.

First, here are some of the functions desperately needed for a Global Government to carry out for the world—not only as a Utopian dream, but as a pressing necessity. We need Utopia. And the recognition of the functions will help to determine the new organisation and structure of Global Government.[109]

1. As is required by the existing Charter, to ensure world peace and security.
2. To prevent **unilateral** armed action under *any* circumstances by *whatever* entity. A corollary to this function is to ensure the disarmament of States and all armies and militias.
3. To destroy all nuclear arsenals.
4. To enable it to carry out 1 and 2 to establish its own rapid deployment force, occupation forces, and other military and naval units. These will be financed through a percentage charge on States calculated on the basis of their current expenditures on armed forces. Such Global forces will also be available to police sanctions and other laws established by the Global Government.

As an important aside, when Global Government is confident of its power and role, it will time to replace lethal weaponry with incapacitating weaponry. Under present conditions there is disgust and abhorrence at the potential use of chemical and biological weapons. They are in crude states of development, subject to the vagaries of weather and designed to create swathes of horrific death. But research is capable of designing protective gear for the users, and forms of such weaponry which incapacitate quickly for say a twenty-four hour period without disfiguring or lasting side effects. This surely would be preferable to the use of high explosives with their high degree of collateral damage.

5. To outlaw arms, including small arms, within State boundaries. Unfortunately, this will not in itself stop mayhem, since one cannot outlaw machetes and knives. Youth Maturity Institutes will eventually help.

6. To establish a global register of arms producers, production and distribution, with each weapon coded for rapid identification (as is becoming the case with diamonds).[110, 111]

In those parts of the world which can least afford it, men women and children take up arms, financed out of desperation by drug and similar traffic, accompanied by brutal suppression, sympathisers cheering from the sidelines, and mystery. Attempts to impose arms embargoes have been weak at best for so-called conventional and chemical-biological weaponry. For the latter, raw materials are not difficult tocombine, and, like explosives themselves, not difficult to plant for individual or terrorist purposes. The hardware for their trajectory, however, is another matter; it is not necessarily different from other such weapons.

There is somewhat more success in controlling nuclear devices, and a great deal more determination. Whereas conventional weapons may blow up the combatants and far-away civilians, nuclear weapons, wherever they are directed, do damage to all of us, and are relatively limited in distribution.

Major industries support the arms trade. Its disappearance over night would create unemployment in producing countries, that is everywhere. Individual countries are in fierce competition to gain market share. While a few countries share the nuclear industry, income can be generated from peaceful power plants, and those countries with political power stand to gain financially from restriction.

Is this too cynical? I do not believe it is. In June 1995 the respected and sometimes iconoclastic **Economist** included one of its famous special surveys, this time on defence technology. The survey treated the armaments industry as an industry just like any other. From that premise the industry should be technologically and financially more efficient, as a contribution to its *growth*. There was no discussion of killing off an industry whose primary purpose is to sell devices which kill humans, destroy cities and cultural treasures, ravage the countryside, cause massive destitution and forced population movements, and a huge bill for the international community to clean up the mess.

There is no will, and I can detect no movement, to suppress the trade in arms. Such suppression is supposed to be impractical.

To some degree it is. Small arms and some large ones can be manufactured in primitive conditions, and escape rigorous controls. In today's world, however, they have limited value for major group violence, especially if confronted with a united Global Government rapid deployment force.

When it comes to international action to stop the arms traffic, critics of the idea will point out how difficult it is to monitor the seas, the air, even forested land borders. Of course it is. But it is by no means impossible.

In the nineteenth century a few navies, operating under international treaties or their State's policies, succeeded in outlawing and reducing slavery to its minimum, despite the fact that slavery was economically significant, well financed, and well organised, with much public opinion on its side. Colonial governments, when they had the will, stopped it in Africa. Like smallpox later, it was almost eradicated.

If it had the will, Global Government could reduce the international arms traffic to a manageable minimum. I doubt if any State in the United Nations has the present will to initiate such a move, even though such a step does not in itself amount to world disarmament. The revised elected membership in the Global Government's legislature which I shall suggest would almost certainly be prepared to do so.

Such a step requires supplementing by requiring junior levels of government, such as States, to introduce full registration of firearms of all kinds, and to eliminate them except for those deemed to have a necessary and positive function outside of human aggression. (Survival hunting might be one such exception.)

It also requires State disarmament, and the accord of power to the Global Government, which I shall argue for below.

Similar controls need to be in place to put a stop to the use of children in armed units. Indeed, since everything cannot be done at once, strategically child armies, such as those creating havoc in northern Uganda, might be the priority target.[112]

In the present world it is too easy for those who use military force to escape international wrath. There is no excuse, save for self-defence. To remove the need for self-defence, the Global Government itself needs the power the United Nations does not have. While the constitution of the United Nations forbids resort to arms, the constitution is seldom used to expel a member. Under a Global Government constitution, States would not be members of the Global Government; populations would. States which defied the Global Government on such a matter would be replaced in law, declared invalid and outlawed, and assured that any gains made by force of arms would not be recognised. I will later argue for Trusteeship.

7. To define terrorism and piracy and to make the planning, financing and exercise of terrorism and piracy crimes subject to international law superseding State law.
8. To codify and clarify all international conventions and treaties which place obligations on governments, organisations and individuals, and to provide for their mandatory enforcement, *whether or not specific nations sign the relevant agreements,* through international courts and systems of policing.
9. To bring under its control and coordination the programmes of what is known as the United Nations family of organisations (UNESCO, FAO, ILO, WHO, WTO and the like) and other organisations established by global treaties (for example, fisheries, environment, airlines).
10. To establish, with the help of appropriate NGOs, including scientific and social scientific ones, long term dynamic development programmes with the aim of reducing global inequalities, expressing localised values, and enabling sustainable self-sufficiency in the context of world trade. The aim should not be the conservation of ways of life, though these should be respected for their positive contributions, but to balance and create equity of opportunity in the global division of labour.

11. To fold emergency relief actions into 9.
12. To smooth the way for refugees and economic migrants, recognising that this implies social tension and change, and alterations in the demographic structure of the world.
13. To direct medical action and research to the types of programmes at present handled by WHO, creating a balance between the needs of tropical countries and others, and between "populist" demands (AIDS, cancer) and those which receive less press attention (malaria, the common cold, arthritis, macular degeneration). Where necessary create drug manufacture and research with the aim of distribution according to ability of societies to pay.
14. To enforce global environmental standards, and to compensate and assist those societies and States for which observance of the standards may create an initial industrial or other disruption. To make wilful environmental damage an international crime.
15. To organise massive support for the training of teachers, therapists and others concerned with youth, and their distribution for enhanced primary and secondary education, and, better, Youth Maturity Institutes as described in Chapter IV.
16. To *require* States to observe conventions with regard to human rights, international courts, nuclear arms, ethnocide, genocide, and the like, *whether or not* the States in question have signed on to them.
17. To establish a system of Trusteeship in which the Global Government would take in charge the administration of failed States, including States that continue to refuse to accept such international mandates as freedom of expression or the criminality of torture.

The concept of Global Trusteeship needs considerable clarification if it is not to be misunderstood. Near-trusteeship UN operations have been reasonably successful in West Timor and Kampuchea, with the agreements of the populations involved, and partially successful in Kosovo. There are countries where the situations underline the difficulties in the application, such a Burundi, Sudan, Myanmar and especially Iraq. But note that these difficulties stem partly from the structure of the United Nations, which is a far cry from Global Government, and from the vested interests of national powers.

Global Trusteeship will be most effective when national disarmament takes place on a world scale, although there will be some instances when a Trusteeship will need to be imposed when a country refuses to disarm. The decision to undertake Global Trusteeship will be most effective when it is based upon a Global Statute of International Law, adopted by an assembly which is that of the people, rather than governments. Only then will it have clear moral and legal authority.

The administration of a Trusteeship requires a civilian executive who is policy oriented. One of the U.S. failures in Iraq has been to make use of an Ambassador with colonial style powers, but no experience in policy making under such circumstances, and no global mandate. Rather the operation is an extension of U.S. culture in which corporate executive and military power values dominate.

Thus a Trusteeship executive must have a United Nations force **under his civilian authority.** The force should be prepared and equipped for police actions rather than for military occupation, though the latter may be necessary in parts of a given country. The Trusteeship executive should work entirely through localized political power, wherever possible, using its authority to educate and/or force the political authority to take remedial steps. The executive may in the early stages, consult with a group of social scientists appointed by the International Social Science Council, as far as possible drawn from the country itself, plus outsiders specialising in the country's affairs; this to assist the Trusteeship executive in refining the problem issues and the approach to their resolution.

Apart from this, officials of the executive, drawn from Global Government resources, would, in principle, be stationed as advisers and monitors to ministries, regional authorities, and the like.

The duration of the Trusteeship would be finite, open to extension. Usually country-wide elections would be expected in a year. Western ideas of appropriate election procedures would not necessarily constitute criteria—there are other forms which might be more appropriate in the short run, and which might be used to create approximate representation to avoid delays in handing authority back to the country.

After such a return to country authority, monitoring would continue until such time as the Trusteeship executive, by now relieved of executive powers, aided by the group of social scientists, could certify to Global Government that the country has satisfactorily resolved, or near-resolved, the issues that caused a Trusteeship to be mandated in the first place.

18. To establish conditions under which political self-determination will lead to State "independence".[113] Currently the situation in such areas as Chechnya, West Papua, Sudan and Kurdistan are examples of a *prima facie* desire for such a change, amongst many others.
19. To make torture, detention without trial, capital punishment and similar offences internationally and effectively punishable, whatever the jurisdiction of the offending system may say.
20. To create an entity which, on behalf of the world's population, will begin the centuries-long task of finding another earth to colonize as a home for humans when the inevitable happens, and the forces of the universe turn this earth into blinding dust.

This is not intended to be an exhaustive list, for there are scores of other issues, from malaria and illiteracy eradication to maritime governance and rights of workers, embodied in the programmes of the United Nations family of organisation and in near-global treaties.

What is different about my proposal is two-fold. The first is the co-ordination of the work of Global Government and *all* the existing independent members of the United Nation family within *one* framework instead of a multiplicity. We shall see that the existing "organisation" is, almost, anti-Global Government. The principle requires major and far-reaching changes in the organisation itself. The second is giving Global Government strengthened legal and forceful powers. This requires fundamental changes in the relationship between States and Global Government.

The biggest bugbear ever to get in the way of a decent peaceful world is the entrenched respect for the autonomy of States, to whom all organisations in the United Nations family of organisations genuflect. Slowly, very slowly, this is modifying. Worse still, any State can get away with almost anything if it simply declares "My crime is my internal affair". Official torture, murder, rape, massacre, bloody internal war, ethnocide, political imprisonment of rather mild dissidents, exploitation of women and children, sexual slavery are blatantly occurring as I write, have occurred consistently throughout the full history of the United Nations, and will be occurring long after you have read this. Indeed these matters were not the primary *raison d'être* for the United Nation's creation. They will continue unless we have powerful, effective, Global Government.

The United Nations has achieved an enormous amount during its short life—half a century. The achievements go largely unnoticed because they are, in terms of the media, undramatic. They do not get attention up front. They seldom make front page headlines. They are based on hard, solid work, enormous diplomatic successes, carried out with minimal fuss and even fewer resources, and with enormously dedicated personnel. Refugee conventions and resettlement; protection of aid operations; development assistance; regional co-operation in research and development; arid land renewal; major successes in the near elimination of disease; mass literacy programmes; mass self-help programmes; population control—one could in fact go on for volumes.

But the moment the United Nations comes up against determined State defiance, it is stuck. It can do almost nothing, except against the relatively weak. Its funds are with-held. Every single State has become an expert in using verbiage and hypocritical legalese to defy. The nose is thumbed.

Every single one of the numerous organisational weaknesses of the United Nations family is a result of the self-interest of States which have put their own power and autonomy first—from the national self-serving and inefficiently hypocritical staffing systems (despite the extraordinary dedication and frustrated competence of the best international civil servants), to the replication of services between organisations, to the costs of translation, to the use of obfuscating UN-ese as a distinct language, to restricting the capacity of peace-keepers; to the enormous costs of numerous and massive governing bodies, to the proportion of funds used for administration rather than programmes; to power-maintaining rivalries and competition between organisations; to programme unworkability because of lack of local·support or international resources; to overlapping rivalries and destructive competition with bilateral aid agencies; to lack of effective use of and decentralisation to competent NGOs; to dependencies on a coterie of "experts" instead of available NGO experts (there are notable exceptions to this); and so on and on.

One could in each case point to speeches in governing bodies deploring such defects, pleas to correct them, funds with-held because they have not been corrected. And one could find the powerful legal resolutions of the governing bodies that override these concerns by *mandating* the Secretaries-General to do exactly what they are in fact doing. Resources necessary for correction are not supplied. Frustrated reforms are contrary to the interests of some bloc, even of States which wish to "banish" incompetent civil servants in their own bureaucracies to one of the UN organisations, or to reward a time-server.

Privately, most States do not *want* the United Nations to be a Global Government. States mistakenly believe that the world can go on as it is, that the public will not rise up in anger at the way States are betraying the future of our grandchildren, are putting the very existence of the world as a planet in danger. States are trying to brainwash the public into believing that Global Government is a danger to their own independence and culture—as if that would matter a tinker's cuss if the globe exploded. States divide the world to conquer it, and in the process create and lose the war.

Consider one major phenomenon. The United Nations system consists of a *family* of organisations. It is literally forbidden for bureaucrats, consultants, or diplomats related to any of them to refer to UNESCO or WHO or FAO or the World Trade Organisation as in any way implying that they are part of, or subject to, UNO, the United Nations Organisation in New York. Forget a governing world system. Instead there is a getting together of grown up independent career-oriented rivalrous siblings.

Result. While some of the organisations are indeed children of one of the foundation organisations and maintain umbilical cords, and while some are not accorded full sovereign status, the primary ones do have that status. Around each of them is a panoply of Ambassadors from the Member States. While there may be smaller executive councils with restrictive powers (of which the primary one is the U.N. Security Council), sovereignty is vested in each of their General Assemblies. Every single one has something of that kind, and most of them bring together full delegations (separate from the Ambassadors) from all the—what is it now—180? Member States once every two or three years. UNESCO's can last up to two months, divided into large sectoral segments meeting simultaneously—and therefore requiring large delegations, to cover each segment, from each of the countries (which many countries cannot afford)—as well as committees and negotiations in the corridors and at restaurants.

In addition, Member States, concerned about the organisations poaching on the mandates of each other, and conducting overlapping activities, insist on intense liaison between them. This is not just general liaison, with, say, FAO having one man in New York who could link up with all the organisations, or even one man in each of the others such as WHO or UNESCO or ILO or WTO or UNICEF—all of which have to do with, say, agriculture or community development. No. It means that every department, every section, has to have someone ready at the drop of a hat to meet with colleagues in each rival organisation (not necessarily simultaneously) at some neutral location to discuss ongoing or proposed activities and to be ready to defend territory and to *object*. You can imagine the proportion of time spent on such exercises, especially in small sections or departments, diverted from substantive work.

Add this up financially—the cost of delegations to expensive capitals for the General Assemblies; the cost of Ambassadors and liaison officers in the same capitals (different Ambassadors for almost every organisation); the cost in time and travel to the organisations themselves for liaison meetings—and with the same money you could possibly create a permanent peace-keeping force, reasonably equipped, or triple the amount spent on development aid. Of course a few highly paid, hubris-creating, Ambassadorial perks would be lost . . .

Aha, say the critics, including politicians who are resisting paying up their countries' assessments, massive waste. Cut back the finances until they get their house in order.

Such remarks, unfortunately typically snide, ignore the fact that every single one of these major wastages, and others such as appointment of staff on the basis of geographical and national quotas instead of ability, derive from binding resolutions of the General Assemblies (composed of representatives of the States themselves) of the organisations, or from equally directive decisions of their Executive Boards. The wastage in the United Nations family is not a result of international servants' decisions: it is the result of decisions by the Member States in the governing bodies—who often act as if they did not *want* the United Nations to work.

The actions of the United Nations with respect to Global Policy are, by constitution, limited and over-ruled by the reserved powers of States which they arrogate to themselves. The United Nations and associated organisations have massive bureaucracies for the implementation of policy, bureaucracies which sometimes, it is true, run away with their own hubris, especially since legislative control is so unwieldy. That leads the public to think of them as having strong executive governing powers.

This is quite wrong. The bodies are much more like associations of States whose resolutions are more like treaties than like laws. States adhere to agreements, or refuse to do so. Many policies are in place only for a minority of ratifying States, lacking global force since a ratification quorum may not be achieved. Important policies, such as the cultural heritage policies of UNESCO, or peace-keeping, are primarily paid for by contributions to special funds outside the restricted and be-ruled general budget. Some such contributions are entirely voluntary; some are governed by principles of payment, which, however, contributors can and do ignore.

Originally, there was some sense to the arrangements. The organisations were small, brilliantly staffed, well focused, a coming together of allies after a devastating war, gradually admitting everybody else who wanted to join. It was thought of less as Global Government—anathema to the peace-time allies—but as a safety valve putting a limit on international snarling, and finding useful international things to do to improve man's lot. Even the last function was in competition with bilateral programmes, which served State interests more directly.

Utopia sees this sort of self-serving Statehood as damaging and as standing in the way of achieving global policies that are urgently and desperately needed. ***Major policies can only be resolved, can only function properly, as global ones.*** Peace, world trade, the relief of disaster and poverty, violence, everything to do with eco-systems, the oceans, the high mountains, desertification, migration, the control of disease and its spread, nuclear policy—make your own list.

The functions of States and Regional Confederations in the global order are to ensure that communes, states or provinces, city governments, and so on, effectively express their local character, administer global laws and understandings in terms of that local character, and make sure that the populations they represent have effective mechanisms for placing their ideas, their point of view, their concerns, before the global policy makers. It is essential, for the Utopia I am conceiving, that the lower levels of government (a) be sanctioned effectively for major and damaging breaches of world policy, and (b), equally significantly, have rights and obligations which enable them to vary appropriate details of global policy to conform with local cultures and conditions.

Let us approach the structure of the Global Government on the basis of what we know of the present.[114]

*If you were to draw up an organisation chart for a State government, would you do the following? Would you divide up the operational tasks into the equivalent of government departments, to deal, for example, with agriculture and fisheries, with health, with labour, with trade, with culture, and so on? I imagine you would. You would also ensure that each department had an effective Director in charge, and an efficient staff to analyse and implement.

Would you then say that each department should have its own elected legislature, independent of whatever there was of central government, and without any obligation to create its rules and regulations to harmonise with other legislatures or departments? That the Ministers in charge should each be a kind of Prime Minister appointed by and responsible to a ***different*** legislature from any of the others?

This in effect, is how world government is organised at present—a range of subject and policy areas, each with its own independent parliament. You might well say that Nation States are perpetuating a divide and rule system in order to prevent Global Government from being effective, or being in fact a Government. It is against their short-sighted interests. They are not ready for it. They must be at some time. We need them to start moving.

So the first major reforms of Global Government would be to:

1. Turn each one of the "family" of United Nations organisations into a *department* of the Global Government, e.g. for global security, military affairs, education, agriculture and fisheries, migration and refugees, culture and science, health, industrial and labour organisation, human rights, and so forth.
2. Change the rank of Directors-General to Directors, except for the one over-all position.
3. Terminate the General Assemblies or equivalents, except that for the Global Government (once the United Nations) itself.
4. Allow the creation of strictly advisory global consultative Committees of Experts, small in size, a-political, and "representative" *informally* of relevant sub-global differences (depending on subject matter the differences could be, for example, geographical regions, the nature of trade, cultural emphases).
5. Restructure the bureaucracy so that it reflects ability alone, administered by an independent tribunal, without reference to group identity, using global examinations to sort entry-level candidates.
6. Vest the General Assembly of the Global Government with legislative powers *in all substantive domains.*
7. The General Assembly to elect cabinet members for limited terms to oversee the departments mentioned in paragraph 1. They would constitute the executive and policy referral cabinet, chaired by a rotating President. The Swiss model might be considered.[115]
8. Laws to be enforceable on States and individuals, through World and Regional courts, appropriately supported, without treaty or ratification.
9. The Global Government to become the sole repository of military forces anywhere. The Global Government

would be the sole authority permitted to have armed forces. It would have its own military command structure and permanent military units, including rapid deployment forces, to contain and eliminate violent flare-ups, aggression between States or their internal units, genocide and the like. The military command would probably also be a police force to supplement State activity directed against such phenomena as piracy and contraband traffic (drugs, slaves, endangered species, cultural artefacts).
10. The division of the political world into electoral Districts. Each large State would be divided into Districts of, say, 10 million people. States between 5 and 10 million population would constitute one District. States with less than 5 million population would combine to create Districts of up to five million. This is an example only.

Whatever the solution, one person one vote will bring about a major shift in power as between peoples. Instead of, according to substantial myth, the values of Western capitalism pervading political and cultural areas from music to computing, that influence would be to some extent modified by the views of major population blocs. We can envisage North America and Europe being counter-balanced by China, India, Brasil, Hispanic America, South East Asia with Indonesia Nigeria, Arabia and African South of the Sahara. Some in the now dominant parts of the world may find this frightening. I would welcome it, provided the elections were free of national governmental control. I trust the common human, but not their rulers.
11. Election to the General Assembly would be on the basis of, say, two Delegates per District.
12. Enumeration for the above purpose would be by *residence* rather than by restrictive definitions such as citizenship.
13. States would be entitled to have *one* Ambassador each to the Global Government.

14. The General Assembly (or global parliament) would elect the Ministerial Cabinet.
15. The Ministerial Cabinet would appoint a Civil Service Commission which would then make *all* appointments to the bureaucracy in accordance with the budget.
16. The General Assembly would approve and amend budgets, preferably with a five year forecast.
17. Income would be based on an assessment to each State, linked to that State's GDP. States would be responsible for the transfer of that assessment to the Global Government within a fixed time period, delays in payment being subject to a penalty, the whole being subject to an "ability to pay" rule set by the Ministry of Finance with General Assembly approval.
18. The operations of the armed forces would be controlled by a Minister, subject to Cabinet directives which would be ratified by the General Assembly.
19. There are to be no vetoes, statutory or otherwise
20. There will be instances, as there are now, where individual States will be incapable of administering their own society. There need to be reasonably clear criteria which could be used to define such a condition, avoiding the danger of cross-cultural misunderstanding. This having been done, Global Government needs to re-institute the category of Global Trusteeship. The General Assembly would then ratify recommendations from the Cabinet to create or terminate a given condition of Trusteeship.[116]

The listing of such principles and reforms is indicative of the major challenges facing reformers of Global Government. Vested interests already built into the system have prevented or stalled the application of timid, try-to-please-everyone changes that blue ribbon and other committees have recommended over the years, including in 2005. It might well be that only a global cataclysm or its imminent threat will force those governments that have the power to change to face reality and act accordingly and in concert.

This is not our Utopian wish. Or, better, a general movement at the grass roots to say "enough is enough" and to mobilise a public opinion fed up with global chaos, sufficiently powerful to wake up State governments to the reality that to continue to obfuscate and defend their powers is to undermine, perhaps destroy, the well-being of the world, including themselves.

Such a re-organisation rests on the premises that inequities in size between voting units (now, States) should be reduced, and that States should be the in the middle, representing their people in their internal affairs and administering policies on behalf of Global Government. In other words, States should be as to Global Government as provinces, *lander,* Swiss cantons and states are to States. And it may well be that between States and Global Government are regional tiers of voluntary agreement. That is the schematic pattern:

The fate of human survival, let alone Utopia, depends on the success with which such reforms can be accomplished, and the effectiveness with which the reformed instrument tackles the issues.

Global Government consists of an organisation to create and carryout policies. Utopia will be reached if the policies are in conformity with more general civilized Utopian values. Writing about a re-organisation will not secure this. We have to set out what we Utopians believe in, and, as in every other domain of life, exert whatever tiny influence we may have to inch forward the generations who follow; to make it a little easier for them to move the next inch.

The previous chapters gave examples of Utopian principles which are capable of being put into practice within the century, and I have elaborated on the requirements of arms control. These are part of the Utopian context and thinking within which the ambitious project of creating a Global Government is situated. It will not do simply to concentrate on creating a world government, since we need to mobilize public action to tackle the surrounding and implied issues as well. A Global Government composed of aggressive individuals would be a disaster. Youth

Maturity Institutes in the majority of populations and cultures is an essential prerequisite for success.

Furthermore, any global government must balance the global "civilized" values it expresses with the justified requirement that peoples—not States—have their own systemic values they wish to preserve. Not only that, but there may be clashes between the local values and the global. Any attempt to impose, internationally, a particular moral code must do so, not simply by expressing a law in an international convention or legislation of the General Assembly, but by intimate and close analysis of the effects of such changes in particular cultures. What does the abolition of *de facto* slavery do? What are the implications of female circumcision or death by stoning for attitudes towards women (who then may be regarded as potential whores), the structure of the family, and the moral system? Thus the law makers must have more than the law itself in mind, but consequent actions to help restore the functioning of society in new forms. This is not an undertaking to be treated lightly, and may require socio-cultural advisory commissions to pronounce on the implications of each piece of legislation before it becomes law.[117]

Reference to the issues of human rights illustrates the complexities with which Global Government will have to deal.

The definition of civil liberties, of freedom itself, which seems so natural to those who live them, is not self-evident to others. It must always be argued for, defined, with passion and clarity and always against the erroneous perspective that civil rights conflict with security. When a Global Government is achieved, it will, I think, reach fruition because of a greater consensus about civilised values and freedoms and responsibilities. If this is not so, Global Government will have an uphill task to establish itself.

While it is relatively easy to define genocide as the physical destruction of members of a defined group,[118] most of the time attacks against groups fall short of this. Attacks against indigenous peoples, minorities, and so forth are designed to strip them of property, prevent them from achieving a secure life-style, force them by social, political, and material pressure to conform to the culture of those in power (not always the majority).

Difficulties in definition arise for various reasons. Ethnocide is held to be the forceful destruction of an ethnos, or traditional culture, whereas attacks against other groups, such as religious cults or followers of alternative lifestyles, are handled separately in a different way. They must be, or else brought together analytically, for they are all cultural variants. Again, some instruments of social pressure are regarded by some as not reprehensible, even good. Religious proselytisation is a major issue of contention in some parts of the world, although its proponents are driven to it by their faiths. Education is a major changer of culture, bearing down on children whose only "defence" is that of their parents, who may be excoriated for resisting a "proper" influence. The Japanese argue that they want a homogeneous society, not one with ethnic variation (although they have religious and other significant disparities). Are such attitudes ethnocidal?

We cannot realistically interpret ethnocide as meaning no change whatsoever in cultural groups. Everything, from TV to the Internet, from pop music to universities, promotes change, and does so unequally. It is therefore necessary to be explicit for a Global Government to be able to face the problem.

Face it, it must. The extreme cases are patently obvious. Rwanda, Burundi, former Armenians, Kurdistan, the Balkans, Brazil, Paraguay, Myanmar, Kashmir. There are troublesome middle cases: Mexico, First Nations of North America, Nigeria, Indian "tribals" and untouchables, and many others.

At least the extreme cases require intervention. At present interference is weak, devoted to human aid, but not facing the certainty that resolution cannot or will not always be achieved by State governments in power. The new government of Rwanda is trying, without means, to achieve a just society. If so, it deserves very much more support than the world is giving it. If that support is given, and it were to turn its back on such a goal, the world is justified in dismissing such a government.

I use the term advisedly. State governments do **NOT** have a God-given right to be in power. Power has to rest in the people. God does not ensure this either. The people have to achieve their powers, governments to earn them. In Utopia both factors will prevail. But they will not arrive automatically.

And in some parts of the world there is no sign of movement in that direction. Again, I do not advocate intervention in marginal cases. But I do most certainly advocate intervention, and strongly, in those instances where governments have over the years shown themselves to be so incompetent as to destroy a reasonable viability of the country, a functional society, or a minimum material base of life. A part of Africa falls into this category. So do Myanmar and Haiti.

Kampuchea may possibly have been rescued from a similar fate by the most unusual kind of intervention, of the kind I am advocating as a first stage of Trusteeship, as was East Timor. That intervention came about through political negotiation and the failure of the Khmers Rouges to maintain their brutal power. That was an opportunity which the United Nations, to its enormous credit, seized. And in other situations, for example, in some parts of Africa, it may not be possible, or the problem may not be political rivalry as much as incompetence.

If a Global Trusteeship system had been in place it might even have helped Iraq and Afghanistan.

We have to stop using the art of being patronising to avoid human responsibility. The State governments in question are composed of adult, usually educated, mostly men. They have had the chance to prove their adequacy. It is not ethical, not human, not responsible, to abandon men, women and children, the very future of large parts of the world, to their fate. Destitution, corruption, greed, brutality, ill-health, misery, food crisis after food crisis, are not to be excused because the government belongs to a different culture, because of the sanctity of the State, because it (supposedly) does not affect us, because the people must solve their problems themselves. These, however justified they may have been at the time of retreat from colonialism, are pitifully wrong now.

A valid Global Government must be prepared to revive and re-define the idea of Trusteeship. It must be prepared to dismiss a State government and to intervene, not only with humanitarian aid (which in the long term can be dependency-destructive), but also with all the tools it can develop to initiate and stimulate the achievement of the *population's* objectives. The process may involve Global Government military intervention, coupled with the best of civil and aid administration.[119]

The subjects that I have used to exemplify policy concerns for Global Government imply decision-making, adjudication, and the power to impose sanctions. Adjudication implies a structure of international courts. These are useless without the power to enforce court decisions against States if necessary. Ultimately, that implies power.

Global Government will require military force to bring about Utopia. There is little doubt that in the first stages it would have to use every kind of pressure, with the threat of force, to induce recalcitrant States (and other organisations, for those there will be) to disarm. Threats are useless unless they are known to be real, as United Nations history has shown.

That implies a military command and military personnel. In Utopia, this would be the only one. En route to Utopia, States would be required to disarm on agreed timetables, perhaps transitionally transferring their personnel to Global Government command.

Global Government will not be cheap. How can we afford it? It is not enough to say, we cannot **not** afford it? We are at liberty to choose ultimate cataclysm for our descendants, to refuse to pay the price for achieving not only what we want but what is necessary for survival. I have proposed a complete restructuring of State fiscal systems, which will simplify national and international public finances.

The challenges are huge, and only partly expressed here. But each one, considered in relation to the others, links to a coordinated march forward, offers hope to populations which may otherwise be cynical about or helpless in the face of the short-term, self-serving, futureless State political systems that so often seem to stand in the way of progress.

We desperately need Global Government. Let's get on with it. How?

XVIII

Epilogue: How to Get There

It is all very well setting out a personal view of where to go in the 21st Century. After all, I won't be there to see it. But brave words are not enough. If I believe we can reach a Utopian goal, it is up to me to suggest how to reach it.

I cannot imagine that your view of Utopia will be the same as mine in all respects. Perhaps you reject the totality of what I have said. You may by your arguments change my view of many things, although I am rather stubborn.

On one matter, however, you are almost certain to be in agreement. We are racing ever and ever faster into the future. Although there are many who attempt to predict the future, and others who discuss ethical and policy issues based upon such predictions, there is considerably less discussion of where we *want* to arrive.

Perhaps you also agree with me that, especially since change is happening so fast, we should be trying to mobilise public opinion to discuss our goals, and to devise ways of influencing our directions. We are not going to agree about everything. So that underlying the effort must be the principle of assessing the compatibility of our differences within one world, non-confrontationally. If they are incompatible for individuals living in one location, they may not be for individuals living elsewhere, and hence can still be functional. But there still may be incompatibilities in the long run that are cause for distrust, violence, vilification. These cannot continue in that form in a Utopian global society. We will have to devise means for recognising the limits, and resolving the issues so that we can live together in respect and peace, if not in total harmony. Utopia is not to discourage difference, which is essential to civilised movement and adjustment; but it is there to remove violence and to turn distrust and vilification into respect.

If you are agreed on this one principle, that it is desirable for all of us in the world to take control of our destiny, that is enough to begin.

There are of course the nay-sayers, those individuals who regard Utopia as an impracticable dream. Their objections are in my opinion simply a refusal to take responsibility, or an inhibited fear of doing something positive. It is easier to let matters and life go by, taking pain or dysfunction as inevitable.

We can identify several of the excuses. "But human nature will never change" is the canard that was thrust against my ideological idealism when I was young, and it's still there. Humans will always be selfish, egotistical, prone to violence. What rubbish! What an excuse for laziness and inaction! There are quite enough people right now who are unselfish, caring and peaceable to constitute a major potential force in world society.

"Human nature", the concept, is an agglomeration of individuals. Individuals, locally and globally, are enormously differentiated. It takes only a few shifts in the *nature of individuals* to change the statistical profile of "human" nature. That is happening all the time. Human nature is highly malleable and highly dynamic. We have control over it. It is up to us to put it right, and not use weasel words to escape responsibility.

Or, "we can't make a change—it's the system". This one has more force. Yes, we as individuals are caught up in systems. Whistle blowers are sacked. Managements, private and public, treat non-conformists with suspicion. The "system" is that great big amorphous nonentity of an organisation in which we poor cogs drive the wheels. Again, this is sheer laziness and defeatism. It is the excuse with which employees at the bottom of the rung give you when your complaints or objections hit the stone walls of organisation stasis. "It's not our policy". OK, get that policy changed.

Or, "we don't have power". Tell that to the people of Georgia and the Ukraine, Iraq Palestine and Afghanistan. For the world's sake, *take the power*. Just taking power won't solve the problems, but it will remove the excuses. And it is much more than simply accepting some version of democracy, which can have dull, corrupt, conservative and banal results. It is a matter of all of us exercising and manifesting will, despite what officialdom, bureaucracy, managers and politicians have to say, and not just at election time.

Just the same, why bother? Humanity has muddled through enormous cataclysms in its brief history, embarking on self-destructive activities like no other species. There are numerous other self-induced threats to our existence, from environmental disaster to national aggrandisement and terrorism, from reproductive disaster to the failure to contain pandemics, from the exhaustion of energy sources to religious myopia. Each of these needs the kinds of resolution that are contained in this analysis. And many of the champions of reform use the theme "If we don't do this, then humanity will disappear"

That's no good. Fear begets more fear, creates disruptive anxiety and strife. This is dysfunctional and it inhibits clear thinking and global rational action. To succeed we need to be positive, set positive goals, abjure the negative. And indeed ask again, why bother? Why waste time abetting the continuity and well-being of humanity? To answer such a question we need to have some kind of an answer to the question, what is the purpose of life, of living?

If your answer is that it is to secure a better place in the Hereafter, then forget Utopia. Utopia doesn't matter, and is not worth the effort, since, although "being good" will no doubt count, all rewards lie fundamentally outside the realm of the defective present.[120]

Insofar as human living has a purpose, in my view it is to improve human living and humanity itself. It is in a way a vortex, each state of life creating a new set of hopes and desires. That is why each of us is here. There is nothing static about it; it is ever moving. It is a secular, a natural, purpose, not a transcendental or religious one. It is down to earth, not airy-fairy. It is of the here and now and also of future millennia. The theme may be expressed in the upbringing of children, in love, in creativity, in the wholesome and infectious joy of life itself, in improving wealth, in everything else we do and experience.

As I mentioned as long ago as the Prologue, the classic argument between the primacy of duty and the primacy of consequences is resolved if we assert that our duty is to humankind, rather than to any individual or part of it, except insofar as the latter contributes to the well being of humankind (as it does for example in a warm and open relationship between a man and a woman). And the consideration of consequences is subject to a time dimension: immediately beneficial consequences may be deadly in terms of the Utopian 21st century achievement.[121]

That is why we need to achieve Utopia—to give expression to the very purpose of being alive. That is why each one of us must find a way, however modestly, to do his or her little bit. And while we may set our goals in terms of what we can achieve in the 21st century, that will not be the end of it. We will simply have learned how to control our destiny, and after the end of the 21st century there will be more challenges, yet other objective for life. What fun! I wish I could be floating around in the atmosphere somewhere with the capacity to see it and understand it all, not as some experts on heaven suggest, to be separate and rejecting interest in it.

Then let us then set about doing it. Every single one of us has responsibility and is in a position to exercise it. At a perfect dinner my friend brought up, as she often does, the huge gap between what we were doing, having dinner, and the pain in, for example, African refugee camps. Should we therefore not have dinner? That by itself does nothing for anyone else, and if adopted universally would mean destroying a valued creative art, to say nothing of restaurant employment. If we were able to turn the cost of the dinner toward a charitable relief, there might be some point. Otherwise it is guilty self-flagellation. And we do not want to **reduce** the quality of life, but to improve and expand it.

No. The aims of world improvement may sometimes be helped by reduction in our own satisfaction. Rich countries will at times have to reduce their riches to meet particular crises, as indeed they do rather miserably now. They devote a proportion of their riches, a tiny proportion, to such needs as charitable responses and peace keeping, and to aid projects that, sometimes, improve the dynamics and viability of poorer countries. This will have to improve.

It will not improve healthily on the basis of guilt. Guilt is an excuse, not a helpful activity. We are not guilty because of what our forebears may or may not have done during the bloody and gruesome history of the world. The past was a step to the present, and hence a step towards Utopia. If we accept guilt because ideologists, frustrated by their lack of progress or power, escape their own responsibility by laying the guilt on us, we will not think or act clearly, and are likely to do as much damage as we wish to repair. Guilt, if there, must be related to a concrete situation for which we have been clearly and consciously responsible, not generalised to everything our civilisation does or has done.

The way we move forward, for those of us who are ordinary citizens, is to exercise our individual creativity and skills toward the common purpose. One of my friends is a teacher. A part of her contribution to the arrival of Utopia is to teach well, and, perhaps within the framework of her discipline, if appropriate, even to discuss Utopia and how we get there. Then as citizen, in social contacts to talk about where we are going. That is enough for many an individual person.

Others will try to amend their personal lives, more consciously asking, is this consistent with a movement toward Utopian goals? Personal relationships, abandonment of jealousies, understanding of others, political action.

Others will go further. They may bring the issues I have raised out into the forum of public discussion, and add other issues to them. At present there are many forums, nearly all around specific, mostly localised, concerns: abortion, euthanasia, logging and fishing practices, peace-keeping, gun control, sexual harassment, substance abuse, child abuse, crime and punishment, the protection of privacy. Nearly all strike me not only as localised in their programmes, as they must be to be effective, but as dealing with the relatively immediate. Nevertheless the immediate relates to long term values—environmental issues to the health of ecosystems; abuse to the health and welfare of citizens; peace-keeping to world order. And by influencing each immediate outcome as it arises, one pushes, however minutely, global society in a direction. It is best if that direction be conscious. Peace keeping as a step toward the global removal of violence, for example. Again, removing jealousy as a step towards both more wholesome lives and reduction in crime and violence, for example.

The point of my argument is to try to bring the *long-term* issues to the fore, to make them more open to discussion and resolution, to move toward the principles that most of us can agree on as representing Utopian values and practices. We must argue about such visions before we can share them.

It should become normal practice for every decision to be conceived, specifically and consciously, in the context of the Utopian goal, as thought of at the time.

To the extent that this is done, the local and immediate concerns become steps on the way to the finer future, a consciously defined future. They are seen as part of a grander movement toward a state of civilised living that is within reach, that can be made real. When your politicians, city councillors and others make a proposal to solve an immediate problem, always challenge them. How does your solution contribute to our Utopian goals?

So that is what I ask of you, the reader. I ask that where you disagree with the vision of Utopia I have set out, you work out in your own mind, or with others, the implications of your disagreement. Don't just say I disagree for this or that reason. In addition, trace through the ramifications of the disagreement for the Utopia you desire for your descendants. Treat what I have written as a draft. Re-write it from your own point of view.[122]

Let the Utopian draft be re-drafted many times. If I am up to it, I may do exactly that in a few years time. For in those years many things will have changed, many elements of knowledge will have become clearer, perhaps my views will have been debated in ways that I for one can learn from. Let others do it also, from their perspectives.

Which raises an issue. I know how very easy it is for a book setting out prescriptive or normative ideas to become the nucleus of a secular cult with emotive overtones and group membership. For many years the environmental movement was almost dominated by such a point of view, which may have helped it get started, and proceed towards more politicised and rationally-oriented actions.

What I am advocating, however, is not as focussed, is more diffuse, and is more open-ended in its objectives. It requires study, thought, exchange of opinions. The mode of action is through personal example, and by persuading sources of power, influence and authority, toward the point of view that innovations should be oriented toward the long-term goal of Utopia, that achieving Utopia must be in the forefront of our strategies.

If this book is to be any use in that process, it can perhaps be thought of as a framework for arriving at socio-political goals that affect our descendants. New beams can be added to the framework, since there are enormous subjects I have not discussed fully, or where my point of view is inadequately informed.

And furthermore it is open for any citizen to take elements in the framework, replacing them with better materials and design. Such changes will be responses to new knowledge, to differing ideas as to what the structure represents, and to improved concepts as to how the beams hold together—what their relationship is to each other. But the building must hold together.

It *is* a structure. So that if you redesign part of the building, work through, to the extent it is desirable, resultant modifications elsewhere in it. Let there be, over time, revised and alternative answers to the question, ***What is Utopia?*** Don't let the question remain unanswered, shoved aside, forgotten.

When smaller issues arise, however emotionally charged or intellectually important, say out loud how they fit with your view of the Utopian goal, how they represent, if done correctly, steps along the way, how they must be judged in those terms. Introduce the long view. Don't let it drop out of sight.

In matters of public policy, or politics at whatever level, more dramatic opportunities exist. The nature of Utopia has to be brought to the forefront. The programmes of political parties for the next five years, if elected, must be related to the ultimate goals. To what extent do those five year plans, or whatever, those massive volumes of legislation, help us to arrive at Utopia—or indeed, do they stand in the way? There are indeed usually long term philosophies at work, but they are often inferred or piecemeal. Individual initiative may be lauded to the skies; but for itself, not because it fits into the grand scheme of a world in which it links up with other significant principles. "We must work toward full employment; and at the same time we must reduce the work force." Such statements are not merely illogical, but indicate nothing about what we *want* life to be like. This, surely, must be the criterion against which policy should be judged—where does it lead us? Toward a Utopian quality of life?

It is time to bring the point to the forefront, to return vision to political agendas. At no time in world history has a global Utopia been within reach to the extent that it is coming to be in reach now. It is not around the next corner. The trail is much longer and more difficult in many countries than it is in others. But, because of the present state of the world, the steps that have to be taken can now be set out with reasonable realism, as being within our power to accomplish.

Governments, as they are structured now, will not do it of themselves. Many changes do not require governmental action.

Many do. This is a potential road block, because governments are typically behind, not in front of, the people's will. Thus it requires intense public mobilisation, with populist pressure, to influence and persuade governments that this or that Utopian goal is within their reach, and will provide them with political dividends. To establish Youth Maturity Institutes for example or to change the interplay between the administration of the law and health services. And I have already referred to the need for international non-governmental organisations to mobilise public opinion to make global government modern and equitable.

In fact international NGOs constitute the strongest institutional apparatus available to advance thinking and action along Utopian lines. They exist to link activists and professionals in every field you can think of, from education to hydrology, from charity to global IT improvement, from economics to UN affairs. To some extent they are rivalrous, establishing competitive boundaries and tapping similar sources of funds both governmental and private. They are naturally and properly focused on their own individual mandates.

This is where I place great hope on students in places of higher education. Every one of them is aiming for a full adult life. Every one of them is in an educational system which requires them to choose a major subject or two of interest. Every one of those subjects has an organisation, an association, which has as its aim the furthering of the professional interests and bases of knowledge of its adherents. And every one of those is linked in a form of international federation which is indeed a Non-Governmental Organisation.

So here is my challenge to the student reader. Join with your fellow and discuss with your mentors the nature of those organisations. Some of your mentors may not even be aware that the national organisation is a part of an international one. Get the relationship out in the open. Then exert pressure, with students from other campuses. To have those bodies seriously address of the Utopian world that are relevant to their interests. Let the international NGOs understand that their members want a better world, and that the NGO is in a position to forward it. This will almost be on the basis of a fusion of religion and science, in the sense in which I have earlier used the terms—science, because rooted in questioning knowledge; faith, because of the belief that Utopia is possible in the 21st century.

Just one example. Anthropologists have their own national associations in many countries. Most of these elect delegations to the International Union of Anthropological and Ethnological Sciences. That body in turn (almost uniquely) is a member of three over-riding major power centres—the International Scientific Union, the International Social Science Council, and the International Council for Philosophy and the Humanities.

Similar links are in every field—education, law, psychology, chemistry, social work, demography, planning, political science, physics, astronomy, economics, branches of medicine and all the others.

But if there has been a sub-text in this book, it is to assert that the issues are interdependent, that we are faced with systemic, not atomised, challenges. "Interdisciplinarity" has been a watchword, often used in vain, within some of the NGOs. In academic life it is difficult to achieve.

Nevertheless, we must try harder.

As a first step I would hope that some of the main NGOs would take the step of creating a World Council of NGOs.[123] The prime first task of such an organisation would be specific. It would be to define and advocate goals to be achieved within the 21st century, whether or not they are thought of as Utopian. It would be to prepare position papers on relevant topics, perhaps along the lines of the topics of this book. It would mobilise debate in each country where the NGOs have national affiliates. Imagine the effect of debates going on in your country within the affiliates of scores of NGOs . . .

This proposal is also in the direct interest of the NGOs themselves. Most are affiliated one way or another with the

United Nations or its agencies, and are critically aware of the defects of the world system in their fields of work. To strive for fundamental long term reforms in a coordinated way can only be of benefit to them.

Then comes the next powerful step. Once the parameters of a global policy on the topic are designed, no doubt with many a regional variation, the power of the united NGOs would be unleashed. This of course would be especially important in designing and implementing Global Government by peoples instead of by States.

The message would in essence by quite simple. "Enough is enough—we the people are tired of myopic views, of petty tinkering with life's challenges. We demand change, and this is what we want". In country after country, until we have what we want.

It may well be that yet a further step will be necessary. States will not give up their control of the United Nations very easily. Indeed it may be necessary to set up the true Global Government outside that organisation rather than reforming it. In whatever way, the International Council for NGOs may have to take the initiative in actually setting it up, designing its charter, funding, and inaugural activities.[124]

This is the time, but let us not expect hasty miracles. I have pointed out that the effects of Youth Maturity Institutes will not be felt fully for maybe fifty years after their introduction. The adoption of other systemic reforms require debate, much more analytic and practical thought, and deliberate implementation, often hesitant, and subject to the criticism of those for whom immediate results take precedence over long term solutions.

But we must begin or it will never happen, and that is too disastrous to contemplate. This is the time to begin. This is our opportunity. Let us start deliberately, no longer feeling like small insignificant cogs rotating helplessly, rather knowing that we have the power—and responsibility—each one of us, to make decisions. And, when we have the courage to do so, to live our beliefs.

We have the means. It is time to have the will.

Acknowledgements

Thanks to SOC Stockholm for their initiative in establishing the World Utopian Championship competition, which I was fortunate enough to win for the competition 2003/5. Accolades to Jon Brunberg and Annika Drougge for their heroic efforts of organisation. Appreciation for the work of the jury, who assessed hundreds of sometimes difficult to read pages and for their youthful enthusiasm. Humble gratitude to Professor Tom Moylan for his over-generous report on the two draft chapters I submitted to the competition.

A number of friends disturbed their schedules to criticize various chapters. I have taken your comments seriously, although you will recognize my obtuseness here and there, which makes me alone responsible for my errors of fact and logic.

It is planned to consider a second edition for the year 2009. Your comments are welcome and will be taken into consideration. You may mail them to Comments, 2901—969 Richards St Vancouver B.C. Canada V6B 1A8 or email them to *cbelshaw@novuscom.net*.

Endnotes

1 And sometimes creating reactionary backlashes.
2 Amartya Sen, *Th Argumentative Indian*, London, Allen Lane, 2005; and the *Bhagavad Gita*.
3 See my *The Sorcerer's Apprentice: an anthropology of public policy*, Oxford, Pergamon Press, 1976
4 See my *Traditional Exchange and Modern Markets*, Englewood Cliffs, Prentice-Hall, 1965
5
6 Pope, Rob. *Creativity—Theory, History, Pracrice*. Abingdon, Routledge, 2005. The book contains an extensive bibliography.
7 There is one attempt, quoted from Henry Petrovski, *Invetion by DesignI* on page 267 which hints towards a generalisation.
8 One study suggests that in advanced countries except the United States there is a strong move towards secularization, and that a high degree of religiosity correlates with social dysfunction. But does religiosity equate with spirituality??? See http://moses.creighton.edu/JRS/pdf/2005-11.pdf 2005 and Gregory Paul, "Cross-National Correlations of Quantifiable Societal Health with Popular Religiosity and Secularism in the Prosperous Democracies", *Journal of Religion and Society*, vol 7 2005, pp. 1-17
9 Interestingly, Robert Rosen, a contributor to the List-Serv *Ideologies of War* suggests that the acceptance of ideologies is an aspect of intellectual laziness.

10 A draft of this chapter is one of two which formed the basis of my submission to SOC Stockholm which earned the title "World Utopian Champion" in 2005.
11 Despite sentences of this kind it is not my intention to imply certainty about future trends.
12 In the late 'forties I had the experience of conducting research amongst units of the British armed forces. The then government was determined to change the culture of the by now professional officer corps. Young officers were indoctrinated with the new ideas, but as they were posted one by one to their regiments or squadrons they rapidly succumbed to the values and culture of the officers' mess.
13 Other institutions such as churches, sports associations and so on normally deal with segments of society, whereas schools, one way or another, penetrate all corners.
14 See Chapters XII and XIII. Utopia will have less mandatory employment, more non-employed activity.
15 How many school career counsellors even imagine the possibility of anthropology as a career, even if they know what the word means?
16 Did—do—schools in Rwanda teach knowledge of and respect for the two competing social groups? How much do northern Sudanese schools teach positively about their southern or their Darfur co-citizens? They don't and they are neither mandated nor equipped to do so. How many Christian schools fail to each Islam or Judaism positively, and vice versa?
17 Note the following by E.M.Forster: "Tolerance is a very dull virtue. It is boring. Unlike love, it has always had a bad press. It is negative. It merely means putting up with people, being able to stand things." Quoted in the *Globe and Mail* July 5th 2005.
18 Cf. Lloyd, Charlotte A., *The Case of the Female Orgasm: Bias in the Science of Evolution*, Cambridge, Harvard University Press, 2005 and also Margolis, Jonathan, *O: The Intimate History the Orgasm* London, Arrow Books, 2005
19 I am indebted to E. S. Turner's review of Francis Wheen, *How Mumbo-jumbo Conquered the World, a short history of modern delusions* Fourth Estate, 2004 in the *Times Literary Supplement* Feb 14th 2004 p. 36 for the choice of epithets.

20 See my *Towers Besieged: The Dilemma of the Creative University*, Toronto, McClelland and Stewsart, 1974 for a fuller discussion.
21 "PLOS" stands for "Public Library of Sceince"
22 I will be showing in Chapter **XII** that this is likely to continue, and that, *properly handled*, our Utopia should want it, not reject it.
23 In late 2005 the press reported that the United Kingdom government is planning to remove schools from Local Council jurisdictions, giving them greater control over their curricula, philosophies and operations. It has been interpreted as moving the principles of the public = private schools into the state sector and giving more weight to independent religious schools. This is a step in the direction toward Youth Maturity Institutes but I have notg seen reference to any required element of material such as risk taking, elimination of violence, or the integration of therapy professionals into trhe system. We do not expect the full implementation of Youth Maturity Institutes to be achieved over night.
24 And it would have an effect on the role of and support for such groups
25 This relates to the Utopian reform of the "justice" system in Chapter **VI**
26 For the attitude of legal authorities to "precautionary risk" see Sunstein, Cass R. *Wars of Fear*, Cambridge and New York, Camnbrfidge Univrersity Press, 2005
27 The latest, and bound to be classical, work on global kinship relationships is the brilliant treatise of Maurice Godelier, *Métamorphoses de la parenté*, Paris, Fayard, 2004 which I believe has unfortunately not yet appeared in English.
28 In journalism and popular talk the work "polygamy" is bandied about. Technically it means a man taking multiple wives, *and* a woman taking multiple husbands—I do not know of such a state, though it would balance the sexes. For a man taking multiple wives the term is *polygyny*. For a woman taking multiple husbands, the term is *polyandry*. Julian Wake informs me of a Sherpani who had five husbands (brothers).
29 This does NOT equate with 75% of the human population.
30 Daphne Branham in the *Vancouver Sun* 2004, 2005.

31 For those interested in the variations in family structure, and their implications for the modern world, I recommend the classic treatise of Maurice Godelier, *Métamorphoses de la parenté*, Paris, Fayard, 2004.
32 Maurice Godelier *Métamorphoses de la parenté*. Paris, Fayard, 2004, p.564.
33 Under existing mores there is also a predatory behaviour dubbed "mate poaching" in which the intiator deliberately tries to move the affections of another person from his or her mate. This is almost deliberately hurtful and bears little resemblance to consensual multiple partnerships. See D. P. Schmidt, "Patterns and universals of mate poaching across 53 nations: The effects of sex, culture, and personality on romantically attracting another person's partner," *Journal of Personality and Social Psychology*, vol 86 no 4 (April 2004), pp.560-584.
34 I am well aware that these assertions will be emotionally abhorrent to many. That fact does not remove the necessity to face up to their illogicality, and the ways in which the issue puts poison into other aspects of Utopian life. If in the long run I am wrong, then other aspects of Utopia will require amendment.
35 This has by no means always been the case. Muslim laws no doubt still have views on cohabitation without marriage. Such laws are still on the books of some U. S. States—in 2005 a woman is being prosecuted under an 1808 statue for cohabiting without marriage. And the European habit of requiring identification from both clients seeking a matrimonial room, and refusing such rooms to the unmarried, gave way only in the late 20th century. The illegality of homosexual interactions and sex is only just disappearing and is not yet global.
36 Dustin Wax on the Anthro-L List Serv, September 13[th,] 2005.
37 However, it is to be hoped that Youth Maturity Institutes will in time reduce the frequency of boredom in the elderly.
38
39 Full graduation from a Youth Maturity Institute could be one element in such tests and ceremonies.

40 The physical abuses of Abu Ghaira and Guantanemo Bay are *not* an aberration. They are part of the hidden culture of United States hard-core prisons.
41 Michael Tonry *Thinking about Crime: Sense and Sensibility in American Penal Culture*, New York, Oxford University Press, 2004.
42 Unfortunately, this is *not* typical of the way authorities handle such trauma.
43 "The no-computer virus", *The Economist*, April 30th 2005, pp 65-7.
44 Unfortunately both have closed for lack of funding. But another has opened.
45 We must be wary of this generalisation. Emergent studies of autism demonstrate that non-sociable individuals frequently have enormously creative intellectual capacities, and most modern creative philosophers have had social differences from the norm, and psychological pains.
46 The destruction of the legal state of British Commonwealth citizen leads to the ambition that in its place there be such a status as Global Citizen.
47 Urban residents the world over are increasingly embracing the foods of other cultures. Pop music, British, Canadian, Scandinavian as well as from the U.S., has an almost universal spread.
48 His paper is on line at the site of the Championship at *http://www.soc.nu/utopian*
49 See Slaughter, Anne-Marie, *A New World Order*, Princeton and Oxford, Princeton University Press, 2004, for a systematic analysis of the activities of international associations, which she believes to be replacing many of the functions of the State. Of which more later.
50 See, for example, André Weckmann *La Roue du Paon*. Strasbourg, bf éditions, 1988, originally published as *Odil eoder das Magiische Dreieck*. Kehl, Morstadt, 1986.
51 Frequently welcomed by feudally-oppressed peasantry.
52 The very title of the fortunately now popular book *Eats, Shoots and Leaves* demonstrates the issue with clarity (Lynne Truss, U.K. Profile Books, U.S. Gotham-Penguin, 2003)

53   Here I have to note my own bias. My awareness of these issues came about as a result of a Canadian Broadcasting Corporation docudrama which centred on a trial in which I was defendant. Not only were facts erroneous, but, more to this point, the fictionalisation of the characters created distortions.
54   There are now numerous language variants in the spell checkers, such a Canadian English, but I doubt if they are used very much, and also doubt their accuracy. For a long time Microsoft's UK English insisted on apostrophes before the 's' of plurals!
55   Paradoxically, many poorer countries experience a cacophony of competing newspaper voices, provided political control holds off.
56   The phrase "natural world" is redundant, for the total world is natural. However the phrase indicates a way of thinking about that world.
57   Clive Bell, *Civilization* Harmondsworth, Penguin, 1928.
58   Martin Cruz Smith, *Wolves Eat Dogs*, New York etc., Simon and Schuster, 2004.
59   The threat of phenomena such as tsunami constitutes another reason for carefully examining the protection and perhaps movement of coastal communities and islands.
60   *Food Crops in a Changing Climate:* Report of a Royal Society Discussion meeting held in April 2005. Policy Statement 10/05 June 2005. *www.royalsoc.ac.uk*
61   For Kenyan pastoralism, see the work of A.B.C. Ochollo-Ayayo.
62   *Nature*, October 27th 2005. Also see *http://www.eurekalert.org/pub_releases/2005-10/nhgr-icc102405.php*
63   This statement anticipates the Utopian argument about guaranteed basic income in chapters XII and XIII.
64   *The Economist* has frequently made similar points even more vigorously. See for example the issue of January 12th 2005 p.28. The number of on line Open Access scientific journals is expanding day by day. (I edit one of them called AnthroGlobe which is multilingual and multi media, impossible in print.) And the Google search engine attempts to separate the gold from the dross by operating special searches which go to the original scientific documents.

65 Some participants did not receive the news and turned up. A strong contingent of Israelis defied the ban, arrived by bus, and held their own scientific sessions.
66 In the years since I first drafted this paragraph there have been revolutionary changes in the techniques of enquiry and the resultant knowledge of the brain.
67 See Gérard Punier's bitter account in his, *Darfur, The Ambiguous Genocide*, Ithaca, Cornell University Press, 2005.
68 See Bernard Lewis, *The Assassins, a radical sect in Islam*, London, Weidenfeld and Nicholson, 1967.
69 See Nevin Halici, *Sufi Cuisine*. London, Saqi, 2005.
70 Political or religious murder has been with us from early days. It was used in the Graeco-Roman world. But its use coupled with propaganda and threats, true deliberate terrorism, seems to have begun with the Assassins, a break away Shi'a-Ismaili sect, and there are passages in the Q'ran which terrorists can use to justify the removal of an unjust ruler by such means. There is a direct ideological link between today's Middle Eastern terrorists and the movements of centuries ago, although no one these days would like Ismaili with the branches of Shi'a which rely on such thoughts. Nineteenth-twentieth century Anarchists often held such views. See the excellent summary in Chapter 6 of Lewis, Bernard, *The Assassins* London, Wiedenfeld and Nicholson, 1967. However a major difference between Assassins and Anarchists on the one hand and modern Islamist terrorists, on the other is that the latter target civilians, for which there is clearly no justification in the Q'ran.
71 For the shameful tragedy in Darfur, which once again demonstrates the self-seeking stance of nation states which I will examine in a later chapter, see Prunier, Gérard, *Darfur: The Ambigous Genocide* Ithaca, Cornell University Press, 2005.
72 For those readers interested in the dynamics and genesis of ideological violence, I recommend the papers contributed to the internet journal *Ideologies of War and Terror* which go well beyond current events at http://www.ideologiesofwarandterror.com
73 A vivid account of the claustrophobic world of Palestine and its relationship to the *intifada* and terrorism is given in Anne-

Marie Olivfier and OPaul Feinberg, *The Road to Martyrs' Square: a journey into the world of the suicide bomber*, Oxford, Oxford University Press, 2005.

[74] In my *The Sorcerer's Apprentice: an anthropology of public policy*, New York etc. Pergamon.

[75] Anne-Marie Olivfier and OPaul Feinberg op.cit.

[76] The young, leaving high school, are increasingly aware of this opportunity, taking time off to backpack around the world before going on to higher education or employment.

[77] Flat tax introduced in Estonia (26% personal and corporate, no deductions) Latvia, Lithuania, Russia (13% personal), Slovakia (19% personal and corporate), Poland leaning in the direction.

[78] I have an account of the webs of reciprocity related to marriage and other events in my *Under the Ivi Tree: Social and Economic Growth in Rural Fiji*. London Routledge and Kegan Paul, 1964 Reprinted in 2004 in Routledge Library Editions.

[79] I give some European examples and examine the technical issues involved in my *The Conditions of Social Performance: an exploratory theory*. London, Routledge and Kegan Paul, 1969. Reprinted in the International Library of Sociology: Theory and Methods, Routledge, 1996.

[80] The 2005 Report on the State of World Population of the United Nations Population Fund at *http://www.unfpa.org/swp/2005/pdf/en_swp05.pdf* singles out gender inequality and reproductive health as the two major factors hindering the ability of populations to take advantage of measures of societal progress.

[81] And we must beware a tendency for crisis-managing NGOs to perpetuate themselves and become businesses in their own right.

[82] *A Critical Analysis of Community Development as an Economic, Social and Administrative Process*. Mimeograph paper for an ad hoc group of experts, Bureau of Social Affairs, United Nations, 1962.

[83] *Under the Ivi Tree: Society and Economic Growth in Rural Fiji*, London, Routledge and Kegan Paul, 1964. Reissued 2004.

[84] When the Community Development movement in India moved from spontaneity to becoming a department of government.

85 This is not unknown in the richer world. I was once called in to report on dysfunctional rivalries in the British Columbia cooperative movement. The C.D. officers were given targets of results to meet, which subverted the underlying principle that the goals of the programmes should precisely reflect the goals of the people.
86 See Jim Igoe and Tim Kensall, *Between a Rock and a Hard Place: African NGOs, Donors and the State*. Durham, University of Carolina Press, 2005, for good case studies and analysis.
87 See my 'Evaluation of Technical Assistance as a Contribution to Development', *International Development Review*, June 1966 vol VIII, no 3.
88 There are unfortunately some NGOs whose purpose is distorted by ideological or proselytizing goals.
89 Jeffrey Sachs, *The End of Poverty: How we can make it happen in our time*. London, Penguin, 2005.
90 See the work of A.B.C. Ocholla-Ayoyo.
91 Cf. my "Evaluation of Technical Assistance as a Contribution to Development", *International Development Review* vol viii, no 2, pp 2-6 and 23, 1966.
92 The shocking slum bulldozing in Zimbabwe in 2005 is but one example, which hit the headlines because it is Zimbabwe. It has also happened in Malawi.
93 See Norenna Herttz, *The Debt Threat: How Debt is Destroying the Developing World*. New York, Harper Collins 2005.
94 In October 2005 African Ministers of Science and Technology committed to integrate science, technology and innovation into their development plans. This is a very small part of the issue for countries without natural resources.
95 Popular music has led the way in many poorer and poorest countries. A number of great architects have emerged on the international scene from Brasil and the Middle East. India has dramatically entered the IT world.
96 A view of the place of States in the world order, consistent with and perhaps reinforcing this argument, is presented in Robert Cooper, *The Breaking of Nations: Order and Chaos in the 21st Century*. London, Atlantic Books, 2003.

97 I have explored the methodological implications of this perspective in my *The Conditions of Social Performance, op.cit*. The unpublished study compares Canada and the Swiss Romande.
98 At present unpublished.
99 Contemporary Swiss labour law and practice, for example, is a result of the horror of the population at the violence and disruption caused by labour disruption during the Great Depression.
100 Vancouver city announcements are regularly provided in translation for such languages. Despite the high Germanic population, German speakers are expected to be natural in English.
101 A Kenyan told me that, at the time, all Ministers were known to be financially corrupt. This was routinely condoned. But if such a Minister fell out with the President the corruption would be made known and the offender would be charged. The knowledge of individual corruption was the President's instrument of control.
102 There are many who disagree with my thesis. Two such are Alexander Gray and Adam Tomkins, *How We Should Rule Ourselves*, Edinburgh, Canongate, 2005. Writing of Scotland, they do not face up to the problem that democracies, as in the Weimar Republic, can go horribly wrong—and then what?
103 An exception is perhaps Thailand, a country of past coups and coup threats. Even here though, the reverence with which the public holds the royal family enables the King to intervene more directly than would normally be the case.
104 See the Epilogue
105 Anne-Marie Slaughter, *A New World Order*, Princeton and Oxford, Princeton University Press, 2004.
106 The evolving draft may be checked for input at http://www.anthropologising.ca/writing/wemovagla.htm
107 Whether this will change as a result of the 2005 G8 summit remains to be seen.
108 President George W. Bush either does not understand or will not recognize this jural position. He gives the impression that his conception of the United Nations is that of just another country to be used or ignored at his will. The United States does not subject its policies to the oversight of the United Nations,

but feels free to accept or reject that oversight as it suits. It is not the only country to do so, but it is the most obvious one, and its example encourages others to do likewise.

[109] As I prepare this text, *The Independent* carries a story indicating that the new US Ambassador to the United Nations is seeking to roll back proposed UN commitments on aid to developing countries, combating global warming and nuclear disarmament. This strengthens my proposition below that States are incapable of objectively operating a world government.

[110] Small Arms Survey Project reports that 640 million small arms and light weapons are responsible for at least 300,000 deaths annually. Graduate Institute for International Studies, Geneva. Oxford, Oxford University Press, 2004.

[111] The Harry Frank Guggenheim Foundation is supporting research in these matters and is considering the possibility of the establishment of a consortium for the coordination of such research. Papers on the subject and the proposal are contained in the Foundation's *HFG Review,* 2005, "Small Arms and Light Weapons". The material is also available at *http://www.temple.edu'cenfad/small*arms

[112] P. W Singer, *Children at War.* New York, Pantheon, 2005 and Lynn Jones, *Then they started shooting: Growing up in Wartime Bosnia.* Cambridge, Harvard University Press, 2005.

[113] I put independence in inverted commas because, clearly, Utopian Global Government implies the transfer of many State powers to the global entity, as is, of course, already the case.

[114] See T. G. Otte's review of George Monbiot's, *The Age of Consent: A Manifesto for a new world order.* in the *Times Literary Supplement,* Sept. 26, 2003 and found his book which is: George Monbiot, *The Age of Consent.* London Flamingo, 2003. Monbiot's scheme for the democratization of the United Nations has something in common with my own. To that extent the heading "Lonely on a Cold Mountain" and the condescending assertion that "even" Monbiot accedes that his ideas are impractical are disproven by the fact that he and I come to similar conclusions independently. In other words, individuals are moving their thoughts in similar

directions. However, in my view Monbiot is so scared of his own ideas he weakens them. He acknowledges the cost of a world parliament as overwhelming—but it would be far less than the combined General Assemblies of the total United Nations family with which I would do away.

[115] The small Swiss Cabinet consists of members of the main political parties in the legislature, not just a majority party. It is chaired by a President, an office which rotate through the cabinet each New Year.

[116] Examples of appropriate conditions might be: failure to maintain a level of living over a given number of years; internal massacres; breaches of human rights, failure to operate an educational system. Trusteeship could be a tool to back up the rapid deployment force (Rwanda) and could have been used to handle post-war Iraq pending the establishment of security and self-government. In a sense something like it has been used for Bosnia and Kosovo.

[117] I am in the process of studying and analysing the relationship between the "Web of Moral Values Globally Approved" and local cultures (from the United States to Papua New Guinea). A very preliminary draft may be viewed at http://www.anthropologising.ca./writing/wemovagla.doc.

[118] As originally proposed, "genocide" included what we now call "ethnocide" but this broad definition was not internationally adopted so that internationally ethnocide without the physical destruction of populations, come under the heading of the right to cultural survival.

[119] For the all important subject of international aid and technical assistance, a major part of the programme of any Global Government.

[120] It is ironic that highly religious movements, believing in a hereafter of Paradise, frequently attempt to achieve paradise on earth through mystical means.

[121] Amartya Sen, *The Argumentative Indian*, London, Allen Lane, 2005, and the *Bhagavad Gita* again.

[122] I hope to revise this text as a result of your input and discussion, and therefore welcome your comments posted to me at 2901-969

Richards St, Vancouver B.C., V6B1A8, Canada. I may not be able to acknowledge every contribution.

[123] The name may have to be adjusted. A quick Internet search brings up an International Council of Voluntary Agencies (concerned with volunteerism), a Council of International NGOs (concerned with Kosovo), World Volunteers for Africa. There is a World Movement for Non-Violence based in southern Brasil which proposes in its constitution a World Council of NGOs.

[124] Per Nor beck, who joined me on the podium as a winner in the 2004-2005 World Utopian Championship, received accolades for a limited but creative and practical initiative. In his home town of Vallentuna, Sweden, he mobilised high school students and other young people to discuss city issues via the Internet. The response was electric, so much so that a non-partisan political party formed and elected a member to the city council, and influenced its policies. Apply such a technique and principle to the national and global stage.